OF GOD AND GUCCI

Keith Rennar Brennan

Beaumonde Press

Beaumonde Press Paperback Edition
December 2025
United States

Copyright © 2025 Keith Rennar Brennan
All rights reserved.
ISBN 979-8-9998507-1-3
No part of this book may be reproduced or portions thereof in any form whatsoever.

Most of the names and identifying details in this book have been changed to protect privacy. Two have not: Keith F. Pecklers and Thomas Stanford – because they earned their place here exactly as they are; predators and child sexual abusers. They are unworthy of the shelter of fiction.

All rights reserved, including the right to reproduce this book or portions thereof in any form whatsoever.

For information, contact info@ofgodandgucci.com

Manufactured in the United States of America.

For Diane

Of God And Gucci

St. Paul's Church

14 Greenville Avenue, Jersey City, N.J. 07305

Rev. Joseph A. Murray, Pastor
Rev. James F. Reilly, Associate Pastor
Rev. Kevin P. Ashe, Associate Pastor
Rev. Patrick M. Mulewski, Associate Pastor
Miss Tina Niehold,
　Parish Council President
Sr. Imelda Marie Hogan, O.P.,
　Pastoral Minister
Sr. Philomena Marie, O.P.,
　Parochial School Principal

Sr. Noreen Conheeney, O.P.
　Minister of Special Education
Sr. Andrea Mueller, F.M.S.C.
　Family Minister
Greenville House
　Hours: 9:30 a.m. - 1:00 p.m. Mon. - Fri.
　188 Ocean Ave.　333-1524
Staff
　Edith Campbell, Social Services

Invites you to celebrate:

THE LITURGY
Sunday
　6:30 p.m. Saturday evening
　7:15, 8:45, 10:00, 11:15 a.m., 12:30 p.m.
　11:00 a.m. Spanish Mass - St. Ann's Chapel
Weekdays
　7:00 a.m. - St. Ann's Home
　7:15 a.m., 8:45 a.m., and 12:00 Noon - Convent Chapel
Saturday
　8:45 a.m. - Concelebrated Mass in the Convent Chapel
Holydays
　7:30 p.m. - prior evening
　7:15 a.m., 9:00 a.m., and 12:00 Noon, 7:30 p.m.

BAPTISMS
1. Parents should make arrangements for Baptism at least one month before the desired date.
2. Parents must meet with the pastor to arrange for the required preparation sessions.
3. Baptisms will ordinarily be celebrated at mass on the fourth Sunday of each month.

MARRIAGES
Arrangements with parish priest 1 year in advance according to Common Policy pastoral preparation for Marriage.

RELIGIOUS EDUCATION
September through May
　for children attending public school
　Grades 1-6: Saturday 9:45 - 11:00 a.m.
　Grades 7-12: Sunday 9:45 - 11:00 a.m.

SACRAMENT OF RECONCILIATION
Saturdays: 1:00 - 2:00 p.m. and 7:30 - 8:00 p.m.

Rectory
433-8500

School
435-8204

Convent
333-2443

Greenville House
333-1524

St. Paul's Church Bulletin (1976)

Chapter 1

I drew St. Paul's Church for the cover of our parish bulletin when I was thirteen years old. Three years later I would daydream about hanging myself in its steeple.

My story begins in September 1976 in the Greenville section of Jersey City. Raised in a devout Irish Italian Catholic family, my parents had hoped that St. Paul's Church would help me find my way. Instead, I would be led down an *un-godly* path paved with sexual abuse, drug dependency, and a proclivity for suicide.

My father, Bill, was the church usher at the ten o'clock Sunday Mass, my mother, Colette, sang in the church choir, and my older brother Billy, was an altar boy. I had joined St. Paul's folk group in the spring of that year, our Country's Bicentennial. It was America's 200th anniversary of the Declaration of Independence, and the first time in my life that I felt free. That summer of '76, Gerald Ford was our president, a company named Apple made some kind of computer, and every boy wanted to be Bruce Jenner, who had just won the Olympic Gold Medal.

Billy and I spent our days playing tag and stickball with the neighborhood kids, but the heart of our family life was St.

Paul's Church. When Billy was in high school, he formed a special friendship with the coolest priest in the parish, Father Tony. He wasn't just a preacher at the pulpit – Fr. Tony became a part of our lives, celebrating holidays and special occasions with us like a beloved family friend.

I received the sacrament of confirmation that spring and received a present from Fr. Tony. A porcelain Hummel figurine of a boy playing his violin for his puppy. Fr. Tony said the figurine was called – *Puppy Love*. The only puppy love I had experienced up until eighth grade was a crush on Miss DiSoto, my confirmation class teacher, and Jennifer Black, my first girlfriend and eighth grade classmate.

Confirmation class was supposed to be about preparing for the Holy Ghost, but for me it was also about preparing for Miss DiSoto every week. Every Tuesday night I got dressed for confirmation class like I was going out on a date; a pressed collared shirt, a hand-knit vest, my favorite bell bottoms and my pecan-colored suede Wallabees. I'd blow-dry my hair to perfection, then complete my routine with a healthy spray of my brother's Aramis cologne - the one that would send him into a total fit if he ever discovered I'd borrowed it.

Darla DiSoto was effortlessly beautiful. Her wavy brown hair bounced like it was being filmed in slow motion and she was part of a Faberge shampoo commercial. Her olive skin was smooth and glowing, but it was her lips that got me – soft pink, naturally shaped like they were mid-kiss. I wanted to ask her to the eighth-grade dance. Every week we sat in a prayer circle on the cold cafeteria tile floor in St. Paul's Grammar School basement. She'd sit cross-legged like the rest of us, but somehow it made her look glamorous. I'd angle myself just enough so I could watch her out of the corner of my eye while pretending to listen about the Holy Spirit. Sometimes I'd say her name out loud for no reason other than to hear it echo in the stale school cafeteria air, the smell of the day's lunch still lingering, impelling her to look at me. "Miss DiSoto, what's the difference between the Holy Ghost and the Holy Spirit?" I didn't even care about the answer. I just wanted to keep her talking to me so that we could look straight into each other's eyes for as long as possible. "Miss DiSoto, what about the Seven Gifts from The Holy Ghost?" I'd watch her purse her lips – explaining the difference between a ghost, a spirit, and the Seven Gifts, and I loved every second of it.

When class ended, I'd wait and linger for all of the other kids to leave. And then I'd offer to walk Miss DiSoto home to Pamrapo Avenue like a gentleman would, even though she was probably ten years older than I was and looked like she could jog the entire way without breaking a sweat. I acted casual, like it was no big deal, like I wasn't dying inside when she'd laugh and say,

"You don't have to, sweetie. I'll be fine." But sometimes she'd let me. And those walks were everything. My heart would thump so loud I was sure she could hear it. I'd glance at her along the way, imagining us holding hands. She smelled so good – like Dove soap and Johnson and Johnson Baby Powder. Finally, we would arrive at Miss DiSoto's front porch and my fantasy would end. I so desperately wanted to kiss her good night. I had already French-kissed Jennifer Black, so I knew how to kiss a girl.

Jennifer was pretty, in that blonde hair, blue-eyed, all-American girl way. Her lips were perfect too, except for the fact that they were perpetually chapped. Like she had just finished running across the Sahara Desert without water. And Jennifer's older sister Dorothea, she looked like a television star. Half-Farrah Fawcett-Majors, half-Jaclyn Smith. Dorothea could steal every guy's attention within a ten-mile radius, and her boyfriend James looked like he stepped straight off the Hollywood set of *Love Story*. If you squinted just right, you could have sworn he was Ryan O'Neil's twin brother. Dorothea and James were always making out and smoking cigarettes – True Menthol. So did Jennifer, but I never told anyone. Jennifer introduced me to cigarettes at thirteen. It took some time to inhale as deeply as they did, but eventually I got the hang of it, even though they made me dizzy.

Dorothea and James fought every weekend, and not just regular fights – epic fights. The kind where Dorothea's voice would go from zero to full on soap opera in about three seconds. One minute they'd be standing on her front steps looking like the cover of a romance novel, and the next, Dorothea would be all dramatic flipping her *Charlie's Angels* hair over her shoulder and saying things like "I can't even look at you right now James!" But James never yelled. He was too cool for that. He'd just stand there leaning up against the porch railing brooding like James Dean, dragging on a cigarette, and staring off into the distance like he was thinking about life and love. His jaw would be all tight and he'd squint in that way cool guys in the movies do, like he was about to say something so deep and poetic that it would stop time itself. Sometimes Dorothea would get James so crazy and frustrated that he would cry out in frustration. I felt kind of sorry for him, but you did what you had to do just to be with a beauty like Dorothea.

Jennifer and I would sit there on the steps, caught in the middle of this hot, hormone overloaded, sexually charged show, pretending we weren't completely fascinated eighth graders, entranced, and turned-on. I know I was. Jennifer would be chewing on her chapped bottom lip and I'd be pretending I understood relationships, nodding to James like "yeah, yeah, I get it." I was captivated by both of them – his charm and her intoxication. James would ask my opinion as to why I thought Dorothea was so emotional – like I was somehow his equal. Clearly, I was not, but he made me feel hopeful, perhaps encouraged by the potential that he must have seen in me. Dorothea would cross her arms and dramatically take extended drags from her True Menthol cigarette and turn away from James like she was officially done with him forever. And that's when the slow, inevitable make up process would begin. James would take his time and flick his cigarette into the street. He'd shove his hands deep into his pockets and sigh like he was carrying the weight of the world on his shoulders. There was lots of running his hands through his hair – classic, dirty blonde, with soft waves that gave it a slightly messed-up look. Medium length, falling just over his ears and brushing against his forehead, James' hairstyle fit the character of Oliver in *Love Story* perfectly. I wished my hair was cool and casual like James, but Daddy made Billy and me blow-dry our hair every day.

James' most calculated move ever, still without saying a word, was simply closing the space between him and Dorothea the way cool guys did. Dorothea would pretend not to notice at first as if she were immune to his effortless charm, but then in slow motion, James would reach out and gently tuck a loose strand of hair behind her ear and just like that, Dorothea would melt, the same way girls would swoon when *Fonzie* snapped his fingers by the jukebox at Arnold's on *Happy Days*. It was predictable, yet mesmerizing to watch. James was a genius! A masterful and accomplished actor in the art of romance. He never rushed, never tried too hard. He just knew exactly what to do and when to do it, as if he had rehearsed the scene a hundred times in his head. I would watch them both taking mental notes and wondering if coolness like *that* was something you were born with, or if it could be learned.

Maybe that's why when Fr. Tony gave me *Puppy Love*, it felt so different. I had always felt like I was on the outside looking in – an observer, a kid trying to figure out the script to a play that seemed to have no lines written for me. I could never be cool like James or Billy. But that day when Fr. Tony gave me the *Puppy Love* Hummel figurine, it wasn't just a gift, it was recognition. Like I was one of them. A moment that made me feel seen, feel important – like maybe I belonged and wasn't just some kid watching a play from behind the curtain. Maybe in my own way, I mattered too. I wasn't just Billy Brennan's little brother. Maybe I *was* special. Maybe I could have a cool priest-friend like Fr. Tony myself one day.

Mommy's best friend Lois, who lived two blocks away, collected Hummels, so I knew that it was valuable. Lois had an Early American hutch in her dining room filled with these little, fragile German boys and girls, but she didn't have this little boy playing a violin for his puppy. *This* Hummel was extra special because it was blessed by a priest. Fr. Tony told me that I was a special person, that I was loved by God the Father, and now that I was confirmed God gave me the gift of the Holy Spirit and I was ready to start my faith journey as a soldier of Christ – just as the Archbishop had told us during our confirmation ceremony. Now at thirteen, I had a spiritual duty to fight the war between good and evil and light and darkness, blessed with the seven gifts that the Holy Ghost had bestowed on me.

The celebration of The Sacrament of Confirmation was a very special day for all of the Class of 1976. It was a who's who of catechists from St. Paul's Church. The adult choir and the folk group were positioned on opposite sides of the altar. Officiating the celebration was the archbishop, who stood in his magnificent robes, embellished with intricate embroidery and rich colors, symbolizing his esteemed position in the church, along with his liturgical headdress that was pointed like a shield and had streamers attached in the back, just like the bishop on *Monty Python's Flying Circus*. Musical director Keith Pecklers, Fr. Tony, Fr. Davis, and Miss DiSoto, were part of the confirmation ceremony, and my brother Billy – along with three of his friends from the parish council, were asked to be speakers.

Wisdom, understanding, counsel, fortitude, knowledge, piety, and most especially fear of the Lord, were the gifts from The Holy Ghost. I also had the gift of the porcelain German boy and his puppy that Fr. Tony had given me, which honestly made me happier than any of the Seven Gifts that the Holy Ghost had given to me that day.

Me (age 13), Billy (age 17), and Fr. Tony at my Confirmation (April 1976)

I kept *Puppy Love* on my night table next to my bed. It was the first thing I looked at when I woke up every morning and the last thing I'd see before I closed my eyes to sleep. Sometimes if I woke up in the middle of the night to go to the bathroom, I would pick up *Puppy Love* and hold the little boy and his puppy in the palm of my hand, but I was very clumsy, so I had to be extra careful not to snap off the boy's violin bow or umbrella handle, or worse, decapitate the boy's puppy.

Puppy Love

Fr. Tony, with his long shaggy hairstyle, resembled Dustin Hoffman. Mommy said that Fr. Tony was down to earth. I knew that meant that he was a really nice person who spoke from his heart and had nothing to do with the fact that he was five foot two. Fr. Tony asked my family to call him by his first name the very first time that Billy had invited him over for dinner. Any cleric, deacon, minister, nun, or priest that visited our home, insisted that we call them by their first names, usually during our first family Sunday dinner together. And in one case, by his nickname *Kunzie,* which was so cool, because it sounded like Fonzie.

Fr. Tony was soft spoken, had kind empathetic eyes, a stout Italian nose, thick dark eyebrows, and was almost monk-like in his demeanor. When Fr. Tony spoke, he spoke with his head and shoulders, leaning in and slowly bobbing into his movements, using words that were equally unhurried and unmeasured. He hypnotized us with his soft demeanor – not unlike every other priest who shared veal cutlets and ziti with meat sauce during a family Sunday dinner, or pigs in the blanket, tater tots, and mini chicken drumsticks on a Christmas Eve, before and after midnight mass. Having a priest come to your home for dinner and holidays was like having Jesus Christ in your home and being able to actually just call him *Jesus* at the dinner table.

"Jesus, would you like to say grace?"

"Jesus, can you please pass the salt?"

"Jesus, would you like more tater tots?"

A priest was seen as a direct connection to God. For our family, having the parish priest as our family friend symbolized that the priests had chosen us, an acknowledgement that we were special and had a unique bond with St. Paul's Church. My brother was so lucky to have Tony and Kunzie as his priest friends. I was in awe of Billy's self-confidence, self-assuredness, and self-esteem. I was having a difficult time finding any *self-anything*. Billy and I, three years and seven months apart, did not get along well because I was Mommy's favorite and Billy was more sports-minded like Daddy. But I still looked up to him. Billy's ability to make friends was something that I craved and aspired towards. Billy was popular, handsome, smart, athletic, and won trophies – and that one summer, when he was a lifeguard at the Skyline Cabana Club, had blonde streaks in his hair. The Skyline Cabana Club in Jersey City was a private swim and tennis club, that in over-hearing a phone conversation between Mommy and Aunt Marie, apparently was also a club where married couples would go if they wanted to have an extra-marital affair.

Sunday dinners were always with Nanny and Poppy, and sometimes, with one of Billy's church friends. Besides fighting with each other, cooking, serving, and table preparation were our parent's favorite things to do, and entertaining Billy's priest friends was more than any family could ask for. We were blessed. After caring for the parishioners and celebrating the sacraments all week, Billy's priests had chosen to often use their personal time to spend holidays and the occasional Sunday dinner with *our* family.

Mom would prepare and fry up three pounds of milk-fed veal cutlets from Maloney's Meat Market and make veal parmesan and ziti with home-made meat sauce with shredded veal, pork, and beef, that Mommy and Nanny called *Pasta Ca'shad*. Mommy would have a custom floral arrangement designed by Johnson the Florist in Bayonne, or Entenmann's Florist in Jersey City -for all special occasions and dinners. Aunt Marie used Entenmann's for decades. They were the only florists they trusted.

Mommy would spend two weeks of prep-time if it were a sacramental event or holiday. Church event related dinners such as communions, confirmations, graduations, and holidays were the best dinner events because Mommy had lead-up time. She needed time to put together her notes, writings, drawings, sketches, and words from torn-out magazine pages of *Woman's*

Day and *Good Housekeeping,* pictures of floral arrangements and table settings. The theme itself was the easy part. It was the special touches and arrangement of details that made Mommy's family dinner events special.

The selected damask jacquard tablecloth that Mommy would dress the dining room table with was hand ironed and placed over the plastic protective tablecloth, which was then placed over the custom-made protective trifold, two-inch thick cork table pad that she kept between her and Daddy's full-size box spring and mattress. Also kept between their box spring and mattress was the three-quarter inch thick, full-sized, forest-green spray-painted piece of plywood that held our mounted Lionel Train tracks. Mommy and Daddy's heads were literally lying on top of a train track 323 days of the year. The remaining forty-two days were a spectacularly miserable time of the year – *the holidays.*

The weekend after Thanksgiving was marked by a holiday ritual in our family. Mommy and Daddy would shimmy the plywood and train tracks out from the foundation of their bed in order to set up our Christmas tree, manger, and holiday village. It was a detailed display of classic Dickens-era scenes and figurines including carolers, figure skaters, and a ballerina posing in a pink miniature thumbnail-size crinoline – all frozen in time and surrounded by a locomotive that blew real smoke and made choo-choo sounds. The vibration from the moving train made the figure skaters clumsily glide across the oval-shaped mirror that Mommy rimmed with artificial snow. The manger, the most important part of Christmas, was placed at the base of the Christmas tree, along with Mary, Joseph, a cow, and a goat with three legs that Mommy leaned against the side of the stable. We even had real pieces of dried-up broken hay laying in the manger and the surrounding area, along with an angel holding a gold star wired onto the point of the rooftop. Mommy kept baby Jesus next to the gold pill box with her saccharine in the gold French-provincial drum table next to the lady's chair until Christmas Eve. In the distance, about nine inches away, towards the skating rink, were the Three Wise Men. Mommy would move them all an eighth-of-an-inch closer to the manger each night after dinner. One of them had a sheep around his neck that was missing a foot. There is a possibility that the sheep and the goat may have been struck by a speeding locomotive at some point, and there may have been a bassinet with the baby Jesus strapped to the locomotive's cab roof.

A white blanket covered the Christmas village like a fresh snowfall on Christmas morning when Billy and I would discover that Santa Claus had visited our apartment and brought us everything that we had wished for and circled in the *Sears and Roebuck Christmas Wish Book* – which was less of a book and more of a controlled substance for kids. Every free moment was spent flipping through its glossy pages lost in a haze of euphoria. But before the magic of Christmas morning, came the three day ordeal known as Family Holiday Decorating Weekend – an event that guaranteed two things (1) Mommy and Daddy's most spectacular Saturday night fight of the year to kick off the holiday season, and (2) Billy getting the actual stuffing knocked out of him as a grim Radio City Christmas Spectacular-esque pre-show to the main event.

The fun always began on Friday night when Daddy, already three beers in, would attempt to untangle the Christmas lights that he swore he had put away organized and every year emerged looking like they had spent the summer in a raccoon's mouth. By Saturday afternoon, Billy was the sacrificial lamb of Daddy's holiday rage and usually found himself on the receiving end of a festive ass-kicking by 8 p.m. All this played out against the sound of Christmas classics playing on our Zenith radio while Mommy methodically draped the gold garland into carefully measured spaces between the branches, placing every ornament deliberately, so as to not to break any balls. We were not the kind of family who used tinsel. Tinsel lacked control. By the time New Year's Day rolled around, after Mommy had been (well, we'll get to that), we were ready to get back to our normal Sunday dinners

Me & Billy (1969)

with Nanny and Poppy and one of Billy's priest friends.

The thick colored grosgrain ribbon that Mommy would handpick at the florist shop for her dinner centerpieces, would be intertwined throughout her magnolia (her favorite) or various seasonally appropriate branches. It was then embellished with greens, seasonal dried berries, fresh flowers, and cut branches that stretched across the center of the dining room table, like open arms embracing our new priest into our family. She would request from the florist a large glass hurricane pillar candle holder in the center of the arrangement to create comfort and warmth and *"set it off"* as Mommy would say. She would write out the little card that accompanied the floral arrangement to whoever the visiting priest was, with one of her pre-written sentiments, color-coded and categorized index cards for every occasion – prepared, practiced and edited, again and again, that were kept in the top drawer of her bedside night table. Most index cards had words that were crossed off, only to be replaced by a more well thought out word, or verse, or lyric, or word or Words, written bigger and **BOLDER,** and then underlined three to five times, to emphasize her sentiment, and get the recipient's full attention. Mommy's handwritten notes were meant to inspire, build confidence, wish luck, and let the recipient know how special they were. She had perfected every occasion, every season, situation, and life event. Mommy used titles and verses from popular hit songs too. All cards were categorized male or female, breakups and breakthroughs, clergy, sickness, anniversaries, birthdays, and death.

"You are THE SUNSHINE OF MY LIFE." – Happy Birthday Sunshine!

"YOU LIGHT UP MY LIFE!" This too shall pass! You are a light to others.

"Love Is In The Air…everywhere I look around." Congratulations on your engagement.

They say that "Breaking Up Is Hard To Do"… but… YOU WILL FIND SOMEONE SPECIAL TO LOVE YOU SOMEDAY!!! (boy or girl)

"Dear (GRADUATE),
*With your **Good Looks** and **personality**, you are sure to go far. Shoot for **THE STARS**, they are yours to **grasp**.*

*"There is no **NEED** to **WISH** you **LUCK**…With your intelligence, talent and determination, you are sure to go **very far**." (perfect for a boy graduate)*

KEEP ON TRUCKING (insert boy's name)! YOU ARE A SPECIAL SOMEONE AND SOMEDAY YOU WILL MAKE A GIRL VERY HAPPY. DON'T GIVE UP! (boy having just been broken off with by his girl)

"Dear Fr. (fill in name),
We are so thrilled to have you at our home for dinner this evening.
"You… are One IN A MILLION! We are lucky to have you!
"You Don't Have To Be A Star"…(Song by Marilyn McCoo)
But you sure are a "SUPERSTAR PRIEST TO US!"
Sign me,
Blessed to call you a friend,
   Colette

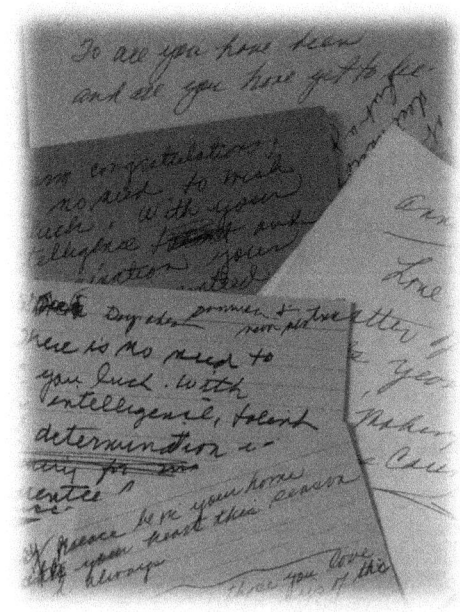

After a priest dinner, our visiting priest would get to take the floral arrangement back home to the rectory, much like the recipient of a red ticket discovered taped to the bottom of a metal folding chair at a St. Paul's School Chinese Auction or tricky tray. Our special prize-winning priest would first be invited by Daddy to say grace, but only after Daddy introduced everyone at the table *formally,* as if the priest didn't already know who we were.

"Father, (Daddy bobbing his head up and down slowly, with his chin tucked down, slightly blushing, humbled, showing respect),

"You know this is my beautiful wife Colette, and Billy and Keith's Mother." Mom delivers her signature double cough. "We want to welcome you into our home with open arms." Daddy says this with his Butler, New Jersey drawl-sort-of-weird-evangelical-speaking-country-voice that he uses when he wants to say something important – a mix of *Gomer Pile* and *The Rifleman.*

"And this is my very special son, Keith, who I am very proud of. Keith is a very talented artist and creative boy, and son, (turning to me), I am so very proud of you."

"And of course, you already know Billy."

Next, Tony or Kunzie would thank my father and we would all hold hands around our dining table and then Fr. Tony or Kunzie would say grace before the meal and acknowledge each of us by name, looking into each one of our faces, like we were the only ones in the world to him and we were having the Last Supper. I always felt weird holding hands with a man. Fr. Tony or Kunzie or someday hopefully my own priest, would lift both hands up a foot or so above the table, bless the food we were about to eat, and bless the wine, which every Sunday was the blood of Christ.

Daddy always drank too much wine-blood and Mommy would give him nasty looks and say that he didn't know when he had enough to drink. *"Now knock it off Bill! You never know when to stop!"* Mommy would say these sorts of things close to Daddy's ear but not close enough that everyone at the table didn't hear what she had said. Just like every wedding that we ever had gone to as a family, they would argue at the table and Daddy would have a few too many drinks and then get on the dance floor. I loved seeing him like this. I mean it's not like he was getting behind the wheel of a car, because we didn't own one, so why not let him drink and dance?

Daddy was an excellent dancer. He would do the worm and jump over his opposite leg and breakdance. He loved entertaining all of his Irish nieces and nephews who would whistle and shout, *"Go Uncle Billy!"* and egg Dad on. There were a lot of them. Dad had two brothers and six sisters, and his young nephews would take part in his uproarious dance show. Everyone roared with laughter, forming a circle around Daddy, clapping, two-finger whistling – the works. Except for Mommy, who was always mad at Daddy for one reason or another, would cry at the table and on the way home, and say things a boy shouldn't hear about their father, like he did not have any ambition or dreams for our lives. Mommy always told me that Daddy was not a *"go getter."*

Most priest dinners ended with Mommy angry at Daddy for over-drinking, lots of sighing, nasty side glances and bickering, resulting in the guest priest feeling a need to share a verse from the bible, or say something that The Lord would say, such as an appropriate scripture to provide solace and make light of the situation.

Ephesians 4:31-32:
Get rid of all bitterness, rage, and anger, brawling and slander, along with every form of malice. Be kind and compassionate to one another, forgiving each other, just as Christ God forgave you."

It seldom worked. Especially the brawling part. This would make Mommy cry at the dinner table while she rolled the crumbs off of the ivory linen damask tablecloth with the crumb-sweeper gadget she bought at Goldman and Barlock Decorators on Broadway in Bayonne – the same place she had ordered the dining room table protective pad and protective plastic tablecloth. Tears rolled down Mommy's face as she vacuumed every last morsel, and every ounce of joy off of the dinner table before serving dessert.

Crumbs popping and jumping inside the clear plastic crumb cylinder reminded me of the Mexican jumping beans I bought at Charlie's candy store at the foot of Neptune Ave. and across the Boulevard. They weren't really beans. I read in *Encyclopedia Britannica* that they were actually seeds from

Mexico that contained moth larvae and when the seeds were heated up, trapped in the palm of your hand, the small insects would jump and bang their heads against the walls of the brown seeds until eventually, when they could no longer withstand the torture, the bugs would die of heat stroke and brain damage.

Rumor had it that the only priest that did not live in the rectory was Fr. Ashe, and that he lived in a Victorian home in Greenville that he purchased with his best friend Ray Ellis. Irish to the core, with graying hair, a ruddy complexion, and smiling sky-blue eyes, Fr. Ashe looked like he could be a priest from a television show, like a younger Buddy Ebsen on *Barnaby Jones*. Ray, one of the catechists in our church, probably a good ten years younger than Fr. Ashe was tall, had dark wavy hair, and wore a mustache like the cowboy in Village People. Fr. Ashe and Ray Ellis were often seen restoring the outside of the home, scraping the old cedar shakes, painting, and gardening together.

St. Paul's rectory and its priests were well taken care of by Willy. Willy was not only the housekeeper, but she was also the cook as well. She was an old woman, probably in her sixties, who spoke with a heavy accent and mostly wore a scowl on her hardworking face. Willy took care of everything that the priests needed, including cleaning the rectory and their personal suites, cooking their meals, and taking care of their dirty laundry. Willy always looked at you like she suspected you were doing something wrong, even when you were simply walking through the rectory parlor, passing the liquor-filled bar and cabinets, to go down the rectory stairs to the basement for bible study and folk group practice.

She was a tiny little woman of four-foot something, full of vim and vigor, or as Poppy would say – *"full of piss and vinegar."* Five-foot Poppy was full of piss and vinegar himself. A pint-sized Archie Bunker with a sawed-off baseball bat stashed under the front seat of his powder blue 1963 Rambler station wagon that he kept handy in case he had to *"hit a coon on the side of the head."* I knew that the word *"coon"* was a bad word, the kind that made grown-ups whisper and shake their heads at, but Poppy didn't really mean it, at least not the way other people did. He got along with everyone. Except Daddy that is.

The relationship between Daddy and Poppy was like something out of *All in the Family* and Poppy played the role of Archie Bunker to perfection. Loud, opinionated, and forever convinced that his way was the right way even when it wasn't. Poppy espoused his wisdom during every chance he could get. Daddy meanwhile was the perfect Meathead, just as stubborn, just as headstrong, and married to Poppy's daughter. Every conversation between them felt like a live taping of an episode – the audience laughter replaced by bickering and talking over each other, until finally, when Mommy and Nanny could not listen to it anymore, would start screaming like Edith and Gloria.

Through cigarette smoke and long swigs of beer and whiskey, Poppy would wave his stumpy-arthritic-cigarette holding fingers at Daddy from across the dinner table like a warning flare.

"You got all these fancy ideas," he'd rasp, smoke curling

from his lips in purposeful plumes, "but you ain't got the commonsense God gave a goose. And no ambition to make anything happen. You have no gumption." Then came Poppy's signature punctuation – his version of Mommy's cough, a thunderous, involuntary stomp. Poppy would slam his right leg onto the floor four or five times. The arthritis tortured him all day and night. I remember going with him twice to Chinatown, slipping down dark alleys into the back of an herb shop where a Chinese woman performed acupuncture. She'd light the needles after she placed them deep into his leg and foot. He would wash the pain away by downing a handful of Anacin.

Daddy, red-faced and quick-tempered, never let an insult slide. He'd bark right back, "And you're just a stubborn old man who thinks the world stopped spinning in 1955."

And Poppy, without missing a beat, would lean back, take a long drag from his Raleigh cigarette, and deliver his final line.

"Well maybe it should have been stopped in 1955 – back when men were men, women were women, and folks had the wisdom to know the difference."

Poppy did have that 1950's kind of wisdom, the kind that was uninvited.

This was the soundtrack of every Sunday dinner, every backyard barbecue, and every holiday – where someone thought it was a good idea to let them sit in the same room. Poppy would puff on his cigarettes like a rooster, and Daddy would push back. For all their bickering, there was something almost enjoyable about it for them. Poppy needed someone to yell at just as much as Daddy needed someone to defy. And just like Archie and Meathead, when push came to shove, they'd sit in the same room, drink coffee and eat their dessert on snack trays and watch *60 Minutes* together, finishing the Sunday night arguing about politics and whether Nixon should have gone to jail. Neither would admit it, but they liked the fight as much as they liked each other. There was always an element of wisdom and truth in the thought-provoking things that Poppy said. He was a provocateur.

I prayed to have wisdom too. Afterall, it was the first and the highest gift that the Holy Ghost had bestowed on the confirmands. At my weekly confirmation preparation class, we learned that through wisdom, we come to recognize the truth, and the ability to distinguish good from evil. If we can turn our heart to The Lord and allow his word and wisdom to guide us, we will live a life embraced with God's love. I prayed to God to use me as he willed, and for me to accept his wisdom with all my heart.

> *"Take, Lord, and receive all my liberty,*
> *all my memory, my understanding,*
> *and my entire will, all that I have and call my own.*
> *You have given it all to me.*
> *To you, Lord, I return it.*
> *Everything is yours; do with it what you will."*
> -Ignatius of Loyola

Chapter 2

We lived in a red brick, three-story walk-up on the corner of Seaview and Old Bergen Road in Jersey City until I was six or seven years old. Our building had that worn-in, lived-in city charm, with fire escapes zigzagging along the facade, becoming make-shift balconies when tenants put their bedsheets and laundry out to dry. Fire escapes that I would imagine myself spinning webs as Spiderman and leaping from landing to landing. This building was the perfect backdrop for my imagination.

The scent of Sunday dinner – garlic, onions, and slow-simmered tomato sauce, drifted through the open windows, mixing with the hum of traffic along Old Bergen Road and the laughter, shouts, and playful squabbles of neighborhood kids playing a heated game of stickball in the street below. Me, Billy and our neighborhood friends would play until it got dark and it was time for dinner.

Our family had a Sunday morning routine. Dressed in our finest clothes – Mom, Dad, Billy, and I would set off for mass. But before we left, there was another ritual that belonged to only us. Instead of posing for photos in front of the brick apartment building that we lived in, we would walk next door to a beautiful, mauve colored brick ranch with a perfectly manicured lawn. Yellow daffodils swayed in the breeze, and a sleek burgundy Cadillac sat polished in the driveway. The home belonged to a kind colored family who never seemed to mind that Mommy pretended it was ours. She orchestrated the scene as if she was setting up for a magazine shoot; making sure every detail was just right. Aunt Rosie, our neighbor from the basement apartment, was the Brennan unofficial family photographer for location shots.

Mommy & Daddy pose with Billy & Me (1965)

  Billy and I darted through the maze of the building's underbelly, passing the swaying rope clothing lines, ducking under the low hanging asbestos pipes, always careful not to brush against the chalky-white limestone encrusted boiler. We'd navigate through the labyrinth of storage units, breathing in the scent of mothballs and damp concrete, until we found Aunt Rosie – ready with her camera. Through the grainy out of focus lens, our lives took shape and were documented in still frames. Mommy directed the scene with quiet determination, and Aunt

Rosie corroborated Mommy's fantasy with each click of the shutter. We looked like a family plucked straight from *Life Magazine*; poised, polished, perfect. Mommy and Daddy looked like movie stars on their wedding day. Mommy looked like she was Snow White, luminous and breathtaking, and Daddy, her prince charming. Mommy was always holding on to that dream, capturing not just an image, but an idea of the life she wanted to live, and a life that she wanted us to believe in. And for those few moments, we did.

Mommy & Daddy

Like most kids, our parents told us to refer to most of their friends and our neighbors as Aunt and Uncle plus their first names. It was a polite thing to do; however, the title was just an honorary one. But honestly, it was a little confusing. You'd go half your childhood thinking you had an army of aunts and uncles only to realize much later, that none of them were actually related to you. Then there were the actual relatives who somehow got bumped up in the hierarchy. On my mother's side, we had cousins, older ones – who were mysteriously promoted to aunt status with no explanation. Apparently calling them by their first names would have been a sign of disrespect, even though by blood, they were still just cousins. It was like a weird unspoken rule – if they were older than Mommy, they automatically became an aunt. You didn't question it. You just went along with the illusion that your cousin was now your aunt. None of this pecking order went on in Daddy's side of the family.

Arnie and Dolores Marino and their two kids, Tracy and Gary, lived down the hall from us. Aunt Lala and Uncle Dinnie were our upstairs neighbors. They were a silver-haired duo in their sixties who had no blood ties to us, but who wrapped us in the kind of affection that made us feel like family. They lavished us with treats during holidays, and birthday gifts wrapped in shiny foil paper. To me, Aunt Lala and Uncle Dinnie felt a little too generous for us to just be neighbors. To me, they felt like Dorothy Gale's Aunt Em and Uncle Henry in *The Wizard of Oz*. They looked like angels to me.

Aunt Lala was petite and wore high heels every day to

work. Her platinum bouffant was a masterpiece of engineering. Beauty parlor teased, sculpted, and lacquered into a cloud of perfection. Her figure was a study in vintage glamour. A full and compacted bosom tapered into a tightly cinched waist, her crisp cotton blouses, three-quarter length sleeves, were always tucked in with military precision – disappearing into the girdle that structured her frame like the secret suit of armor that Wonder Woman wore. Aunt Lala was Dolly Parton with a dash of Mae West. Sharp-witted and unshakably confident for being all of four foot nine. Her small, manicured hands, tipped with immaculate and precisely painted polish, moved with precision, whether smoothing a tablecloth or tucking a strand of hair behind my ear when saying goodbye.

Every morning Aunt Lala went to *"business"* as they called it, heading to the textile company on Culver Avenue where she worked for the president – which sounded important. What mattered most to me though, were the fabric scraps she brought home to me every week. Glossy polyester, sturdy denim, pieces of ultra suede, glitter lurex, and slinky fabrics that I used to create costumes and art. Rich decorator textiles like the ones in the windows of Dell's Creations on Danforth Avenue and the fabrics that Cher wore on *The Sonny and Cher Show*. I would run my fingers over them, feeling the stories they held, the countries that they came from, imagining the costumes and clothes that I would create. Uncle Dinnie was a lather and a union man, a builder of bones and backbones, helping to shape the New York skyline building the World Trade Center with his own two hands. Uncle

Dinnie carried the scent of sawdust and steel, a hint of oil, and the musky scent of a day's labor lingering in his collar, all of which I could smell when hugging him hello. Uncle Dinnie didn't talk much, but when he did, it made you feel important, like you mattered, like it was coming to you by way of Mr. Rogers, or Captain Kangaroo. Gentle, soft-spoken, and effortlessly kind.

The best part of the day was when Aunt Lala would come home, and as if by magic, produce one of my favorite surprises – a bubble bath container shaped like one of my favorite cartoon characters, bright and plastic, their colors electric against the muted tones of our bathroom. I loved them. I loved the way their heads unscrewed, releasing an addictive, intoxicating fragrance that filled the bathroom with something both sugary and clean. Inhaling the thick glistening liquid soap inside Tweety Bird's head, wrapped around my brain the same way St. Paul's church incense did. It numbed me. Freed me. Made me high. My bath time was never routine. I always made it into a production, a play or a movie, even a Sunday mass, with my television cartoon friends lined up along the space between our clawfoot tub and the wall. My disciples were Tweety Bird, Sylvester the Cat, Bugs Bunny, Elmer Fudd, Dick Tracy, and Bozo the Clown. Tweety was my choir director, his wide yellow head tilted just so, overseeing the sacred water, giving direction with his speech impediment. *"I tawt I taw a puddy tat!"* Bugs Bunny, Sylvester, Dick Tracy, and Bozo were the priests, and Elmer Fudd, eternally confused, was a nervous altar boy. "Shhh...be vewy, vewy, quiet," I murmured to him before dunking his bald little head beneath the surface, sealing his fate by the weight of my hand.

Like sepia tone Kodak photographs at the start of every family photo album, some colors have faded. But some family memories you never forget. It wasn't all cartoons and bubble baths at that apartment building. One memory burned into my mind is of Billy, wide-eyed and trembling, his seven-year-old frame shaking, running through our four-room apartment screaming and terrified. Earlier that afternoon, Mommy was cleaning and dusting the shelves while a Marx Brothers movie played on the television set in the background, and she stumbled upon a discovery that would haunt Billy for a lifetime. Harpo Marx, the scary, mute, albino looking, wild-haired clown – with his shock of blonde curls and unsettling silence. Billy's reaction to seeing Harpo on TV was instant – his face drained of color, his breath hitched, his body frozen in sheer panic. And once Mommy knew, once she had witnessed Billy's reaction, once she discovered his Achilles heel, she knew just what to do.

Harpo Marx

The weeks that followed turned his fear into a disturbing game for the three of us. Draped in a tan trench coat, a black rain hat slouched over her brow, and a curly blonde wig that made her almost unrecognizable, Mommy became something out of Billy's nightmares. Snow White turned into a sinister vision of Harpo Marx. Mommy would lurch toward Billy – her arms outstretched in eerie silence with the exception of an occasional deranged grunt and moan, which amplified through our apartment and amplified Billy's horror. Billy would bolt, shrieking, crying, and scrambling around the glass kitchen table, running in and out of our four rooms. I hid under the kitchen table on the cold linoleum floor with my hands pressed tightly covering my face and my half-closed eyes. Peeking out through the cracks between my fingers, pinning my four-year old body firmly against the wrought iron bars of the kitchen table, I hid –my body partially camouflaged by the fake ivy that Mommy planted in a green Styrofoam ball and arranged to cascade from the black ironwork that was suspended and welded into the center of the table base. The same floral arrangement that I would hide parts of my dinner, like liver and lima beans, squeezed into a wet ball of partly digested food that I carefully managed to spit into my hand. The same kitchen table where so much of our family life played out. Where birthday cakes were cut, where we bobbed for apples, where Nanny and Poppy lingered over coffee, where serious conversations took place, and now – this.

The Keeping Room was the name of our kitchen, and ground zero for the start of all of their fights. Anything said, screamed, whispered, or witnessed in that room, around that glass and wrought iron table, or any other room in our apartment for that matter, was not to be discussed, shared, described, mentioned, reported, or told to *anyone*. Mommy had purchased an avocado wooden plaque with black letters spelling out "The Keeping Room" at our parish craft show. It matched our avocado appliances perfectly. She hung it above the Harvest Gold metal kitchen cabinets six feet above the cabinet that my father kept his liquor in. On Saturday mornings after breakfast, Mommy marked Daddy's whiskey bottle with a pencil before she would leave for work at the collection agency so she could determine how much he drank, sometimes adding warm water to the bottle from the kitchen faucet when the whiskey level was only an afternoon away from empty.

Me, Mommy, Daddy, Nanny, Poppy and Billy (1964)

My other favorite thing to do at five besides taking bubble baths and creating costumes in my playroom, was playing house with Tracy in the backyard of our apartment building. We were married. Tracy was eight. Mommy told me that it was a May-December romance, but I had no idea what that meant. Our dream backyard, just beyond the white picket fence in our imaginary play world, was a deep lot of dirt, patchy grass, gravel, and cigarette butts – surrounded by a six foot chain-link cyclone fence, with steel wires that ran vertically and bent into a zig-zag pattern – with razor sharp metal hooks protruding up and out to prevent five years olds like me from climbing up and over like Tarzan onto the neighboring tree to fetch the string beans that my eight-year old bride told me to fetch for our imaginary dinner.

Once landing in the neighboring yard alongside the cyclone metal hedge, I filled my baby-blue and white striped seersucker shorts with as many bright-green string beans that my five-year old pockets could hold. Some green beans, nearly as long as my forearm, had to be pushed into my elastic waistband so that I could begin my ascent climbing back and over the six-foot fence to arrive home to my wife Tracy. The man of the house bringing home dinner. I loved being married.

The short journey home and jumping over the razor-sharp zig-zag hooks, proved more challenging than my developmental brain had anticipated. As I leaped up and over, I forgot to lift my little left arm higher into the beautiful blue summer afternoon sky and was suddenly snatched at my left wrist by the razor-sharp zig-zag jaws of the metal cyclone monster. I had impaled myself, as Tracy and I had just begun our honeymoon.

Tracy started screaming with the over-effectiveness and bravado of any eight-year-old girl witnessing her five-year old husband skewered and bleeding to death. She was minutes away from becoming a young widow, traumatized for the rest of her life. Forty-three inches of kindergarten body weight and blood-soaked seersucker, hanging from a hook, dangling from underneath a string-bean tree. Our mothers, during the entire duration of our young marriage that afternoon, gossiped about our neighbors while sitting on the concrete three-foot basement stair wall, fifty feet away from the graveled death trap that Tracy and I called home.

Mommy and Dolores ran to my hanging, dangling, bleeding body, feverishly trying to push the dead weight of my limp five-year-old frame upwards, each of them balancing on their tippy toes, holding onto my little calves and floppy ankles to prevent further tearing and damage to my wrist. A flash of white bone was exposed. I was hanging from a main tendon, no longer able to support my head which was now draped down onto my right shoulder. I dangled like a broken marionette.

My short life pumped out of my wrist and down the small curvature of my forearm. A steady stream of warm strawberry Jello flowed into the tiny crevice of my arm pit, welling up into rivulets, and then, a small spring, and then within seconds, a river of blood flowing down across my protruding ribs and caressing my soft baby belly.

My bleached white tee shirt, now blood saturated and tie-dyed crimson, was no longer tucked into the elastic waistband of my crisp baby-blue striped cotton seersucker shorts that held a handful of limp bloody green-beans in my right pocket. A handful of additional green-beans slowly slipped from my lame grasp, while others lay strewn across the nicotine infused gravel carnage. The steady stream of candy-apple-red cascaded down into my shorts and thighs, collecting into the hem, now blood-soaked and dripping, splattering onto my black and white saddle shoes, the pair Mommy let me play in, before plopping and hitting the hard tamped dirt and dust-covered gravel graveyard, mixing my bright pure life into a muddy, burgundy, coagulated sauce.

The world between my shutting eyes was narrowing. My vision blurred, tunneling inward. Sounds were muffled. I don't remember experiencing any sort of pain or screaming for that matter. My blood tickled me as it moved – deceptively gentle considering that it was draining me.

Mommy, my mother-in-law Dolores, and my beautiful eight-year-old wife Tracy, all screamed for help as I hung crucified for picking string beans. The carnage was able to attract the attention of Uncle Martin, our thirty-something, relative-bachelor-neighbor, from the third floor back apartment, who was washing his cereal bowl in front of his kitchen window and was able to see the bloodbath happening below. Uncle Martin bolted down three flights of apartment stairs to rescue my near lifeless body off of the fence. His breath was ragged, his heart pounding through his shirt as he gripped my shredded arm and without hesitation, lifted me, tightly grabbing my ripped wrist just before the bone, a gushing of blood, of flesh, an open vein. Uncle Martin ripped his belt from his now blood-soaked jeans and made a tourniquet. Next, he quickly ripped open his button-down shirt and ripped the sleeve off and then made a proper tourniquet. The fabric was soft and warm from the heat of his body but quickly became saturated with my blood as he wrapped it tightly around my mangled wrist to stop the flow of my short life spilling out onto the pavement. He carried me, his arms trembling from the rush of adrenaline and horror, like one of the fallen soldiers that I played with in my playroom earlier in the week that had his arm blown off. My body slumped limply against Uncle Martin's chest as Mommy climbed into the backseat of his yellow Ford LTD, her arms outstretched, her lap becoming my stretcher. Martin laid me across her. My tiny blood-drenched body folded into her as she clutched me, pressing her hand gently against the makeshift bandage and whispering frantic prayers between choked backed sobs. The engine roared to give me life, tires screeching against the gravel as Uncle Martin gunned it down to Jersey City Medical Center – the only place that could save me.

But as we sped down the streets, I felt it again, that slow creeping blackness at the edges of my vision, the way the world tilted and blurred, the heat of my mother's frantic hands wiping the sweat from my forehead, her hands pressing against my stomach, her touch the only tether holding me to this side of consciousness. Uncle Martin swerved into the emergency entrance of the hospital and jumped out of the driver's side within seconds. His white tee shirt was blood-stained and wet. As the rear door swung open, my otherworldly sight focused on its hulking brick facade resembling something out of an insane asylum. Cold. Merciless. A place where horrors lived and breathed. It was not a place of healing, but a place where the desperate clung to life, where the fluorescent lights flickered, where the sterile smell of antiseptic barely masked the musky smell of sweat, blood, and sickness. We were on a battlefield. I was quickly placed onto a stretcher and whisked into the emergency room. Mommy kept trying to wipe the blood that had splattered onto my face while I was hanging. Once into a makeshift room, there were nurses and doctors running frantically around me, with instruments and long needles. And then, the stitches. I stared in a trance at what looked like *Dr. Frankenstein* – sewing each of the sixteen stitches that held my wrist and hand to my arm, pushing arm innards back through the gaping hole in my wrist, and pushing a curved needle and thick black thread through my flesh. It all seemed to be in slow motion. The *Frankenstein*-esque repair job that curves grotesquely around my wrist looked like I cut my wrist open with the plastic saw-toothed blade of my crafting pinking shears in an attempted suicide. But that would have been a decade premature.

Chapter 3

Arnie and Dolores, our upstairs neighbors, had done it. After years of scrimping, saving, and eating Chef Boyardee, they finally bought their own piece of the American dream; a two-family house on Neptune Avenue, just one block over from the apartment building we all shared. It wasn't just a house; it was a step-up. A declaration that they had made it. A place where life would unfold in a new, bigger, better way. And when they asked us to be their tenants, it felt like a step up for us as well.

    I loved Dolores. There was something about her that made the world feel lighter when you were around her, like she carried her own sunshine with her wherever she went. She was pretty and petite and wore her short blondish-brown hair always in a modern style. She wore jeans and sweatshirts and even though she was close in age to Mommy, they were worlds apart as far as style. I never saw Mommy in jeans. Ever. I don't think she owned a pair. Or sneakers for that matter. Dolores' smile was quick and easy too. She drove a blue Mustang; the kind of car that made people turn their heads when she cruised past. Just being in her presence made things feel less heavy. On the other hand, Arnie, her husband, was a big, towering Italian guy with thick black hair, broad shoulders, and the kind of presence that filled the room with his anxiety. Arnie worked at General Electric alongside my dad, but I couldn't tell you what they both did. I have no idea. But Arnie had figured out how to get a home for his family. A wife, two kids, a dog, and the crown jewel – a pool. A twelve-foot round oasis. A glistening paradise under the punishing Jersey summer sun. Was there ever anything so wonderful and utterly exciting as a backyard pool growing up? For roughly eighty-days of the summer, taking into consideration rainy days, I would watch from our bedroom window with my chin resting in my hands staring out at them. A few yards away, there was Tracy and Gary splashing and streaking their golden tan limbs, jumping through the water like fish. The sun kissing their skin, the water catching the light, and everything around them looking magical. It was a summer long reminder that a magical life was not for everyone.

  Billy and I were rarely invited to swim, maybe a handful of times the entire summer. Our neighbors, the Smiths, also had a pool. A larger pool that was oval. A pool that could easily have fit all the neighborhood kids and may have once or twice. But Billy and I were spectators, sitting at the edges of their magical worlds – watching, waiting, hoping. It wasn't cruelty – it was just the way things were. The pool belonged to them. And we were on the outside looking in. Their laughter carried through the heavy, humid air, mixing with chlorine and the hum of distant lawnmowers. Our windows were open all summer because we didn't have air conditioning.

So, I sat there, my face against the screen, staring at Tracy and Gary diving for pennies, with my fingers digging into my cheeks, swallowing a lump in my throat, pretending that it didn't matter. But it did. The water rippled into a feeling of not belonging. It mattered in a way that only a seven-year-old could feel, that deep ache of exclusion, the quiet, unspoken reminder that no matter how close we lived, and how much stickball we played in the colder months, there were invisible lines drawn between neighbors and friends during the summer.

Me and Billy

We lived next door to a neighbor just like Gladys Kravitz, the nosey neighbor on the television show *Bewitched*. Gladys and her retired husband Abner lived on Morning Glory Circle next door to Darrin and Samantha Stephens. Gladys Kravits was convinced that there were strange things going on in the Stephens home – and she was right. Samantha was a witch. But no one ever believed poor Gladys. Not the neighbors. Not Abner. Only Gladys could see through Samantha's suburban housewife act.

I always loved it when Samantha's cousin Serena would show up – her sexy, jet-black haired cousin with the heavy eyeliner and devious attitude. Serena had no interest in hiding her powers or playing nice. The wildest part was that they were both played by the same actress: Elizabeth Montgomery. Even at ten years old, I found her incredibly attractive. Samantha was dreamy, but Serena was dangerous – and somehow, even better.

One Sunday afternoon, our suspicious neighbor – "*Mrs. Kravits,*" while doing laundry, looked through the window past the alleyway and into our basement, and in-between the asbestos pipes, just before the old oil furnace, saw Arnie masturbating over the slop sink. She phoned my mother and said that we were living with a sicko. That evening, my parents sat me down at the kitchen table, the nine-inch black and white television turned off for added seriousness. Daddy looked uncomfortable and spoke in his country voice.

"Mrs. Kravitz called Mommy this afternoon and said that she saw Arnie…touching himself. Masturbating."

I stared at the glass table, Mommy and Daddy reflected upside down as usual. Then, as if she had been waiting for this opportunity, Mommy leaned in over the glass and added, "That's why you must never go to the bathroom alone in a movie theatre. Some men cut off little boy's penises."

That was it. That was the warning. No follow-up. No added addendum. Just one of Mommy's helpful parenting tips tossed in with a crazy accusation. We personally had never seen Arnie do anything strange, so we continued to be happy as their tenants and never gave it another thought. A few years later, Mommy fell down the back stairs leading out to the yard because the old wooden steps needed to be replaced and there was no railing to hold on to. Arnie was sure that my parents were going to sue him. We never would have – and didn't. It was, however, the reason why we ended up moving to Bayonne.

The only lawsuit my parents ever had was against the Boulevard Pool, when Daddy dove off of the high dive and when he pushed off of the bottom of the pool – he sliced his hand on a broken bottle. Daddy sued the pool and eventually received seven-hundred and fifty dollars which barely covered his medical expenses. The worst part was that we were never allowed to swim at the Boulevard Pool again.

Every summer Paula and Claudia, our neighbors across the street, vacationed in Miami Beach on Collins Avenue, bringing with them Laura Ann and Kara. That only left Tracy Gary, Jimmy, and Bruce to play with. Jimmy liked being by himself mostly.

Paula and Claudia paid me to feed the cats in their yard every summer. It was my very first job and I loved it.

"Psps... Psps...psps…psps psps…." I crouched low to the ground channeling my best Marlin Perkins from Wild Kingdom- whispering into the humid air – calling out to mama and her five kittens. They were skittish, their tiny bodies darting like shadows beneath the porch steps, eyes wide with suspicion. I liked to pretend I was tracking them in the wild as though I was some great explorer earning their trust. But they never let me get too close, not like Tommy.

Tommy was the neighborhood stray. A sturdy gray alley

cat that claimed our front porch most days as his throne. I had claimed him as my confidant and I'd sit beside him for hours, my knees pulled up to my chest, stroking his rough, long spine as I whispered plans, secrets, and movie ideas. I shared with Tommy the things I couldn't say to people. He never judged or questioned; he only listened. His tail flicking lazily, his head tilting just so, like he understood everything I was saying. Tommy was a comfort on days when the world felt like it might swallow me whole, like days when I would have to go shopping with Mommy and Daddy to Union City.

Mommy and Daddy would take me to Schlessinger's Men's Store in Union City to buy my clothes. They said I was now *husky*. My weight, when I turned twelve, fluctuated like Mommy's. It may have had something to do with the medication that Dr. Shapiro prescribed for me. I was in eighth grade when they had me fitted with the cement-colored leisure suit that I wore for my confirmation and graduation. I stood on the worn-out-gold-colored carpeted wooden box while the tailor, an old Italian man who smelled of cigar smoke and Paco Rabanne cologne, pinned the hem of my husky-sized slacks and jacket sleeves. The carpeted box, now weathered, its once vibrant jewel-tone pile the color of corn on the cob, had faded to a mashed, muted cream of corn. Once plush and inviting to stand on in only your socks or bare feet, had become dirty, with matted fibers frayed in places where countless chubby eighth-grade pubescent husky boys like me stood in similar leisure suits. The exposed wooden sides of the box bore the marks of time, with subtle scratches, nicks, and the occasional staple that grabbed and sliced at your ankle in one pivot as you disembarked from the magic carpet and connection to a bygone era. You were stepping off into the unknown world of elegance and craftsmanship in your cement-colored leisure suit, ready to receive the sacrament of confirmation or your grammar school graduation diploma.

It was also the same leisure suit I wore when Mommy had professional photos taken in our apartment of me sitting on my brother's knee. Mommy said the suit color was taupe. It looked and felt more like cement to me. I wore a hunter-green tie with cement colored decoy ducks. Billy wore a matching cement colored leisure suit but sported a silky Quiana open collar shirt with a hunter-green floral print. The photography session involved a wardrobe change half-way through in order to show a more casual side of me. A stiff, starched cotton, spread-collared shirt with a stencil-stamped batik floral design, in shades of hunter-green and cement.

My brother and I were positioned into the corner of our parent's bedroom for a week of pre-production, staging, costume design, and wardrobe fittings. Mommy would stage photography sessions in multiple rooms to view and pre-select our best angles.

First pose: I would sit off to Billy's right side for one of Mommy's test shots, shot in between her two hands, joined at the tips of her chewed-up fingers into a rectangular shape as if she were looking through a real camera lens. The next set-up would be a run-through with me sitting on Billy's *left* knee and then sitting on *both* of his knees and facing straight ahead with his hands on my shoulders, which felt weird. And then another pose with me kneeling *beside* him with my arms and hands draped across his knees, and then multiple shots were taken with both of my legs tucked under my own knees with just my head slumped over resting on his leg like I had fainted. Or was dead.

Some shootings were orchestrated seated on Mommy's gold brocade lady's chair, next to the gold French Provencal drum table where she kept her gold tone footed pill box that held saccharin, and baby Jesus during the Holidays. By the time Billy and I were professionally shot at the ages of thirteen and sixteen, we had hundreds of poses down.

Shooting practice (1974)

My parents' bedroom was the first room off of the front hall. It was a living room typical of many two-family homes in Jersey City, but our parents used it as their bedroom. Mommy's preparation behind the scenes was three weeks of selecting wardrobe and location scouting within our five room Jersey City apartment. The day of the Edward Martin shooting, after our parents cooked up the usual Saturday breakfast large enough to satiate and send four child murderers to the electric chair, we prepared for the arrival of Greenville's local photographer.

Billy (age 16) and Me (age 13)

Mommy had heard of Mr. Martin's fine reputation from Aunt Marie and Aunt Angie, who by the way could have been cast as *Carmela Corleone* in *The Godfather*. That's right, Francis Ford Coppola himself had wanted Aunt Angie to play Mama Corleone – Vito Corleone's wife in *The Godfather,* but the role eventually went to a real actress. But that could have been Aunt Angie swishing around in an apron making sauce and dramatically clutching her chest during Sunny's funeral. But no, Uncle Johnny had to ruin it, and according to Mommy, Aunt Angie had to turn down *The Godfather* role, not because she didn't want to do it, but because Uncle Johnny said *no*, and not because he was just a controlling husband either. The real reason according to Mommy was far juicier. Uncle Johnny was fautching around. And not just with some random floozy, but with Aunt Claire! Yes! Aunt Claire who is Uncle Johnny's sister-in-law! What made this whole story even more absurd was that Aunt Claire herself was the least likely mistress in the history of mistresses. Aunt Claire was a certified chain smoker, very petite and sickly looking, always coughing, always in a cloud of Virginia Slims. Anxious and nervous to the point that her arms and legs were constantly shaking. How could Aunt Claire withstand the sloppy weight of Uncle Johnny on top of her? I mean the physics alone were baffling. She would need to have some hidden core super-strength we didn't know about, like some secret weight-bearing mechanism that allowed her to survive the weight of Uncle Johnny without shattering like a piece of fine china.

Aunt Angie was the complete opposite of her sister Aunt Marie and was discovered by Edward Martin. Somehow or another, Mr. Martin knew someone who knew someone, and was able to get a photo of Aunt Angie to Mr. Coppola. Edward Martin knew talent and exactly what Francis Ford Coppola would want his Mamma Corleone to look like. Aunt Angie was a size sixteen with a full, round face and soft lines surrounding her eyes. Her dark hair, streaked with silver, was always swept up and pinned neatly around her head, framing her head like a crown. She was always seen in her apron, tied loosely around her waist, its cotton worn and stained from years of stirring sauce, rolling out dough, and preparing endless meals for Uncle Johnny and Little Johnny.

Me, Uncle Johnny, Daddy, Poppy and Uncle Joe (partially seen)

Uncle Johnny was creepy, and reminded me of Curley, one of the Three Stooges. He would yank me too close to his mole-infested-jaundiced face – a constellation of waxy brown Raisinets orbiting his bald, greasy head, each currant a marker of his excesses. Uncle Johnny, holding me too tightly against his fat Italian gabagool-stuffed pot-belly, forced me to breathe in his scotch and soda, halitosis, cigarette breath – shotgunning streams of Chesterfield smoke directly from his blackened, tar-encrusted lungs into mine and leaving a trail of noxious echoes in its wake. A boisterous laugh filled the kitchen with his slapstick gurgle, spraying brown saliva from his mouth as he jerked his head around like one of the Three Stooges, overacting for the laughter and applause that Daddy, Poppy, and Uncle Joe, Nanny's older bachelor brother, would not give him. Daddy and Poppy did not like Uncle Johnny. I don't think Uncle Joe cared one way or the other. Uncle Joe was invited to every holiday from Thanksgiving through Easter Sunday. He mostly observed us and said very little.

Uncle Joe looked like a perfectly groomed gentleman of his time. Even though it was 1976, Uncle Joe still dressed like it was 1952 and he had somewhere important to be. A white cotton shirt, starched and ironed to perfection, and tucked into pleated camel colored wool gabardine trousers, cognac colored, leather lace-up dress oxfords, and a matching leather belt. Uncle Joe finished off his ensemble with a healthy splash of English Leather aftershave. At sixty-something, Uncle Joe's hair was more salt than pepper, parted with obsessive care and slicked to the side with pomade so thick it gleamed under the dining room light like polished marble. He wore a tan cashmere overcoat in the winter which he never removed until he was good and ready. The only two things that seemed off with Uncle Joe was that he belched and farted at the dinner table and that he sexually assaulted Mommy every holiday.

On Thanksgiving, Christmas, New Years, and Easter Sunday, Uncle Joe would slip Mommy a hundred-dollar bill at some point between the antipasto and Nanny's homemade lasagna, and then he would make his move on Mommy while her head was in the oven. He would press the front part of his pelvis into Mommy from behind, grabbing her at the hips and bending over her, grinding his private parts into her rear-end, his hands reaching around her waist, then feeling her breasts. *Yes*, I personally witnessed this.

Mommy would yell, "Uncle Joe! That it is not nice to do

that! I'm your niece! Knock it off."

The assault always took place in the Keeping Room. Nanny would be at the sink washing dishes and would twist her head and shout without turning around.

"Joe! What the hell is the matter with you!" Sounding like an angry Edith Bunker yelling at Archie for saying something off-color, her hands dripping pearls of sudsy water onto the linoleum like nothing was all that unusual. I'd stand there, frozen in place with my hands full of black olives and celery sticks smeared with cream cheese and dusted with paprika, staring at this scene like a deer caught in the kitchen headlights. I don't know if Daddy knew that Uncle Joe was molesting Mommy. Maybe he didn't want to know, but if Daddy knew that Uncle Joe was feeling Mommy up during every holiday for a hundred bucks, he never let on. Uncle Joe would back away – smoothing out the pleats in his trousers, adjusting his wilted erection, and then ask when coffee and dessert were being served as if this was completely normal. And in a way, it was. I had personally witnessed at least five hundred dollars' worth of molestations over the course of a year and a half.

Back at the dining room table, Uncle Joe would nonchalantly *let one rip* - once again no warning, no apology – just the long bubbling sigh from deep within his bowels, followed by absolute silence, as if we were all supposed to politely ignore the fact that we were about to launch into a beautiful ricotta cheesecake dripping in strawberries. Nanny would smack her white cloth napkin against her thigh and mutter, "Jesus, Mary, and Joseph!" but never directly at Uncle Joe. After all, he was still her older brother.

Mommy would always tell me to never repeat what I saw and heard, and I would always promise not to tell. I had to double promise and pinky swear to Mommy the time that I overheard Mommy talking to Aunt Marie about her husband, my Uncle Nick, tying her up and locking Aunt Marie inside her bedroom closet all day until he came home from work. Something like that could never get out, but me and Mommy were best friends. Billy called me *"Momma's boy,"* which was fine because *he* could have Daddy. He could be a *Daddy's boy*, but I was Mommy's favorite. I guess Billy liked getting beat up. Mommy explained at an early age that Billy and Daddy had more in common with each other, like baseball and sports, and that we had more in common with each other in the same way, only we liked movies, television shows, fashion, and shopping.

Besides nearly discovering Aunt Angie, Edward Martin had shot Aunt Marie's daughter Elaine, and according to Mommy, Edward Martin was able to capture Elaine's gazelle-like beauty and fine features. Elaine looked like a high-fashion model.

Mr. Martin was on time as instructed and in accordance with the contract that Mommy insisted they both sign. He arrived promptly at our apartment at 2 p.m. doused in Pierre Cardin cologne. His perfectly styled hair was pomade slicked over to the side. He methodically set up his camera equipment and lighting, taking intermittent direction from my mother. My father sat in his club chair off to the left of my mother's makeshift studio. Staging was everything and there would be no rankling of unceremonious temperament on my mother's seat. My father knew his place and any arguing was better left for later.

The final proof sheets of photos and poses were narrowed down in the course of a week, with Mommy magnifying our details with a loupe she special ordered at Mr. Martin's photography studio. The finished portrait, thirty-six by twenty-four, custom framed in an Early American wood frame, satin finish, with non-glare glass (as soon as there was such a thing), hung above my mother's gold embroidered French Provincial lady's chair for three decades. Mommy told me that I could be a model.

Billy (age 16) and Me (age 13)

Chapter 4

I had that Donny Osmond kind of hair. Thick, dark brown hair that was always a little too long and hung over my forehead no matter how often I tried to push it back. My smile was a little crooked, and my eyes, hazel with flickers of blue, never seemed to match up either, the right one slightly lazy and a little larger, making me look perpetually confused. And my teeth, a jumbled mess. But I knew how to dress. Even as a kid, I had a sense of style that made me feel I belonged, even in times that I felt I didn't.

  Every couple of weekends, Mommy, Daddy, and I would catch the Bergen Avenue bus from Neptune Avenue to Journal Square. Mommy and I would go straight to Danny Mack to find her shoes and Rags To Riches for my colored chinos. Daddy would head straight to Lorsche Men's Shop, which felt less like a store and more like a private men's club, with polished wood floors and the hush of old money. If we really wanted to make a day of it, we'd take the train to Newark, to the grand department stores – Hanes, S. Klein, and Bamburgers – each one its own cathedral of display windows, perfume counters, and escalators that were a bit of a bumpy ride and came with a price. Without fail, the day ended in a fight. Maybe it was the crowds, the money, the unspoken tension that came with wanting more than you could afford but later that night, something always exploded.

Still, they bought me anything I wanted when it came to clothes. That was our family's love language. Our family said I love you through collars, cuffs, and careful tailoring. Daddy had his French-cuffed shirts custom made at Lorsch, his initials monogrammed on every one: WLB. William Leo Brennan. He always had a silk pocket square folded just so, perfectly matching the tie he'd carefully chosen for that day. Everyone said he was a sharp dresser, and Mommy loved that about him. It was one of the things that she loved the most. It made her feel like the world saw them the way she wanted to be seen – elegant, stylish, and put together.

Mommy and I would have lunch at Journal Square at either Boulevard Drinks, for grilled hot dogs, or Liss Drug Store, for grilled cheese sandwiches, and as Mommy would always say, "*a side of French*," which meant an order of French fries. Mommy was just like Poppy in saying words in make-believe French, you know, words that you add onto an ending, or make into an adjective. Poppy would declare something *"good and Frenchie,"* which, in his world, meant the absolute best – as if it came straight from the Champs-Elysees. Mommy's *"side of French"* wasn't just a food order; it was a performance, a nod to some dream of elegance just out of reach.

Sometimes Mommy and I would go visit Aunt Marie, who worked at Marion & Rose Lingerie Shop on Bergen Avenue just before Journal Square. It was like stepping into a scene from one of those million-dollar movies that played on Channel 9, the kind that starred Lana Turner.

Aunt Marie had jet black hair that cascaded in soft sculpted waves against her alabaster skin which seemed to glow under the store's bright lights like she was on a Broadway stage. Every inch of her corseted frame was meticulously perfected, like a Hollywood makeup artist had done her face at the start of every morning. Aunt Marie penciled in her beauty mark, ensuring it was the perfect shade of black. Her eyebrows were precisely drawn, arched in charcoal to match her eyelashes and lined eyes. Her lips, a rich, deep red, precisely drawn and filled in, revealed her dazzling white teeth. Aunt Marie was by far the most glamorous aunt that Billy and I had.

Marion & Rose was a hushed, intimate world, draped in silk and lace with racks of delicate negligees in shades of champagne, blush, and midnight black. The golden light of the

Saturday afternoon sun filtered through the lingerie shop's windows, casting a kaleidoscope of lace patterns onto the mannequins – like shards of glass splintering across delicate peignoir sets. I loved the mannequins that had hair and makeup, and I was especially attracted to the blondes. I would stare at their painted faces, frozen in perfect beauty, studying their sculptured features along with every smooth curve of their plastic bodies, while subconsciously listening and recording every word that Mommy and Aunt Marie were gossiping about. Their dramatic stories sounded like a made for television movie. I absorbed every rise and arc in their storytelling, the gasps, the laughs, and the tears. There were always tears. And anger. Most conversations ended with talking about Daddy and my Uncle Nick.

The mannequins called me. I was drawn into their silent glamor. I imagined the stories and secrets they were certain to have heard and witnessed. Every part of them molded and defined except for their ability to speak. Or move. But they could read the truth behind the human faces that visited the lingerie shop, like a *Twilight Zone* episode. These mannequins had seen and heard it all. Silent witnesses to an endless stream of humans, mostly women, that passed through the lingerie store day after day, night after night. Some whispered betrayals – confessions made in hushed tones over racks of slips and corsets. These women, their voices low, sharing stories of sins better saved for *keeping rooms*. They finger the delicate lace of a chemise, while sharing bits and pieces of their lives, tiny holes that weave a story. The mannequins had seen their share of teary-eyed women searching for versions of themselves they once knew. Standing perplexed at why and how their figures had shifted, how and why they had put on weight. The *real* women would telepathically ask the mannequins, *"Do you think I still look beautiful?"* Just as well that the mannequins could not speak. Some of the women had obviously given up.

Some came in groups of two or three girlfriends. The younger women would laugh, embarrassed by the sexier underwear that the shop sold, holding panties up high and giggling, a few spinning the lacey string around their finger like a lasso. These women were still excited to get dressed up in beautiful negligees for the men in their lives. And some women came alone, their hands trembling as they unfolded a slip in the softest, flush pink, trying to remember what it felt like to be held by a man, or to be made love to.

And then there were the men. Oh how the mannequins noticed the men. The ones who entered the shop with cheap smiles, clutching expensive bags with fidgety hands, stammering about something in black, something… a little daring and …sexy. Some of them were husbands who were still young and had wives that still wanted to have sex with them, and some older husbands were there to buy a gift of hope for what they had lost. A handful of times the mannequins had seen men purchasing sexy lingerie for themselves. These men were often sweating and stammering. But the saddest of the men were the ones with eyes filled with only obligation and emptiness.

There were others, the mannequins knew them instantly, that were not shopping for their wives. They moved with confidence but whispered names that didn't match the wedding bands on their fingers. The mannequins watched as they traced the footsteps of *these* men in the store. They were not to be trusted. They watch as the men trace the silk with the same fingers they will use to trace their mistress' skin that night. They see these men slipping a crisp ten-dollar bill across the counter to ensure a quick transaction so that they can scurry out, their secrets tucked into elegant paper bags, sealed with a pink scalloped sticker by Aunt Marie, the top saleswoman and top secret keeper.

Lastly, at the end of each night, the mannequins would see Aunt Marie run her fingers over the silks at closing time, adjusting and finger-spacing each ivory satin-charmeuse quilted hanger, each piece of pleasure and pain, depending on the scene, always with a distant stare, as if imagining another life that had escaped her. Perhaps a life with a French or Italian lover, or perhaps simply a husband who didn't tie her up and lock her in a closet on her days off. But the mannequin's job was to stand there, to observe in silence, in secret.

Sometimes after visiting with Aunt Marie at the lingerie shop, Mommy and I would meet Nanny for lunch at The Canton Tea Garden for Chinese food. It was located at the beginning of Journal Square. I would only have the clear broth and fortune cookie, because Russel, the fifteen year old red-headed, freckled troublemaker who lived up the block from us (who was thrown out of St. Paul's for disciplinary problems), said that at some

Chinese restaurants, they lock-up a monkey in the middle of the table and diners hit the monkey on top of his head with a rubber mallet until his head splits open and they kill him, and then the family eats the hot monkey brains right there at the table directly out of the monkey's head. He said that it was a delicacy and that it was real. It was the most disgusting thing I had ever heard, and it made me so angry that I could cry, and I hated Russel for putting that into my head forever. I loved monkeys. Mom and Dad told me to stay away from Russel because he was nothing but trouble and was going to wind up missing or dead someday.

I always wanted a monkey, but I knew that it was out of the question. I did get a pet mouse one Saturday after having lunch with Mommy in Woolworths on Broadway in Bayonne after an afternoon of shopping. Mommy and I would sit at the counter and order our usual grilled cheese and a side of *French*. Woolworths had a small pet department tucked between the toy aisle and the register – parakeets, goldfish, and cages of twitchy little hamsters and mice. That afternoon, one of those mice spoke to me. Not literally, but with eyes that told me that we belonged together. He was white, no bigger than a cotton ball with ears, and I knew instantly that he was my Topo Gigio, like the mouse on *The Ed Sullivan Show*.

We bought him everything he needed. A rectangular glass tank, balsam wood shavings, nesting cotton, a water bottle to clip on the side, a squeaky metal wheel, a full-blown Habitrail that I could create into a castle, and a clear plastic ball that he could roll across my playroom in. I named him Billy Jack (BJ for short) after a character in the movie that had just come out. I spent all of my time in my playroom making clothes for Billy Jack, who was named after the Navajo Green Beret Vietnam War veteran, and martial arts hero who could chop bad guys in their throat and kill them. Billy Jack defended the Freedom School and the students and townspeople against the bad guys. Billy Jack goes through a Navajo initiation with his tribe, where he was purposely bitten by a large rattlesnake, so that he would become the blood brother to the snake and become a hero. I loved films with heroes.

In no time, I was able to create an entire wardrobe for BJ. I made him tiny capes, action-hero tunics, and even a miniature Dracula costume complete with a high collar to match mine. His favorite costume was Mighty Mouse. He would climb into the palm of my hand without hesitation; his tiny whiskers twitching with excitement and scurry up my arm nestling into the curve of my ear tickling me with his soft little mouse nose. I'd lift him up by his tiny face, pressing a delicate kiss onto his miniscule mouse-mouth, and then our favorite part, I would grip his pink leathery tail and swing him high through the air. BJ would soar like Mighty Mouse, his cape billowing behind him, before landing safely into a pile of soft fabric I had spread out on the floor as a makeshift runway for his heroic landings. And just like clockwork, BJ would scamper back over, leaping onto my outstretched hand, eager for another flight. Over and over and over and over, he would fly through the air until it was time for dinner.

My playroom was technically an eight-foot by ten-foot

bedroom that my parents allowed to be my playroom. It was the best gift that my parents ever gave me. Here I was the creator, the inventor, the architect, the builder, the fashion designer, the actor, the singer, the writer, the artist, the magician, the director, the editor, the makeup artist, the movie star, the race car driver, and most of all – Dracula.

In the center of the room was my card table. It had a wood-grained vinyl top and two folding chairs, one for me and one folded and kept in the closet. Under my card table was my electric racetrack. Just big enough to produce car crashes and highway death scenes. One corner of my playroom was where I kept my electric organ and guitar. Across from that sat my Easy-Bake Oven, Creepy-Crawler Bug Maker, and stacks and stacks of monster magazines. Hanging on a hook, my Dracula cape that I designed and made myself using a yard and a half of black velvet that Nanny had gotten me, and part of a cake box from Greenville Bakery that I spray painted black and sewed onto the top of my cape as the collar. I made a vampire walking stick from a broken broomstick, a glass doorknob, and black electrical tape. My fangs, fake blood, and Dracula jewelry were kept in a shoe box that I made into a small coffin. There, at the end of my shelf was the blonde wig, the very same wig that Mommy had worn while chasing Billy around our apartment. It had now found a new purpose, and on Sunday nights, it became my *Phyllis Diller* wig, and a crucial part of my weekly performance for Nanny and Poppy as well as a yearly holiday performance for our neighbors.

During the week, every night after dinner, Mommy and I would eat penny candy from a small brown paper bag that had a serrated edge along the top. On my way home from school, I would stop at Grocer's candy store and buy a dollar bag of Red Hot Dollars, chocolate covered jelly rings, rainbow colored circus peanuts, coconut slices with three colored stripes, wax bottles filled with sugary colored liquid, and red cherry licorice shoestrings. Next, Mommy would go into the kitchen and take out the vegetable oil and glaze the bottom of the Sunday sauce pot with enough vegetable oil to cover the kernels to make popcorn. After every kernel was popped, Mommy would then drizzle it with a quarter of a cup of melted butter, toss in a handful of salt, and sit with me in my bedroom on my brother's twin bed, our snack trays set up to watch our favorite television shows together.

We loved *The Sonny and Cher Show, Laverne and Shirley, Happy Days, The Captain and Tennille,* and *Donny and*

Marie. Our Friday night favorite was *The Partridge Family.*

Shirley Jones played a widowed mother, and her real life stepson, David Cassidy, played her son on the show. Keith (the star of the show), after his father dies (no reason is given and he is never spoken of again), convinces his mother to quit her bank teller job and form a band with his four other siblings.

The Partridge Family recorded an album in their garage and became famous and traveled the world in a brightly painted school bus. Keith Partridge was everything I wanted to be. Handsome, funny, talented, wore fashionable clothes, and was loved by all the girls. I loved to entertain. Mommy said that it was a sign that we were both named Keith.

The neighborhood kids, myself and Billy included, formed a band and practiced in Tracy Marino's upstairs apartment. We all played instruments, kind of, and sang, sort of. I knew for sure that we would become famous after people heard us perform. We decided on the song *Windy* to be our first hit, but the band had creative differences, and we broke up a week later. I was so upset. I was sure that we were going to be famous. Keith Partridge was always on the cover of *Tiger Beat Magazine* and Mommy told me that I could be on the cover of *Tiger Beat* myself one day if I get a lucky break and get discovered.

Saturday nights, after my parents were done screaming, cursing, and fighting with each other, Mommy and I would spend the remainder of the night together watching our favorite nightly television shows. We would set up our faux-marble plastic snack trays, which were kept under my bed, to watch *The Carol Burnett*

Show in my bedroom. Mommy would close my wood-grain plastic accordion door and call my father a bastard or an asshole under her breath.

More than once, Mommy told me she should've married Leo – the guy she not so secretly dated while Daddy was in the army. Mom and Dad were engaged. Daddy was a Morse code operator in the Korean War. When I would question him about it, Daddy would use his right pointer finger and type in the air *dots, dits,* and *dahs,* which he said meant words in Morse code. Daddy said that skilled Morse code operators, like himself, could understand code in their heads at a rate in excess of forty words per minute. I could not imagine him being able to do this.

Mommy showed me the photo of Leo she had shown me multiple times throughout the years, that she kept in her wallet, tucked safely behind credit cards and receipts, its edges yellowed and bent at the top right corner. Leo was tall and had dark wavy hair. He was the total opposite of Daddy except they were both tall and thin and dressed well. Mommy's touch was always gentle when she traced Leo's face and body with her index finger, feeling the warmth of the boy who made her laugh while Daddy was off at war. She didn't speak about Leo often, but enough for me to know that she openly allowed herself to remember the love letters, the dances, and the way Leo looked at her. Many Saturday nights I wished that Leo was my father. I would wonder to myself how she even ended up with Daddy anyway, because all they ever did was fight.

Mommy and I would laugh so hard during *"The Carol*

Burnett Show!" Tim Conway played businessman Mr. Bernie Tudball, and Carol would play Mrs. Wiggins, his dumb and sexy secretary that he called "Mrs. Uh-Whiggins." Mr. Tudball said that she was a *"Bimbo who the IQ-Fairy never visited."* Mrs. Wiggins was constantly filing her nails and the sketches centered around Mr. Tudball's frustration over Mrs. Wiggins' dimwittedness, such as not being able to use the office intercom system and how she walked across his office in her tight skirt. Tim and Carol would send Mommy running out of the bedroom because she would wet her pajama bottoms from laughing so hard.

Although our favorite part of the show was the question-and-answer segment when Carol would take questions from her audience and perform her Tarzan yell. It was at the end of the show when Carol would sing "I'm So Glad We Had This Time Together" which would bring us to tears. Carol would tug at her earlobe and say goodnight to the grandmother who raised her.

> *"I'm so glad we had this time together,*
> *Just to have a laugh or sing a song.*
> *Seems we just get started and before you know it,*
> *comes the time we have to say, so long."*

This meant that the Carol Burnett show was over and Mommy would cry while sitting on the edge of my brother's twin bed across from mine, still chewing the sides of her fingertips, tugging and pulling, tiny teeth-torn flaps of flesh, ripping at the outermost corner of her fingertips with her front teeth, eating mostly her pointer, her middle finger, and her thumb, especially her thumb, always leaving the pinky alone. Gnawing at the part of the finger where the cuticle meets the nail bed at a ninety-degree angle, Mommy would rip at it – stretching the cuticle thin enough until it snapped and bled, then sucking the blood from the freshly made tear – applying pressure with alternating fingers until the bleeding stopped.

The Carol Burnett Show

I would rub her back through her pajama top and tell her that everything would be ok. We would then break down our snack trays and clean up, and I would give Mommy a kiss goodnight on her cheek. Mommy would go into her own bedroom to get into bed with my father who was already asleep from a Saturday of binge drinking beer and whiskey. We would need to get up early the next day for Sunday morning Mass.

Ready for Sunday Mass.
Mom and Dad, Billy (age 10), and Me (age 7)

Chapter 5

Some summer Sundays after Mass we would go with Nanny and Poppy on day trips. We didn't own a car. We had never gone on a family vacation, *ever*, except for one nightmarish week cut short in 1971, in Beach Haven, New Jersey, with Mommy and Daddy, Nanny and Poppy, and Billy. I was nine years old, and it was hotter than hell that week. Mommy said so a hundred times, mopping her forehead with a kitchen towel as Daddy loaded up Poppy's station wagon. Poppy stood in the street smoking his cigarette, making snide comments about the way Daddy packed the luggage. I thought Daddy's head would explode.

After driving for almost five hours counting bathroom breaks, we finally arrived at the house that we rented, which turned out to be a shanty bungalow with a clay dirt floor, an old, splintered driftwood-esque picnic table, that served as the dining room table and required a certain amount of bravery just to swing your legs over its wobbly benches without getting seriously slashed and stabbed by rusty hardware and splinters the size of toothpicks. Grey field mice ran through the rooms.

Nobody could sleep because the fans just kept pushing the

hot air around. Mommy kept saying that it was like being in an oven. Daddy was sweating buckets, pacing around in his white crew-neck tee shirt, muttering under his breath about Poppy. And then there was Billy. He'd been annoying and teasing me all week, and it was only Wednesday. Flicking my ear, calling me a baby, shooting spitballs made out of toilet paper into the back of my head like he had a dart gun. The old wooden floors kicked up a mixture of clay dirt, crushed gravel, and dust while walking through the shanty rooms in our white Keds, creating dust bowls as my brother and I scuffled, wrestled, and slapped each other around. It was out of control.

I had finally been pushed too far. I grabbed an old rusty kitchen knife just lying on the table and lunged at him. I could not take another minute of his teasing, spitballs, pinching, and prodding. I hated Billy by this point and remember wishing that he would get cancer and die. But before I could stab Billy in his heart, Daddy's hand came out of nowhere, smacking me so hard I flew off the bench and landed on my back. The knife fell, clanging against the timeworn dusty floorboards like a scene out of *Bonanza*. Billy sat there, wide-eyed for once, his stupid smirk gone.

Daddy was towering over me, his face redder than ever, the veins in his neck were popping out like he was in a Saturday night fight with Mommy.

"What the hell is wrong with you?" he bellowed, shaking the sweat off his forehead.

I just laid there, staring up at him crying. Poppy of course was laughing from his spot at the head of the picnic table, like the whole thing was the best entertainment he'd had all week. So, after five torturous days, we loaded up Poppy's powder blue Rambler Station Wagon and headed back home to Greenville. Our family was better suited for day outings to lakes, our local pool, and a yearly late summer day trip to Sterling Forest Gardens.

Sterling Forest Gardens had sixty acres of lawn, ornamental grass, flower beds, interconnecting ponds, and mosquitoes, located in Tuxedo, N.Y, a three-hour car ride from Jersey City. Mommy and Daddy would be up and at 'em at 6 a.m. packing lunch, singing, and whistling. Daddy was a big whistler. We would eat an early breakfast, go to 8 a.m. mass, and then get ready for Nanny and Poppy to pick us up for our road trip in their Rambler. Daddy would brush my brother's and my teeth on mornings of special occasions and Sunday Mass. Sterling Forest Gardens was a special occasion. Daddy said that me and Billy were not doing a good job at dental hygiene and that our teeth were yellow, so he would call us both into the small five by seven-foot bathroom and mash down our tooth-brush bristles into a mixture of hot water, peroxide, and baking soda, and scour our teeth. After scrubbing our gums bloody with his caked-up, chalky, salty, and burning concoction, Daddy would make us smile at him, checking for missed tartar and stains, using a silver dental pick to remove the sepia tone crusty deposits trapped beneath our forced smiles. Next, he would move onto our scalp and hair. He would grab my face with his strong athletic grip, sinking his thumb and forefinger into my six-year-old jaw, steadying it for hair product and combing. Daddy would then mix his homemade pomade in a metal cup he placed into the center of the white porcelain bathroom sink covering the drain. He waged a weekly war on our hair, due to its unruly texture and natural ability to have a mind of its own. He was determined to tame it. After mixing a concoction of shea butter, honey, and vegetable oil into a thick yellowish goop, he would scoop it from the cup with his right hand and slather it into our hair, first messing it up roughly at the roots with both of his hands, sometimes ripping out long stray hairs by accident, shaping it forcibly. Then using the comb to dig deep into our tender scalps eventually wrestling every cowlick into his desired growth pattern. Nearing the complete look, Daddy would clip runaway hairs surrounding my ears with long pointy steel barber scissors, sometimes inadvertently catching the thin membrane surrounding the top portion of my earlobe. Tears would press out from the corners of my tightly closed eyes. Daddy would ask if I wanted something to cry about. I would whimper no, barely audible, with the taste of peroxide and warm salty paste dripping down my throat, my tightly squeezed eyes trying to hold back a river of tears.

    My brother and I would wait on our front porch for Nanny and Poppy to arrive, having already started the morning traumatized by having our smiles taken away. Our salty gums and mouths were left throbbing, swollen and bloodied; our scalps raked tender down to every hair follicle and nerves on our heads. Mommy would dress my brother and me as twins in nearly identical outfits from Schultz's Department Store, even though we were three and a half years apart. Navy and white henley jacquard knit tops over white or blue denim shorts, with white crew socks, and Keds. We were color coordinated as an entire family most of the time. Shades of yellow, shades of tweed with taupes and sandy undertones, shades of gray and black, shades of aubergine, mauve, and eggplant, but we wore mostly shades of blue, especially navy.

Me, Nanny, and Billy. Sterling Forest

We would arrive at Sterling Forest four and a half hours later due to my frequent need to urinate at rest stops along the way. The nervous condition I was in the process of developing was becoming more and more visible and physical. My ticks were becoming out of control. I suffered constant pain in my neck and shoulders from ticking, shrugging and jerking all day and all night. I was no longer able to cover up what was happening to me neurologically, and I could no longer control my bladder. Not that I would wet the bed or have an accident – I would simply need to urinate every thirty minutes. The final pitstop in Orange County, just before we would arrive at Sterling Forest, was always the Red Apple Rest. It was a cafeteria style restaurant that had trays to gather your food on and slide around the aluminum rails picking out whatever you wanted. Nanny and Mommy would always have a piece of the homemade apple pie that the Red Apple Rest was famous for. My brother and I would get an order of *French* – and a Coke. Daddy and Poppy weren't snackers so they would continue their bickering and name-calling.

Red Apple Rest

My father would accompany me to the Red Apple Wash Room, which was located outside in an attached building, and stand behind me, waiting for me to pee into the five-foot tall, white, urine stained cracked porcelain urinal. As my anxiety attacks began happening more frequently, I would have difficulty emptying my bladder completely and was often only able to leak out a few drops at a time but felt the constant pressure of a full bladder. Doctor Shapiro called it *"bashful bladder syndrome,"* but the scientific name he said was *Paruresis*, a psychological disorder in which a person is unable to urinate in the presence of others, such as a public restroom.

There were no dividers between urinals. Men peed out in the open. Sometimes you would walk into a men's room and there would be a ten-foot-long porcelain trough to pee in. Like a barn animal. Daddy explained to me that in Ireland the pee-trough is common and that it was a good idea to pee in the trough because you didn't have to touch anything other than your own penis, and the only thing that gets dirty is the sole of your sneakers from the sticky urine where the men stand, dribbling and shaking the excess urine off before tucking in and pulling up their flies. If there were other men at the pee trough, I would pretend to pee and then shake and zip and quickly walk out of the bathroom praying not to wet my pants until the bathroom would be empty and I could pee into the pee trough by myself, praying that no one would walk in on me, which would result in me stopping mid-stream and leaving the bathroom feeling like my half-full bladder was going to explode. I would stand at the urinal or pig trough, anxious, crying and shaking, with Daddy trying to contain his increasing pent-up anger less than eighteen inches behind me, not at me, but with Mommy and Poppy, asking what was taking so long. He wasn't being mean, and he really did have a lot of patience with me. I truly was taking a long time to pee. Daddy was just mentally exhausted from fighting with Mommy and Poppy.

    Now, at the age of ten and a half, suffering from constant crying jags, anxiety, tics, and now, the inability to urinate in a public restroom, I would need to be medicated. I was becoming the mental case that Billy said I was. Doctor Shapiro told my parents that my symptoms were indicative of growing pains. He prescribed *Stelazine*. Tiny red lacquered pills that he said would help me breathe, easing the sharp stabbing pains in my chest, that at first would paralyze me, and then drop me to my ten year old knees, trembling, crying, unable to breathe, knife-stabbing pain into my heart, a sense that I was being smothered and that I was going to have a heart attack and die. I would discover years later that my tiny shiny red pills were used to treat certain mental disorders such as schizophrenia, psychotic disorders and hallucinations, none of which I believed I had, unless you consider the persistent inner voice that had convinced me that I would be famous one day.

If it was growing pains, my waistline was beginning to grow as well. My weight fluctuated like Mommy's. My parents told me that my tiny red shiny pill would help relax me and make me less nervous. I took the recommended Stelazine dosage prescribed by Dr. Shapiro for twelve years even though years later I would discover that the recommended maximum dosage time was actually twelve *weeks*. Taking Stelazine longer than twelve weeks could raise the risk of *Tardive Dyskinesia*, a condition affecting the nervous system that could cause permanent damage, including involuntary and abnormal movements of the lips and tongue, facial grimacing, sticking out your tongue, or in rare cases, sucking and fish-like movements of the mouth. Luckily, the only side effects I seemed to have developed after the twelve weeks, were the permanent jerky movements of my head and shoulders, blinking my eyes, and later, beginning age twelve or so, the incessant combing of my hair with a silver aluminum comb that I kept in the back pocket of my pants at all times, whipping it out, raking my hair every two minutes until my scalp was sore and bloodied. Thank God I didn't start sucking like a fish. Stelazine, however, had increased my penchant for sleepwalking, and after I tried to unlock the front door and escape, in my pajamas, while my parents were watching the *Doris Day Show* one night, incohesive and babbling something about being chased by a giant frog, my parents called Dr. Shapiro for advice. Dr. Shapiro told my parents that thirty percent of children between the ages of five and twelve experience a sleepwalking episode, that persistent sleepwalking was stress induced, and only afflicts one to six percent of children. He told them the dangers of waking up a sleepwalker and that studies had been inconclusive as to whether or not waking a sleepwalker could cause permanent brain damage. Dr. Shapiro told them to sleep with one eye open and report back with any adverse behavior.

Urinating on my brother's *Abbey Road* and *White Album* at two in the morning qualified as adverse behavior. Billy was screaming at me but somehow, I managed to continue sleepwalking. He could have caused me to have had permanent brain damage. Dr. Shapiro questioned if there was unusual stress in the home. This was not the first time that the question of stress in our home had come up. My Kindergarten teacher Mrs. Edmondson had noted on my report card in the comments section that I was exhibiting signs of stress and anxiety. She requested to speak to my parents in school during parent/teacher night and Mom and Dad were able to convince her that everything was fine in our home, and that they would take me to our family doctor for observation.

Everyone adored Dr. Morris Shapiro. It was as if he were a priest. He had so many women patients, and they worshipped him. His waiting room would be filled with women of all ages and sizes. Women waited for hours to receive their weight loss medication.

Dr. Shapiro was a manic bundle of energy. A bespectacled, six-foot tall, slim, Jewish man in his mid-fifties with a receding hairline and oversized Geoffrey Beene tortoise shell eyeglasses. He would run from examining room to examining room, racing through the adjoining doors, slamming each door behind the other. His waiting and examining rooms reeked of rubbing alcohol. His patients could hear him yelling "We're here! We're here! We're here!" running from each examining room, happening upon his next patient. We would sit in the waiting room for hours before he was ready to see us. Dr. Shapiro was very hopped up, like the Roadrunner, and If I had known better, I would have thought that Dr. Shapiro was on drugs himself.

I would be so embarrassed during my bi-yearly physical examination by Dr. Shapiro. Mortified and humiliated to unbutton my pants, pull down my underwear, and have Dr. Shapiro check my testicles for hernias and abnormalities with his nurse standing beside him writing notes on a clipboard.

"Cough. Again. One more time. Cough." Inspecting my ten-year-old scrotum for deformities with his cold hands in full view of Mommy, Daddy, and his nurse, who Doctor Shapiro

ended up marrying after his wife (who was the head nurse of his office) died of cancer. I didn't understand what coughing had to do with having a hernia, but I was too embarrassed to ask.

    The worst medical examinations were saved for St. Paul's Grammar School, however. Every October from the age of ten, the school nurse would assist the local Doctor in the annual St. Paul's Grammar School Hernia Hunt. Boy after boy would line up single file in front of the hall lockers and into the assistant principal's office. Six boys in, we were instructed by the nurse to unbutton our pants and pull down our zippers. Our scrotums would be flash frozen with panic and fear. Finally reaching the doctor and the school nurse, we were given further instructions to pull our pants down to expose our underwear. Our testicles would be hard as walnuts – it was always freezing in the principal's office. We were then told to lower our underwear and expose our genitals. Our cold penises retracting like baby turtles sticking out our heads a few centimeters in search of safety. It was terrifying. Apparently, there was an excess of testicular abnormalities back in the sixties. The doctor would grasp one testicle at time, rolling it gently between his thumb and first finger to feel for lumps while the nurse looked on. The most humiliating act that a boy can go through, with the exception of when Gerald Lapnicki got so nervous that he threw up through his nose and Dan the janitor had to sift cherry-scented sawdust over the floor to cover his green putrid nose-plosion.

    You would pray to Jesus Christ, God the Father, and The Holy Ghost that you would not get an erection during the ball rolling. In fifth grade Thomas McNary got so nervous that he peed on the doctor's hand when he was instructed to cough. The nurse verbally castrated Thomas in front of all the boys on the line and then made him clean his puddle of urine with brown paper towels. The doctor, now pissed on and pissed off, was more intent than ever to produce a hernia on one of us, and a not so lucky sixth grader would be sent for further observation and diagnosis. I would thank God that I was not picked out for further observation for testicular cancer or hernia. No, I was now being observed for a very different situation.

Around this time, Joni Ann, the daughter of my mother's friend Chicky from the collection agency that they both worked at, was getting her doctorate in child psychology and asked my mom if she could write her thesis on me. It would require her observations of me over a two-week period which would entail three or four visits to our home. My Mom thought it was a great idea and asked me if I would like to be the subject of Joni Ann's psychological thesis. I quickly said yes, excited to do anything that was different from my day to day.

Joni Ann arrived with the confidence of someone who had read every book on child psychology. But she hadn't met a child like me. She had a tote full of notebooks, a pretty smile, and a reassuring personality that made me feel like I was about to do something important. I was super excited to be a part of a study.

When Mom told me about Joni Ann's thesis, I felt as though I had been cast in a lead role. Finally, my life was going to have some sort of purpose beyond existing in my playroom dressed up as Dracula. Upon meeting Joni Ann, she told me and Mommy what to expect from our sessions, our interviews together. She told me that she would see me the following week.

That Wednesday, Joni Ann came to see me. After our greeting, she asked me if I could draw a picture of my family. We sat in my playroom at my card table on tan metal folding chairs. Joni Ann had taken a sketch book out of her tote bag, placed it on the wood grained vinyl card table top, and opened it up to the first page. I turned the sketch pad horizontally and began drawing my family with the new box of Crayola crayons that Joni Ann had provided. Joni Ann and Mommy told me to take my time and that they would be chatting in the Keeping Room until I finished with my drawing. I could hear their conversations trail off as I focused on the task at hand; a family portrait, drawn and colored.

After ten minutes or so, I finished coloring our family portrait and poked my head out of my bedroom door jamb to tell Joni Ann that I was finished. Joni Ann was excited to see my artwork. Mommy had been telling Joni Ann what a talented artist I was – that I was a creative child. Joni Ann excitedly headed back into my playroom to see what I had drawn. As Joni Ann got closer to my card table and closer to my drawing, pulling the metal folding chair out from the card table while still trying to make out what exactly I had drawn, I could see the concern on her face grow. Joni Ann's head was tilting, her mouth began to gape, and her eyes were squinting as if she was confused by what she was seeing. The drawing was of me, Mommy, Daddy, and Billy. In the sky I had drawn a small yellow sun in the far-left top corner that was barely visible. Covering the sun were black and charcoal gray storm clouds that I had drawn and colored to cover the entire top portion of the 8x10 sketch paper. Mommy was standing next to me in the drawing, crying with two dotted lines falling from her eyes all the way down to the brown crayon wax dirt ground that she was standing on. Daddy with his face colored red and purple, and Billy with red Crayola blood spouting from his nose like a faucet. Joni Ann was shocked. She then tried to use what she was going to school for. She had surmised that I was depressed and suffering from serious anxiety.

Well, Joni Ann began speaking in a different voice than the one she came in with. It was much slower, sing-songy, and carefully measured as if she had stumbled into a crime scene and didn't want to spook the suspect. Mommy however, just behind Joni Ann, was forever my cheerleader. *"Well this is very expressive! Isn't it great Joni Ann!"* Joni Ann nodded but she was clearly recalibrating her entire thesis in real time. What was supposed to be the simple case study of an average kid from an average family had just taken a hard left turn into something else entirely.

"So, Keith, tell me about the storm clouds." she asked, her voice light like she was inviting me to explain a choice of wallpaper instead of my obvious descent into existential despair at age nine. I shrugged. And ticked. And shrugged some more.

"The storm is always there Joni Ann." I said simply without any emotion. Joni Ann took a long pause after a deep inhale, followed by a slow nod. She had a troubled look on her

face. This was something deeper, darker, and probably way more interesting than her thesis would have been. Joni Ann then flipped to a fresh page in her notebook and clicked on her pen.

"*Okay Keith.*" her voice - gentle, but serious.

"*Let's talk about these storm clouds.*"

I'm sure plenty of kids in Greenville had seen their parents go at it – screaming matches, slammed doors, fathers disciplining sons with fists, punching walls, storming out into the night. But Mommy always said that she was lucky. While other men headed straight to Tierney's bar after a blowout with their wives, Daddy would slip into a dark empty pew at St. Paul's Church, his head bowed down in silence. He'd pray for forgiveness, for the strength to be a better husband and father. And if he was lucky, a priest might be there to hear his confession.

Mommy always said that Daddy was a family man and not the kind of husband that ran around. And he never hit her like Mommy's friend Maryann's husband did. Uncle Frankie gave Aunt Maryann a black-eye once or twice. Daddy never hit Mommy, but I still just wanted him to leave, like the father in *The Partridge Family*. Not to die, but just get divorced so that Mommy and I could live on our own, like Shirley and Keith Partridge. I knew that money was the root of all of our family issues, and they couldn't afford or even know *how* to get divorced. Lack of money was all they ever fought over.

We would finally arrive at Sterling Forest by 2 p.m., just in time for the last aqua adventure show. I would eventually, while medicated, be able to urinate in public restrooms like at the

Red Apple, if accompanied by the constant flushing sound of the urinal, finding a spot to fixate on the bathroom wall, and distracting my *Paruresis* disorder with images of dead babies when absolutely necessary, and reserved for the most dire of circumstances such as being forced to urinate into a pig trough.

Seated together in the first row – in the only six seats available for the dolphin show, we were splashed and soaked with dirty, cold, dolphin water. We dried off while walking a quarter of a mile in the blazing August sun, sticky with swamp-butt, to find shade under the bronze *Time and Fates Sundial* near the center of the Gardens. Collapsing into more grass, we would eat our salami and cheese sandwiches and drink our Yoo-Hoo while gazing silently across Memories Lake, which was filled with dozens of colorful, happily painted pedal boats in the shapes of frogs, rabbits, and tropical fish.

I would daydream of falling out over the side of the pink rabbit in the middle of the lake in full view of Mommy and Daddy, Nanny, Poppy, and Billy, swallowing as much swampy lake water as possible, gulping the biggest gulps my lungs could hold, imagining that I am being pulled down into the abyss by the *Creature of the Black Lagoon*, gasping and struggling for air before sinking to the bottom of Memories Lake, never to be seen again.

After having spent the last five or six hours name-calling, bickering, fighting, and teasing, it would be time to get back into Nanny and Poppy's Rambler and begin our four hour plus, bashful bladder journey back home to Greenville.

Finally reaching Greenville by nine or ten p.m., Billy and I would retreat back to our bedroom and fall asleep listening to the sounds of our parents still fighting, juxtaposed against the pure gaiety of a midsummer night swim of kids in our neighboring backyard pools. *"Marco Polo. Marco Polo. Marco Polo."* A symphony of *Marco Polos* repeated what sounded like thousands of times until I finally cried myself to sleep, with Billy in his twin-bed two feet away from me. Salty, dirty, sticky dolphin tears stuck to the corners of my tired eyes, sealed themselves shut from the hot breeze of the floor fan. I am stirred by the reminder of the start of our day, my gums still sore, my body still overheated, a day spent with my family stuck in a labyrinth of gardens.

Sterling Forest Gardens (1974)

Chapter 6

Our family celebrated the holidays together with Lois, John, and their two sons Joseph and Richie, who lived two blocks over on Gates Ave. Lois was Mommy's friend with the Hummel collection. We would celebrate Christmas Eve in our apartment, and New Year's Eve at Lois and John's home. I was best friends with their son Richie between the ages of eleven and thirteen. I would stay over on Saturday nights. Richie and I would build a fort and watch science fiction and war movies. Lois would give us ice cream sandwiches for breakfast, and we would laugh as Lois would tell my mom over the phone that she had made a beautiful breakfast. Lois would then open her candy cabinet and freezer. The Connors were the antithesis of the Brennans, but with Mommy and Lois, opposites definitely attracted. They were lifelong friends. There weren't many rules at the Connors home, and I loved being there.

On New Year's Eve 1974, I sat on Richie's twelve hundred piece model of the Japanese battleship Nagato shown in the beginning of the film *Tora, Tora, Tora!* Richie had painstakingly built Nagato from a model throughout the entire summer. He ran through his house screaming and crying "Tora, Tora, Tora!" Thank God my butt bombing did not dissuade Richie from going on to protect our country. He joined the Army five years later. Richie and I slowly started to drift apart when Richie began high school, and I was still a year behind in eighth grade. My new friendships at St. Paul's were beginning to blossom and I began spending all my free time at the church.

In the fall of 1976, I had started preparing to receive the Holy Sacrament of Confirmation, which among Christians, is when a child reaches the *"age of reason,"* or early adolescence. Prompted by my mom and dad, I decided to nervously join our parish bible study group. Nina, my new best friend, was a year or so older than I. She was President of the Parish Council. Nina wore tortoise shell horn-rimmed glasses and had dirty blonde hair cut to her shoulders. She sang soprano and played the tambourine in the folk group and also worked at the rectory a few nights a week as a part-time receptionist. My parents were so pleased that I had so many new friends at St. Paul's. I was making my confirmation in April, and religious community service and church engagement were part of our instruction.

That April, the Archbishop confirmed me as *"Steven"* – chosen after Doctor Steven Kiley, the young assistant to the older and wiser *Marcus Welby, M.D* from the hit '70s ABC television show of the same name, and admittedly, the object of a slight boy crush. Steven Kiley, portrayed by a young James Brolin, rode a motorcycle to see his patients and spent his days off sailing. I had wanted Steve to be my confirmation name only after first pitching Jesus and Elvis. I didn't see what the big deal was. It was immediately shot down.

James Brolin as Dr. Steven Kiley, Marcus Welby, M.D

Fr. Riley told our religion class that we must be named after a saint. There was no Saint Steve, however there was a *Saint Stephen*. Steven was close enough and was condoned by the Pope. I read about Saint Stephen in our Encyclopedia Britannica and discovered that Saint Stephen was Christianity's first martyr, accused of blasphemy and stoned to death. He sounded perfect to me.

Making our sacraments, serving God, and saving ourselves for marriage were top priorities and frequent dinner conversation in the Keeping Room. Seated at that kitchen table, my brother and I had taken an unspoken vow of chastity to our parents to save ourselves for marriage, to remain virgins and to never have intercourse outside of marriage. Engaging in *outercourse*, however, was never discussed, and in hindsight, probably should have been covered.

There was always a question-and-answer period with Mommy and Daddy at the end of our sex education seminars. Daddy, impeccably well-groomed and health conscious, showed my brother and I how to properly care for our circumcised penises and foreskin at an early age. Daddy was uncircumcised but took Billy and me into our bathroom one night after one of their lectures, the three of us pulling down our pajamas, and showed us how to properly and efficiently maintain good penile hygiene.

Brennan family doctrine, like the church's, was strict and unwavering. Cursing or breaking one of my father's mandates would often result in corporal punishment. At least in Billy's case. Billy was beaten up routinely, but Billy deserved it. He was argumentative and annoying. If Daddy looked at me angry, I would immediately begin to cry. He never hit me. If we weren't home for dinner on my father's first sounding whistle, you would be given a final warning whistle. His warning whistle was never directed at me. I was always seated at the dinner table on the first whistle. Not Billy. One 6 p.m. dinner whistle resulted in having my father issue a final warning whistle to Billy because he was still playing football in the street with the neighborhood kids. That whistle call ended badly. After finally coming through our front door and into the kitchen hallway, my father grabbed twelve-year-old Billy by his arms and shoulders and began thrashing him through the hallway like a six-foot hammerhead shark attacking a sea lion. Billy, flailing and floundering, was being dragged and bounced off the hard white plaster walls headfirst. Slipping in his own blood and trying to stand, but being punched down onto the yellowed, worn marble linoleum six or seven times, blood was splattering everywhere, out through Billy's nose and split lip. I was crying and shaking, crouched down against the door jamb of my playroom and my mother was screaming for Daddy to stop.

"BILL! STOP!! STOPPP!!! YOU'RE GOING TO KILL HIM!!!"

Mommy screamed that she was going to call the police. Daddy finally let go of Billy after what seemed like twelve rounds. Billy never cried during or after his beatings. He took it – and gave Daddy a nasty look to boot. Thank God Daddy never hit me. I think he felt sorry for me. All he had to do was look at me and I would start crying. I was scared to death of him hitting me, so I would collapse into a pool of tears, literally on the floor. The only time I came close to being hit was the hot summer day when I accidentally spit into the passenger side of a moving car and spat into a woman's face. I know I spit, I can remember the exact moment, as well as the car stopping and the man, his wife, and a child in the backseat, all screaming and yelling at me until my parents came out and discovered what had happened. I didn't spit into the car on purpose, but had a difficult time explaining that it was simply poor timing, or an involuntary movement caused by the *Tardive Dyskinesia*. It was the one and only time that Mommy washed my mouth out with Ivory soap for lying, even though I had held onto the belief that it was purely coincidental that I happened to spit into the street at the exact moment that the car was driving past me. I would never spit into someone's face on purpose, but they didn't believe me. My parents decided the next day to send me to a Christian camp in Jersey City on Duncan Avenue for the remainder of the summer.

It took me two days to come out of my shell. I loved putting together outfits for my next day at Christian camp, and it was another place that I could perform. I had the hair, the fashion, and the talent. I could be famous like Keith Partridge, and I knew it. I already shared his first name! I told my parents that I needed to learn how to play the guitar, and two weeks later, they bought me an acoustic guitar and signed me up at Freddy Gifford's School of Music. I would learn to play the guitar and maybe one day I could audition for the church folk group, and like Keith Partridge – I too would be discovered.

Christian Camp (1973)

Chapter 7

Even though I was completely uninterested in sports and spent every waking moment drawing, designing costumes, and making movies, my father forced me to play baseball like Billy. I tried out and made the major league in the Greenville American Little League on my first try. It wasn't that I couldn't do it, I just didn't find it interesting. The baseball team was sponsored by King Lincoln Mercury, the car dealership down the block from our house on Neptune Avenue. Our uniforms were red, white, and blue.

The baseball field was five or six blocks towards Bayonne on Kennedy Boulevard, just past the roller-skating rink where I spent every Saturday morning before going steady with Jennifer. I was twelve and loved couples skating. I had a rotating cast of giggling girls to choose from. But to get to the field, you had to run the gauntlet, and by that, I mean you had to pass the Finkelstein shack at the end of our block. It wasn't a house. It was a shack. Like a legit horror movie shack. The kind of place that the Frankenstein monster stumbled into while being chased by torch-wielding villagers out to kill him. Inside lived Mr. and Mrs.

Finkelstein and their retarded son Jeffrey, who to the neighborhood kids was the human embodiment of chaos and sheer horror. Jeffrey had some kind of unpredictable superpower. He'd burst out of that shack escaping like a bat out of hell, shrieking and flailing like Jerry Lewis in *The Nutty Professor*. His shaved head would glisten in the sun as his tongue flicked in and out like a lizards, and his eyeballs – enormous, rolling, possessed – seemed to track all of us playing in the street at once. You could hear Jeffrey before you saw him, like a tornado warning.

"AHHHHBLUGGLUBLUGGAA!" he'd scream, tearing down the block, arms windmilling like he was trying to fly. And trailing behind him, like some cursed shepherd of madness, came poor Mr. Finkelstein hunched over, his long scraggly gray beard flying behind him, dressed in what looked like a scarecrow's leftovers yelling:

"JEFFREY! JEFFRREEEY! STOP! FOR THE LOVE OF GOD! STOOPPPPP!"

But Jeffrey never stopped. He accelerated.

Eventually poor Mr. Finkelstein would catch up to Jeffrey, usually on someone's porch, sometimes in a neighbor's garden, and wrap his arms around him like a net around a wild animal. The chaos would finally stop. Mr. Finkelstein would cry as he cradled his son, rocking him gently, whispering whatever magic words could soothe the monster until he could guide him back into that haunted little shack they called home. After surviving Jeffrey, I'd finally make it to the baseball field. Not that

I wanted to.

I hated baseball, not because I was bad at it, but because everything about it felt *wrong*. The thick polyester uniform trapped every ounce of the summer heat making me feel like I was baking in Saran Wrap. Why in God's name does it have to be made of thick polyester? The hat? That was the worst part. It flattened my carefully blow-dried hair, the same hair I'd spend hours combing. No thanks. What I really looked forward to once I got to the baseball field was the icy cold Yoo-hoo and Sabrett hot dog and getting lost in my daydreams as I picked dandelions in the outfield near the railroad tracks. I wasn't there to catch fly balls – I was there to make wishes. While other kids played shortstop and screamed for pop-flies, I was in the outfield blowing feathers off money-stealers, watching the trains go by, imagining that one day I would be the one going somewhere far away. I didn't know where or how, I just knew it wouldn't be with a bat in my hand. I was never going to be a famous baseball player. That I was sure of.

Billy, Gary Marino and me (1972)

Eventually, my coach Mr. Geary told me in front of my teammates that I was better off quitting, that he could tell I was not very interested in baseball. Mr. Geary was right. I felt relieved. I was happy that it was over – but a nervous wreck to tell my father. I walked home the same way I came, walking on the stone five-foot high embankment. When I told Daddy what had just happened, he made me go with him back to the field so he could speak to Mr. Geary.

Dad nearly got into a fist fight with Mr. Geary. Apparently, Dad told Mr. Geary that he had better rethink his decision to throw me off the team. I'm not a hundred percent sure what Dad had said to Mr. Geary to get him to change his mind, because at one point Dad had told me to start walking home and that he would catch up with me. I turned around when I got to the sprinklers in the center of the park and could see Dad with his hand close to Mr. Geary's face while he was speaking to him. That night, Mr. Geary came over to our apartment and he talked to me like I was Mickey Mantle and told me that I had great baseball potential and he wanted me on the team. He was so nice to me. This was very confusing. I knew I didn't have that kind of potential, and after Mr. Geary left, Dad finally agreed to allow me to leave the team. And he told me that I was a good baseball player and that I did a great job making the majors and that he was very proud of me. Now, Dad was fully onboard with me becoming a famous actor and entertainer.

Gifford School of Music was a few blocks from our house next to Gino's Italian Delicatessen on Kennedy Boulevard. A white brick apartment building with shiny black letters above the windows of the first floor. I was a nervous wreck. Dressed casually in blue jeans, a white turtleneck, and my green suede Puma sneakers, we walked six blocks through Greenville to the music school with my guitar in tow. We were the only family on our block that still did not own a car or a color television. Nanny and Poppy would pick us up in the Rambler for weekend trips and errands, like going to Sears and Roebucks in Union City. On weekdays we were on our own, either walking or taking buses.

We arrived a few minutes early for my first Saturday afternoon four o'clock lesson. Daddy knocked on the door of the music school as Mom adjusted the hemline of her dress, smoothing away the wrinkles. She coughed, twice, as usual, and always in preparation for putting her thoughts together. She licked her two fingers, her pointer and her middle fingers, and tried in vain to slick down the flyaway hairs from my side-part. Daddy shot me a stern look, the kind that would usually start me crying, and questioned whether I had used the blow dryer on my hair that morning. I had.

Just then the door opened, and a young woman invited us in.

"Hi. I'm Freddy's wife, Linda. Freddy will be with you in a few minutes. Make yourselves comfortable."

We were early for everything and then would have to walk really slow or hide around the corner in order to arrive at our destination exactly on time. Not a minute before or a minute after.

Linda was blonde and pretty. Five-foot two, with brown eyes and scattered freckles, she appeared to be in her mid-twenties. Fashionably dressed in the bohemian style of the day, Linda wore a chestnut colored, faux suede, shoestring lace-up, buccaneer styled blouse, topped off by a wide-spread wing collar. Adorned with brass-tone grommets and twin cuff buttons at the bottom of her sleeves, she tied a colorfully patterned silk scarf tightly around her small waist. Her hip hugger bell bottom jeans, with tattered and frayed edging, fell gently over colorful suede patchwork platforms. Linda's hair was cut into a shag, with soft bangs, layering at her crown, and wispy tendrils that cascaded gently to the top of her shoulders. She wore no makeup other than the slightest, palest, hint of pink on her lips. The next thing that we noticed was that we had actually stepped into the front vestibule of their home. The music school was in their apartment. And then Mr. Gifford appeared.

"Hi there. I'm Freddy Gifford. Welcome to Gifford School of Music."

He reached out for my dad's hand first, shaking it quickly but deliberately. Mom coughed again, twice, then slowly extended her hand to Freddy. Mr. Gifford gently twisted the first third of my mom's hand over, pulled it in slowly towards his face, and then kissed it, rolling his eyes upward until his eyes met her eyes. It was a move straight out of *Dark Shadows* – when Barnabas Collins, freshly undead, kisses the hand of Josette De Pre after recognizing her as his reincarnated soulmate from two centuries ago. Except, this wasn't 1795, it was 1975 and we were in Jersey City.

Watching Freddy kiss my mother's hand, I realized I had seen this before – not just on Dark Shadows, but in myself. Because I, too, had a double life. After school, while other kids were playing stickball, I was locked under Laura Ann's front porch dressed as Dracula. I had asked to be locked in there so that I could lie in the dirt, eyes wide open, the scent of mildew and old wood above me, cold earth pressed into my back, the sweet taste of fake blood as it pooled around the corners of my mouth. I could hear Paula, Claudia, and Laura Ann giggling above me through the rusty iron gate as they sealed the wooden door, leaving me to prepare for my resurrection once dusk came.

The girls would return, reverently creaking open the door to my crypt, and I would emerge. Slow. Controlled. Swishing my velvet cape across my face. A crimson ascot cinched tight like a noose of elegance around my neck. I would rise, with all the drama of a silent movie, into the dimming light of Greenville, and then speak "Looook into my eyes. You are getting sleeeeeepy. You will obey…my eeeevery…command."

Paula, Claudia, and Laura Ann would scream and run away, Claudia, my favorite, would collapse in a swoon and I loved it. Because as Dracula, I was powerful. I was magnetic. I was free. Dracula didn't shrink under the weight of his own thoughts. He didn't worry about fitting in or speaking up. Dracula commanded the room. He didn't ask for attention, he took it. And if people didn't like it? He turned into a bat and flew away. I loved his exit strategy.

And there, in that music studio, as Freddy kissed Mommy's hand, I realized that he was not only my guitar teacher, he was *my kind*.

"My name is Freddy. Freddy Gifford." Mom was clearly impressed with Mr. Gifford.

"Colette." Mom coughed. *"My name is Colette Rennar."*

The only time my mom would use her maiden name was if she was trying to impress someone. There was a lifelong disagreement of spelling and pronunciation concerning my grandfather's last name, between his brothers and himself. Poppy insisted on "Rennar," with a French accent over the "ar." His brothers spelled their last name "Renner." No French accent. No vowel "a." No pretense. Two plumbers, an electrician, and Brother William, the enigmatic invisible uncle never to be seen or spoken to, who gave his life to God and The Ghost, at the age of twenty-two, all spelled their name *Renner*. But my grandfather – *Nick Rennar* – had a certain savoir faire.

"Oh, what a beautiful name! Are you French, Colette?"

"I am...in part." Mom answered demurely. The other *real* parts were mostly Italian and one part Irish. I stare at Mom and Mr. Gifford, and then at my dad. My mom pulls her hand slowly away from Freddy, tucking it within her other hand, pulling it towards her bosom. We all realize after Freddy's hypnotic spell fades, that we are in the midst of greatness. Or at the very least, in the presence of an Elvis impersonator. Freddy was at least six foot two with piercing blue eyes, thin build, jet black hair, slicked and shaped into a pompadour, and lamb chop sideburns. He was

dressed in a belted, buckled, and buttoned, midnight-blue velvet, hip length vest. Underneath he wore a white acetate shirt with a long pointed collar, offsetting the black knit dickey that covered his neck, protecting his instrument. Sporting tight-fitting black polyester pants and short shiny black boots, Freddy was still the 1968 version of Elvis, married to Priscilla – fashionable, healthy, and virile. The 1973 girdled, drugged, sick bloated Elvis would never be in his repertoire. Freddy took me through the living room and into the studio. Freddy showed me how to hold the guitar, pressing the fingers of my left hand firmly against the six strings, while guiding my right pick holding hand to create music. Freddy told me that in a few weeks we would be playing songs like *"My Sweet Lord"* and *"A Horse with No Name"* together. It would take me six months of bloodied and calloused fingers to master *"A-Tisket, A-Tasket,"* *"Away In A Manger,"* and *"Beautiful Brown Eyes,"* but I was determined to praise the Hindu God Krishna by playing and singing George Harrison's song duet with Freddy. It felt as though I had entered an alternate universe. It felt very different at Gifford School of Music. There was something magical and otherworldly when Freddy spoke. It seemed that he was channeling Elvis himself.

"Now Keith, I want you to hold that guitar and feel the notes when you hold them. Use the talent that God has given you to reach others and inspire them with your voice!"

I stared at Freddy trying to absorb every word he said, every note he played, every song he sang. "I will Freddy. I will."

Freddy would weave inspiration into every music lesson

and told me that when Elvis was a boy he was a dreamer; and that he would go to movies and imagine himself as the hero of every movie. Freddy told me that I could be a hero in my own life too; by praising God with whatever gifts he had given me and not being afraid to show them to the world.

Chapter 8

Saturday mornings started out like every other, like a cheerful rerun from a show that hadn't yet been cancelled. My brother and I slept in an 8X10 foot bedroom on twin beds. The only thing separating us from the rest of our apartment, and any illusion of privacy, was the faux-wood accordion door which snapped open like a magician's trick and held itself closed by a magnet, offering as much soundproofing as a wet napkin. We would wake up to the soundtrack of what sounded like domestic bliss, but Billy and I were not fooled. Mommy would be singing in the kitchen like a lounge act at the Tropicana, and Daddy would be whistling like a Disney character while prepping breakfast. The Zenith radio, the size of a breadbox and framed in walnut veneer, would be playing the sunny sounds of *Lawrence Welk, The Lennon Sisters, Connie Francis, and Bobby Darin.* Mommy would belt out *"Can't Take My Eyes Off of You"* like a Frankie Valli backup singer, or her all-time favorite, *"More"* by Bobby Darin, to my father, as he fried up the bacon, eggs, and home fries like the man of the house.

Mom and Dad would dance around the hot stove every Saturday morning, bumping hips by the frying pan like they were auditioning for *The Newlywed Game,* but within an hour or so, somewhere between the second cup of coffee and the last home fry, the weather in the Keeping Room would shift. Mommy's singing would abruptly end, and Daddy's whistling would take on a sharper, more impatient tone, like a tea kettle or pressure cooker about to blow. Someone must have said something to the other or perhaps a nasty glance had been shared. The show was over. We all knew that the 8 a.m. sweet aroma of eggs and bacon would be replaced by the 5 p.m. creeping stench of whiskey, beer, and disappointment. Everyone knew that later that evening the curtain would rise on Act II, which Billy and I called "Saturday Night at the Fights."

Mommy would leave at 10 a.m. for work on Saturday mornings, but not before marking Daddy's whiskey bottle with a pencil when the bottle was an afternoon away from empty. Billy would be playing sports or out with friends from St. Paul's, and I would promptly sequester myself in my playroom, making sure to avoid my father as much as possible. He would be in the living room in his club chair, watching sports and drinking boilermakers – a beer cocktail consisting of a glass of beer with a shot of whiskey mixed in. Daddy would call me out of exile for lunch, making the best grilled cheese you ever had by placing a small plate on top of the sandwich while in the frying pan, and then placing a water filled teapot on top of the plate. Yellow Velveeta would ooze out from the sides of the bread and caramelize into a salty, buttery, crispy delight. I had no idea what he did for a living, but he was by far the best at making a Velveeta grilled cheese. During lunch, I would ask him a million questions about anything that came into my head. He really wasn't that bad; I actually felt sorry for him. Me and Daddy got along so much better when my mother and brother were not around.

I would sit at my card table watching Creature Features on my nine-inch black and white television, completely lost in the world of old horror films, dressed and made up as Dracula. I was fully immersed – cape draped over my shoulders, hair slicked back, and just the right amount of white face powder to look like I had recently emerged from my coffin. One of the scenes I had seen so many times and the one that never stopped fascinating me was the scene from *Frankenstein* – the moment when the monster meets the sweet innocent little girl Maria by the lake. Maria, just six years old, was the picture of childhood innocence. She played with her kitten and picked daisies in the soft glow of the daylight, unaware of the horror that she was about to experience. When the monster stumbled upon her, Maria didn't see a monster at all. She saw a friend, and without hesitation, she took Frankenstein's giant stitched hand into her own tiny fingers and led him down to the water's edge. There Maria showed him her game, how she could pluck daisies, toss them into the lake, and watch them float like tiny delicate boats. She giggled, handing the monster a flower, encouraging her new friend to do the same. After a few brief moments, the daisies were all gone and the monster, the poor confused tragically unaware *Frankenstein* monster, looked at Maria and saw her as an innocent daisy and thought, why not? With the same innocence she had shown the monster, before she could protest, little Maria was tossed into the water. But she didn't float like a daisy. She drowned. It was just a misunderstanding. Maria didn't know that she was with a monster.

Frankenstein 1931

I would stay in my playroom all day until Mommy would come home a few minutes after six. Daddy continued drinking boilermakers all day watching sports from his club chair. I grew more anxious with every hour until Mommy arrived home. The front door would open with the telltale jingle of Mommy's keys, and the whole apartment held its breath. First, she would check the cabinet to see if the line had moved. Even though Daddy was adding whiskey shots into his beer all day, he thought of a rather clever way of fooling Mommy by filling the whiskey bottle up to the line he had discovered, with tap water. Then he could say that he only had a few beers.

The real fighting would take place after 7 p.m. on Saturday nights; the culmination of a week-long build-up of nasty glances, sighs, and curse words like asshole, God dammit, hell, bitch, and bastard. They were living ticking time-bombs.

Over dinner, what started as a simple comment would trigger the first round, which started with Mommy tossing words like *"you always"* or *"you never."* My brother and I would retreat to our respective corners, Billy pretending to read his Mad Magazine and me scampering into my playroom for refuge, quickly cloaking myself in my Dracula cape. The fights would always be about money and my father's inability to generate extra income. Mommy had flyers and business cards printed for Daddy's floundering weekend painting business, and on Sundays after mass Mommy and I would place flyers on windshields and in the mailboxes of homes in Greenville and the neighboring more affluent community of Country Village, in the hope of generating extra money for our household expenses, and the possibility that one day we may be able to try another family vacation or be able to afford a car. Those rare times that Daddy would get a painting job, he would always underestimate the price, resulting in only covering the cost of the paint supplies plus a small pittance. This would inevitably make Mommy go crazy, often forcing her to call the customer up to try and renegotiate the price for an extra twenty dollars. Aunt Marie would hire him to paint her apartment every Spring. He would hear her boastfully telling her girlfriends over the phone that she had her contractor there painting her apartment. It would make him lose his mind.

Some Saturday Nights at the Fights were worse than others. Immediately after dinner, the only sound would be the hum of our old fridge and the muffled rerun of *Hee Haw* on our black and white television, reminding us that once upon a time, this Saturday had started with keeping room dancing, singing, and whistling. Mommy was a master at pressing all my father's buttons, provoking him just enough to dance along the edge of disaster, but never quite going over. Until that one night.

This particularly gruesome fight ended with Daddy nearly slicing his finger off at the knuckle with a carving knife while he and Mommy were fighting as he was slicing the London Broil. There was blood gushing onto the meat and splattering onto the glass kitchen table, rolling off the beveled glass edge, seeping into the wrought iron edge, running down the iron leg, and plopping onto the linoleum. Mommy had worked all day and came home to my father having consumed too many boilermakers. He was never outwardly drunk – just combative when provoked, and my mother provoked him as much as possible without getting strangled.

Mommy took Daddy's cigarettes, tapped the pack upside down on the edge of our glass and black wrought iron kitchen table three times, turned it back over, raised the pack to her red lipstick-stained lips and pulled a Kent out of the silver paper lining with her teeth. She stared at my father, her brown eyes lined black with anger, her lips ready to launch words that could cut him down. She struck the match on the first attempt, and then fake chain-smoked while they yelled and screamed at each other. They usually kept it confined to the Keeping Room, but this Saturday Night at the Fights could not contain it. It had spilled over into my playroom.

Weekends in our apartment were their stage adaptation of *"Who's Afraid of Virginia Woolf"* starring Mommy and Daddy as Elizabeth Taylor and Richard Burton, but without the funny parts, where Mommy, as Elizabeth Taylor, laughs hysterically while she's drinking. Mommy and Daddy knew how to keep the fighting to a minimum without the police being called. The playroom brawl was a one-time exception, a film noir memory of Daddy strangling Mommy with his bloody hands in my playroom closet. The protagonist, Mommy, as Kim Novak or Tippi Hedren is trapped in a web of dire circumstances, about to be thrown off a cliff or have her eyes pecked out by the birds. In the movies, a hero always steps in, the music swells, and the villain is defeated. But this was no Alfred Hitchcock film.

My playroom closet had double sliding doors and a high wooden shelf that Mommy and Daddy hid our Christmas presents every year. Billy and I would always find them and know the big things that we were getting from Santa. That Saturday Night at the Fights, the hollow wooden doors of my playroom closet crashed to the floor like broken bones, knocked off their tracks by Mommy's desperate kicks. Daddy pinned Mommy against the walls of my closet. His finger, hastily wrapped in a torn dish rag, a loose hose, sprayed fresh blood onto the alabaster walls. They wrestled in the closet like animals in a cage, their bodies tearing down all of my carefully colored arranged clothes and costumes. My wooden hangers snapped like matchsticks bouncing off of the surrounding woodwork and ricocheting off the hardwood floor. I cowered under my card table, clutching my Frankenstein Monster doll, crying and burying myself within the comfort of my thick black velvet Dracula cape, rubbing the soft edge of the gold satin lining against the edge of my lips to soothe myself. Mommy gasped with Daddy's hands around her throat, both of their faces purple and their eyes bulging, Mommy's eyes popping out and upward all the way up to the Christmas shelf. I screamed and cried at them, ruining the golden lining of my cape with open-mouthed, sobbing-wet imprints of my fake blood-stained lips. Streams of snot dripped from my charcoal eyeshadow-smudged nostrils, rolling down the shiny gold satin interior in a gobbly-goop of saliva, snot, and tears, which was already stained by fake blood, white pancake powder, and black eyeliner. Billy and I begged them to stop. I prayed to Jesus on the cross that hung crooked from its nail above the doorway – tilted by Mommy being roughed up in my closet. Saturday Night at the Fights had never ended so badly as this night. Billy and I had never seen Daddy get physical with Mommy. We were a close-knit family. Other than Billy getting beaten up a few times a month, no one in the family had ever been hit or strangled before. A fight of this magnitude would need to be compartmentalized in a place that could not be accessed for at least a few decades. As usual, the next day, we would all have breakfast in the Keeping Room and then get dressed in matching outfits ready for Sunday mass as if nothing had happened the gruesome night before.

    I was always wishing that I was older than I was so I could get away and create a life for myself. I wanted to be an adult. I wanted to belong somewhere. I so desperately dreamt of a different life, a life that I could feel happy in, and I believed that being older would allow me the freedom that I craved. I was just so sad and depressed. And I knew what depression was because Nanny and Little Grandma (Nanny's mother from Italy who lived in the apartment across from them and sat in a rocking chair in the middle of her kitchen, only spoke Italian, and only wore black,) and Nanny's side of the family, all suffered from depression. Aunt Minnie, Nanny's sister, was not only suffering from depression, but she also heard the instrumental version of *"Somewhere My Love" (Lara's Theme* from the 1965 film *Doctor Zhivago* movie soundtrack) played over and over again in her left ear. Aunt Minnie described it as the music that plays when you are on a carousel and you can't get off or a small music box stuck in your ear with a tiny ballerina dancing around. Mommy told me that Aunt Minnie suffered from *musical ear syndrome –* which is a real thing, and that the medical term was *Tinnitus.*

    Nanny and my cousin Anthony had electric shock treatment a few times and went to psychiatrists for medication. Nanny had been sent away to the Carrier Clinic twice. I knew what electroconvulsive therapy was, and it was very, very, scary. It was just like it was in the movie *"One Flew Over the Cuckoo's Nest."* That was one of the only two movies that Daddy had taken me to see. I was twelve. The other film was *The Exorcist* the following year. So, I knew what *depression* was, and what can happen. Like the time when Poppy said he was going to throw Nanny out their third story bedroom window. That was the last time that Nanny had shock treatment.

Nanny and Keith (1965)

Nanny slept in a twin bed in a separate bedroom of their four hundred square foot apartment. It was Mommy's bedroom when she was a teenager. Mommy and Daddy slept in that same twin size bed when they first got married and were saving money to get their own apartment. Nanny had a gold gilded birdcage the size of a teapot, that had a wind-up dancing yellow finch inside it. Poppy would wind up the music box finch to awaken Nanny every morning. I loved Nanny more than anyone. She was my safe place, my favorite person in the whole wide world, and sometimes after school, I'd stop by Nanny and Poppy's apartment unexpectedly just because I wanted to see her. I never knocked, I just walked right in, straight to her bedroom and sat on the edge of her delicate bed. "Nanny," I'd whisper, "I'm here." Nanny would slowly open her eyes, still soft with sleep, and smile that smile; the one that made my chest feel warm and safe.

Nanny's arms, thin and bruised, with swirls of purple, blue, and burgundy, struggled to free themselves from the tight white cotton sheet and duvet that Poppy had tucked around her like a papoose, but she always got them loose enough to hug me. Her room smelled like her. Gentle. Like powder and something sweet, something warm. It smelled like love. I could just stay there forever just lying next to her, but she always got out of bed and walked with me into the kitchen, her soft hand resting on my shoulder or wrapped around my waist with her head on my shoulder. We would sit at the kitchen table talking about the day, while she'd mend a garment that needed fixing. Nanny was always sewing. Not simply mending but creating magic. Fabric holes the size of a dime could magically be mended away after they had looked like they had been eaten by a moth or caught on a nail.

By the time I was six or seven, Nanny had taught me how to sew. How to thread a needle without pricking myself, how to hem a pair of pants, fix a sweater hole, and even sew a French seam and back stitch. It was something special we shared.

I could talk to Nanny about anything. Sometimes I just rambled about school or friends but other times I talked about things that sat heavy on my heart, and when my words disappeared, my throat got tight, and my eyes stung, Nanny would ask me if I wanted her to scratch my back. I'd pull up the kitchen chair right next to hers just to the right of the rotisserie where she made her eye-round every New Year's Day. Nanny would reach out with her soft, gentle hands, scratching my back just the way I liked. Never in a rush. Never pulling away too soon. It was one of those small perfect things that made me feel like nothing bad could touch me as long as I was sitting here with Nanny. I worried about Nanny though. The refrigerator side-shelves were now overflowing with ketchup and duck sauce that Nanny was now eating straight from the condiment packets, in addition to Karo Corn syrup that she had begun drinking straight from the bottle.

I would dream wildly and believe that another life was possible for me. A life without fighting, worrying about money, and depression. A life with family vacations. A life like Keith Partridge had, famous and traveling the world entertaining people. Or a life like Dr. Steven Kiley had, working for Marcus Welby and healing people, riding motorcycles and sailing. Or life as an account executive at an advertising firm, like Darrin Stephens from *Bewitched*, married to a wife as pretty and smart as Samantha and living on a cul de sac. I could be all of those professions, but what I really wanted to do was to just be famous. I knew that I was destined for fame, but for *what,* that was the big question.

Finally after a year and a half of guitar lessons with Freddy, I could play my guitar adequately enough as long as there was someone else playing along with me to compensate for my mistakes and mischords. Freddy and I would eventually move on to *"Seasons in the Sun,"* *"Sunshine on my Shoulders,"* and Ringo Starr's *"You're Sixteen."*

I spoke to Freddy about the possibility of my auditioning for our church folk group, singing and playing my guitar, and he was very encouraging. In celebration, Freddy sang for me the Elvis gospel song *"You'll Never Walk Alone,"* looking up at the heavens through the ceiling tiles, crooning in full vibrato the whole way through. He said it was a song about faith and going through life's storms. Freddy believed, like Elvis, that all good things came from God, and that he didn't believe he would sing the way he did if *God* hadn't wanted him too. Freddy said that there was a plan for the talents that God gave to me and that it was my job to discover what that plan was. Freddy gave me hope and the feeling that I could belong. It was time for me to leave Greenville's Graceland to serve the Lord, serve Jesus, and serve the Ghost, using my musical God-given talents. I was ready to love God in the deepest way possible. Maybe I could be in the church folk group one day! Like being in the Partridge Family! I could be another Keith Partridge!

Keith Patridge

Chapter 9

Greenville had it all. Our own Graceland was just the beginning. We had Martin's Bakery for Sunday rolls and doughnuts after Mass. We had Grocer's Ice Cream parlor and candy shop for ice cream sodas, candy necklaces, and flying saucer penny candy that my friends and I would make believe was the host during pretend mass. We had Gunther the barber for tight fades and uneven bowl cuts, and Schultz's for underwear, sneakers, and Buster Browns. Winfield Pharmacy was where you went for Russell Stover's, Whitman Chocolates, and Heaven Scent dusting powder to buy for holidays and birthdays when you didn't know what else to buy. The brunette counter lady wore the same Heaven Scent perfume as Mommy – it hit your nose like a powdery cloud of baby angels, right before the butcher shop next door smacked you in the face like death. Dan the butcher ran the meat shop with sawdust on the floor to soak up whatever may have been leaking.

A block after was Sodano's Chicken Market, which wasn't a market so much as a live-action horror movie, chickens clucked one second and were gone the next. The screams, the feathers, and the bloody runoff snaking across the pavement were enough to send chills down your spine. You learned quickly to walk in the street on Ocean Ave. until you were ten steps past it, holding your breath and saying a quick prayer for every chicken you'd ever eaten. And then there was Murray's Department Store – our very own one-stop shop for everything from lamps to lunchboxes. It was on aisle three, somewhere between the spiral notebooks and the pencil cases, that I lodged the eraser end of a number two pencil so far up my nose it vanished. One second, I was goofing off, the next I was being rushed to Greenville Hospital with Mommy and Nanny yelling at me while I tried not to sneeze it deeper into my brain. A doctor removed it with forceps while I screamed like one of Sodano's chickens being massacred.

Just a block up from Murray's on the corner of Ocean and Bartholdi, sat Greenville's very own haunted house in plain sight – Tierney' Tavern. Tierney's wasn't just a bar; it was a warning. Its whiskey-soaked breath leaked into the streets on weekend nights, a stale fog of beer, bourbon, and broken dreams. The place had a pulse, and it beat loudest on Friday and Saturday nights when the neon sign buzzed above its pie-sliced facade like a bad moon rising, like a wolf calling on his pack of scoundrels. Inside? Chaos. Fights broke out every weekend, usually over something stupid – a spilled drink, a wandering hand, a glance that lasted too long. Fast girls clung to leather-clad guys with sweat slicked tattoos, and there were always whispers about who was selling what and who got stabbed in the bathroom that weekend. The stories, whether true or not, were endless – gunshots in the alley, someone ODing in the back room. Greenville's gateway to hell. Then there was Jigger the one-armed bartender. Nobody knew how he lost his arm, and no one dared to ask. He slung drinks like a machine and could break up a fight using only his stump and a glare. Some said he once knocked a guy out cold with his bar rag. During the week Tierney's took on a more ghostly vibe. On slow Monday afternoons, you could always find some bleary-eyed regular slumped on the old bar stool tied to the column outside – not to keep it from being stolen, but to keep it from becoming a weapon again. Word was someone had used it once to cave in another guy's skull over a pool game gone wrong. Even as a kid, walking past Tierney's gave me the heebie-jeebies. It hummed with something dangerous. You didn't have to know the rumors to feel it in your bones – this place wasn't just bad news; it reeked of it.

Tierney's Tavern

Continuing on a safer path, across the street, and up half a block further down Ocean Avenue, was the post office and the Greenville Trust Company Bank. It was a weekly stop for Mommy and me. The Trust Company was a serious bank. It was a half-block long brick building with a palatable prison-like feeling to it, with its twelve-foot-high black iron gate. A guard – dressed in Military Blues, stood armed and ready, guarding the biggest black safe you had ever seen and hundreds of shiny long brass boxes with keyholes and numbers on their front panels that slid in and out of their metal casings. It was very formal, like you were at Fort Knox. Mommy and Nanny would fill out a slip of paper, hand it to the bank official who would then sign it, passing it onto the military bank guard. After proper identification was presented and inspected, the guard would permit Mommy and Nanny to look through Great Grandma Finizia's pewter box in a private three-foot by four-foot closet. Mommy and Nanny would visit the bank box and go into the closet twice every year to check on Nanny's engagement ring from Poppy and a platinum and diamond cocktail ring that Nanny promised to Mommy upon her death.

Greenville had its own unmistakable rhythm – a place where everyone knew your family and a nickel could still buy you something sweet. No matter where you went, the air was filled with the sound of church bells, the aroma of fresh pizza and bread, and the comforting hum of parish life that made the whole neighborhood feel like family. We lived, laughed, worshipped, and loved every last bit of it.

My brother and I would run to our grandparents' apartment on Pearsall Avenue every school day at noon to have our lunch. St. Paul's Grammar School was only a block away. Nanny and Poppy were the only grandparents that my brother and I had, and I adored them. Nanny and Poppy would have our snack trays set up in front of their French Provincial sofa stocked with the usual accouterments – a white paper dinner napkin folded on the diagonal, an eight ounce glass bottle of Coca-Cola with a white and red swirl bendy straw placed at the far right corner, a package of Drake's Yodels to the left, and a set of miniature silver and glass salt and pepper shakers in the center of each of our plastic faux-wood snack trays.

Nanny would sashay into the living room dressed as a waitress, wearing a white cotton apron tied around her small waist. Her hair would be pulled up into a chignon with a little cotton waitress hanky on her hair, holding a small white order pad, pulling a number two pencil from over her left ear, and taking our lunch order. There were assorted choices on Nanny's luncheonette menu – grilled cheese cut into fours, frozen Celentano pizza cut into thirds, pastina, and hot dogs that Poppy would slice open, fry in butter until crispy brown on all sides, served with a thick golden stripe of Gulden's mustard, wrapped in a papoose of soft white Wonder Bread. If we got extra lucky, our hamburgers, complements of Dan the butcher, would be accompanied by a side of *French* – Poppy's freshly made French fries, peeled and pressed through a magical metal apparatus, fried in scalding hot oil, tossed with coarse salt, and piled high into a brown paper cone that he would make from left-over grocery bags. Nanny would serve Heinz ketchup on the side in a white milk glass toothpick holder. My brother and I would watch *Bewitched*, and three quarters of the game show *Password*, before running back to St. Paul's to finish out our school day. After school Nanny would be home in our apartment, four blocks away, doing laundry and ironing. Daddy didn't like the way Nanny ironed his shirts, with a crease down the center of the arm. He preferred it ironed flat, and Mommy had to tell Nanny not to iron his shirts any longer. I knew Nanny was hurt. From then on, only Mommy ironed Daddy's shirts.

One day after school, before dinner, Nanny and Poppy told my brother and me that Mommy and Daddy were on their way home with a big surprise. Mom and Dad had been hinting for some time that a little one would soon be joining our family circle. For years Billy and I had been praying and begging them for a puppy. Temporary family pets had made their way in and out of our young lives. First, there was Arizona the turtle. When Arizona was a year old, our father inadvertently fed him a garden worm that he had sprayed with insecticide and killed him. Then there was Sniffles the rabbit. He ate the kitchen linoleum and suffered from irritable bowel syndrome. Next, we had Blueboy the parakeet. Gone. Too dirty and noisy. There were countless other new arrivals that would inevitably come down with mysterious afflictions that we were told made it impossible for us to care for them. My parents were suffering from some sort of Animal Munchausen syndrome by proxy. One by one they would be taken away by my Uncle Tom or Uncle Joe to the farm. The farm was described by my mom and dad as some glorious vacation resort owned by Jesus for special pets that could no longer coexist within the boundaries of family life. On the farm, Arizona, Sniffles, Blueboy, and the others, could run free and enjoy their remaining years being loved, nurtured, and well taken care of by Jesus and his mother Mary.

Finally, our day arrived. Mom and Dad were on their way home with the puppy of our dreams! My brother and I danced in joy, still dressed in our baseball uniforms from practice an hour earlier. We sat on the edge of the couch, our imaginations running away from us! Maybe an Old English Sheepdog like Tramp on *My Three Sons!* Or a dog like Tiger on *The Brady Bunch!* Or maybe a dog like Fonzie's Spunky on *Happy Days*! Or Scruffy on *The Ghost and Mrs. Muir*! We had never been so excited!

The doorbell rang. The door opened.

"Boys, close your eyes! Daddy and I have a surprise!" Billy nudged me. "Here we go," he whispered, eyes alight with excitement. We waited for the unmistakable sound of paws scrabbling on the linoleum, a joyful bark, or maybe the sight of a wagging tail in the doorway. Instead, Mom and Dad walked in holding a small, white puffball of a dog with apricot-colored ears. It didn't bark. It didn't wag its tail. It glared.

"Oh," I said, trying to mask my disappointment. "A...dog?"

"A French poodle," Mom corrected, beaming. "Isn't she beautiful?"

Billy shot me a look that said, Beautiful? Is she joking?

Mom continued, lifting the dog like she was a prize.

"She's a purebred. Look at her coat! Look at her apricot-colored ears! She's a show dog! She's been professionally groomed!"

"She's got a nasty attitude," Dad muttered, trying to rub a bloody scratch on his hand.

We sat there frozen. This wasn't the scruffy, ball-playing, stick-fetching dog of our dreams. This was a dog that looked like it belonged on Mom's French Provincial gold-brocade lady's chair wearing a pearl necklace.

"Don't worry," Mom said, oblivious to our disappointment and shock. "I already have her pedigree papers." She pulled out a folder like she was unveiling the Constitution. "And guess what? I already named her after me! Gina La Colette! Isn't that just perfect?"

My brother, finally finding his voice, blurted, "You named the dog after yourself?"

Mom nodded, smiling proudly and then presented Gina La Colette's official papers from The American Kennel Club for me and Billy to inspect, proving that Gina was a purebred, the daughter of Loveable Dancing Playboy and Dolly of Limerock.

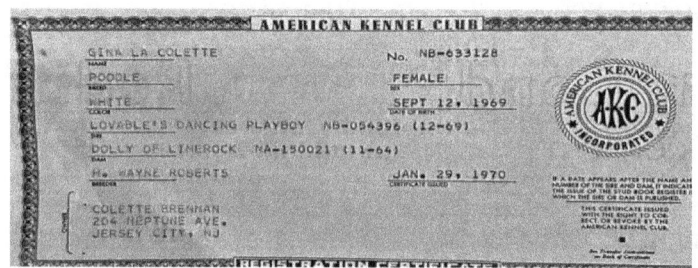

"She's disgusting!" Billy yelped, jumping back into the couch, punching the throw pillow.

"She's beautiful," Mom corrected Billy. "You'll learn to love her."

"Where is Limerock?" I blurted out.

Gina shot us a nasty look as my brother and I glanced at each other, silently mourning the golden retriever that never could've been. It was official – we were now stuck with a snooty French poodle named after our mother.

My first thought was where is this farm? I'll take her there myself. No one seemed to think it was odd that my mother named a French poodle after herself? Her friends? Her Cousin, Aunt Marie? Daddy said *nothing?* It became clear that Gina La Colette was here to stay. She would be placed in some sort of Mothers' Pet Protection Program. Billy and I both immediately hated Gina. It was one thing we had in common and agreed on.

Me and Gina La Colette (1970)

Gina La Colette had a perfectly coiffed white fur ball on her head and wore a bow off to the side of her pom-pom. Mommy would change her bows according to the occasion or holiday. Red for Christmas, pink for Easter, green for St. Patrick's Day, orange and black for Halloween, and red, white, and blue for the 4th of July. She had apricot cascading ears, a black shiny nose, and a twisted smile. Her thick ankle poms, perched upon her tightly shaved paws and manicured, painted nails. Mom and Dad loved Gina La Colette like she was their third child. My father was constantly brushing her. He even brushed her teeth regularly too, and when Daddy would get too rough, Gina La Colette would growl at him. Daddy would take his hand, grab her by her long snout and crush it tight. Not enough to hurt her, but enough for Gina to yelp out. He wanted her to know that he was the boss.

When Gina La Colette turned three, Mommy and Daddy decided to mate her with Pepe, our neighbor's dog. Pepe was black. Mom, Dad, and my father's brother, Uncle Joe, turned my playroom into what looked like a makeshift wrestling ring with layers of scattered newspaper pages of the Jersey Journal scotch-taped in place like a tarp, and taped at the corners onto the worn oak floor beneath my crafting card table. For his services, Pepe's owner would get a free puppy of my mother's choice, the one that was of least value, to keep, or sell like my parents were going to do. The sale of Gina's puppies would enable Mommy and Daddy to finally be able to buy a used car from Daddy's brother, Uncle Tom.

It felt strange that Gina was going to be forced to have sex so that we could get a used car, but it seemed like the only way, and suddenly the appearance of Gina was all beginning to make sense. Mommy figured out that Gina could get us a used car. Mommy always found a way. She had to, because after all Daddy was not a go-getter. We were one of the only few remaining families on the block that did not own an automobile. Depending upon the size of Gina's litter, it could also mean driving lessons for Mom and Dad, and possibly an air conditioner for our bedroom.

Gina La Colette had her period and was bleeding those

last few days leading up to her intercourse, leaving blood stains on Mom's gold jacquard lady's chair the day before, which Mommy had to treat with Carbona stain remover. Gina was gross when she had her period. Her vagina would pulsate. This particular night, Gina La Colette was placed in the center of the wrestling ring with Pepe, but Pepe was smaller than Gina and he could not reach her vagina, so Daddy got the idea to put Pepe on the stepstool that Mommy kept in between the refrigerator and the wall. Once Pepe jumped up onto the stool, he grabbed onto Gina's hips and mounted her. Pepe's penis was disgusting. It was super skinny, and its penis-head was a shiny, misshapen, hot-pink mushroom the size of my thumb. Two minutes in, Pepe's right hind leg slipped off of the stool, and Pepe flipped over the back end of Gina in a roundabout wrestling move, and now they were both stuck on their sides laying on the blood-soaked *Jersey Journal*. An acrobatic move on Pepe's part, but Pepe's poor dismount had caused his gross penis to be lodged backwards.

Watching Gina get raped like that and then become twisted and locked butt to butt with Pepe was difficult for Billy and me to watch. Not that we *had* to, but Daddy encouraged us. He said it was part of nature and how babies were made. But Gina was being raped under my wood-grained vinyl covered card table. My sacred altar. It had turned into a bloody wrestling match. And Gina was yelping. And it was just like they say about watching an accident – it's difficult to turn away.

It was like that one summer afternoon the little blonde girl up the block, the eleven-year old that looked like a dirty Cindy

Brady, was playing hopscotch in the street in front of our house and got hit by a speeding car. It came out of nowhere, barreled into her, bounced her off of the windshield, rolled her down the hood of the car, tossing and lashing her long pigtails in the air around her head like the two ends of a loose jump rope, and then tossed her onto the asphalt. The assailant drove around her pint-sized body as she hit the pavement and sped off. The little girl immediately jumped to her feet, hysterical and in shock, waving her arms frantically in the air up and down, screaming at her highest pitch, like Jeffrey the retarded boy. Looking down to scan the outcome of her near-death experience, we could all see that her transparent Casper-like skin had been ripped off her forearms, elbows, knees, and shins, and her blood had begun to reach the surface. It was like watching a real-life horror movie.

There was no running away for Gina, and in a mean way that I feel really bad about, I was kind of happy that she was getting what she deserved. I know that sounds terrible. She was just – so mean – like Billy.

Daddy and Uncle Joe had to separate Gina La Colette from Pepe Minelli physically, by forcibly removing Pepe's skinny, hot pink, twisted, backward penis, from Gina's backwards bloody vagina. There was blood everywhere. They had wrestled their way into a lockdown on the pages of *The Jersey Journal* and activated the black ink on the sports pages and classified ads, staining Gina La Colette's perfectly coiffed, perfectly white, perfectly controlled self. What's black and white and red all over? Gina. And she looked as if she had gone through a Saturday Night at the Fights with Pepe Minelli.

Gina sat ringside for three years watching Saturday Night at the Fights with me and Billy. It was her turn.

After nine weeks of pure hell while Gina was pregnant, she was finally ready to deliver her litter. This time Mommy and Daddy transformed my playroom, and wrestling ring, into Gina La Colette's nursery. Her birthing bed would be a large box from the produce department of the A&P located two blocks away which was found waiting among piles of cardboard boxes left for garbage. It was the same spot where someone had set the homeless man on fire with gasoline a few years later. When Daddy got home, Mommy lined the box with an old baby blue terry cloth bath towel that had bleach spots on it. After Gina's water-sack broke on the kitchen linoleum, Daddy picked up Gina, cradled her in his arms, and placed her in their makeshift delivery-room box until her puppies started coming out of her vagina. I was frozen seeing Gina's bloody glop coming out of her vagina, and in a weird way, made me feel like I was dying. The last puppy, number five, was black with a white diamond on his forehead. Daddy had to stick his hand up Gina's vagina one final time in order to pull this last puppy out, who had stopped breathing. Daddy laid him gently on his lap and performed CPR, massaging the little puppy's chest, and breathing gently into Little PJ's mouth. Mommy had already named him – P.J. for Pepe Junior, and we all decided as a family, at that moment, that if Daddy could save little P.J. we would keep him and not sell him for a used car. But in our family, surprises like this almost never happened, like making a spur of the moment decision or planning an unexpected day trip. Everything was planned weeks and months in advance. Meals were planned a week to ten days out. Every day's dinner coordinating with a certain day of the week. Pasta was a Sunday meal. Friday night was pizza. Saturday night was beef – T-bone steak, London broil or burgers and fries. Wednesdays were especially horrible for some reason. Sauteed liver dredged in white flour, two pounds of bacon, onions, and brussels sprouts. We were planners. We certainly could never keep this black diamond puppy. It was just talk. Just procrastination so that an unexpected, happy, spur of the moment, wish upon a star, dreams come true moment, could seem possible for our family.

Mommy and Daddy didn't take risks or ever act on a whim, like the time that Daddy was offered a promotion and relocation for his job at Allied Chemical. We had a choice to relocate either to Dallas, Texas or Atlanta, Georgia. This was the most exciting thing that I had ever heard being discussed in the Keeping Room! I wanted to relocate to Dallas as a *family*. I even prayed for my mom and dad to stay together, backtracking to Mommy for a short time on my encouragement to divorce him so that we could live together on our own like Keith Partridge and his mom, or look-up Leo again and start a new life for the three of us. The relocation out of state would mean we could start a whole new life together. This felt similar to the time that my parents were considering buying Fat Timmy's two-family house up the street with the narrow alleyway that he got stuck in while trying to retrieve a half-deflated basketball. The entire neighborhood was cheering and jeering Fat Timmy on.

"Free Fat Timmy! Free Fat Timmy!

Anything that happened in the middle of the night was exciting.

Fat Timmy was an arm's-length reach to the partially deflated basketball. He cried helplessly and wailed from 9 p.m. until 2 a.m., trying unsuccessfully to wiggle himself free. Stuck in a two-foot wide alley between two sides of green asbestos shingles, Fat Timmy's swollen ankles lifted somehow an inch or two above the wind strewn tunnel of the alley, which collected Dorito bags, McDonalds Cheeseburger paper wrappers, greasy paper plates, fast food napkins, and Budweiser cans. He helplessly kicked assorted garbage beneath his feet. It took until 2 a.m. for the fire department to be able to free Fat Timmy.

Of course, my parents chose not to start over in Dallas, and also chose not to buy Fat Timmy's house. Mom and Dad decided not to become homeowners because they would have needed to borrow the down payment from Uncle Bob, who had generously offered to help. Despite his brother-in-law giving him the chance to own his own home, my father was reluctant to accept help. He told Mommy that he did not want to feel obligated to anyone.

Billy, Daddy, Gina La Colette, and me (1972)

Chapter 10

On laundry days, Mommy and I would walk over to The Trust Company Bank to see Pedro the Peruvian hot dog man. Pedro had a gold tooth and sold delicious Sabrett hot dogs and homemade orangeade that contained orange rind shavings the texture of shaved balsa wood. We would eat our hot dogs sitting on portable, child sized, cotton canvas folding stools. Mommy would make a special stop at Triangle Square Bakery for spice cakes when she wanted to treat herself to something special. I would get a home-made waffle ice cream sandwich. Mommy was now described as heavy weight. Poppy would make off-handed remarks about her weight and make her cry. One Thanksgiving, Poppy slapped Mom on her butt and said that she had put on a lot of weight. Mommy started crying and we thought Daddy was going to hit Poppy. Mommy no longer looked like the movie stars on Million Dollar Movies. Gone was her twenty-four-inch waistline. Things were changing.

A few Saturdays in the summer, we would go as a family to the Boulevard Pool – five blocks south towards Bayonne, located on the city line. Daddy would take me and Billy into the men's changing area to put on our swimsuits. The floor was slick with sunbathing lotion and tropical oils making it necessary to hold on to the walls to get to the locker area as if you were ice skating. The attendant would give Daddy a metal wire basket to put our belongings in and a locker key with a thick elasticized cord to wear safely around his ankle. We would undress in the open cement cell. The concrete holding areas and open showers reminded me of scenes from prison movies. I felt strange taking off all my clothes. It was the only time that you would see a penis other than your father's and brother's. I would sneak glances at as many penises as I could without ever making eye contact or looking obvious.

Mommy would sit poolside, her plump legs dangling over into the deep end of the pool while my father would climb his way up to the highest of the three diving boards, perching himself for exhibition. Clinging to the rough concrete top side of the pool, I would relieve myself into the cool, suntan oil-slicked water, warm urine sedating my fear and anxiety, while my father launching into a reversed two and a half somersault dive in a tucked position.

We would leave the pool at 6 p.m. and find ourselves back at the cement prison changing cell to shower and get dressed to start our walk home. Mommy undoubtedly was annoyed or crying over something my father had said earlier in the afternoon, the two of them not speaking since 2 p.m.

The fun ended halfway through the summer at the Boulevard Pool the summer Daddy tried to impress us all with his famous two-and-a-half double tuck dive. He sprang from the high dive like a torpedo, twisting upward with the same swagger he brought to every family swimming escapade. But this time, the splash wasn't met with applause. When he surfaced, his hand shot up first, then the blood followed. It came in bright red ribbons, swirling through the blue chlorinated water like dye from a ruptured firework. Kids screamed. Lifeguards blew their whistles. The pool had to be evacuated, cleared like it was a crime scene.

Billy, Me, and Daddy. Boulevard Pool, Jersey City (1967)

Mommy was furious. Not just about the blood or the ruined afternoon, but about the jagged shard of glass buried at the bottom of the deep end. She said the pool should pay for their negligence. She insisted that Daddy sue. Of course he didn't want to. That wasn't his way. But she pushed, and eventually he gave in. Months later, a check arrived – $750. Barely enough to cover the attorney and the stitches.

Every Sunday we would head to the 10 a.m. mass at St Paul's – all of us in matching outfits, still groggy from Saturday Night at the Fights. Right after Mass came the real holy ritual – a pilgrimage to Martin's Bakery on Ocean Avenue. "Okay," Mommy would announce as the bells from the church faded behind us. "We need a dozen donuts, six seeded rolls and two of the jelly donuts that your father likes." "Make sure I get the chocolate donut," Billy would say while elbowing me in my ribs. He knew I only ate chocolate donuts.

Uncle Tom waited for us on our front porch every Sunday morning, arms folded grinning ear to ear, his shiny new Buick parked in front, waiting for us to arrive home. "Look who it is." Daddy would say, *"The King of North Arlington."* Uncle Tom was Daddy's younger brother and the only uncle who visited us regularly. "Let's cruise," Uncle Tom would say as Billy and I would tumble into the back seat of his car, the smell of Armor All and air freshener hitting us like joy in a can. Uncle Tom told the worst jokes which of course made them the best jokes.

"So a horse walks into a bar," he'd say, glancing back in the rear view at Billy and me. The bartender says, *"Why the long face."*

"Why did the tomato turn red?" he'd ask. "Because it saw the *salad dressing*!"

I'd shout before he could finish, laughing like it was the funniest thing on earth. Billy would roll his eyes and would say that I ruin everything. By late afternoon around 5 p.m., Nanny and Poppy would arrive for Sunday dinner. Nanny always brought us two bags of wise potato chips, and a quart of chocolate ice cream packed into a white cardboard container and topped with a five-by-five sheet of wax paper from Grocer's candy store. We sat around the television after dinner for our sacred family viewing of *60 Minutes, Wild Kingdom, The Wonderful World of Disney,* and *The Ed Sullivan Show*. But right before Ed could introduce Topo Gigio, another plate spinner or a tap-dancing dog, the real headliner took the stage – me. At exactly 7:45 p.m. I'd clear my throat dramatically and announce, "Ladies and gentlemen, for one night only – the fabulous, the fantastic…*Keith Brennan."* The living room rug was my stage, the playroom my dressing room. I transformed into Phyllis Diller using Mommy's blonde curly wig – the one she would wear chasing Billy around the apartment, with long white gloves, a cigarette holder that I made from a straw and electrical tape and spew out jokes that I had memorized from seeing Phyllis Diller perform on *The Mike Douglas Show*. "Take my husband. Please! Take my mother-in-law…" With my hand on my hip, like impersonator Rich Little, I dove into my act, performing impressions, singing, dancing, and most of the times, all at once. And when Gina La Colette came into our family, I'd dress her in something that I had created that afternoon using fabric scraps, pipe-cleaners, and scotch tape. Mommy and Nanny would howl with laughter. Daddy would clap and say, "That's my star!" and Billy would glare at me with his arms crossed, looking like he was being tortured.

"You're not funny," he sneered.

"Why does he have to be so weird?"

"You're just mad because you were born without stage presence," I chewed back. "Your *beige* Billy. You have no talent. You only know how to catch a baseball."

At the end of every performance, Mommy would smile and say, "One day sweetheart, you're going to be discovered. You just wait and see," followed by Billy groaning, "God help us."

Me as Phyllis Diller (1968)

Before Nanny and Poppy would leave for the night, Nanny would sit on the edge of our bed and scratch our backs with her soft, gentle hands until our eyes grew heavy, and our breathing slowed. *"Good night my monkeys,"* she'd whisper in our ears, kissing our foreheads. And then in came Poppy. Poppy never rushed bedtime either. He'd settle himself at the foot of the bed, legs crossed and reach into his pocket like it was a magician's hat. He'd pull out a worn book of matches, always with a slow deliberate flair like he was a real magician. We knew what was coming and we braced ourselves every time.

"All right boys," he'd say with a twinkle in his eye, peeling one cardboard match from the booklet, its jagged edge perfect for the game.

"Let's see what kind of steel you're made of tonight." Then Poppy would yank the match from its roots.

Billy, ten and forever trying to act unfazed, would lie back, arms crossed behind his head.

"I'm ready," he'd say cool as ever. Me, seven and determined to match my big brother's grit, would nod silently, pressing my lips together to stop a smile from forming. Then Poppy would begin. The matchstick would trace the edge of our toes, slipping in-between them like a feather, and glide across the delicate arch of our feet. Poppy's foot torture was incredibly intense. The matchstick danced across our skin slowly and intentionally, just enough to send jolts of ticklish anticipation up our spines. Poppy would work his way to our ankles and then back again – in and out of each toe, never speeding up, never easing off. We'd hold our breath. Squirming was defeat. Laughing was weakness. And so we lay there, locked in stillness, breathing through our noses in long, even meditations. Rigid.

"Poppy," I'd whisper, my voice tight with restraint, "I'm not laughing. Not even smiling."

"Oh, I can see that," he'd grin, never breaking rhythm.

"You're a statue tonight. You're like the Statue of Liberty."

Billy would chime in, half-laughing, half-choking. "Bet he can't get through the pinky toe without cracking."

"Wanna bet?" I'd hiss back, gritting my teeth.

"Shhh," Poppy would say, with mock seriousness. "Focus. Focus like a warrior. This is the final test. You feel nothing. You are rigid."

Poppy made us believe that if we could withstand the matchstick torture, we could withstand anything. And somewhere inside us, we believed him. He taught us that there was strength in stillness. There was power in not giving in. When the ritual was over, Poppy would toss the matchstick aside and tuck the blankets up to our chins.

"Now," he'd say, settling between our two in beds, "it's time for a story."

"*Billy Know-It-All?*" I'd ask, hopeful.

"Of course," he'd smile. "Who else? Tonight's story is called *Billy Know-It-All and the Mountain of Doubt.*"

Billy groaned. "Ugh, not the Mountain of Doubt again. He always climbs it. He always wins."

"That's right," Poppy said, his voice low and warm, "because he never let anyone tell him he can't. Even when the wind screams in his face, and the rocks beneath him crumble, Billy Know-It-All keeps going. You know why?"

Poppy shoots me a look. "Because he believes in himself. Billy Know-It-All believes that anything is possible." I mumbled half asleep. "Exactly," Poppy would say, "and when you believe in yourself boys, even the tallest mountain isn't so tall. Even the scariest night gets brighter. Even the hardest day ends with the story. Everything you need is within you. If you believe in yourself, you can accomplish great things." He would reach out to ruffle my hair and then Billy's.

"Goodnight boys. Always remember to be rigid."

Me and Poppy (1965)

Chapter 11

The first time I remember hearing the name Keith Pecklers was when I joined St. Paul's Glee Club. It was the Spring Concert. I had just turned eleven, and while I wasn't exactly sure what being in a glee club meant, I figured it had to be more interesting than sitting through another boring afternoon class. Besides, I was selected to be Mr. Spring. I got to water my classmates with strips of paper inside my watering can.

Keith Pecklers was St. Paul's musical director, and he played the organ. Not just any organ, but a massive, towering beast of an instrument that sat in the church choir loft, stretching towards the ceiling like something in a grand cathedral from *The Phantom of The Opera*. When it played, the whole church seemed to vibrate. It wasn't just music, it was power. The kind of sound that made you feel you were close to heaven. But that spring it wasn't Keith Pecklers in charge, it was Mr. Max Mendenhall, who was a real orchestra conductor, the kind you saw on PBS leading an ensemble of musicians in tuxedos. He had the presence of someone who had studied in Vienna or Paris but somehow, he ended up here in Greenville coaching a bunch of Catholic school kids through a spring concert. Unlike Lawrence Welk, who smiled his way through every polka and waltz, Mr. Mendenhall took music very seriously. There was no fooling around on his productions.

Live performances were a big deal in our parish – spring concerts, Christmas shows, carnivals, school plays, and the annual parish variety show in St. Paul's auditorium. But on Sundays, the music belonged to Keith Pecklers. He stood up in front of the choir loft, conducting with quiet command. I'd sit near the front of the church, tilting my head back to watch him. One Christmas Eve, Mommy sang Ave Maria from the choir loft during midnight Mass, and Keith Pecklers accompanied her.

He was something of a prodigy but had a strange way of conducting. His left hand would be on the organ, while his right hand moved in a peculiar, almost masturbatory motion to guide the choir behind him – his half-closed hand, moving it up and down and sideways, shaking and rattling through the Frankincense incensed church air. He had a speech impediment, speaking with his tongue glued to the inside of his bottom lip.

I met Keith Pecklers on an unusually warm spring day in March of 1976. I was thirteen and I was drawing St. Paul's Church from across the street, sitting on the curb on Old Bergen Road in front of St. Anne's Home for the Aged. Something had told me when I jumped out of bed that morning to go to St. Paul's and sketch the church. So that's what I did.

The sun cast a warm glow over Old Bergen Road, softening Greenville's edges with the gentle touch of spring. A light breeze carried the mingled scents of daffodils, hyacinths, and diesel fumes – vanilla and honey layered with exhaust. Buses and cars rushed by, some just inches away from my feet, but I hardly noticed. I was deep in a spell of my latest creative fixation – capturing the grandeur of St. Paul's Church. Perched on the curb, I sketched with quiet intensity, a number two pencil in hand, tracing the church's facade with reverence. The cries coming from the nursing home behind me barely registered. Somewhere, someone was screaming, but I remained locked in, consumed by the way the light pooled in the mortar between the red bricks, the way it flickered along the copper steeple, now worn to a soft, greenish patina. I marked the moment I began – 12:16 – etching those numbers into the tiny clock face on the steeple.

Keith Pecklers

As the late afternoon descended upon me, clouds suddenly drifted quickly across the sky like ghosts holding hands, their foggy forms casting dark shadows over the church and parish without a minute's notice. It felt like the heavens themselves were reaching down to embrace the ground below and suck me up into the clouds. The church steeple, a beacon of God and hope, had now appeared cloaked in clouds of mystery. The ghosts engulfed the rectory, the convent, and my grammar school rooftop, veiling the grandeur of the church's architecture in what looked like a shroud of danger. Suddenly I heard someone approach me, a figure rising from beyond the ominous clouds. It felt dramatic.

"Hi. Aren't you Billy Brennan's little brother? I'm Keith Pecklers. A friend of Billy's."

Startled, and slightly buzzed, I looked up to discover an uninvited, ominous namesake.

"Yes, I am. And my name is Keith too." I continued sketching, thinking that Pecklers was simply crossing the street.

"Wow! That's really something! I guess we were meant to meet!"

"What are you drawing? Are you an artist?" Pecklers asked.

Pecklers was backlit by the sinister darkness of the foreboding sky. It suddenly looked like a scene from *Dark Shadows*. For a moment, I was blinded by the hazy sky, but as he moved closer, I could see Pecklers more clearly. Six-foot tall with bad acne on his face and neck, inflamed pimples and pustules masking his Irish impish face.

"I am. I'm drawing the church." I replied.

Who knew that my pencil-drawn amateur thirteen-year-old drawing would be on the cover of St. Paul's Church bulletin for more than two decades, or that the name – Keith Pecklers, would be etched into my memory for a lifetime. I was about to receive the second gift from The Holy Spirit; the *gift of understanding*. This gift allowed us to see the hand of God at work in our lives, and through prayer God can reveal to us the spiritual reality that underlies sensible appearances. Although I was considered the class artist in eighth grade and could draw well enough, I never fully thought of myself as an *artist*. I was more of a creative kid – a visual thinker, an idea person. Drawing was just one way that I made things real. What I truly excelled at was bringing ideas to life – creating something people could see, feel, experience. Like movies. That's where my imagination felt most alive – when a story became something more than just a thought in my head. Something you could watch unfold.

For our final grade in 8A religion class, we were assigned a project on the seven days of creation. Most kids were probably going to write an essay, maybe do a poster board or some boring handout, but I wanted to do something different, something big. So, I created a book entitled *"It Happened Like This"* – the title underlined four times and bound together in a binder covered in adhesive wallpaper of little boys and girls. In retrospect, this was so creepy. But it was the only wallpaper that made sense at Paul Brothers' hardware store on Ocean Avenue. On the last page, my teacher scrawled in red pen: *A, excellent. May I have it?*

I was thrilled. Beaming. At 13, it felt like I had arrived – writing a book of God's origin, no less, and getting high praise for my creativity, my writing, and even my drawings. I proudly signed the last page, *The Author*. Maybe I would be a famous writer one day. I told Mrs. Muller she could borrow it, but I needed it back.

I'm glad that Mommy saved a few projects like *"It Happened Like This"* to document important dates and times in my life. They serve as little markers of where I was developmentally and creatively. But reading it now, I'm a bit taken aback. The writing seems much more juvenile than I remembered, certainly not the work of a nearly high school-bound 13-year-old. The angel on the title page, once so majestic in my mind, now looked more like a Rorschach test. Still, *"It Happened Like This"* seems like a key of some sort. A puzzle piece. Because just a few months later, I'd be graduating grammar school and heading off to Hudson Catholic High School for Boys. My childhood was beginning to slip away, but before it did, I managed to leave behind a peculiar little book – a creation on creation, – capturing somehow, exactly who I was in that moment.

Keith Pecklers and I continued speaking.

"But I also like to do other things too; like singing and playing the guitar, writing music, making movies and stuff."

"Wow! It sounds like you are very talented." Keith Pecklers said to me as the afternoon sun had completely been overtaken by darkness. Then Pecklers sat next to me on the curb in front of the nursing home as I continued to sketch the steeple. The screams from St. Anne's Home for the aged grew stronger, angrier, and more desperate. Old people slumped over in their wheelchairs moaning, some balling, some cursing. An old-age prison.

"Wow! You're amazing! That looks just like the church! You are very talented Keith!*"*

I remember it sounding strange to be called Keith by another Keith. It felt odd. There were plenty of Mikes, and Bobs, and Jims, and Johns, but I knew of no other Keith other than Keith Partridge and Keith Pecklers.

"You know that I am the musical director of the folk group. Well, I actually need someone just like you."

Pecklers spoke to me as he stretched and spread his legs out in front of him as wide as he could and within two feet of the slow-moving Old Bergen Road traffic of cars, and city buses. He makes me extremely nervous, but I managed to awkwardly respond.

"Of course I know who you are! You went to school with my brother Billy. You are the organ player for the spring concerts and glee club too. I sing in the glee club, and I play the guitar."

Pecklers was graduating high school with Billy. Their paths crossed every so often; they ran in some of the same circles and shared a few mutual friends. Both had served as spiritual teen leaders on Search retreat weekends, a Catholic youth program designed for kids sixteen and older. I wasn't old enough yet, but I was already counting down the days until I could go on one myself. It was a youth talking with youth Christian peer program. During a Search retreat, you are given an experience of Christian community; something you may not have experienced in your home, school, or parishes, the way that Billy and I did. An atmosphere of love, caring, and openness is created during the weekend so that the "candidates" – the kids, can let down their defenses and take an honest look at themselves. Search retreat weekends were for anyone who was looking to strengthen their relationship with The Lord or even begin a relationship with Christ for the first time. The emphasis of the retreat is not to overload the kids with doctrine, but rather make the love of Christ come alive through shared experiences and storytelling. Teenage life can be difficult and confusing, and pressures can be difficult to handle. On Search weekends, they taught you how to keep Christ in the center of it. The retreat also gave you the opportunity to think about your life – what you can change and where you may have been keeping the Lord out. The weekend consisted of members of the church – a priest, a nun, four or five teenaged spiritual leaders, and a married couple who were the example of Christ. Billy had been on multiple Search weekends. So had Pecklers. And I wanted that too.

My parents had been asked by Monsignor Davis to be the married couple on Search 28 a few months earlier. They showed the kids that weekend what it's like to be married in Christ, to live with a joyous heart, and to have a marriage filled with love. It was a big honor.

Search weekends were a rite of passage – intense, emotional, a little theatrical, and occasionally terrifying. They were packed with raw personal testimonies, skits, music, tear-streaked faith walks, and something called *palancas*. We were told it means "lever" – as in, something that helps move what's otherwise unmovable, like your hardened teenage heart. Or your unresolved family issues. Palancas were the secret letters from your family, friends, and church community meant to be read during a particularly fragile moment of the retreat. You weren't supposed to know they were coming, which only added to the emotional ambush. After hours of crying, singing, confessing, and sleep deprivation, the arrival of those surprise letters were guaranteed to hit you in the gut with a spiritual sucker punch. Kids wept. Some found Jesus. Others had complete mental breakdowns.

But the real test of your faith came later that night, during what was referred to as the *promise walk,* which was really just a blindfolded journey into the woods of Blairstown, New Jersey. You'd be led by strangers holding your elbow, through a maze of twigs, pinecones, and unforeseen emotional landmines, while a whispering team member clung to you telling how the Holy Ghost changed their life.

At some point during the promise walk, things would take a turn – from eerie to downright scary. This was the *trust walk* segment. Arms stretched wide, blindfold still on, you're told to fall straight back. No warning, no countdown. Just fall. And somehow, just before you are about to hit the ground, you're caught – scooped up into the arms of your guide, who now symbolically represents Jesus. Surrender. Trust in the Lord – or at the least, the upper-body strength of a 17-year-old volunteer from Paramus.

Keith Pecklers wrote a beautiful palanca on official St. Paul's Church stationary for my parents during their first Search weekend when they were invited to be the designated married couple.

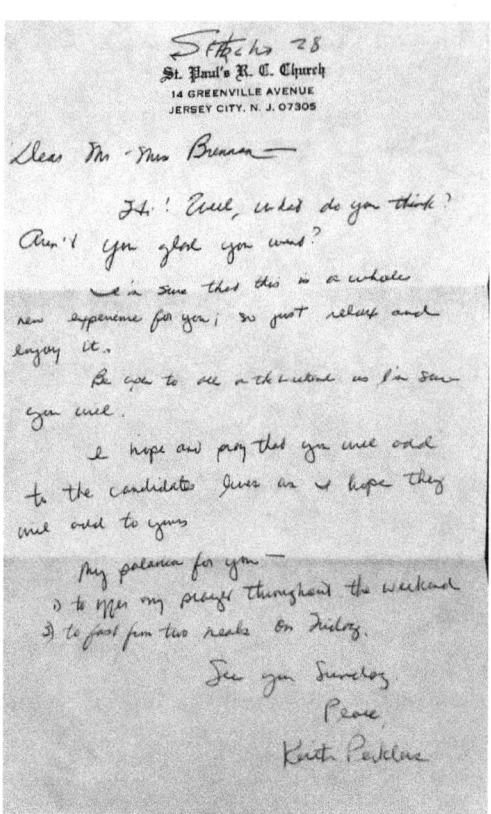

Search 28.

"Dear Mr. and Mrs. Brennan –

Hi! Well, what do you think? Aren't you glad you went?

I'm sure that this is a new experience for you; so just relax and enjoy it.

Be open to all in the weekend as I'm sure you will.

I hope and pray that you will add to the candidates' lives as I hope they will add to yours.

My palanca for you –

1) to offer my prayers throughout the weekend
2) to fast for two meals on Friday.

    See you Sunday.

    Peace,

    Keith Pecklers

In the palanca, if you are a friend, you write encouraging words and convince the kid to give themselves to Christ for the weekend, but you also tell the person on the retreat that you will "*fast*" or give up something in their honor and pray for them the entire weekend.

Sunday is the *"Homecoming."* The spirit filled yellow school bus pulls up to your church. You have just spent the past forty-eight hours being overtaken by The Holy Spirit. There are dozens of family and friends gathered to welcome and support you on your new Christian journey. As the candidate steps off the bus into the arms of their sponsor, they are either laughing or crying and wearing a four-inch wooden cross on a leather cord tied around their neck. The cross was a symbol of devotion. It reinforced our faith and was a reminder that we could be a better Christian.

Keith Pecklers continued to make small talk with me as I finished sketching the iron railings of the church, the bushes, and Mother Mary, finally completing my masterpiece and signing with my initials KB at the bottom right corner. He said he was very impressed with my attention to the details and was so complimentary.

"What is the symbolism of the time? 12:16?" Keith Pecklers asked me.

"I'm not sure," I continued. "I don't have to be. It will reveal itself. It may be a date and not a time."

He said that apparently *talent* was a Keith thing! And next came what I was dreaming of happening since I began guitar lessons with Freddy.

"Hey Keith, have you ever thought about playing your guitar in our folk group? We play during 11 a.m. mass every Sunday. It just so happens that I am holding auditions after Sunday Mass in two weeks. Why don't you try out? I bet you would be an excellent addition to our folk group."

Having Keith Pecklers invite me to audition for the St. Paul's Folk Group was a dream come true. I was elated and felt so mature. Finally, I was ready to be a part of St. Paul's and use my God given talents to praise the Lord and celebrate Sunday mass and the Holy Spirit in my own way, and to do so as part of a musical group was just the icing on the cake. This was everything that I had prayed for. This was the gift of *Understanding* from The Holy Ghost. All of my lessons with Freddy, playroom practice, and impressions of musical legend Keith Partridge were finally about to pay off. This could be the lucky break that I was waiting for. The kind that Mommy spoke of. I would need to prepare with Freddy a church song that I could sing and play for Keith Pecklers during the audition which was only two weeks away.

But what would I play?

Finally, after much deliberation and suggestions from Mom and Dad, I decided to perform *"Be Not Afraid."* Freddy wrote down all of the chords for me so that I could practice in my playroom, and Freddy and I were able to practice together twice that week before the folk group audition.

Be Not Afraid

G	C	G	C	G	G	D/F#

You shall cross the barren desert, but you shall not die of thirst.

C	C/B	Am	D

You shall wander far from safety though you do not know the way.

B	Em	Am	F	C	G

You shall speak your words in foreign lands and all will understand.

G	Em	A	D	D/C

You shall see the face of God and live!

G	C	G	D/F#	Am	D	G

Be not afraid, I go before you always.

C	Am	Bm	Em	Am	D	G	C

Come follow me and I will give you rest!

G	C	G	G	C	D/F#

If you pass through raging waters in the sea you shall not drown

C	C/B	Am	D

If you walk amidst burning flames you shall not be harmed

G	B	Em	Am	C	F	D	D

I stand before the power of hell and death is at your side If you

G	Em	A	D	D/C

Know that I am with you through it all!

The day of the audition snuck up on me like a stomach bug. One minute I was rehearsing *Be Not Afraid* in the bathroom mirror with dramatic reverence, and the next I was doubled over in bed gutted by cramps so sharp they made my knees jerk involuntarily. I vomited twice, had diarrhea three times, and by the time the sun was up, there was absolutely nothing left in my body but nerves and desperation.

I tried on six different outfits, maybe more. None of them felt right. Too stiff, too flashy, too *"please pick me."* I eventually settled on my navy cords, and the hand knitted vest Nanny gave me for my 13th birthday. Nanny's friend Madeline, who lived in the apartment above Nanny and Poppy's, had knitted it for me. It was five inches of thick yarn and shifting shades of blue, ranging from powder blue to cobalt, and rimmed in a dark navy trim. That vest felt like armor – like something knitted with love, worry, and old-world strength, and I needed every thread of it.

Mom had made me Carnation Instant Breakfast, which I sipped nervously, knowing it wouldn't stay down. I was right. I'm pretty sure she snuck a raw egg in it, her go-to protein trick ever since food became a battle zone. Breakfast had become its own war. The only thing more stressful than actually eating was watching my parents prepare the meal while arguing about money. Slamming pots. Slamming utensils. Slamming each other with their words. By the time we sat at the table, it was a minefield of sighs, side-eyes and nasty comments. Dinner always ended the same way – Mommy crying softly into her napkin, Daddy retreating to the sink to wash dishes in icy silence, then grabbing Gina's leash and taking her out for their nightly walk, just the two of them. Gina loved her solo time with Dad. She even had a sound she made – two sharp coughs, just like Mommy's, the minute he grabbed her collar. It was like they shared a secret code. Meanwhile, I was gagging on my vegetables, chasing cauliflower with milk, packing my cheeks like a squirrel so I could excuse myself to use the bathroom and flush the half-chewed mush away. Once they realized I was playing games with my meals, they came up with a new system: whatever I didn't eat, whether it was eggs and toast at breakfast or liver and brussels sprouts at dinner, I had to finish the next day. Cold. Congealed. Punishment food.

All they really had to do was stop fighting.

That Sunday, Mommy gave me a Stelazine and sent me on my way. I was thirteen, anxious, sweaty, and wired on antipsychotics, lugging my guitar down the five blocks to St. Paul's for the folk group audition after the noon mass. I was a mess – anxious, awkward, and desperate to be chosen, but convinced I wouldn't be. My stomach still hurt. My armpits were soaked. My brain was cycling through every possible social disaster. I couldn't stop thinking about how ridiculous I'd look in front of the other people if I hit a wrong note. But somehow, that vest gave me courage – and so did the prayers. I whispered Hail Marys and Our Fathers all the way to St. Paul's.

There were about ten of us gathered in the side chapel after the noon mass, scattered like sheep waiting to be sorted out. Most were teenagers – older, cooler, confident in the way I wasn't. A few adults lingered, guitars slung across their chests. I recognized some faces – one girl from the 10 a.m. choir, a boy I had seen collecting hymnals, and Jess Parker, who already belonged to the folk group. Jess played guitar and sang harmony like she was born doing it. She also knew Billy through Search weekends and the church, which made her more intimidating. My friend Nina, who I had met at bible study, was also already in the group, playing the tambourine and singing. We were told only three new members would be chosen that day. My legs were trembling. I had barely enough voice to speak, let alone sing. But I knew that I had to force myself to do this.

Jess strummed something easy, a warm-up chord progression. The room buzzed with casual confidence of those who already belonged to the group, not those who were bleeding for the chance to belong. I watched Keith Pecklers across the room as he conducted the auditioning kids with that same peculiar signature-style hand motion. Part conductor, part something that looked vaguely inappropriate.

When he called on me to perform, by the power of God, my mouth miraculously opened and I sang *Be Not Afraid* like it was a cry from the pit of my stomach. My voice was a little shaky at first, caught in between terror and a trance, but something inside me pushed forward – the fear, the fasting, the raw egg and Stelazine, the vest, the endless prayers. It all surged forward like it had nowhere else to go. And when I finished playing the guitar and singing, the room went quiet. Not in awe – just still. Keith Pecklers nodded.

That was it. A nod.

Like I was marked.

And with that small nod, my world had changed.

Keith Pecklers had discovered me.

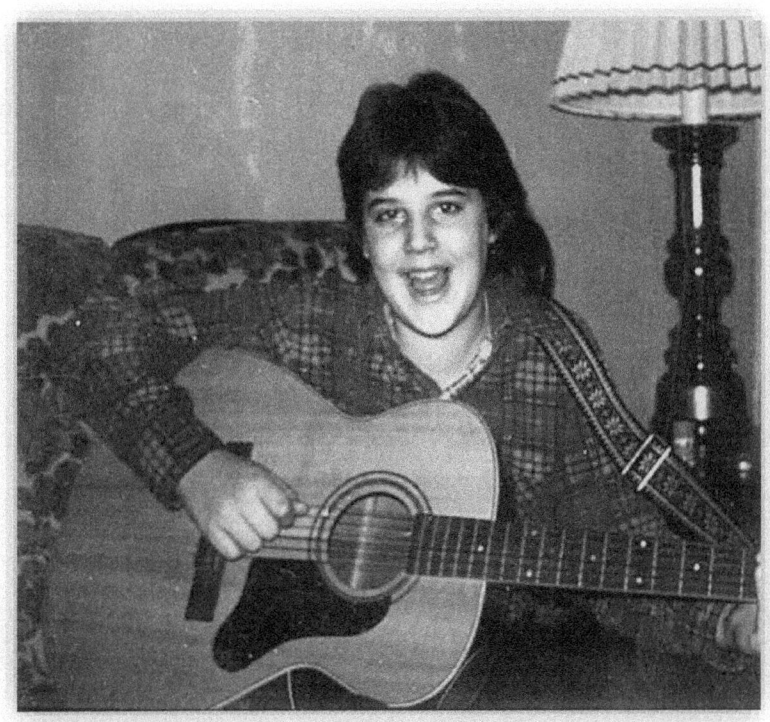

(1976)

Chapter 12

I received a call that Sunday evening from Keith Pecklers. I could hardly catch my breath. I was so excited. Keith was officially welcoming me into St. Paul's Folk Group! I had done it! Mommy said that I was on my way! I was the third Keith! *Keith Partridge, Keith Pecklers, and me, Keith Brennan!* Keith, Keith, and Keith! Like The Holy Trinity! I believed that God had a plan for me. This was the very first time I had ever felt chosen. This team wanted me. I was full of God's spirit, love, and energy. The Holy Ghost was opening my heart and mind through the folk group, and I couldn't be happier. I was learning to trust completely in the power of The Holy Spirit. This was the most exciting day of my life, and it was even better than winning the leading role of Lil' Abner in our eighth-grade play or Mr. Spring in our third-grade production of *"Welcome Springtime."* This was different. I was a lead guitarist now. I had accomplished what I had set out to do, and was part of St. Paul's church family. I was part of a community, a parish. Just like Billy.

Keith Pecklers immediately picked me out as having potential and being the perfect addition to the group. He kept his eyes on me during the entire audition. Mommy told me that it was because Keith Pecklers had seen something very special in me. The only time that I had been this happy was when Fr. Tony gave me the *Puppy Love* Hummel for my confirmation. Mom and Dad were so happy that I was part of the church, and it was even better that I was serving God by using my God given talents. I understood that this was the way that God was working through me, so I prayed to God to increase my faith in Him and say yes to everything that The Holy Ghost had required of me. Freddy helped me so much along the way. He filled me with hope and encouragement every week during my guitar lesson.

That June, a few months after joining the folk group, I was about to graduate St. Paul's Grammar School and Keith Pecklers signed my graduation autograph book! What a thrill! On page one I wrote *Professional Actor* for profession. I was sure that I would end up in Hollywood someday.

8th Grade (13 years old)

It was so cool to have friends who were adults and older than me. It made me feel special. I felt important. Keith Pecklers wrote that he was glad to have *"gotten to know me!"* I couldn't believe how lucky I was to know him. This is what Keith wrote to me:

June 1976

Keith –

I'm glad I've gotten to know you, through our (excellent?) group. I wish you peace & success in the future, with whatever you choose to do.

Good luck at Hudson, and enjoy it!!!

Peace,

Keith

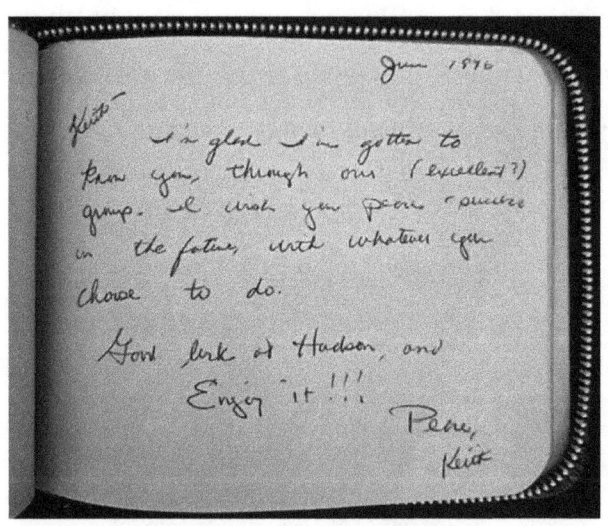

8th Grade Graduation Autograph Book (June 1976)

I did wonder why Keith had placed parentheses around the word "excellent" and why did he use a question mark. We were an *excellent group* weren't we?" We were a family. I was part of a group. It was like one of Mommy's notes. Only I was the recipient.

Joining the church folk group was like finding a missing puzzle piece. After wandering through our neighborhood depressed every day, feeling adrift and uncertain of my purpose, the sense of belonging that came with being part of the group was profoundly comforting. This was my first time feeling like I belonged somewhere. I made so many new friends.

When Mom and Dad were asked to be the married couple retreat leaders again on a *second* Search weekend, Jess, the adult guitarist in the folk group, wrote Mom and Dad a beautiful palanca. Jess's palanca had everything a Brennan could love, and when Jess wrote in the palanca: *"and Keith, well, he holds a real special place because of his ambitiousness,"* I felt complete acceptance and so much love.

Dear Mr. and Mrs. Brennan,

I just can't express how happy I am that you have joined the Search community at St. Paul's. Seeing you at the prayer times or special occasions is great. I just wish more people (parents) had an interest in what their children were doing. God has blessed you both with two great boys. Bill, he's a true gentleman, and Keith, well he holds a real special place because of his ambitiousness in the Folk Group. You are so filled with God's spirit, it just seems to radiate to all. You are two of the nicest people I know and I pray that God continues to help you grow in love and that his peace and joy are always with you.

For your weekend, I offer my daily masses and communions.

I will also sleep on the floor and abstain from eating for 24 hrs.

Thanks for being you!!!

Love,

Jess

The summer of 1976 was off to an exciting start. Beginning high school at Hudson Catholic in September seemed like a lifetime away. I wanted this summer to last forever. I was spending all of my free time at St. Paul's and I was high on Christ and growing more in love with the Holy Spirit every day. I was now trusting God to guide my life completely. Between the bible study group and the folk group, I was at St. Paul's two to three times a week, mostly meeting in a room in the rectory basement which was adjacent to the main open part of the basement where Keith Pecklers had his office. Then in June, something new started happening.

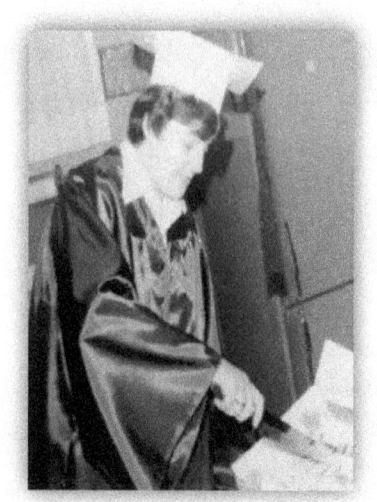

Grammar School Grad. (1976)

Keith Pecklers began calling me every night at 10 p.m. on my red push button phone that my mom had recently bought for my thirteenth birthday. It had only been two months after auditioning and joining the church folk group, but already Keith and I had so much in common. I joked that we belonged to the *Keith Club*! We were both musicians, like Keith Partridge, and St. Paul's was our family, just like the Partridge Family. I was shocked that he was calling me so late. I had never had someone older, someone important, take this kind of interest in me before. I sat up straighter in bed, the receiver pressed tightly to my ear.

My hands were damp with nervous sweat, but I forced my voice to sound casual and grown up.

"Hey," I said trying not to sound too eager. "Hello there. How are you?" Keith's voice came through the line smooth and familiar, like we had been having these conversations for years. "I just wanted to check in and see how everything is going."

It was the kind of thing adults said to each other to check in, like I was a part of something. I mostly listened when Keith talked. I didn't know what to say to him and I didn't want to mess up the chance of becoming closer friends with him. Keith spoke about God and stuff – about what it meant for him to play the organ and lead the choir, to be a Search retreat leader, and stuff like that. He talked about how meaningful it was to be able to meet kids like me, and how he got to know my parents during the retreat that he had been on, when Mom and Dad were the married couple. Keith Pecklers said they made such an impression on him, and that I was so lucky to have parents like them. I swallowed.

"And your brother Billy, he's such a solid guy."

I agreed, unsure what else to say. I felt something swelling in my chest, a sense of suddenly being proud of Billy. I couldn't mess this up, so I made sure to sound interested in everything he was saying and I carefully inserted what I thought were smart adult-like comments every few minutes just enough to make it seem like I belonged in the conversation. "I can't wait to go on a Search weekend myself," I said at one point and Keith chuckled. "Yeah Keith, it's an experience. You're going to love it and meet so many cool people. This is going to change your life in so many ways."

For the first week or so, we talked about how practice went that week and how the harmonies came together just right at Sunday Mass. Stuff like that. But then slowly things started to change.

"You ever think about girls?" Pecklers asked me this question one night, his voice markedly lower, more personal. I hesitated because it was not a topic we had ever covered.

"Yeah of course!" I said. Pecklers laughed. "Yeah, I mean we all do. It's normal for guys to talk about this kind of stuff. You know, guy stuff." Pecklers chuckled.

It made me sit up a little straighter.

No, I didn't know. I didn't know how to speak about *"guy stuff"* really. It's not like Billy and I had conversations about anything, and most of my close friends in the folk group were girls.

I felt like I had just been given access to a new level of conversation, so I tried to keep my voice casual to meet his, like we were just swapping notes on everyday life. Guy stuff. Pecklers continued speaking.

"It's normal too, you know – to jerk off ."

My throat went dry. I didn't say anything. I didn't move. Even though Pecklers was nearly three blocks away sitting in his own house, I felt like he could see me. And he didn't stop there.

"How many times a day do you jerk off?"

My body stiffened and I felt the sudden rush of heat run from my legs to my head and face.

Embarrassment.

Confusion.

Shock.

The kind of shock that doesn't make sense and sneaks up on you for hours and days after the fact and keeps tumbling around in your head like, what just happened? I had no idea how to respond, but I also knew I couldn't respond like a nervous, anxious kid, so I forced a laugh out trying to play it off like this was just normal guy talk. I didn't answer Pecklers hoping that he would move on and that it was like a joke or something in passing and he didn't really expect an answer. But he did. And he asked me a second time.

"How many times a day – *do you jerk off?*" Pecklers was persistent.

After a five second pause, I reluctantly told Pecklers between four and five times a day, which was true more or less. I felt my stomach tighten. I felt the ground beneath me starting to give way, but I couldn't back out. I couldn't very well hang up on him.

Pecklers' voice stayed light like we were just still talking about music or bible study. But what Pecklers said next to me made the world stop. I completely froze.

"Have you ever gotten a blowjob?"

Now I could hear the sound of my own breathing in my ears, but I didn't dare make a noise. My mind was scrambling for what to do and how to answer. I had only recently turned fourteen and had never gotten past first base with Jennifer, but I was not about to let him think I was just some inexperienced dumb naive kid. I had gotten this far; I wasn't going to blow it on a blowjob.

I forced myself to let out a breath, willing my voice to come out. My fingers tightened around the phone receiver, twisting the cord around my free hand like a tourniquet. I swallowed hard and I answered, my heartbeat pounding in my ears. I had no idea what to say, so I backed up a little bit, and said "*no*" – my voice barely audible.

"I mean...not yet." I stumbled with finding the right words, but finally blurting out a further response, hoping that he would believe me and still wanted to be friends with me. I try to use my acting abilities. Even so, my voice seemed high-pitched.

"I mean, I know what it is of course." I laugh and continue to try to explain myself.

"I know that I act and look much older than fourteen, but I haven't gotten to third base yet with my girlfriend. You know, she's only just graduated grammar school."

I try to laugh it off the way that I could only imagine a guy doing with his buddy, but I honestly didn't know what to say to him. I had only French-kissed Jennifer.

It was really embarrassing, but I was so excited that Pecklers wanted to be my friend. I wanted to be anything other than who I was. I wanted to be the kind of guy that was given high-fives and was clued in to inside jokes (and sometimes even crude jokes), or said the occasional curse word.

Over the course of a couple of weeks, it became normalized listening to Pecklers say sexual things. Guy stuff.

Night after night, Pecklers would describe the sex that he was having with his girlfriend.

After another few weeks, Pecklers was successful at finally convincing me to masturbate while we were talking on the phone with each other. I felt *really* uncomfortable and weird, and I was incredibly embarrassed. He told me that he and his other friends do it and that it was no big deal.

Within a week or so, the topic had turned to blowjobs again, and that's when Pecklers told me that his girlfriend loved giving blowjobs as much as she loved Jesus, and that she would give me my first blowjob.

The only other time I had heard an adult talk about sex, was with my parents in the Keeping Room. It was always clinical and biblical, and blowjobs had never been covered, with the exception of that one time that Mommy made fifteen-year-old Billy an appointment for a haircut by her hairdresser Henry at Greenville Coiffeurs. Henry had cut Mommy's hair for years. He was the only gay person in Greenville other than Gene the Flame.

Billy and I would accompany Mommy every Thursday at 4 p.m. to have her hair washed and set. We would drink Fanta orange soda in a bottle from the vending machine and wait while Mommy and a half dozen or so of other ladies would sit under what looked like the top portion of a rocket ship that blasted hot air over the entirety of Mommy's head to thoroughly dry each section of hair that was wrapped in rollers. The process would take two hours.

Mommy had made Billy an appointment with Henry one

afternoon after school. Billy nearly came home with something more than a haircut. Henry had told Billy that he wanted to give him the gift of his first hand job with a woman that he was friends with. I had never heard *hand job, blow job,* or any *extra job* ever spoken in our house. I didn't know technically what a blowjob was, but I figured it out soon enough. A man could be inflated by blowing into the hole of his penis, and it must feel amazing.

Mommy stopped going to Henry. She went to Jim, the owner of the beauty parlor, after Billy's near hand job incident. Jim was very understanding and very apologetic. It was awkward however, because Henry was doing blow-outs in the next chair, three feet to Mommy's right. Mommy explained that it was difficult to find a good beautician, or a florist for that matter.

I remember the blow job that I tried to perform on myself to find out what it felt like. In our bathroom, seated on the white toilet across from our white clawfoot tub, one school night while Mom and Dad watched TV. Dr. Shapiro had said that I had a mild case of scoliosis, and I could barely bend over to grab my calves let alone reach my penis to blow it up with my mouth. So, I came up with the idea of taking a flex-straw, actually two flex-straws connected. You can tuck the sides of the top or bottom of a plastic straw and force it into the end of a second straw by making a little side pleat at the end. I held the two-foot makeshift straw and firmly planted it against the hole on the head of my erect penis. Blowing into the straw as hard as I could, I caused the glands on the side of my neck and up into my ear canals to inflate to the point where I started to feel a tearing sensation in my neck, like a splitting sensation and noise. I could feel my lymph nodes inflating and the sounds of crystals popping and then exploding in my eardrums like it does when crunching down with your teeth on the colored pellets inside the fake Eucharist candy flying saucer. It felt like my glands would be inflated like that forever. Like a human blowfish. It did take away from the feeling of having my urethra blown out through a plastic straw, which in itself was excruciatingly painful and anything but pleasurable. I did not understand what I was doing wrong? Why was this so painful? Why would anybody want a blowjob?

    I needed to believe that Peckler's girlfriend blowing me up would feel a thousand times better than blowing myself up with two plastic flex-straws. I must be doing something wrong. Anyway, I was able to convince Pecklers that the reason I had never gotten a blow job, was more a matter of just not having gotten around to it, and eventually Pecklers let it go.

Chapter 13

Only a month ago I was cutting my graduation cake and signing yearbooks with messages like *"Never change!" "You're gonna do great things!"* and *"2 Young +2 Drink = 4 Roses!"* Now, I was pacing through locker-lined hallways where no one knew me, where my creative side had no context, and where the arts were swallowed up by pep rallies and varsity swagger. My freshman year at Hudson Catholic had just begun that week, and I felt like I was barely hanging on. It all felt like a dream speeding forward without giving me time to adjust. A blur of half-days drifting by in a haze of notebooks and bells.

Keith Pecklers called my bedroom phone at 7 p.m. that Wednesday evening to tell me that our folk group was going to practice at his house the next afternoon at three. What a thrill to be invited to the musical director's home! Keith lived on Bartholdi Ave. at the top of the block, at the opposite end of Tierney's, with his mom, dad, and brother. He was a college student at St. Peter's University and on his way to becoming a scholar and Jesuit priest. Keith told me over the phone that the folk group would be practicing at his house because the rectory, church, and school were being occupied for something else. I felt so grown up and so excited to be part of St. Paul's inner sanctum. I gave Keith Pecklers a big yes and told him I was looking forward to seeing everyone the next afternoon. Wow! What an invitation! It was the beginning of everything.

I rushed home, peeled off my school clothes, and changed into my play clothes. I grabbed my guitar, and I made the short walk to Keith Pecklers' house. For the first time in what felt like *forever* my life was happy. And more than that, *I* made it happen. It wasn't because I was Billy Brennan's little brother. I may not have been athletic, but I was talented. I could sing and play the guitar. No one gave that to me. God had answered my prayers. The Holy Ghost had taken up residence in my heart, filled my head with light and made me feel like I was no longer just a kid trying to escape. It was the first time in my life that I felt free.

I stood there on Keith Pecklers' porch, one foot in my old life, the other trembling on the edge of something new. My hand gripped the neck of my guitar like it was the only thing anchoring me to earth. On my way walking over to Keith's house, I kept thinking of Billy – how easy it all seemed for him. How natural he was at sliding into every room like he belonged there, always in the center of something, composed and articulate. I wanted that. Desperately. To walk into a room and not feel like an imposter, to feel like I belonged. This was my chance.

I stood waiting – twitching and shrugging. I couldn't help it. I waited for the other members of the folk group to arrive.

I waited.

And waited.

My neck and shoulders became sore from my constant shrugging.

Nothing.

No one.

My heart hammered fast and unevenly.

I wiped my damp hands on my jeans.

My armpits were wet, and perspiration was seeping through my button-down shirt. I looked up and down the block scanning for any sign of the folk group. I hadn't had time to phone anyone the night before.

Nina, Jimmy, Denise, Jess?

Where is everyone?

I was sure that they were on their way. I second guessed that I had gotten the day wrong. Maybe the time was wrong?

No. This wasn't a mistake. I'd been told to come.

I swallowed hard.

My neck was wringing wet now too.

I had never done anything like this before by myself. I didn't feel so mature at *this* particular moment. I felt like the fourteen-year-old kid that I was, anxious and nervous at not knowing how to seem or act like an adult in a situation like this, a kid playing at being important, and any second someone was going to tell me that I didn't belong.

I could hardly control my nerves. I looked side to side from the wooden porch, up and down Bartholdi Ave. to see if I could see any other members of the folk group coming. My heart was racing. I searched down to Tierney's squinting, cupping my hand over my eyes to block the sun, tracing the two sides of the street, my eyes darted up and down – picturing Jess turning the corner of Old Bergen and Bartholdi with her guitar case in tow.

But nothing.

I leaned forward and tried to peer into the top glass pane of the oak door, its beveled glass darkened by an ivory lace curtain. I stared into the reflection, adjusting my hair, combing it frantically with the aluminum comb that I kept in my back pocket at all times. And then – *movement.*

A shadow.

A tall figure.

The sound of slow, heavy footsteps on the other side of the door.

I stopped breathing.

And then a deep metallic click echoed from the deadbolt.

The doorknob turned.

And then the door creaked open.

It was Keith Pecklers.

The following section is based on my original responses from a legal intake form submitted during my case. Some details of my legal correspondence have been redacted, expanded or supplemented to preserve emotional boundaries. The core truth remains unchanged.

Stephen C. Rubino
Attorney at Law
CLIENT INTAKE FORM
FOR SURVIVORS OF CHILDHOOD OR ADULT SEXUAL ABUSE

(PLEASE USE ADDITIONAL PAPER IF MORE ROOM IS NEEDED FOR YOUR ANSWER)

I, KEITH BRENNAN OF THE TOWN/CITY OF BAYONNE, DO SOLEMNLY SWEAR OR AFFIRM THAT THE ANSWERS AND INFORMATION THAT I HAVE GIVEN BELOW ARE TRUE.

February 2, 2008

PART 1: BACKGROUND INFORMATION

1. Please state your full name: Keith Brennan
2. Please state your phone numbers:
(a) Home: ▮
(b) Work: 973-555-0080
(c) Cell Phone: ▮
(d) Fax: _____
(e) E-Mail Address: ▮
3. What is your date of birth: ▮

4. Where were you born? (please provide city, county or province and country)

Jersey City, N.J.

5. What is your current address? (Please provide street address, city, county/providence, country and postal code/zip code): ▮▮▮▮▮▮▮▮▮▮▮▮▮▮▮▮

6. Please list the mailing address you want to use if it is different than the address listed in question 5 above.

7. SCHOOLS: Please list all of the schools which you have attended, the city or town in which the schools were located and the years in which you attended each school.

SCHOOL	CITY/TOWN	YEARS ATTENDED
St. Paul's Roman Catholic Grammar School,	J.C., N.J.	– 8 yrs.
Hudson Catholic High School,	J.C., N.J.	– 4 yrs.

8. What is the highest grade of school that you have completed? 12th

9. **POST SECONDARY EDUCATION**

(a) Did you attend college, university or a trade school?

    YES [ ]   NO [X]

10. If you did, please list the institution attended, the city or town in which it is located, the program you took and the years that you attended.

SCHOOL	CITY/TOWN	PROGRAM	YEARS

11. Did you receive a university degree or diploma?

    YES [ ]   NO [X]

12. If so, please describe:

_____

_____

13. **EMPLOYMENT - CURRENT**

(a) Are you currently employed?

    YES [X]   NO[ ]

(b) If you are employed, do you hold that job throughout the entire year (annual) or is it seasonal?

    ANNUAL [X]   SEASONAL [ ]

(c) If you are currently employed in a job throughout the year, please list the name of your employer, company address, how long you have been employed there, your job description and your annual salary/income.

    EMPLOYER: Neiman Marcus

    ADDRESS: 1200 Morris Turnpike, Short Hills, N.J. 07078

    JOB DESCRIPTION: Sales

    YEARS: 2 ½   ANNUAL SALARY: ▮▮▮▮▮

(d) If you are currently employed in a seasonal job, please list the names of your employer, how long you have held that seasonal job, your job description, the number of weeks in a year you do that job and your weekly income.

    EMPLOYER:_____

    ADDRESS:_____

    JOB DESCRIPTION:_____

    NO. OF WEEKS:____WEEKLY INCOME_____

(e) Do you have any other source of income?

    YES [X]   NO [ ]

(f) If you do have another source of income, please list what that source is and how much income you receive annually from that source.

Wife's income. Realtor

We share our income as husband/wife.

14. **EMPLOYMENT - HISTORY**

Please briefly describe your employment history by year, if possible:

I was self-employed for twenty-five years as a fashion designer. I owned my company – Rennar Designs, a clothing designer/manufacturer. 1980-2005. Then I went to work for Neiman Marcus.

15. **INCOME TAX RETURNS**

(a) Is the income listed in questions 13 and 14 above, declared in your income tax returns?
    YES [X]   NO [ ]

(b) If it is not declared in your income tax returns, please list any other way that you can prove that income.

___

16. Have you ever been convicted of a crime?
    YES [ ]   NO [X]

If yes, where, when, for what offense?

___

If more than one offense, briefly describe your criminal record

___

PART II - SPECIFICS OF THE ABUSE

17. Abuser's full name, including middle initial:

    Keith F. Pecklers, Fr.

18. If your claim is based on abuse suffered at an institution, please identify the institution (school, parish, hospital, private residence, etc.)

St. Paul's Parish, Our Lady of Perpetual Help, Pecklers' family home, Stanford and Frank Maione's home, my family home (as a child).

19. Date or dates of abuse, or period of time during which you were abused or assaulted:

    1976-1980

20. During this time period, approximately how frequent were the acts of the abuse or assault (i.e., how many times per week or per month) and what was the approximate duration of each act (i.e., several minutes, half an hour, several hours)

State the detailed specifics of the abuse you suffered i.e., violent acts, acts of a sexual nature, emotional abuse:

Pecklers: Once every week or two. With Pecklers, the duration was usually half an hour or so.

Keith Pecklers: Pecklers was our church musical director. A couple of months after joining the church folk group, Pecklers began grooming me, calling me every night at my home, asking me about sex and stuff. I had my own phone.

Pecklers would be talking dirty to me, asking me about masturbation, and wanting to know how many times a day I masturbated and things like that. He would describe to me sex he had with his girlfriend. Pecklers told me that his girlfriend loved sex and gave great blowjobs. I told him that I was a virgin. Pecklers told me that his girlfriend would give me oral sex. This took place over a month or so. He would call me every night and tell me to masturbate while he spoke to me and he would do the same, all the while talking about what his girlfriend was going to do to me sexually.

I would meet Pecklers and our folk group every week for practice and play at mass on Sundays. I sang and played guitar. Pecklers told me to come to his house for practice after school one day. This was September 1976. I had just entered high school.

I finished school that afternoon early, got home, changed into my play clothes, got my guitar, and walked over to Keith Pecklers house for folk group practice. He had an organ set up in between the living room and the dining room. This was his parents' home. We practiced for a while, maybe thirty minutes or so, and I questioned him as to when the other folk group members were coming, and then Pecklers reached down to get sheet music out of his music bench. Instead, he pulled out two pornographic magazines. There were naked images of men having sex with women and women giving blowjobs to men.

My heart was racing. I was shocked after looking at them. After a few minutes Pecklers told me that this was my lucky day and that his girlfriend was coming over to give me a blowjob. We went into his bedroom and sat on the edge of his bed. Pecklers took off his shirt and unbuttoned his pants pulling them down, kicking off his sneakers and told me to do the same, that she was coming any minute. He then pulled down his underwear and had an erection. (refer to #34 for supportive evidence)

The next few minutes happened quickly. He tgrabbed me by the back of my neck and forced my head ▆▆▆▆▆▆▆▆▆▆▆▆▆▆▆▆▆▆▆▆. He then grabbed me and yelled at me never to do that again. He then pushed me down onto my back as he did the same to me. I thought that it was over and tried to get up but Pecklers pushed me down onto his bed and got on top of me. He began rubbing and humping his body against mine. I remember trying to move my face because he was trying to put his tongue into my mouth.

Just then Pecklers suddenly pulled himself off of me, his body and neck arched in panic. We could hear the rustling of keys. I immediately thought that it was Peckler's girlfriend arriving too late to have sex with me.

I was wrong. Pecklers said it must be his father coming home early from work. Pecklers darted off the bed yanking me up from my arm. I grabbed my clothes and sneakers and ran naked into the bathroom across from his room, adjacent to their kitchen. I could hear his father's heavy footsteps as he came closer to the bathroom and into the kitchen where Keith had run. Mr. Pecklers had caught the back of me running into the bathroom. He knew that someone was hiding. I cracked the door open for a second to see Pecklers trying to button up his shirt.

His father began screaming at him and I slowly turned the glass doorknob and closed the door tight with my back against it. I was crying, shaking, and hyperventilating. My heart felt so heavy pounding through my chest.

Mr. Pecklers was screaming at Keith.

"What are you doing?! Why are you doing this?! You promised us that you would never do this again!"

Mr. Pecklers then started yelling for me to come out of the bathroom, not yet knowing who he was about to find.

I was frozen. Paralyzed.

Mr. Pecklers continued to scream for me to come out of the bathroom.

I was sobbing.

When he saw me, recognizing me from church, realizing who I was, that I was a Brennan, Mr. Pecklers fell back into the kitchen chair and put his face in his hands.

His face and neck were purple. He looked like he was having a stroke. He stared at me and started weeping. Keith Pecklers nodded for me to leave.

I ran down the hall towards the door with my sneakers in my hand, stopped suddenly because I realized my guitar was still in the living room and I darted to get it. I bolted out the front door and ran three blocks stopping at the top of my street to gain my composure before going home.

Abuse continued every week at St. Paul's rectory and church. Pecklers had an office in the rectory basement and would abuse me after practice and mass. In the choir loft-during mass, Pecklers pulled out his penis and ███████████████████ ███████████████████████.

Another time during a young couple's wedding ceremony, he performed ███████████████████████████ and ██████████████████████ while the couple exchanged their wedding vows.

Another time he put his hands down my pants and masturbated me in the sacristy.

No place was off limits. On a retreat at someone's home down the Jersey Shore, Point Pleasant, he performed oral sex on me as I lay on the family couch while everyone on the retreat slept around us on the floor in sleeping bags and comforters.

Pecklers abused me in the front office of the rectory in between masses.

PLEASE TAKE AS MANY BREAKS AS NECESSARY

Chapter 14

God,

I am so tired. I am lost in the heaviness of the air that I breathe. I am smothering and it is a slow and painful death.

I inhale a thickness of fog, confusion, and darkness, and walk the neighborhood searching for a meaning.

Crying, raging at myself. I am worthless. I am pathetic. I am diseased in my mind. Mentally ill like Nanny. God am I her? Am I worse?

I am the Un-Dead. I have become a monster. A haunted thing walking among the living, I can't feel joy, only sadness.

I can't see light, only darkness.

And now, something inside – Something dark, and sick, and crawling inside of me is whispering

"Just give in. Give up. Let it end. I can help you."

And I am afraid. I am afraid because a part of me is listening. Part of me is ready.

Please God if you can hear me – Reach into this night, into my bed, and take me. Rescue me or release me.

Save me.

Lift me up or let me go.

I cannot carry this.

A new deacon had been assigned to St. Paul's Parish to prepare for his ordination and his name was Father Thomas Stanford. Fr. Tom was unlike any priest we had ever seen before. Thanks to the changes brought on by Vatican II, priests and nuns no longer had to dress in traditional habits and clerics could now dress as if they were normal. Our congregation was prepared during masses leading up to it.

The priests at St. Paul's, still stuck to the old ways, wore black buttoned up clerical shirts with the white priest tab inserted at the collar. But not Fr. Tom. He looked more like a camp counselor or a folk singer than a priest. The first time we saw him outside of the church he was wearing a tee shirt, jeans, and sneakers; like a guy who'd just stepped off a beach in California. Imagine that, a priest in a tee shirt and jeans. It was mind-blowing! Even his clerical shirts weren't the usual standard black. Fr. Tom wore a burgundy one, a grey one, and a khaki color one. No one had ever seen a priest dress like this. Everyone wanted to be around him.

I met him for the first time after that introductory Sunday mass. The entire church was buzzing, you could feel the excitement, like an energy was running through St. Paul's. It was like God had picked the coolest priest on earth and dropped him right into our laps. Pecklers played the organ at Fr. Tom's introduction mass to the congregation. The deep powerful notes rolled through the church like a royal procession, introducing St. Paul's new prince.

There was incense wafting through the aisles and into the pews. Daddy was the usher. The choir voices, including Mommy's, soared across every inch of the vaulted ceilings. And then there was us – the folk group, playing *"On Eagle's Wings"* right up on the altar, Jess and I sharing a music stand and microphone. This wasn't a routine mass; it was a debut concert, and Father Tom was the headliner we never knew we were waiting for. And then Fr. Tom stepped up to the altar – cool, confident, and smiling like a rockstar.

After mass, at the church social, Pecklers introduced me to Fr. Tom. Our parish was ready for a younger priest since Fr. Tony had been transferred to a new parish. Someone would have big shoes to fill. We sure were missing those Sunday dinners having been blessed by the presence of Billy's priest-friends for the last couple of years.

That Wednesday, I bumped into Fr. Tom at the rectory just as I was heading in for folk group practice. He was coming down the hallway, humming a tune under his breath, his black cassock flowing behind him like a cape.

"Hey, superstar," he said, flashing his big white smile. I turned quickly, sure that he was speaking to someone behind me.

"You doing anything after practice tonight?"

I shook my head. "No, not really."

"A few of us are heading over to Fossetta's for burgers and pizza. Jess is going, and two of my friends – Fr. Frank and Sister Martha. You should come. I want you to meet them."

My stomach flipped. Me? *Meet them?* Pizza with two priests, a nun, and Jess? That wasn't just hanging out. That was something else!

"Oh wow. Yeah – yes! That'd be amazing," I said, trying to keep my voice from cracking.

"I just have to give my mom a call."

"Great!" Fr. Tom beamed. "Use the phone in the office. I can't wait to meet your folks once I'm settled. Hopefully, Sunday after mass. Make sure you come and find me to introduce them. It's my first homily. I'll need all the support I can get."

That night, we were all packed into a corner booth at Fossetta's. The place smelled like garlic knots, tomato sauce, and lemon furniture polish. Fr. Tom introduced me to his closest friends – Father Frank, who was a few years older and had once been his theology professor at the seminary, and Sister Martha. She was older than both of them, short and stocky, with a no-nonsense air that made her seem very uptight. She wore a black skirt with a matching blazer over a white blouse, and her veil was more like a snug white cap that hugged head like a uniformed nurse from another era. She was also Fr. Tom's closest friend.

We laughed loudly and ate pizza and burgers. Fr. Tom, Fr. Frank, and Jess ordered a pitcher of beer, and Sr. Martha and

I, a pitcher of Coke.

They made me feel included, not just like a kid tagging along. I wore my favorite jean shorts to folk group practice, the ones that ended a few inches above my knee. I remember clearly, we were halfway through the first pie when I felt a hand – not just a brush, or bump, but a firm resting hand on my leg. I looked down quickly – then over at Fr. Tom. His hand didn't flinch. He just looked at me and smiled softly, like nothing had happened. Then he slowly pulled his hand back to his own lap and went on talking to Fr. Frank about the homily he was working on. I sat frozen for a minute chewing pizza crust, wondering if maybe he had thought that it was *his* knee. Or maybe because the booth was cramped, it had been an accident. Maybe it was my fault, and I accidentally brushed against *his* knee.

"This is my *guy*," Fr. Tom announced to Fr. Frank and Sr. Martha.

"He's got the voice of a teen idol and just wait until you see him play the guitar."

They all laughed, even Jess smiled at me. I sat up straighter. I felt taller, older – that I belonged., like this was what being chosen felt like. Walking out of Fossetta's, Fr. Tom asked me if I wanted to take a ride with him that coming Saturday to run a few errands. I quickly said yes.

That Saturday, around 10 a.m., I heard the sharp honk of a horn and ran to look out my parent's bedroom window. There he was – Fr. Tom, in a green Plymouth Duster, gleaming in the sun like something out of *The Dukes of Hazzard*.

"Hop in!" he called – his face, sunglasses, and big wide smile gleaming.

Fr. Tom leaned over and pushed the passenger door open from the inside, still flashing that signature grin. I hopped into the bucket seat. The windows were already rolled down – it was a warm day, seventy degrees and climbing. The breeze smelled like spring, and the Jersey City sidewalk was already baking under the sun. Fr. Tom wore a fitted white tee shirt, blue jeans and white sneakers. His gold watch caught the light every time he turned the wheel, reflecting in his gold aviator-style sunglasses. His car was filled with the scent of coffee, cologne, and cigarettes, still strong, even with the windows open. Fr. Tom was nothing like any priest I had ever seen, not even Tony or Kunzie.

"You good?" Fr. Tom said to me before pulling away from my house.

"Yes! I'm great!" I try to seem relaxed, even though it felt like I swallowed a blender. We pulled down Neptune Avenue, my house beginning to shrink in the side mirror, and with it, the little bubble of my world.

I sat trying not to look too stiff, impossible actually with the amount of twitching that was going on.

"You sure you're good?" Fr. Tom repeats to me when we get to the light.

"It just feels weird being out with a priest, that's all."

"Well, I'm not wearing the collar, so you're safe for now." Fr. Tom chuckled.

"I don't bite."

The wind whipped through the open windows. My guitar-callused fingers drummed on my knee as he lit a Benson and Hedges Menthol cigarette and started talking fast – casual like we've been friends for years.

"I've got to pick up some mail at my parent's place in Belleville," he said. "Should only take a minute. You'll get to meet my old man." He didn't seem thrilled about it.

When we pulled up to the modest home, he flicked his cigarette out the window, stepping on it after getting out of the car. Walking right into the house, Fr. Tom motioned for me to follow him. Inside everything smelled fresh like spring cleaning.

"Dad? It's Tom."

Suddenly a man, appearing to be in his late fifties, stepped through the dining room and walked into the foyer where Fr. Tom and I were standing. His father barely looked at me, which seemed odd.

"This your new helper?" he grumbled to Fr. Tom.

"Something like that," Fr. Tom replied, brushing it off with half-of a smile.

On the wall, I spotted a framed photograph. Fr. Tom – younger, and in a blue suit, with his arm around a beautiful blonde girl in a light blue dress. They both looked like they were in their twenties. It looked like it could have been an Edward Martin shooting.

"She was his girl," his father said without looking at me. "Before all of this *priest* stuff."

I glanced at Fr. Tom. His jaw tightened for just a second,

squaring it off sharply, accentuating the cleft in his chin.

"Well, the Lord had a different plan for me, Dad. I got the calling." Fr. Tom said this, turning to me, this time smiling with his lips closed and pressed together.

"Well, the poor girl. *Poor, confused,* Mary Catherine. For the same thing to happen to her *twice* must have been devastating. Your Mom bumped into Mary Catherine's parents at the market, and it seems that poor Mary Catherine is suffering from depression."

"Ok Dad. We really can't stay. I just wanted to pick up my mail. I still need to change my address from Sacred Heart Seminary to St. Paul's. We'll let you get back to cleaning. Give Mom my love." The vestibule felt as if the temperature had dropped twenty degrees and a chill ran through my body giving me goosebumps.

Back in the car, Fr. Tom quickly lit another cigarette, inhaling deeper than I had ever seen someone do other than Uncle Johnny. He then rolled down the window and let a long forced stream of smoke shoot towards the house, like a line dividing him and us from the life he had left. We didn't speak right away. He pulled down the block and off onto the highway. There was an empty, uncomfortable space. The radio was off and the only noise was the humming of the road beneath us.

"Mary Catherine was the love of my life. We went out for a few years. We were engaged to be married."

I looked at him, unsure of what to say, or if I should say anything. It was a shocking revelation. I hadn't thought up until that point that priests were even human. I know that sounds ridiculous, but I had never really given any thought that a priest actually had a normal life before getting the calling from the Holy Spirit.

"I left Mary Catherine for the seminary."

I continue to stare at Fr. Tom. I am hardly blinking. He drove with both hands on the steering wheel, his cigarette dangling out of the corner of his mouth like Steve McQueen as he continued his story.

"And *then*, I left the *seminary* for Mary Catherine."

I took a second, trying to understand, trying to comprehend what he had said to me.

"And then, for the final time, I left Mary Catherine *again,* practically on the altar. This time for good." Fr. Tom flicked his ash out the window.

"Thought that I could have a different life. But something kept pulling me back. The Holy Ghost, I guess. I don't know." He paused. "Some things are just meant to be," he continued, "Besides, what's done is done. You can't change the past. At least I get to meet cool kids like you."

I didn't know what to say. I was only fifteen, but I knew the feeling of being caught between two lives. Fr. Tom turned to me, his gold aviators flashing glare into my eyes temporarily blinding me at that second.

"You ever feel torn? Like you are being pulled by an energy greater than yourself but unsure what that force is?"

"All the time," I said softly.

He smiled. "Good. That means you're listening. You have to keep saying *yes*. We must say *yes* to the Lord and *yes* to what is asked of us. Now let's go get a burger. I'm starved."

That afternoon I told Fr. Tom my dreams of wanting to be an actor and filmmaker and Fr. Tom told me about how he chose a life of Christ and what his faith meant to him. It felt like we had been best friends for years. When Fr. Tom pulled up in front of my house later that afternoon, the green Duster rolled to a soft stop in front of my house like it had delivered me from one world into another. He put it in park, let the engine idle, and turned to me with that familiar mix of warmth and slight mischief in his voice.

"You know," he said, adjusting his sunglasses. "In two years, I'll be looking to get a new car."

I looked at him, not sure what he meant.

"And when you turn seventeen – *this one's* yours. The Duster. It'll be yours."

My jaw dropped.

"Wait – are you serious?"

He smiled, that big white movie star smile.

"Dead serious. So don't go crashing your bike before then."

I laughed, but inside, something changed, something felt different, quiet and grateful. I felt safe. That was it. I felt *safe* with Fr. Tom. Fr. Tom was becoming the big brother I had never had. Someone who saw me and understood me. Someone who was going to give me his Dukes of Hazzard's car!

I imagined him coming over for dinner and for the holidays, and within a few weeks, my wish had come true. Tom was like a member of our family, sitting across from me at the table, leading us in grace, laughing with my family at my stories, then watching *The Wonderful World of Disney* and *The Sonny and Cher Show* on the couch.

In a moment of rare courage, I opened up to Fr. Tom. He had picked me up at Hudson Catholic after school like he often did, and we drove down to the park in silence, the weight of something unsaid filling the space between us. When we parked beneath a bare-limbed tree, I broke down.

"I need to tell you something," I whispered, my voice already unsteady and breaking, "about Keith Pecklers."

Tom didn't move. He didn't interrupt me, he just listened.

And then, as if a dam gave way, I sobbed – full, body-shaking sobs that came deep from my soul. I told him everything. Every horrible detail. What Pecklers had done. How scared I was of him. How I didn't know what to do, how the folk group and St. Paul's had become my entire world.

Tom reached over, put his hand gently on my back, and pulled me toward him. I cried into his chest like a five-year-old.

"I've got you," he said quietly. "I hear you. And I believe you."

I couldn't respond. I just nodded through the tears, shaking, letting his words wrap around me like a blanket.

He waited until I calmed down and said, "I'm going to talk to him. I'll take care of it. You don't have to carry this anymore. And don't worry, I'll see to it that you remain in the folk group."

And that week – he did.

It stopped. Keith Pecklers left me alone. Completely. No more nightly calls. No more awkward glances. It was over. It was as if Fr. Tom had reached into a nightmare that I couldn't escape from and plucked me out of it. From then on everything changed. I was able to completely block out anything that had happened with Pecklers. My parents had become very close to Tom, and within a few months, they began going to see Tom separately for spiritual counseling – marriage counseling.

One Sunday over roast beef and mashed potatoes, Tom casually turned to my mom and dad and said, "I was thinking, next weekend, would it be alright if I took Keith down to the Jersey Shore? Just a weekend, a get-away – there's a little motel I know down near Atlantic City."

My parents lit up like Tom had just offered me a scholarship.

"Oh my God, that would be wonderful," Mommy said, coughing twice, cupping her mouth with her hand. "What a beautiful experience to have that kind of time with someone like you."

Daddy nodded, and then in his Butler, New Jersey weird voice said, "You sure he's not going to drive you crazy?" he joked, nudging me with his elbow. Tom laughed and reached across the table to mess the back of my hair – he knew better than to mess up the front.

"Nah. He's good company."

I couldn't believe it.

A weekend away?

With my best friend?

A priest!

With someone who got me, who actually wanted to spend time with me. *Me,* who had always felt like the tagalong kid, the outsider, the one peeking in from the hallway while Billy and his friends laughed in the kitchen. And now I had my own *Tony*. My own *Kunzie*.

We drove down to Atlantic City on a Friday evening after school with the sun dripping behind us in gold and red streaks. Tom sang along to the radio – Neil Diamond, Jim Croce, even some Beatles. He knew every word. I remembered thinking this is what friendship feels like.

The motel wasn't fancy, but to me it was magic. There were two queen size beds in the room and the one that I claimed was a coin operated *Magic Fingers* bed that made the whole mattress shake when you dropped a quarter into it. I had never seen such a thing! Tom found a few quarters, popped them into the coin-slot and gently pushed me against the headboard. "Relax!" Tom said. We both laughed as the bed began to shake like Linda Blair in *The Exorcist!*

Tom removed his collar, tossed it onto the bed, and unbuttoned his black clerical shirt. He stood in front of me in his white tee shirt, the same kind he wore when we'd drive around town doing errands.

"I'm going to take a shower," he said, tossing his shirt over the back of the chair.

"Okay," I answered, barely looking up from the TV. I was happy watching TV and just enjoying the fact that I was away somewhere on a vacation.

A few minutes after saying he was going to take a shower, Tom walked back out of the bathroom. His hair was still dry. He hadn't taken a shower. He moved slowly across the room, out of the bathroom, and bent over the nightstand next to my Magic Fingers bed where I was still sitting with my back against the headboard, still shaking. Suddenly, at the sight of Tom, my skin turned cold. I was literally frozen.

Tom picked up his pack of cigarettes, tapped the pack on my nightstand, removed a cigarette and struck a match, lighting it as it hung from his mouth. He waved the match to put it out and tossed it into the ashtray, raised his head, inhaled deeply, and blew his stream of white menthol smoke toward the yellowed popcorn ceiling. Next, he opened the top drawer while wondering out loud if there was a bible. There was. "Thank God," he joked. I followed him with my eyes, my eyeballs bobbing, my head shaking – held onto my body only by my neck and shoulders. I didn't know where to look. I was seven years old again at the Boulevard Pool in the men's changing cell.

"Are you alright with this?" Tom asked.

I didn't know what *"this"* meant. Not really. Everything in my body screamed to move, to run, to disappear, but I couldn't. I felt like I was paralyzed. I fumbled and stammered, my voice didn't even sound like mine. I remember being shocked that he was so hairy. No one in my family had hair on their chest.

"*Yeah,* I guess I'm okay," I managed, my voice trembling between trying to sound polite and trying to keep breathing, while literally shaking.

Tom nodded. And smirked.

"God made our bodies. There's nothing to be ashamed of. Being *naked* – it's natural."

He sat gently on the edge of my bed, still shaking from fifty cents ago.

Then he looked at me and said it so calmly, so casually, that it took a second for the words to penetrate my brain.

"I'm *gay*."

Tom paused, as if he were waiting for a reaction. I gave him none. I couldn't. I just stared into his eyes. My brain was still trying to catch up to what was happening. The only *gay* people I knew of were Henry – Mommy's beautician, and Gene the Flame from Greenville.

"But *you're* not gay," he added quickly. "I *know* that you're not. Don't worry about that. You're *not.*" I didn't need convincing, I knew I wasn't gay.

Then Fr. Tom continued, like he was telling a story over coffee. That he'd been in love with a priest who was his professor while at the seminary – *Fr. Frank*. The same Fr. Frank that I recently sat across from with Sr. Martha, having pizza. Fr. Tom explained that he and Frank had been lovers at the seminary and that it had recently ended, and that they now remained close friends.

Lovers.

I could barely make sense of that word. I could hardly think of that word coming out of Fr. Tom's mouth. It didn't belong in the same sentence as seminary. Or *priest*.

He said all of this in the same easy tone he used when talking about a Broadway show, or his car, or the Holy Ghost, as if this was just another thing, just another piece of himself to share. Then he stood up again, stepped out of the smoke, rubbed his cigarette butt in the ashtray, and walked into the bathroom, closing the door behind him. I just sat there alone. As straight as I could, backed up against the headboard, praying for the shaking to end.

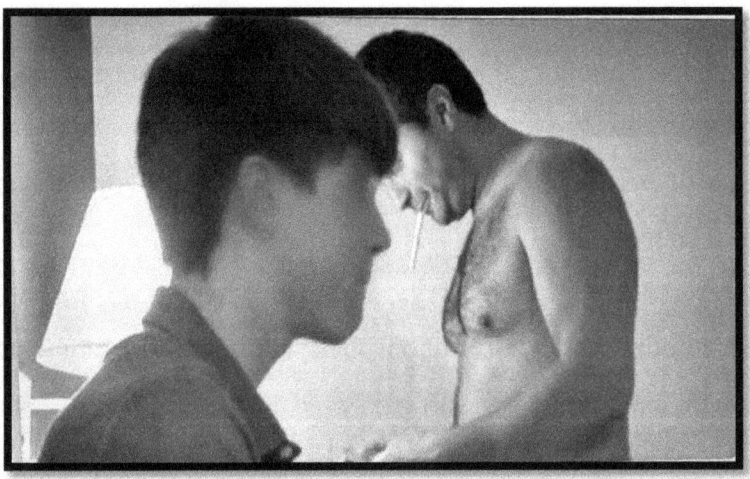

Of God And Gucci (2011)

Finally, it stopped. I stared straight ahead, hardly breathing, trying to understand what had just happened. My mind raced and spiraled, unable to land on anything that made sense. I felt like I had been in a washing machine for the last ten minutes.

My thoughts flicked around my brain like broken film loose on a reel. Maybe I was dreaming. Maybe I was having one of my night terrors. Maybe I was going to wake up and realize I peed on Billy's *Frampton Comes Alive* album and this will all just be one weird nightmare. But I didn't wake up. The bathroom door stayed closed and I sat there on that motel bed in the glow of a television that I could no longer hear, trying to figure out what Fr. Tom had just said to me, and what it really meant.

Even though everything that happened at the motel had left me feeling confused, like I'd stepped through some invisible curtain into a world I didn't understand, it still felt good to be away on a vacation. Fr. Tom took me to breakfast, lunch, and dinner – restaurants that had tablecloths and chandeliers hanging, wine lists, and waiters in tuxedos. Fr. Tom even bought me little things I never would have asked for – like cool sunglasses, a leather bracelet, even a record album I mentioned in passing on the boardwalk. That night he took me to dinner at Resorts International. Just walking into a place like that made me feel as if I was in a movie. Somewhere between the entree and dessert, Fr. Tom slid a small box across the table.

"What is this?" I asked.

"Just something to remind you of this weekend," he said smiling. Inside was a silver watch. Sleek. Like an adult would wear. Like Tom wore.

"Tom, this is too much."

"You're worth it," he said, "You've been through a lot lately. I want you to know how special you are, and that I'll always be by your side to help you through. That's what real friends do for each other."

And that's what made it all so confusing. I did feel special. After everything I had gone through with Pecklers, Fr. Tom had been the only one that I could truly trust, the only one I told. He had protected me. He stopped it. I felt safe with Tom. He was the only adult I could really talk to. I didn't know where I would be without him. And there was no way I could lose that. So, I kept showing up. I started spending as much time with him as I could – riding in the Duster, helping him at church, hanging out with that small group of friends from the parish.

And then there was Jennifer. I kept Jennifer separate from everything else at the church. Her family was not religious and I'm not even sure if they regularly went to mass. She didn't know about Fr. Tom – not really. It felt safer that way, like my worlds couldn't touch or they'd unravel, but she met him once briefly, Jennifer holding my hand and looking beautiful in her denim skirt and wedge sandals. Fr. Tom stepped out of the church vestibule and waved.

"You must be Jennifer," he said, shaking her hand. "Keith talks about you."

"She's pretty," he told me later. "You've got good taste."

It was Jennifer's birthday. I wanted to get her something special. It isn't every day that your girl turns fifteen. Thanks to Tom, I knew what a special night out was supposed to feel like, you know, with dinner and all. I took Jennifer to The Gallery -the new restaurant on Danforth Ave. that Billy had started working at as a bartender. After dinner, we were all set to go see *Rocky* at Cinema 440. I wanted it to be the perfect date. During dessert I presented Jennifer with a present that I had purchased with the help of Mom. It was a diamond butterfly necklace from Kay Finlay Jewelers on Journal Square. I questioned the saleswoman as to how many carats the diamond was.

"Is this real?"

"It better be," she replied, "After all, *it is $29.*"

"It's a total of .002 carats, sweetheart. She's a lucky girl. She's going to love it."

I could afford it; I was working as a busboy at a local Italian restaurant where Billy was a bartender as well.

Jennifer wore an orange butterfly print qiana dress. She looked especially beautiful that day. And yet, even with that sweetness, something inside of me felt split – like I was two people living in one body.

Jennifer broke up with me a week after giving her the butterfly diamond necklace. The one I had so carefully chosen at Kay Finlay. The one I had proudly paid for with my hard-earned busboy money. What happened to Mommy and the saleslady standing beside me over a velvet viewing tray – telling me how girls remember gifts like this – *forever?*

Forever turned out to be six days.

Jennifer said something about how things were changing. About how it wasn't me, but of course it was. And then, the very next day, I found out that she was now going out with Gavin Simms, who could not be more opposite than me. I was an artist, an actor. Gavin – well, he looked like someone who would become a scientist.

When I was *Mr. Spring* in the Spring concert at St. Paul's, Gavin was *Father Time* and apparently, my time was up. Jennifer had chosen the boy who made sense. The boy who could give her a future. And maybe I couldn't anymore, and she knew the difference. Because truth be told, I was starting not to recognize myself either.

ST. PAUL'S PLAYERS — Keith Brennan sprinkles water on his fellow classmates, the flowers, during the third grade play previously at St. Paul's School, Jersey City.

Had Pecklers turned me into something? Was Jennifer pulling away from me because of what happened that night in her alley a week before – when I tried to touch her beneath her butterfly-print dress, our heads barely two feet below the kitchen window where her mom and grandmother were laughing, sipping coffee and eating Entenmann's crumb cake? Was it because I tried to rush things? Was I too fast now? Did Jennifer break up with me because I was now becoming someone else? *Something else?* Was I becoming a monster now having been made the *un-dead* by Pecklers? Didn't Dorothea and James like me any longer? Was Jennifer pulling away because she could feel it? The sickness in me? The *secret*? My heart broke clean in half that night. And in my head, a cruel soundtrack on repeat. All I could hear was *Chicago's "If You Leave Me Now,"* like Aunt Minnie's soundtrack of *Laura's Theme* playing over and over in my brain – only for me, it felt like a funeral march and not a lullaby with a miniature ballerina stuck in my head.

*If you leave me now
You'll take away the biggest part of me
Ooh-ooh, no baby please don't go
And if you leave me now
You'll take away the very heart of me
Ooh-ooh, no baby please don't go
Ooh-ooh, girl, I just want you to stay*

*A love like ours is love that's hard to find
How could we let it slip away?
We've come too far to leave it all behind
How could we end it all this way?
When tomorrow comes and we'll both regret
The things we said today*

*A love like ours is love that's hard to find
How could we let it slip away?
When tomorrow comes and we'll both regret
The things we said today*

*If you leave me now
You'll take away the biggest part of me
Ooh-ooh, no, baby please don't go
Ooh, girl, just got to have you by my side
Ooh-ooh, no, baby please don't go*

~ Chicago

The first person I thought of calling was Fr. Tom at the rectory. I didn't even hesitate. I ran crying, shaking, completely shattered, to the phone booth at the end of Jennifer's street on Ocean Avenue. My fingers fumbled the coins into the slot, the cold metal, slippery with sweat, pressing the buttons as fast as I could, slamming the glass bi-fold door behind me, my breath hitching between sobs.

Thank God Tom was there. The second I heard his voice on the other end I broke down all over again.

"Tom," I gasped. "It's me."

"What's wrong?" His voice sharpened, but calm. It tumbled out between gasps and sobs. How humiliated I felt, how gutted.

"Jennifer broke up with me…she's with someone else…I gave her the necklace, and I thought… I don't know…I just…I feel like I'm dying."

Fr. Tom's voice was steady and calm.

"Okay, he said firmly, "Take a deep breath. I'm right here for you, okay. Come on over to the rectory. I'm home all night on call. I'll meet you at the front door. Don't ring the bell."

I ran sobbing three blocks to St. Paul's rectory with *"If You Leave Me Now"* on auto-play in my head.

Fr. Tom was already at the door waiting for me. He opened it just enough for me to slip inside and once inside the vestibule, he leaned into my ear and whispered to be very careful and quiet going up the stairs, we don't want to disturb the other priests in their rooms. I nodded through my snot and tears running down my cheeks. I was surprised that Tom didn't lead me into a den or the side parlor where parishioners had counseling. Instead, he turned and started up the stairs. I had been in the rectory to get to the basement for bible study and folk practice, but never like this, never sneaking, never feeling like I was somewhere I wasn't supposed to be.

I followed Fr. Tom, my footsteps light, my heart heavy with grief, up two flights of stairs to get to his room. When we got to his suite I collapsed onto the love seat, my body giving out from the weight of everything. The crying started again. I couldn't stop it, it just kept coming like a flood, my body still shaking.

Fr. Tom moved across the room, opening a small wooden cabinet that sat between his small living room and bedroom. He poured two drinks.

"Here," he said, handing me a glass.

"Drink this. It'll calm you down."

I lifted the glass to my lips. The glass was short and heavy. The drink was sweet, warm, and smooth. It was my first drink.

"It's Dry Sack." he told me. I nodded like I knew what that meant, then he casually pulled out a pack of Benson and Hedges Ultra Deluxe Menthols and offered me one. I didn't let on that I had smoked cigarettes before with Jennifer. I took the cigarette from him, my arm outreached and trembling, after he lit it with his own cigarette that was dangling from his mouth.

"I think it would be a good idea to give your mom a call to let her know that you are here."

Fr. Tom was right.

"After all, it is a school night. Why don't we tell her that I'll drive you home at ten. Is that good?"

I nodded my head at Fr. Tom taking the phone.

"When you're done talking, let me say hi so she knows

you're safe." I nodded to Fr. Tom.

"Hi Mom? What? No, I'm not ok. I'm with Fr. Tom at the rectory. Yes, I am crying. Jennifer broke up with me. Just a few minutes ago." I immediately start crying again.

Fr. Tom took the phone from me.

As Fr. Tom spoke to my mom, I looked around his small living room and noticed a metal record stand filled with albums. The alcohol was beginning to relax me. I kneeled down on the carpet to go through his collection while he spoke to Mom.

"Colette, it's me, Tom. Of course. I was just glad that I was at the rectory. Yes, he ran right over. We're going to spend a couple of hours together, listen to some music and talk it all through. No, I didn't know Jennifer. I just met her briefly after mass this past Sunday. Yes, a beautiful girl. I know. Oh, believe me, I know what it feels like. I was in love once too. I sure was! And then the *calling* came. No, (chuckling), it was The Lord. I know. Yes, I was a good catch! Well, that's true, but if I were married and had a different life, I would never have met kids like Keith. I agree. He is very special. Don't worry Colette, he's in good hands. I'll have him home at ten, ten-thirty. Ok, you too. Ok, I'll tell him, Colette. You too. Goodnight."

Fr. Tom hung up the phone and knelt down next to me as I shuffled through his albums.

"Your Mom said that she loves you very much. You're a lucky guy to have folks like them. See any albums that interest you?"

Fr. Tom had an array of albums. Barbra Streisand's

Superman, Barry Manilow, Peter, Paul and Mary, *Jesus Christ Superstar,* and Captain & Tenille, which was playing on his record player.

Fr. Tom softly sang the verse.

> *"He is now to be among you at the calling of his hearts*
> *Rest assured this troubadour is acting on his part.*
> *The union of your spirits here has caused him to remain*
> *For whenever two or more of you are gathered in his name.*
> *There is love, there is love."*

Still on the carpeting, we slid over to the loveseat and sat with our backs up against it. Within a few minutes and a few sips of my second drink, I began drifting in and out, lost somewhere between being awake and sleeping. I was completely exhausted. I could feel Fr. Tom's arms around me, pulling me in, guiding my head against his chest, and then softly, he began to sing to refrain of the Captain & Tennille song, his voice low and steady, almost hypnotic, blending into the haze of sherry, cigarettes, and emotional exhaustion.

I wasn't sure how long I dozed off, but then there was movement. Something shifted. I began to stir, and my body moved very slowly, before my mind caught up. My head was spinning and my stomach churning in an awful combination of grogginess, nausea, and something else I couldn't quite place. I kept my eyes half-closed, they were too heavy to fully keep open, adjusting to the dim light, trying to figure out where I was and what was happening. My brain felt thick and slow, struggling to make sense of it all, and then slowly I could hear sound – the music, Captain & Tennille's *Muskrat Love* looping over and over in my head.

I'm not sure how long I dozed off. My head was spinning, disorientated from the sherry and cigarettes I suppose. I had never felt like this before, but I had seen Daddy looking like this as he would awaken from his Saturday afternoon booze naps.

I realized slowly as I began to come back into my body, that I had fallen into a sound sleep. I felt immediately embarrassed. The first thing I noticed was that the lights were off and there was only the smoky filtered light of the street post coming through the blinds and that it was considerably darker than when I had arrived. *What time was it?* I thought, still on the floor.

And then, groggy and disconnected, the sudden realization that Fr. Tom was now leaning over my ribs and stomach area. I could feel the weight of him. My eyes were trying to focus, my arms and legs were dead to my sides. I could not move them. What was happening?

Just then, I noticed my button-down shirt and tee shirt had been pulled out of the front of my jeans, my belt buckle had been opened, and the button of my blue jeans had been undone.

SURVIVOR INTAKE FORM
Please Take as Many Breaks as Necessary

21.   State the names of any person or persons who were aware of the acts of abuse or assault against you:

Fr. Tom Stanford: Abuse lasted approximately one year total with Pecklers, at which point Fr. Tom Stanford took over. After confiding in Fr. Tom that I was being abused by Pecklers, he promised to speak to Pecklers to get him to stop.

He did and then began grooming me for himself.

With Fr. Tom, there were upwards of one hundred incidents of sexual abuse that began when he came to St. Paul's as a deacon and lasted until October 1980 when he was a priest at Our Lady of Perpetual Help in Oakland, N.J.

Fr. Tom asked me if I wanted to get a burger with a few friends one night including his best friend Fr. Frank Maione.

Sitting in a booth across from Fr. Maione, I felt Fr. Tom's hand on the inside of my thigh, rubbing me. I thought I was imagining this or that he thought that it was actually his own thigh that he was rubbing.

He started taking me on errands. He drove a green Plymouth Duster.

The first time he picked me up in front of my house, he promised to give me his car when I turned seventeen. I would later total this car, with him in it, in a car crash.

He asked my parents if I could go away with him and stay in a motel near Atlantic City.

As I lay in bed watching television, Fr. Tom said that he was going to take a shower. I could hear the water running.

The motel had a vibrating bed called "Magic Fingers" that had an electric device that was mounted at the top of the headboard. Fr. Tom put a handful of quarters into the mechanism and told me to relax.

Five minutes later Fr. Tom walked out of the bathroom, directly to the left of the TV completely naked. Fr. Tom asked me if I was "okay" with it. I nervously said yes but felt very uncomfortable. I had never seen a naked man before other than my father and my brother.

Fr. Tom walked over to the bed night table and lit a Benson and Hedges cigarette. He made small talk and talked about being naked and how God loves our bodies and that I should not be ashamed. He walked around the bed to where I was laying, bent over the night table, opening the drawers in search of a Bible.

He then sat on the bed, still naked, and told me that he was gay.

I had no idea what he was talking about because I knew that priests did not and could not have sex. Priests could not be gay. They took a vow of chastity.

He continued and told me that he and Fr. Frank had been lovers for a few years, and that they met in the seminary.

Fr. Tom told me that I was not gay and that I should not worry about that because he knew that I wasn't.

He walked into the bathroom and took his shower.

Nothing else happened that night.

A few weeks later, growing closer in friendship, I went to see Fr. Tom at the rectory because my first girlfriend had broken up with me. I was upset and crying. He took me up to his room. It was my first time in a priest's room.

Fr. Tom had me telephone my mom to say that I was with him in the rectory and that he would drive me home by 10 p.m.

He gave me a cigarette and told me I needed a drink. He gave me Dry Sack (sherry) in a glass and had one for himself. We continued drinking while we sat on the floor against his loveseat. We listened to Captain & Tennille.

Now drunk and crying, I dozed off.

I awoke to Fr. Tom unbuttoning my pants and fondling my penis.

I was paralyzed. Unable to move. Disorientated. Fr. Tom performed oral sex on me and I ▮▮▮▮▮▮▮▮

Abuse took place everywhere.

His car in Staten Island after shopping at the Staten Island Mall one afternoon.

Fr. Tom pulled down a deserted road and performed oral sex on me. A police officer pulled up to us and began questioning us. The officer questioned Fr. Tom and he told him that he was a priest and that he was helping me, counseling me. That I was having a family problem with my parents.

He let us go.

Abuse happened often with Fr. Tom in his room at St. Paul's rectory.

I would go to the rectory after school, and my parents would let me stay with Fr. Tom until nine or ten p.m. and then he would drive me home. He would give me liquor and play albums, and we would have sex in his bed and inhale Rush liquid incense, which is Isobutyl Nitrate to get high.

Fr. Tom gave me a trip to the Bahamas for my sixteenth birthday.

Abuse every day.

Fr. Tom took me on a bus trip to Disney World for a week that summer as well.

Fr. Tom told me that if anyone were to ask about our relationship that we would say that Fr. Tom was my uncle.

One time Fr. Tom took me to Sr. Martha's summer home during the winter to check her pipes to make sure that they weren't frozen.

Sr. Martha's vacation home was in Long Branch, and it was the middle of the winter. Fr. Tom and I went in. It was freezing cold in the house.

Within a few minutes we were in Sr. Martha's bed having sex. Neighbors called the police and when we wouldn't answer the door, they threatened to break it down. I ran into the bathroom and refused to come out.

Police forced me out and I was visibly shaken and flushed. I could not catch my breath. The police kept asking me if everything was ok. I said yes and Fr. Tom talked his way out of it and the police left.

Fr. Tom also would abuse me in my own home with my parents

there.

Once he asked my mom and dad if he could stay and sleep over after dinner. It was the night that he came over to convince them that nothing bad was happening. He slept in my room in my brother's twin bed when my brother was away. My bedroom was ten feet from my parent's bedroom and the door on our bedroom was an accordion style folding door.

Fr. Tom climbed into my bed and performed oral sex on me while my parents slept. There were endless times of abuse. The Jersey Shore, mountains, hotels, motels, and rectories. I stayed at Fr. Tom's and Fr. Frank's house in Manahawkin. They built a home on a cul-de-sac at the point of a lagoon.

I stayed many times. Fr. Frank had sex aids in his night table next to his bed like stuff that made your penis feel hot when you blow on it. Fr. Tom would use these on me and on himself.

With Fr. Tom, abuse lasted up to several hours as there were visits to the rectory, overnight visits, and weekends away. Also Fr. Tom took me on vacations/trips to the Bahamas and Disney World. (see attached)

22(a). State the detailed specifics of the abuse you suffered i.e., violent acts, acts of a sexual nature, emotional abuse:

With **Keith Pecklers**: On an emotional level he told me that my brother was also involved sexually with other males. There was force used at times. Pushing me to my knees. Holding me down as he would masturbate himself on top of me and also leaning on top of my body to masturbate me. Forcing my head down to give him oral sex. Pecklers would get on top of me naked holding me down with his weight and try to kiss me, rubbing himself against me until his climax. At times Pecklers would make me masturbate him. All times of abuse would end with his climax. Pecklers ███████████████████████████████would ██████████████████████████████████ and onto my body at other times.

With **Fr. Tom Stanford**: Emotional abuse included him telling me over and over again that the greatest gift, praise, that you can give to God is the gift of yourself. Using your body by making love to another human being was a union with God Himself.

Tom, being a priest, was the ultimate gift to the Lord.

Over and over again Fr. Tom would say that our making love was a gift that God was giving us, that it was beautiful. To deny sharing ourselves with each other, we would be denying something that God blessed us with. That sharing our bodies by making love was the same as making love to God.

He manipulated and brainwashed me to believe I was special; chosen and blessed to be in this special, exclusive relationship with him.

Fr. Tom infiltrated, tricked, and befriended my mother and father and gained their love and trust.

Fr. Tom knew that I was taking the prescription medication Stelazine for anxiety and panic attacks since I was 11 or 12 years old. At times I literally could not breathe and would hyperventilate and gasp for air. I had taken medication at times in his presence. There was no physical abuse w/Stanford, however, after sexual abuse had stopped, I developed an eating disorder (undiagnosed) and had notable weight loss. I can document this through photos and will expand on this.

Sexual abuse with Fr. Tom included oral sodomy and masturbation – on me, and to him. Fr. Tom would ejaculate into ▇▇▇▇▇▇▇▇ and onto my body and would have me do the same to him. Fr. Tom would lay on top of me, or have me on top of him, and rub our bodies together to achieve orgasm.

Fr. Tom used various sexual positions including ▇▇▇▇▇▇▇▇▇▇▇▇▇▇▇▇▇▇▇▇. Fr. Tom used alcohol, marijuana, and Rush (Amyl Nitrate) during my abuse.

PLEASE USE ADDITIONAL PAPER IF NECESSARY

Chapter 15

ACTORS PROLOGUE THEATER: ACTORS WANTED
Auditions at The Hotel Plaza 91 Sip Ave. Thursday 7pm.
All actors should come prepared to deliver a monologue.
Call 201-555-4252 for additional information.

I read this half inch by two-inch ad in the Jersey Journal classifieds after school one day, and once again my world was about to change. I had received another gift from The Holy Ghost. This time it was the gift of *Counsel,* which allows a man to be directed by God in matters necessary for his salvation. I needed God as my director and salvation as soon as possible, with not a moment to spare. The gift of Counsel enables a person to judge individual acts as either good or bad. The Holy Ghost will help you understand what is necessary to be carried out, or if something is evil it should be avoided.

When I got home from school that day, I made myself a Buitoni Instant Pizza in the toaster, and opened *The Jersey Journal* to see what movies were playing that coming weekend at Journal Square. We had recently moved to Bayonne. Mom's friend Maryanne, the one whose husband gave her black eyes, finally left him and was moving out of town. Before she left, she offered Mom and Dad her apartment.

I always read the classified section, my second go to after the movies, and discovered this small two-inch ad for an acting class. I read and re-read it at least one hundred times, twitching and shrugging my shoulders. I still had faith that God had a special plan for me and that I would be famous someday. That was if I didn't kill myself before then.

I was now spending all of my free periods at St. Aedan's Church across the street from Hudson Catholic, praying for a miracle. I felt so incredibly confused. I would cry in the dark pew and pray for a way out. I couldn't understand why loving the Lord was so painful. Physically, mentally, and spiritually, I was at my breaking point. I was deeply, desperately depressed. I wanted to end it all. I prayed for God to either kill me or help me. And quickly. I was weeks away from killing myself.

I would pray for God to send an angel to save me. Over and over and over again. I knew that it was possible. God had sent the angel Gabriel to Mary to tell her that she would give birth to the Son of God and God sent an angel to the shepherds to tell them of Jesus' birth. God sent angels to protect the tomb of Jesus after they crucified him, and the angels also rolled the boulder away from Jesus' tomb so that he could rise from the dead and walk out. God sent an angel to Daniel in the lion's den and directed the angels to shut the mouths of the lions so that no harm would come to him and that the lions would not eat him. And God sent the angel Clarence to Jimmy Stewart in *It's a Wonderful Life* when his character in the movie, George Bailey, had so many problems that he was thinking of ending it all by jumping off of the bridge in Bedford.

I knew that God sent angels to help and protect people and save them from danger and trouble, so I knew that God could send an angel to help me. But in-between praying for a miracle, I would daydream of ways to kill myself. I became fixated on hanging myself in St. Paul's steeple, the same steeple that I sketched a few short years ago when life was simpler in my playroom – designing costumes, creating and building castles, playing with my mouse. The only thing I had to think about then was how bad Mom and Dad's fighting would be that Saturday Night at the Fights, and if Daddy was going to beat Billy up that weekend too.

In one suicidal daydream, I would climb step by step up and around each worn wooden landing, having been led there by Pecklers. Up to the steeple on the top of St. Paul's Church, we'd pass the stained-glass windows, their vibrant colors and intricate designs casting holy shadows across the stairwell. Each pane told a story – scenes of saints, miracles, and martyrdom. But to me, they looked like cages. The thick lead strips that held them together kept everyone paralyzed, even Jesus and Mary.

As I climbed higher, the windows bled light. Jeweled toned reds, purples, and golds slashing across me like knife wounds. The bell tower wasn't a beacon any longer. It was a trap for me. A holy prison. When Pecklers was done with me, just like in real life, he disappeared. And I stayed behind. Alone. In this dream, I take the brown braided belt from my jeans and thread it around my neck, then loop it over the chain that rang the bell. And then I jumped. My body would swing between the bell and the surrounding structure, limp and broken, clanging my head again and again, against the ironsides. My eyes would bulge like Mommy's did when Daddy strangled her in my playroom closet. My feet, swollen with blood, would sway back and forth until one of the volunteer church cleaners found me early the next morning. Tangled in rope, chain and silence.

That was one version. My other favorite suicidal fantasy took place in the choir loft. I would stand in the back, by the enormous brass organ pipes, take a running start, sprint past the bench with Pecklers conducting Mommy as she sings *"Ave Maria"* at midnight mass, and then I'd leap. *Soar.* Fly over a sea of worshipers like a fallen angel crashing through the stained-glass sky. A final performance. A perfect ending.

But still, something flickered deep within my soul.

Something whispered: *"Not yet."*

St. Paul's choir loft

Saturday Nights at the Fights and family time spent in the Keeping Room taught me well. What to show and what to hide. How to look normal. How to keep the volume just right, the tone believable. No one knew. Not Mommy. Not Daddy. Not even Billy. No one would ever know about what was happening to me with Pecklers, and now with Fr. Tom, so maybe I was a better actor than I thought. I had fooled everyone into believing that I was thriving in my new life at the church. That I was safe. That I was blessed. That I was just like Billy.

But I was still nervous to act on stage. I spent time hidden behind Phyllis Diller and Harpo's blond wig and Dracula's black velvet cape only a few short years ago, but now as a teenager, I could hardly rely on a wig and a cape to cover up. When I saw the ad for the acting class and took it as a sign from God. I needed a sign. Any sign. And there it was – printed in black ink. I worked up the courage to call the phone number for more information.

Phone ringing…

Click.

"Hello, Actor's Prologue Theatre. Brenda speaking."

"Uh…hi. Um…I saw your ad in the Jersey Journal…for the acting class?"

"Yes! I'm so glad you called. Are you calling about the audition?"

"Yeah…I mean, I think so. I – I've never done anything like this before. Not really."

"That's perfectly ok. We welcome all experience levels. The class will be a mix of beginners and more seasoned performers. We focus on confidence, movement, and self-expression."

"Okay. Um…it said something about a *monologue?*"

"Yes. For the audition, we ask everyone to prepare a short monologue or soliloquy. Something that shows a little of your personality and emotional range. It doesn't have to be long, just a couple of minutes."

"Okay. Um…Thank you, that helps. I have never acted in a *monologue* before."

"You'll do great. Just calling is the hardest part sometimes."

Brenda was right. I could hear Poppy whispering in my ear to be rigid.

"What is your name and address? I will send you a letter in the mail with more information. In the meanwhile, go find yourself a monologue!"

I gave Brenda my name and address and then hung up the phone. The perspiration ran down my forehead and into the phone receiver.

The letter arrived in the mail three days later. There, tucked in between a PSE&G bill and a coupon book from the A&P, was a long white envelope with my name and address written on it and *The Actors Prologue Theatre* written on the top left corner. I tore it open and pulled out a sheet of single folded stationery with typing on it.

An audition. An acting class. I quickly looked up the word *prologue* in the dictionary.

"An event or action that leads to another event or situation." I still was not sure if I was meant to be an actor, even though I clearly declared myself a future professional actor on the first page of my St. Paul's Graduation Autograph book, the one Pecklers signed. I also wrote on page one that I was class president. Anything that I had once been proud of, any hint of achievement, had been replaced. Washed away by depression, swallowed by self-loathing, drowned in suicidal thoughts. That boy had died.

I folded the letter gently and placed it in my top drawer, pulling it out every twenty minutes, re-reading it over and over, tracing the words with my finger as if the ink and indented typewritten words could make me braver.

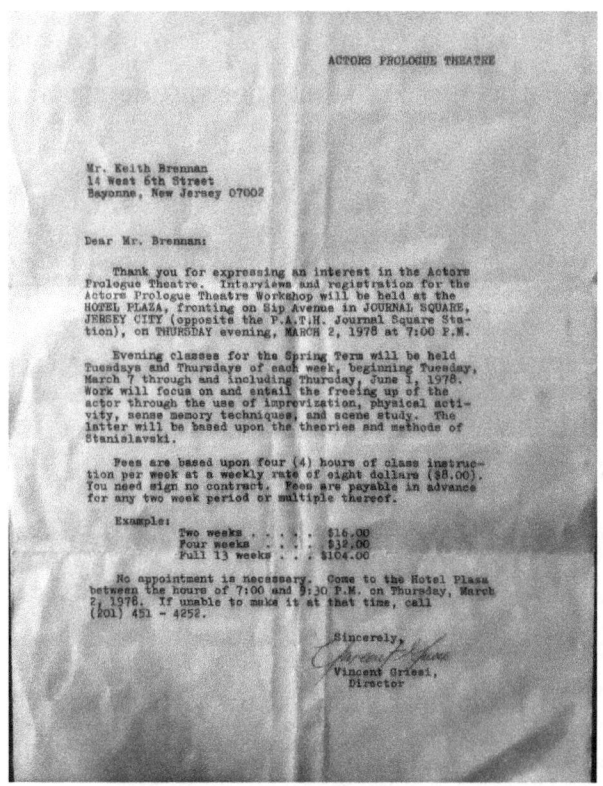

My anxiety disorder was now out of control, and I was becoming sicker by the day. My neck and shoulders were in constant spasm from jerking and twitching all day. Pimples surrounded my mouth and chin. I couldn't picture myself being anything more than dead. The heaviness of my depression and anxiety pressed down on me – my stomach aches, my ticking, my shoulder shrugging, my sleeplessness, my lack of focus at school, my dropping grades, my depleted energy, my weight loss. And let's not forget my incessant hair combing. My scalp hurt. My brain hurt. I was now inhaling liquid *Rush* all day long. It was the only way to slow down the uncontrollable thoughts traveling between my brain and my body. As hard as I tried, I could no longer pray it all away.

I loved the cold glass rim of the brown liquid incense bottle touching the warm rim of my nostril. The smell of *Rush* liquid incense, that odor of sweaty feet and dirty socks, numbed me instantly. The slight sting and burn of chemical liquid peace first making contact against the delicate membranes of my fifteen year old nose, holding the shot glass sized bottle of *Rush* against one nostril at a time while pressing the alternating nostril closed with the opposite thumb, breathing into the depths of my nasal cavity as hard as I could, its fumes providing instantaneous relief, intoxication and self-detachment. Total loss of all inhibitions. I could feel my blood flowing through every vessel in my body. The increase of oxygen and chemicals rushing to my brain.

Inhale.

Deeply.

Slowly.

Every muscle in my body breaks free from my self-imposed imprisonment. I am warm inside, and I imagine that it must feel this way when I die. This is what freedom feels like. The sounds that surround me – music, voices, the ringing in my ears, the reverberation of whatever is happening in the near distance, over and over and over.

Ahhhh. I am euphoric for three to four minutes at a time and it is all so worth it. The fleeting high was worth the impaired judgment, the visual distortions, the instantaneous pounding headaches, the irregular heartbeat, the nausea, the disorientation, and the constant state of confusion, followed by the suicidal thoughts that last for the twenty minutes until my next huff. It made the night terrors last a shorter amount of time if I huffed throughout the night when I get up to pee, which was usually five to six times a night. It broke up the time spent being chased by the monsters. The benefits outweighed the negatives. I could lose myself. I was in control as long as I was using.

It was also worth the dry mouth, worth the burning sensation that rushes up my neck and into my head, setting my neck, ears, and face on fire. The *Rush* rocket that is launched directly into my brain – orange and red, exploding directly on contact, causing a temporary loss of vision that sometimes returns minutes later, and sometimes *not*, teasing me with spots and dark shapes that float across my eyes, like unholy ghosts whose only job is to terrify me and drag me deeper into the darkness of despair. They threaten me through temporary blindness, reminding me that I have entered hell.

I'm high for such a small fraction of time. This is *exactly* the reason why I need to huff twenty to thirty times a day now. What started out as a way to allow the Holy Ghost to enter me more freely, to lower my inhibitions – to make love to God through Fr. Tom easier, had now become an addiction. I was literally a Channel 7 *Afternoon Special*. I was now addicted to drugs, sex, and God. I was truly the *un-dead*. Not a vampire, because in order to become a vampire you must bleed out completely and then the vampire must give you some of his blood to infect you. Pecklers and Fr. Tom were not that generous. Being *un-dead* is the state between life and death, and your soul is forever trapped in the prison of your decaying body.

But even living with all of that, the idea of acting still felt like a magnet. It would not go away. I felt an attraction that I could not get rid of. And so, I re-read that classified ad at least a hundred times. It pulled me in. What did I need to prepare? What was a *monologue*? What was I to deliver? I was having trouble now speaking on the telephone to people. How could I perform in front of an audience?

I looked up the word monologue in our Encyclopedia Britannica.

Monologue, in literature and drama, an extended speech by one person. The term has several closely related meanings. A **soliloquy** is a type of **monologue** in which a character directly addresses an audience or speaks his thoughts aloud while alone or while the other actors keep silent.

This was my chance to become a famous actor like the ones I had watched on *The Mike Douglas Show,* but I had to deliver a *monologue*. The only acting experience I had, if you could even call it that, was performing in my own homemade movies. My first film was a *Frankenstein* remake. I was twelve years old and had just received a Super 8 camera and a film projector from my parents for my birthday. It was my prized possession – my portal to another world. The best gift they ever gave me besides the orange Raleigh bike. I cast my best friend Richie as the monster and directed it in his backyard, with all the drama and chaos of a real Hollywood set. Richie's backyard became the monster's lair, and his plastic military playset and toy soldiers stood in for the ill-fated village. We blew up the military base using firecrackers and I shook Richie's mom's baby powder through the air like it was fallout from the explosion. As costume designer, which I also was, I crafted Richie's *Frankenstein* body out of black trash bags, rubber latex gloves for the hands, and a Clorox bleach bottle – cut in half and spray painted black, for the square top of his head. I taped screws from his dad's toolbox to the sides of his neck for bolts and wired a coat hanger into them for his electrified awakening scene. We used Richie's dog's heavy silver chain for a scene where Bobby from across the street, playing the angry villager, whipped the Frankenstein monster in slow motion. I filmed the entire movie and then spent the week editing it, cutting and splicing the film together in my playroom. I already had a film projector for my movie premiere, which was that Friday night in Susan's basement. I made popcorn in

Mommy's sauce pot and sold it in individual baggies with a paper cup of Strawberry Kool Aid. I sold my movie combo for fifty cents. It was my first film and I had grossed five dollars. I was the writer, director, and film producer. I was the costume designer, the sound engineer, the cinematographer, the make-up artist, the stunt coordinator, and the proprietor of the concession stand. I did it all. I knew how to do this somehow, and I was good at it.

My second film was *The Magician*. I shot it on location, meaning in front of Richie's house on Gates Avenue and around the corner at #30 School where I had gone to kindergarten. In this film I played the magician. My power – making things disappear. I'd lift my hands dramatically, say some type of made-up spell, and poof, cut to an empty frame. It was editing magic, or at least my version of it. The finale was Richie getting hit by a car – carefully choreographed, of course. Though to this day I can't believe we pulled it off without a single adult questioning what the hell we were doing. I loved bringing a story I had written and directed to life on film, sitting back and watching people view it, completely absorbed in the world I had created. In those moments behind the camera, I was someone else. I was something else. Maybe a filmmaker. Maybe a storyteller. Maybe a magician.

The audition was a week away and I had to prepare my monologue. I went to the Greenville Library and checked out a book about Stanislowski, the greatest acting teacher of all time, along with a book of monologues for beginner actors. This was my shot. My *Mike Douglas* moment. My chance to be discovered.

But I was terrified. I chose a monologue that was about losing your socks in the laundry – how they disappear. It was funny. Age appropriate. I made cue cards on 5x7 index cards, highlighting my lines in yellow crayon over thick black Magic Marker. I rehearsed in my bedroom with the door shut, pacing like I was delivering Shakespeare to an empty stadium. Every so often I'd hear Mommy through the door. "Slower Keith. Don't rush the words. Enunciate! Speak from your diaphragm."

I didn't even know where my diaphragm was. Mommy believed in me. She leaned against the door frame and said, "Keith. All it takes is one person. One person who believes in you – can change your life." She told me about movie stars who were discovered at soda fountains and on Hollywood Boulevard. "Sandra Dee was born and raised in Bayonne and look what happened to her!" Mom went on. "Look at Brian Keith from *Family Affair,*" (one of our favorite shows.) "I bet you didn't know that he was born in Bayonne too. And Frank Langella! He's starring in *Dracula* on Broadway now! That's proof that you can be a star!" I *didn't* know that there were so many stars from Bayonne. Even in the middle of my unraveling, even while carrying secrets and shame that no boy should have to carry, the thought of it still excited me. I was ready to try.

Mom drove me to the Hotel Plaza that night. Until then the only places I was allowed to go alone was St. Paul's School, the church, and the rectory. They knew I was safe there. I was a nervous wreck. I had taken a Stelazine before leaving the house, just a half-tablet to take the edge off. My stomach was in knots and the cramping had become a nearly daily punishment ever since Pecklers. The pain had moved in like a permanent squatter in my gut, stealing my sleep most nights, waking me up with night terrors. I would wake up screaming – Mommy would run in – switch on the light and rub my back until I calmed down. I was always exhausted. Always floating just outside of things like I was stuck in a snow globe, and someone was shaking it. Nothing felt real. Adding to that, I was now high most of the time. And now, this *hope* – that maybe, just maybe, I could still do something big with my life, something important. Something I could call mine.

We got to Journal Square early. The sky was deep violet, already veined with the glow of streetlights, with the red Jersey Journal sign lit up next door to The Hotel Plaza. Mom found a parking spot across from the hotel. We were still driving the used car we were able to purchase from Uncle Tom thanks to Gina La Colette. Before going in, Mom turned to me. "You okay?" she asked, "You'll be great! Just be yourself. Or be like Sandra Dee or Frank Langella."

I shot her a look. The Hotel Plaza sign looked like a movie marquis. Ok – I said in my mind. Be rigid. You can do this.

The Hotel Plaza was a full service hotel with 190 rooms and several dining rooms such as the Wedgewood Dining room, cocktail lounge, and men's bar. The banquet hall, decorated in French and Italian Renaissance style, became a gathering place for political and social events in Jersey City. Politicians frequently staged rallies in the ballroom for upcoming elections and those who disagreed with the current political leaders and mayor, or disrupted the meeting, were physically ejected onto the streets of Journal Square. Jacqueline Kennedy came to the Hotel Plaza during John F. Kennedy's campaign for presidency in 1960, but it had since fallen into disrepair.

The hotel was red brick trimmed with limestone and white marble. It had a colonial style main entrance, a lobby and had a marquee over the entrance. My mother and I walked through the grand lobby and sat on a long, tattered black leather sofa. Brenda, the director's girlfriend that I had spoken to on the phone, greeted us. She had short jet-black hair cut into a shag and she wore an apple-green paisley kerchief tied around her neck like she was either about to go on a safari or host a game show. Brenda was nice though, and she spoke to me like I belonged there.

"Mrs. Brennan," we should be done by 9 p.m. if you want to stop back then. Don't worry, Keith is in good hands." Not the first time I had heard that. Brenda spoke to Mom while glancing back with a smile for me. After some small talk, a tall, older man in a turtleneck and a corduroy blazer walked over to where we were sitting.

Brenda lit up like he was Dino De Laurentiis.

"Keith, this is Vincent," she said, "he's the director." Vincent shook my hand like I was someone important even though my palm was clammy and my voice cracked when I said hi. Just then, over Brenda's shoulder, I could see out of the corner of my eye that the brass doors to the hotel lobby were opening and in walked a girl who was making her way over to where we were gathered. She said that she was there for the acting class and introduced herself as *Diane*. Brenda practically jumped off the couch to greet her and bring her into the group. She introduced her to Vincent and the eight other wannabe actors sitting on the couch and random chairs someone had dragged over to form a semi-circle.

"Everyone, this is Diane!"

Everyone mumbled a polite "Hi" or waved. But I wasn't looking at *them*. I couldn't.

I could not take my eyes off of *Diane*.

There was something about her that hit me like lightning. Not the love *at-first-sight* kind they show you in cartoons like *Peppie La Pew* with hearts popping out of his eyes. This was something else that I had never experienced before. Diane had something that captivated me instantly. I couldn't shake the feeling that we knew each other somehow. With her brown loose curls and a cupid's mouth, Diane seemed like an actress straight out of a 1940s movie. As I watched her, I felt a connection so profound that it bordered on the supernatural. When she looked at me, the world fell into slow motion. I tried to act cool when Brenda introduced us, but I think I said something like, "HiImKeithniceboots."

Diane's heart shaped face glowed. She was petite and wore a short denim jacket, ivory cotton button down shirt tucked into denim gauchos and brown Frye boots. I felt zapped into her eyes. At that moment, I felt as though I was gazing upon an angel here to save my life. My *Clarence*. As we exchanged introductions, I could not help but feel a surge of excitement coursing through my body, as though divine intervention and fate itself had brought us together on this exact night.

March 2, 1978 would be forever etched in my memory as the night that I met Diane. The night I fell in love. I knew at that moment that there would never be enough time to spend with Diane. There would never be enough time for me to look at her, to hear her stories, to listen to the way she said her s' and the exaggerated movement of her long eyelashes, like dark wings that suspended the oceans of her blue eyes. Just being next to Diane pulled my soul into hers. And I had just met her only a few moments ago. God had heard my prayers.

After Vincent and Brenda introduced themselves to the group, they explained that we would be taking the elevator to the top floor studio for further instructions and to prepare for our auditions.

"We'll be heading upstairs to the rooftop studio," Vincent said, clapping his hands together like we were already in a Broadway warm-up. "It's where we will hold auditions and class sessions. Just follow me and Brenda to the elevator."

Diane and I, along with eight other actors and actresses, made our way up to the rooftop studio by way of the hotel elevator. An original 1920's old-fashioned cage elevator operated by Sam the elevator operator – an old, colored gentleman. The building had eight floors and the ride to the top was jolting. The cavalcade of directional arrows, brass buttons and clanging motor sounds of shifting gears and pulleys caused me slight alarm, like the pulley could snap any second and kill us all. I edged in and positioned myself closer to Diane, our legs pressing lightly together in the crowded elevator. I closed my eyes and inhaled the sweet spicy scent of her perfume washing over and calming my anxious heart. Our fingers touched ever so lightly as the elevator stopped. It was a shock – more like an electrical current, running down our arms and into each other's fingers, jolting us abruptly at our destination, and back into our bodies. We  looked at each other with amazement. And excitement. Lots of excitement. Just being next to her felt like my soul was floating. Like it had reached out without asking me and curled itself around hers, as if we were already connected from somewhere else, and I had only known her for twenty minutes.

"Step down. Careful stepping out." Sam repeated this several times until all of us were able to slowly edge ourselves past the elevator gate and door and into the studio. A wall of black iron cased windows faced the fading sun setting across the New

York skyline. We all stopped to look in awe. We were told by Vincent to take a seat. There was a small cabaret style stage and a dozen tan metal folding chairs set up in front of it. Diane and I sat next to each other. Vincent welcomed us to the *Actor's Prologue Theater* – a theater workshop, that if accepted, would last for thirteen weeks. Two hours of class instructions would take place on Tuesday and Thursday evenings, at a weekly rate of eight dollars. The money wasn't an issue for me, I had two jobs as a busboy at two different restaurants.

The rooftop studio wasn't what I had expected. No red velvet curtains. No spotlight. Just a big open room with scuffed wood floors and a small stage with two lights at each end barely holding on to broken stands. Vincent stood at the front of the stage with a clipboard in hand. Brenda sat off to the side of the stage with a yellow legal pad and a pen on her lap. "Alright," Vincent announced, clapping once as he held the clipboard under his arm. "Who wants to audition first?"

I immediately looked down at my shoelaces like they had suddenly become undone and needed my attention. A guy named Tony bravely volunteered. He did a Shakespeare monologue that had something to do with dying with nobility. He even had hand gestures. I didn't hear most of it because my heart was thumping so loudly. Then Vincent looked directly at me.

"Keith? Keith Brennan?

It wasn't a question.

I stood up fast, knocking the script with my monologue to the floor. I bent down to pick it up, then dropped my cue cards, two of them scattering under chairs in the next row. So, I was off to a strong start.

"Take your time," Vincent said kindly.

"I'm good," I squeaked, as if I had just inhaled helium.

I walked over and took one step onto the stage. It felt like I was walking the plank. Diane was sitting cross-legged near the back, her elbows on her knees watching me. I could feel her eyes on me. I cleared my throat with a *Mommy two-cough*, closed my eyes, and began speaking.

"Ladies and gentlemen of the jury – because let's face it, I'm being judged here – I present to you Exhibit A: one lonely sock.

A lonely, confused, *innocent* sock that went into the laundry with its identical twin…and came out alone.

Where did its partner go?

Did it escape the spin cycle to pursue a solo career as a dust rag?

Or is there a secret society of left socks living in a vent behind the Maytag?

Because I swear up and down that I put both socks in the hamper. *Both.* Every time!

But when the laundry day comes, it's like – BOOM. One of them goes missing!

Gone. Abducted by aliens.

Meanwhile, I'm left digging through my drawers, trying to make a match – like I'm on a dating show for footwear.

'Bachelor Sock Number One…meet a completely

different shade of blue who has a toe hole.'

And they say a teenage life is hard?"

Everyone started laughing – really laughing. Even Vincent was laughing. Brenda looked over at him and Vincent smiled. Then she scribbled something quickly on the pad. I shrugged my shoulders to the audience and took a half-bow, jumped off the stage, and returned to my seat. I had made it through. Diane was next.

Diane took her time making her way to the dark stage, navigating through the darkness, maneuvering through the tan, scratched metal folding chairs. She was petite and ethereal. Once center stage, Diane began to act as if she was standing in front of a mirror and putting on her makeup. She slowly brushed the imaginary blush back and forth across her cheekbones and pushed the curls away from her forehead as she dusted her face with imaginary powder. She filled in her eyebrows with an imaginary brown pencil, applied eyeshadow, and applied lipstick as if she were a famous Hollywood actress. The stage was now lit with the brindled light shining through the dirty windows facing Manhattan. She tousled her shoulder length chestnut brown curls with her fingers, gently causing tendrils to unwind around her heart shaped face. Slowly she lined her lower lids, using her forefinger to ease down the translucent skin surrounding the lower part of her eyes. Tossing her head up and to the side, she applied invisible mascara, her eyes opening wide like a silent film movie star. Opening her slight mouth, she positioned the lipstick at her cupid's bow, dragging it to the furthest point on each side, then rolling her plum-colored lips inward, and then at ease, blotting her mouth with an imaginary tissue from her imaginary dresser. She then proceeded to act putting imaginary earrings into her ears, wincing at not being able to find the holes, staring through us, using us as the *fourth wall* that I had read about in *An Actor Prepares* that I had on loan from the library. Diane produced the entire monologue to us without saying a word. Diane was brilliant. A brilliant star, a shining light cast against the New York skyline. Everyone clapped and then Vincent spoke.

"Actors. What we just witnessed Diane perform was *sense memory* using the audience as *the fourth wall*. Bravo Diane! Beautifully acted."

I didn't know what he was referring to as the *fourth wall,* but Diane was magical.

The audition seemed to fly by in a blur, and the connection between Diane and I was growing stronger with each passing moment. When the time came for the class to be over, I seized the opportunity to offer Diane a ride home when my mom came to pick me up. I was eager to spend any time with Diane to prologue the evening. I wanted Diane from the moment our blue eyes met. I hadn't known that I was saving myself all along for *Diane*, but now it all made perfect sense. Diane would be my *one and only true love* in this lifetime. God had sent me the angel that I had been praying for and keeping chaste for. Well, for the most part. And it would not be like making love to God with Fr. Tom. It would be like saving myself for *marriage,* the way Mom and

Dad had prepared Billy and me.

It was now 9 p.m. and the class was over. Vincent had miraculously paired Diane and I as scene partners to study and prepare. We had all made it through the audition and were officially part of the *Actors Prologue Theatre Troupe!* I planned to ask Diane if my mother and I could drive her home, but as we made our way towards the lobby of the hotel, my heart sank at the sight of a man entering the hotel lobby with two young boys in tow, a telltale sign of family life. Confused, I turned to Diane, my voice trembling as I asked her the burning question in my mind.

"Who are they?" I whispered close to Diane's ear, my heart already heavy with disappointment.

And with those words, my world came crashing down around me as Diane revealed the truth that I had been too blind to see. Diane was not the single, fifteen-year-old, unattached girl that I had imagined her to be, but a twenty-six-year-old married mother of two young boys.

The revelation knocked the wind out of me. I asked Diane to tell me the truth of what my eyes could not see, what my heart did not want me to feel.

"Yes, I am married and have two children. A few weeks ago, I had a lump removed from my breast and biopsied. I made up my mind that if I did not have breast cancer, that I was going to live the life that I dreamt of, and I had always wanted to take acting classes." Diane's husband had questioned her as to how they could afford the eight dollars per week for the classes, and she told him that she would find a way.

We had only known each other for two hours, but I had never had a feeling like this. It wasn't sick, sour, or painful to feel. Diane lit me up from my insides out. She lit my soul on fire. I was instantly in love with her.

Chapter 16

Diane and I met every Tuesday and Thursday evening at 7 p.m. at The Hotel Plaza over the course of thirteen weeks and became friends. And *yes,* I dressed as if I were going on a date with Diane every Tuesday and Thursday evening. Time spent with Diane was different. We had an unexplainable comfort with each other. We finished each other's sentences, made the same vocal inflections to recognize things together, simultaneously. We were one hundred percent plugged into each other's energy, found the same things funny, and the same things worth an eye roll.

We would take the rickety elevator at The Hotel Plaza with Sam, down to the lobby to get snacks from the cafe adjacent to the hotel, bringing back ice cream sundaes or chips and sodas up to the rooftop studio. We would dream out loud together while looking over at the New York City skyline, the twilight hours of the day drifting away from us. In-between scenes, I would show Diane my dance routines. Disco dancing was all the rage.

Once I asked Diane to allow me to demonstrate a new dance move that involved grabbing your partner by the wrists and pulling them to slide in between your open legs, quickly spinning around to lift them by their wrists. When I attempted this on Diane, she nearly flew out the open window. We had never laughed so much in our entire life.

I could not tell Diane or anyone else that I was living a double life. My life at St. Paul's and my new life meeting Diane were completely separate worlds, and one of them was out of control. I was going down a dangerous path, and it felt that way.

As our acting classes were coming to an end, Diane and I made a promise to stay in touch, but God had a different plan. At first, we called each other once or twice a week, then it was once every two or three weeks, and then eventually, our calls stopped altogether. Diane was married. And had two children. What the heck was I thinking? I was fifteen for God's sake. So, Diane and I drifted apart. But I knew that Diane and I were meant to be together. It didn't matter to me that she was married, and I was in high school. None of it made sense. I knew what I felt in my heart. Diane was the one that I was waiting for. The angel that I had prayed for.

But as time passed, I had no other choice than to fall more deeply in love with St. Paul's. I attended Search retreats and homecomings as often as I could, bible study and folk group practice each week, and played at mass every Sunday. I needed God and the Holy Spirit more than ever and prayed for the Holy Ghost to bless me with the gift of *Fortitude*. I desperately needed the strength to go on. I longed for escape and could not shake the feeling that the monsters were closing in, their icy grip tightening around my soul with each passing day. I was falling into a deeper depression – no, a psychosis unlike anything I had ever felt and had only experienced by watching Nanny slip into the same darkness of depression. I was getting closer to shock treatment every day.

I had seen a report on venereal disease on television – some late night-night PSA with diagrams of infection. Suddenly it all clicked. I became convinced that Pecklers had infected me with something monstrous, and I needed to find a cure. My soul depended on it. He infected me with a fatal disease. A sickness. A curse. I had been bitten by a vampire, and I knew it. Not the kind on *Creature Features*. Not the kind that wore plastic fangs or fake capes. Pecklers was real and he had passed something into me. Some rotting poison. Some dark, crawling thing. It was now inside of me and I had to kill it before it killed me. I knew what I had to do.

Nanny had taught me how to thread a needle and sew by hand at eight, and I could hem a pair of trousers by ten. She also was skilled at removing splinters with a sterilized needle, teaching me as patiently and gently as possible to first insert the needle to break the skin, then to search for the splinter, and then the extraction. And Poppy had taught me how to be rigid, so I was confident that I could carry out my mission.

First, I took a Stelazine from my bedroom night table, and then I walked into the Keeping Room to get my father's bottle of Johnny Walker from his cabinet. I drank two whiskey shots directly from the bottle, replacing what I drank with tap water from the faucet, and then I reached into my pants pocket to get my *Rush*.

Ahhhh.....breathe in deeply, one nostril at a time. Ok. My head spinning. On fire. I was disconnected now. Unplugged. Numb. I was ready.

With a *Rush* fire burning in my stomach, I got the sewing box from the bottom of my mother's closet and searched to find the tomato pincushion that had assorted sewing needles stuck into it like a crown of thorns. I turned each needle slowly, inspecting. Too thick. Too thin. Too warped. Then – this one. Just right.

I lit the first burner on our gas stove. The blue flame clicked, then roared. I held the needle over the flame, carefully holding it by the edge of my white tee shirt. I watched it glow orange, then black. The soot hissed as I stretched out another part of the hem to wipe it clean. Then I turned and walked to the kitchen table.

I stood before my reflection and took three deep breaths. I positioned myself directly beneath the ceiling fixture – that big black light had lit up the Keeping Room for every moment of our family life. That ceiling light had hung over meatloaf Mondays and Sunday pasta nights with Nanny and Poppy. It hung over all of our celebrations, priests saying grace, Carvel sheet cakes, and birthday candles burning down to the wax. It had seen it all. That thick glass table was like a second set of eyes. It had mirrored everything. And now it reflected something heinous.

I opened my belt and unbuttoned my jeans, pulling them down. And then I pulled my underwear down. My body trembled as I stared before my reflection. Half-boy, half something else. I was about to rid myself of a curse that had been driven into me, deep inside, rooted like rust spreading in my bones. Rotting marrow. I wasn't trying to hurt myself. I was trying to save myself. Trying to remove the mark of the Devil that was left inside of me by one of his disciples. I held the needle over me and whispered.

"Get it out of me. Get out."

And then I began.

I guided the glowing tip toward a place only I could name. There was no scream. No pain. Only the breathless silence of holy violence. My hand moved up and down, mapping the geography of the curse. Searching for its entrance, creating ways for the poison to exit. I was rigid.

"Get it out! Get it OUT!" I yelled.

This was the only logical way to kill what Pecklers had done to me, had given me. I needed to kill the smell and taste of him that would not go away, no matter how much I prayed. Then, with a trembling hand and a moist paper towel, I'd wipe away what remained – metallic, raw, stinging. My body flushed, shaking, tender in places I could barely touch now. I repeated the ritual until eventually pain overtook purpose, until tenderness became inflammation, and the soreness morphed into something darker, something that warned me that I was drifting toward danger. Infection. Madness - definitely.

I was back in St. Aedan's church now every day before and after classes, and questioning God as to what was happening to me. Why did I meet Diane? *God, why did you take my angel away from me?* I cried silently in the church pew. How could Diane be married when I was certain that we were meant to be together? Why have you forsaken me? How can I get out of this without killing myself? My angel is here to save me.

I sit here in silence. A dark church, feeling lost.

I'm begging you, please, either let me find my purpose in this suffering

Or let me find peace in death.

I need your guidance more than ever, God.

Show me that there is a reason for all of this, that there is a light at the end of this tunnel.

Help me to see that I am not alone, that you're here with me, even in the darkest moments.

Give me the strength to keep going, to keep fighting, even when it feels like I can't go on anymore.

Help me to find hope amidst this impending doom, and to trust that you have a plan for me, even when I can't see it.

Please, God, hear my prayer and guide me through this darkness.

Amen

Chapter 17

For my sixteenth birthday, Mom and Dad invited Tom to join us for dinner to celebrate. Mom made my favorite – veal parmesan and ziti, with plenty of garlic bread, and a Carvel Fudgie the Whale birthday cake for dessert with *Happy Birthday Keith* written in blue icing. Tom wore his burgundy clerical shirt, open at the collar. His sneakers were kicked off and halfway under the table. Dinner conversation was our usual mix of school, church, and current events. Dad made a birthday toast, and we all clicked our wine glasses together. I was allowed to have a glass of wine at Sunday dinner if we were entertaining a priest-friend. They had no idea that Tom and I were drinking in his rectory suite a few nights a week. Let alone the drugs.

After dinner, Mom dimmed the lights and brought out my birthday cake. Dad started singing "Happy birthday to you, happy birthday to you…" and Tom and Mom joined in as I made a wish and blew out the candles.

And then Tom cleared his throat and began gently tapping his wine glass with the edge of his teaspoon. Mom let out her signature double-cough and then Tom spoke.

"Before we cut the cake, I have a little something I'd like to present to my favorite sixteen-year-old."

I told Tom that he didn't have to get me anything.

"Oh, but I did. And more importantly, I wanted to. The truth is, I need this gift as bad as you do!"

Mom and Dad laughed along with Tom, looking at each other like they were all in on a secret. Tom continued.

"Keith, I already spoke to your mom and dad last week about this, and they gave me their blessing."

Tom reached into the inside of his jacket which lay beside him, pulled out an envelope, and placed it on the cake plate in front of me.

"Open it." Tom said, grinning ear to ear.

I hesitated, slightly embarrassed, then opened the envelope. Inside were two airplane tickets, white with blue trim, the words "Newark to Freeport" printed in bold letters.

I stared at them, confused.

"Wait…this is –"

And Tom burst out, "It's a trip. For us. For you! Your first real vacation away! On a plane! We're going to the Bahamas! Beaches, blue water, no homework, no stress, just you and me! Six days and five nights! Happy birthday kiddo."

I was stunned.

"To Keith. And to new adventures!" Dad said, raising his wine glass.

"And to *wonderful* surprises." Mom added. *"And to having a best friend like Fr. Tom."*

"And aren't you able to get your driving permit?" Tom continued.

"Well, kiddo, let's start driving practice as soon as possible." Tom added. "It won't be long before I get that new car that I told you about, and that beauty parked outside is all yours."

Mom and Dad could not have been more delighted. Tom was the best thing that ever happened to me.

Two weeks later, I was sitting on a beach in the Bahamas. The sun was brighter and hotter than I had remembered Seaside Heights to be, although I had only been there once or twice. The ocean was most definitely bluer. My first flight. My first vacation. Paradise. Liquor. *Weed.* Local weed. And it was strong. Tom called our vacation, *a celebration of me.* But once we checked into the resort, the lines between celebration and obligation blurred.

Tom and I discussed and rehearsed our response if anyone got too close or nosey and started asking questions. He was always my big brother or uncle. But I was not just a normal sixteen-year-old kid on spring break. Even though there were moments when I felt grown up, none of it felt *normal*. Tom and I ate at the best restaurants and liquor was included. I drank and smoked *a lot.*

Two weeks later, as promised, Tom took me to Bayonne Park to practice driving. When we got to the park, Tom pulled alongside the fountains so that we could switch seats. I turned the key, the engine started right away. A powerful engine. I looked over at Tom, my heart pounding with excitement. I had dreamed about this moment from the very first time that Tom had mentioned it to me, when he took me to his family home in Belleville and promised to give it to me when I turned seventeen.

We rolled through the park, slow and smooth. I was doing it – really driving! Tom was smiling.

"This'll all be yours next year," Tom said. "Maybe sooner. We'll see how things go."

I nodded, my throat dry. "That'd be amazing."

Eventually it was time to leave the park.

"Let's drive back to your parents' house," Tom said, "I'm sure you can handle driving down to 6th Street." But just then, I was somewhere else – off in my head, daydreaming.

That's when I missed it. A flash of red. A STOP sign. Tom yelled. I never even saw the stop sign. One second, we were cruising through Bayonne Park, the next metal shrieked, glass exploded, and we were embedded in the side of a Chevy Impala stuffed with teenagers. I sat dazed in the driver's seat, my mouth bleeding, hands cupped over my mouth that I had hit on the steering wheel. I wasn't sure if my teeth had been knocked out. And then I started screaming.

"Oh my God! Oh my God!" again and again. Tom was already telling me to let him over into the driver's seat. I climbed over his lap while he shimmied into the driver's seat. Our blood was everywhere. Tom quickly buttoned up his khaki collared clerical shirt, grabbed his white-collar tab from the car console, wiped the blood from his forehead, and slid into priest mode. He turned quickly into Father Tom. This time with blood on his hands.

By the time the ambulance and police arrived, I was still dazed, cradling my bleeding mouth in my hands. The officer leaned into the Duster.

"You alright Father?"

Fr. Tom nodded solemnly, voice low. Then, without a word, he raised his hand and made a sign of the cross – not over me, not over himself, but over the crumpled wreckage of the Impala, as if absolving the bloodied teenagers for the sin of being in our path.

"Kids. We had the right of way and all of a sudden, they sped out directly in front of us." Fr. Tom continued, "There was nothing I could have done. Hope they're alright. Seems like *St. Christopher* was looking out for *all of us* this afternoon. To make it out with only a few bumps and bruises is a blessing."

"Well, that's a good way of looking at it Father. The only bad thing is that it looks like your car is totaled." The police officer continued, "I have a tow truck on its way, Father. We'll take good care of you."

Tom gave the officer the sign of the cross and said a prayer.

"Thank you, Father. God bless you."

After the tow truck arrived, Tom and I took the Boulevard Bus to my parents' house. I sobbed on the bus ride there. Tom had his arm around my shoulder and told me that everything would be ok.

When we walked into my parents' house covered in blood

Mom and Dad were in the kitchen preparing dinner.

Mom gasped. *"What happened!!!?"*

Tom told them. Matter of factly. Said that I was driving. That I missed the stop sign. That I totaled his car.

They were upset of course, but most especially that I totaled Tom's car. He assured them that he planned on getting a new one and that he would get a rental until he figured out what to do. He knew how to soothe us. He was the adult in charge.

At this point, my parents noticed that my behavior was becoming more erratic. Night after night, my sleep was plagued by vivid and terrifying nightmares, each one more chilling than the night before. Monsters and vampires invaded my dreams, their sinister presence threatening to consume my very soul. The screams that pierced the silence of the night would send Billy catapulting from his bed. They would find me thrashing and sobbing, tangled in bedsheets drenched in sweat, my eyes wide with terror as I struggled to escape the clutches of my own imagination. How was I to sleep in my twin bed, having slept in it with Fr. Tom – spooned as tightly as possible to fit the two of us without falling off? A threesome with Fr. Tom and The Holy Ghost ten feet away from my parent's bedroom. Separated by a plastic accordion door with a magnetic lock.

How was I to feel now that I had experienced the feeling of my head and body lying on Fr. Tom's hairy chest, his hairy arms around me, feeling his hairy legs against mine and at times holding me down? How could I *un-feel* the sensation of his five o'clock shadow, like a piece of sandpaper across the soft skin on my cheeks, or his swollen, nicotine and coffee-infused tongue having been in my mouth and down my throat a hundred times by now? The worst part, and I know that this sounds crazy, but it felt normal to lay in bed naked with Fr. Tom. I felt incredibly confused, but I loved him and my body continued to convince me that God was in control, and that I was giving God the most beautiful gift a teenage boy could give. In addition to Tom, I was also having sex with Nina's older cousin Marilyn, who I had recently begun seeing a few times a week and I was also seeing Becky as well.

I was now experiencing the gift of *Piety* from The Holy Spirit. A generous and childlike love, so that a person wants to please God as a loving Father, even if it means making sacrifices. Fr. Tom told me that our relationship was not homosexual and that I was not gay, and that because it was *of God,* that it was holy. It was *holysexual* I suppose.

Tom had convinced me that intimacy with God was the ultimate gift, the sign of ultimate love and obedience to God. And yes, I believed him. Showing our love to each other was a gift of understanding, a gift of obedience, a gift of intimacy with God, and I believed him because why wouldn't I. Fr. Tom was the closest thing to God I had ever known. This is what it meant to be chosen. This was the highest calling.

The weight was falling off of me. It wasn't intentional, at least not at first. Food, even the foods that I liked, just didn't have a taste anymore. The breakouts on my face were relentless. Mom, ever attuned to appearances, decided something had to be done and so we found ourselves in the waiting room of Dr. Good, a well-known dermatologist in Jersey City Heights. Dr. Good made me think of the doctor from Bugs Bunny with an oversized head mirror ready to yank out a molar with a wrench. He looked like he was 100 years old, and his office reflected the same era. The wallpaper was the color of old teeth, the chairs were relics from another century, and the smell of antiseptic and mothballs clung to the air like a ghost that refused to leave. When he finally shuffled into the examining room, he peered at me over his glasses and made a series of noises as he poked and prodded my face and then came his diagnosis. I was going through puberty and my body was changing. He then shuffled around his cabinets and handed me a bottle of medicated drying solution. I stared at the bottle. It was the color of a sickly beige Band-Aid and when I put it on my face, it didn't so much blend into my skin as sit on top of it, like a layer of death. I looked in the mirror and realized with grim amusement that I now resembled one of the *undead,* which ironically felt fitting because that's exactly what I was – a shell of a person. I was going through the motions of being alive, but I felt dead inside. Completely numb. I was spinning an intricate web of lies trying to keep my mother and father convinced that Fr. Tom was nothing but a mentor, a guiding light in my life. The truth was unthinkable, but the weight of it was getting heavier, juggling it all – my parents, my church friends, school, my faith, my confusion, my secrets, my survival. It was like trying to hold on to a thousand fragile glass bowls at once, and I was beginning to drop them one by one. I could feel everything slipping away.

I wrote my parents long letters trying to convince them that I was ok and that Fr. Tom and I were just close friends. Mom would keep my handwritten letters for safe-keeping and give them to me three decades later, along with photos of me and Fr. Tom, which unknowingly would help me piece together this part of my life with new eyes.

The first letter I wrote to my mom begins with my reference to the night that my family sat me down in the Keeping Room and interrogated me until I came apart at the seams. I had just gotten home from being at the rectory with Tom. Sometime after midnight, Tom said that he had better get me home, after all, I was sixteen, and he still had to put the finishing touches on his homily for Sunday morning mass. We had been in his bedroom suite at the rectory since 7 p.m., drinking Dry Sack, smoking cigarettes, smoking weed, huffing *Rush*, and having sex.

Our apartment was dark just as it always was at this hour by now. My parents should have been asleep, exhausted from their Saturday night battle, and Billy should have been out somewhere in the city with his friends. This was routine. But as I stepped into the foyer, I sensed that something felt *off*. The lights were on in the Keeping Room. Just then I heard Mommy's double cough, and a chill ran through me, immediately chasing away the drunken haze and the lingering effects of huffing all night and smoking pot all night with Tom.

As I approached the Keeping Room, my body knew before my mind did – this was an ambush. I rubbed the sleeve of my shirt across my mouth and my chin, then frantically rubbed around my neck to erase any scent or residual of Fr. Tom off of me. His sweat, his cologne, his nicotine, his alcohol, his saliva, his everything had been all over me only minutes before.

Mom, Dad, and Billy stood in the Keeping Room surrounding half of the kitchen table. Their faces unreadable, their bodies rigid. I was still fighting my high. Mom coughed again. She looked to the side, first at Daddy, then Billy, and then settling on my face like they had a plan in place. They were warped. Not in anger, but I could sense something worse was at play. My father told me to sit down at the table. This was going to be an interrogation. My emaciated body sliding against the back of the black metal wrought iron chair felt like a human cheese grater. And then, another cough. And another. *What the hell was going on?*

And then Mom began to speak – slowly like she was about to light a stick of dynamite.

"Keith, we want to discuss something with you."

I thought I would die right there. They found out about Tom and me. That must be it. The secret is out. My stomach flipped violently, and bile shot its way up my throat. The pain throbbed, hot and sour, from the base of my spine to the roots of my teeth. A wave of nausea surged so hard it felt like my stomach was turning inside-out. My skin turned ice-cold, and I could feel the blood draining out of me, like a plug had been pulled.

This felt like the time when we had to sit Nanny down in her kitchen and tell her that she had to go to the Carrier Clinic for electric shock treatment. The silence. The terror. The look in her eyes – vacant and betrayed, as if she already heard the hum of wires and knew her mind was about to be jolted into silence. And now, sitting in the Keeping Room, I could almost hear the humming of the electrodes. Mommy continued speaking.

"Keith, your father, (cough), and Billy and I, (cough-cough), have noticed that you are not acting right. You are very nervous, (cough), and anxious, (cough), and have been shouting and talking in your sleep every night. You're not interested in school, and your grades are dropping. (Cough, cough, LOUD cough). You are no longer interested in your artwork, or acting, or drawing, or designing costumes, and you spend all of your time at the church and rectory. Now me, your father, and Billy want to know…*what exactly is going on?*

"Going on? What do you mean *going on?"* My words stumbled out of my mouth like I had been drinking. "There's nothing going on."

But Mom's coughing said otherwise.

I answered them while staring down into my reflection. The last time I looked into this glass table I was performing self-surgery. What could be wrong? Their reflection made it appear that there were half-a-dozen of them glaring at me. They wanted a confession, and I had no way out. I was cornered. Outnumbered. I would need to confess it all. Well for the most part.

I told them that Pecklers had begun calling me every night shortly after joining the folk group and that he was having phone sex with me – talking dirty about masturbation and the sex that he was having with his *"girlfriend."* I told them that Pecklers had tricked me and told me that the folk group practice was going to be at his house one day after school. I told them that I was playing the guitar and singing as he played his organ and I was waiting for the rest of the group to arrive, growing anxious by the minute. I told them that he pulled pornographic magazines out of his bench instead of church sheet music. I told them that Pecklers told me that his girlfriend would give me a blowjob. I told them that I hadn't even known what it was. I told them that Mr. Pecklers had walked in on us and was screaming at us. I admitted *everything. Everything* that I needed to admit, that is. Everything except the fact that I had a self-diagnosed venereal disease, was self-mutilating, and that I was now in a *spiritual menage-a-trois* with Fr. Tom, The Lord, and sometimes The Holy Ghost. I also held back that I was addicted to inhalants, alcohol, and sex, and that I had just started dating Nina's twenty-one-year-old cousin Marilyn who looked at least forty.

First Mom and Dad wanted to call the police and then my father wanted to go to the rectory with Billy and John Connors and beat Pecklers up. They were screaming at me and at each other. It was complete chaos in the Keeping Room that night, like we were the Tyrone family in *Long Day's Journey Into Night*. A family in-crisis being ripped apart with blame, addiction, secrets, and emotional chaos.

I was crying hysterically, collapsing into the wrought iron kitchen chair, and sliding down onto the linoleum floor. I screamed at them that I would kill myself. I crawled on the kitchen floor like a trapped animal, heaving and sobbing hysterically, my hands slipping on my falling tears, my bitten fingernails and gnawed cuticles gliding across the vinyl. I was completely unhinged.

"I will kill myself if you dare tell anyone! I swear to God – I will cut my wrist with a razor or jump off a building! The church is my entire life! Please, I made a mistake!!! I was tricked by Pecklers!!! I never wanted to have sex with him! Pecklers told me that Billy was having sex with guys too."

"That's a lie!" Billy screamed.

"Pecklers told me after he did what he did to me, that you were having sex with Vic Cain from the parish counsel."

"That's a *God-damn* lie," Billy screamed. "I'm going to *kill* him!"

I screamed to them that I meant it – that I would kill myself, that I had already planned it. That I would do it. Screaming and crying, I gasped for air, unable to breathe, grabbing my chest, being struck to my knees with chest pains so severe that I thought my heart would stop right then and there. This was by far the worst thing to have ever happened in the Keeping Room – or any room, besides the night that Mommy was strangled by Daddy.

Daddy and Billy picked my wet, sweaty, fragile body up off the floor and sat me back onto the wrought iron chair. Then Dad brought up the *make-up*.

For the last month or two, I had begun wearing make-up. At first to cover my pimples, but then I kind of liked it. I felt incredibly ugly, and I seemed to gain relief when I started lining my eyes, using blush, and adding an eyebrow pencil, which apparently was the last straw for them all. They were admittedly *pointy* eyebrows, like a vampire's, or Mr. Spock's from *Star Trek*. I even had begun penciling a clef in my chin because Fr. Tom had one. Actually, maybe *that* was the last straw. I no longer looked like myself. I looked like a heroin addict. Like Al Pacino as Bobby, the junkie in *The Panic in Needle Park*, but I could not stop it once it had started. Somewhere along the way, I had read that an actor should look the role at all times, because you could be discovered *anywhere*. And so, I knew that actors and rock stars wore make-up, so it didn't seem odd to me.

What they did not know at the time was that it had already *ended* with Keith Pecklers months before, and that I had gone to Fr. Tom to help get Pecklers to stop.

What they did *not* know was that I was now in a sacred spiritual union with Fr. Tom, God, and The Holy Ghost, and that I would do anything to protect what God had wanted of me, what God had asked of me and Fr. Tom.

My parents were in shock once I told them what Pecklers had been doing to me. They made me tell them every disgusting detail. It was too late to do anything to Pecklers. It was over, with the exception that he may have given me a fatal disease. And they had no way of knowing that I had also become hyper-sexual and was now juggling two to three girlfriends at any given time, along with my relationship with Fr. Tom. Up until this point, I had dated Jennifer, Janice, Janine, and Mary. Maria, Shelly, Karen,

Colleen, and Kelly. Elaine, Becky, Marilyn, and Fr. Tom. And I was barely sixteen. I would have given them all up just to be with Diane.

Marilyn worked at *The Jersey Journal* on Journal Square. She had been in a years-long relationship with Joe, an older guy, probably in his thirties, who had a job, nice clothes, and a fancy car. Marilyn was in love with me right away and would allow me to drive her white Plymouth Volare even though I was only sixteen and had no permit. Once I was driving on Kennedy Boulevard and stopped at a red light. When I glanced over into the next lane, I realized that it was my father driving the blue Skylark that Gina had gotten us. I took a quick left turn to avoid him seeing me. He didn't mention anything to me when I returned home that evening, so I guess I got away with it.

Marilyn and I would park down Roosevelt Stadium on a Friday night and make out and get to third base every time. I would go as far as I could without officially breaking my vow of chastity. At least my definition of it. One Friday night at the stadium, Marilyn and I were parked, with me in the driver's seat. Suddenly a deafening tap-tap-tap rattled the driver's window. A flashlight beam sliced through the window nearly stopping my heart. A police officer's face appeared in the window, and I was ordered out of the car – shoes on, with my pants around my knees. I had remained committed to the chastity vow that Billy and I had made to our parents and was saving intercourse for marriage, however, I was now committing *outercourse*.

I shuffled out into the dark parking lot while the officer

held the flashlight on me. Marilyn sat in the passenger seat wide-eyed and mortified. The cop asked me a few pointed questions, nothing I wanted to answer in front of Marilyn, and finally told us to go home after we were officially embarrassed.

Nothing like this ever went on with Becky. Becky came from a nice family. I felt like a normal teenager when I was with her, and I enjoyed our age-appropriate dating. But the reality was, I was a sophomore in high school and having sex on average three to five times a week. Most Saturday nights I would go out with one of my girlfriends and then would spend 11 p.m. until 2 a.m. at the rectory with Fr. Tom.

I was exhausted from lying to my parents about my comings and goings, and at one point, my house of cards came crashing down. My Mother was on the Bergen Avenue bus coming home from work one day. The bus rattled along its usual route, stopping and starting on Old Bergen Road to the jerky rhythm of the city traffic. My mother sat near the middle of the bus, lost in thought, running through her mental grocery list and silently flipping through her *Reader's Digest*. Then Mom heard a voice from the seat in front of her, enthusiastic and chatty.

"Oh my God! He's adorable! My cousin Marilyn is crazy about him! She's been dating him for a few weeks. Shhh...she's a few years older than he is! He's only sixteen, but Marilyn said he acts very mature for his age. He is starring as *Billy Bigelow*, the lead actor in Holy Family Academy's production of *Carousel*. He's just so talented. *And cute!*" The two women laughed and giggled while telling the story.

Mom's ears perked up and she tapped the woman on the shoulder.

"Excuse me, (double-cough), *who* are you talking about?"

The woman turned to my mother beaming.

"Oh, my cousin Marilyn is dating this adorable guy who is the lead in *Carousel* at Holy Family Academy. His name is *Keith* and he's five years younger than my cousin!"

"Shhh! Don't tell anyone!" He's only sixteen! Hahahaha! He's at our house a few times a week. He drives her car!"

"Oh, do you know *him?*" asked Marilyn's cousin.

Mom coughed, kind-of more like a gag reflex actually, and told her who she was.

"Well, I gave *birth* to him!"

Marilyn's cousin's eyes widened, and my mother sat back in her seat horrified and totally flabbergasted.

Mom was furious. A twenty-one-year-old woman. After everything else that took place within the last few months with me, and now this. Most shocking of all was the fact that I still had time to dabble in community theatre, but I knew that I could meet more girls. Especially because Holy Family was an all-girls high school. Of course, the first person Mom called when she got home was Fr. Tom. The receptionist put her right through to his room. I happened to be there.

"Tom what the hell is going on with Keith?"

Tom grabbed the phone and sat down beside me on the loveseat holding the receiver to both of our ears as my mother told him about what she had just experienced on her bus ride home from work.

It was the beginning of the end. Mom and Dad were shocked that all of this could be happening right under their noses. First Pecklers, and now a twenty-one-year-old woman. And Marilyn *looked* like a mature woman. There was no way around her bustline or the fact that she appeared at least ten years older than her age. They would faint if they ever saw her.

The walls were beginning to close in on me, and Marilyn had to be sacrificed in order that no one would discover my relationship with Fr. Tom. I knew I had to divert my parent's attention. Marilyn would be the perfect distraction. Besides, Marilyn had always said that something else was going on between me and Fr. Tom. She said it was obvious. She would tell me that Fr. Tom was in love with me.

I guess there may have been people that chose not to see what was taking place with me and Fr. Tom – like my family, friends from the folk group, and close friends of Fr. Tom, like Fr. Frank and Sister Martha. Or my best friend Nina. Or my fifteen-year-old high school girlfriend Becky. People didn't know about things like this back then. There were no words. Even the Jesuit Brothers from Hudson Catholic, when I convinced them to allow Fr. Tom to be a substitute teacher for our religion class. I suppose they didn't realize something was off. Or the police officer that questioned me and Fr. Tom when we were discovered in Fr. Tom's car pulled off the highway onto a deserted dirt road after shopping at the Staten Island Mall. No one would dare question a priest. He was God on Earth. Tom even fooled the two Long

Branch police officers who questioned Fr. Tom and I, when they threatened to break down the front door, and then the bathroom door when I was having a panic attack on that cold February afternoon when Fr. Tom took me to Sr. Martha's house to check on her pipes, and we ended up having sex in her ice-cold queen sized bed.

A neighbor had called the police to report a man and a boy had entered Sister Martha's home at four o'clock on a cold Winter afternoon; however Fr. Tom was able to convince the police officers that I was his nephew, that we were there to check on frozen pipes and that I was emotional because I had been going through a difficult time at home. Even the five priests, who along with Fr. Tom had rented a Seaside Heights bungalow together in the summer of 1979 and allowed me to sleep in the same bedroom with him must not have realized that something criminal was taking place.

My parents insisted that I break off all relationships at St. Paul's including the folk group, the bible study group, all Search retreats, my best friends Nina and Lucas – one of the twins from Union City. And most of all, my relationship with Marilyn.

My life was falling apart, and I had to do all I could to convince my parents that I needed to save my relationship with Jess and Fr. Tom. I was in survival mode. They were the only ones left and who had my best welfare in mind and were stable and reliable friends that I could depend on to help me through this stage in my life. I had no one else. Reluctantly Mom and Dad agreed that it would mean my total destruction if they were to prevent me from at least having two friends in my life to get me through these growing pains. Besides, Mom and Dad loved Fr. Tom like a son and still believed that he was helping all of us as a family get through a tumultuous time because of Pecklers. We relied on Tom's spiritual guidance and Mom and Dad continued to see him weekly at the rectory for spiritual guidance. We all needed Tom.

Chapter 18

I wrote my mother long letters during this time, trying to convince her not to believe what she was feeling, what she was seeing. In the letters I speak of being able to cut off friends at St. Paul's, specifically the folk group, that my parents did not think were good for me, in order to save my relationship with Fr. Tom. I had to give up Nina because she was Marilyn's cousin. I hated having to end my friendship with her. But I knew that I couldn't live without God and I couldn't live without Fr. Tom, and she was getting dangerously close to finding out – or admitting to herself, that something was not right with our friendship.

She asked me point blank one afternoon if I was in love with him. We were driving in the car, and she asked me at the stop light. I told her no, and that I loved him as a friend. The truth was that Fr. Tom and I had discussed leaving the country and running away together.

Dear Mom,

I really don't know quite where to begin. I feel that if i say what i want to say in letter form it may come out more adequately. When i got off the phone with you, i felt pretty lousy inside. Do you remember when we sat down, all 4 of us at the kitchen table and had that talk about everything? Well yous all had some questions to ask and very openly & honestly i answered them. I could have kept everything inside and denied certain things but i figured that my family should still be able to love me for the mistakes i've made in my past. Those few weeks i did a lot of thinking about my life, who i am, and where i'm going. I may not have said so, but believe me, i did a lot of soul searching. I came up with a few answers for myself for some of my questions. To begin with i decided that for once and for all, "i like myself" and that truthfully, i was much better off without St. Paul's and the people who went with it. I did however keep two friends who meant something to me; Jess and Tom. As for Jess, sure, i know what she's all about and i know she likes to talk but i can honestly say up to now she has been a friend. When i say friend, i guess i have two meanings; a person who will support you and be there to have good times as well as bad and second - by, as a friend to me is someone whom you can tell anything and always trust, a person who you can share common feelings with and have things in common. Jess is a good person in my eyes and as far as i know, she has never done me wrong.

As far as Tom, i don't know where to start. I met him about a year ago this week. Even when i first met him he came off as being a very special person. I think I was thrilled at the fact that i was friends with a "Priest." i was thrilled to be able to see him ordained a priest. That is one of my most meaningful days so far in my life. Sure everyone has problems, some worse off than others, but as far as i can see, he is one of the most sensible, logical, and stable persons i've ever met. Often when i have a problem or when he does, he tells me the best thing to do is pray. He has a very deep faith & trust in God, in ministry and this is one of the things in him that impresses me the most. I've met many priests and have been on about 5 retreat weekends as you know and never have i've seen anyone so gentle and loving or priestly for that matter as he is.

When you said what you did in the car i didn't realize you wanted a response from me. I've never felt that, or thought even, that i have to "convince" you, my own mother, that I don't have anything other than a friendship with Tom. For one thing, i'm not gay. I may have been confused say when i was 13 or so but at almost 17, i know where i'm at. Secondly, if i ever found out that Tom was having relationships, i think it could really destroy my outlook on him as a "Priest" and that would hurt more than anything. He studied 8 yrs. to get where he is today and after all those years i'm sure his commitment to God is very strong. He had many opportunities to leave, and did twice, yet he came back and finally decided that the priesthood was what he wanted. I know that i wouldn't be able to sleep with myself, nevermind anyone else, if i were a priest and broke my vows for someone. One of the things i've looked forward to all year was when he's able to say mass and break bread. Sunday night mass for me was something very beautiful and special. I'm proud to be able to call Tom a "friend" and i'm very proud that he is a priest.

So Mom, i guess the best thing we can do is to just talk a little bit more often and let each other know what we are really thinking. I love you very much and don't want to keep anything from you or daddy – all i ask though, is for your trust and for yous to believe in me.

Love always,

Keith

The truth was that I would have done anything that Fr. Tom said or suggested in order to please God. If Fr. Tom had asked me to jump off of a bridge, I would have. If Fr. Tom told me that God wanted me to drink poison, I would have drunk poison. I would have probably killed my parents if Fr. Tom told me that God was asking me to.

Fr. Tom explained to me that The Holy Ghost had conspired with God and Jesus to bless us with the love that we shared, and that our love was our greatest gift to the Lord. Tom's job now was to convince my parents that there was nothing going on.

Around the same time that all of this was taking place, as

if I wasn't nervous and anxious enough, Tom began receiving cryptic type-written letters from a stalker that knew everything that was going on with us and threatened to expose us if we did not end our relationship immediately. The letter writer described me as a "*Young Buck*" and that sometimes "*Young Bucks meet an early demise.*" I was terrified. The typed letters were out of a horror movie, complete with a stuck key that drove home the point that someone wanted to kill me.

I know wh-t is going on. I have been w-tching the two of you closely! You are making a terrible mist-ke to not end your relationship now! Young bucks c-n sometimes meet -n early demise! Some young bucks die by being run over by c-rs, or poisoned, or shot to de-th!

Young buck…you are not -lone! There are others! If this does not end immedi-tely, a letter will be sent to your mother and f-ther!

I know where you live!

That week I was nearly run down by a speeding car that intentionally tried to run me over in front of St. Paul's Church. I fell backwards landing hard onto the sidewalk as the car barreled passed me, missing me by inches. I grabbed my heart which was jumping out of my chest and in just a flash, the car was gone. What if my parents find out? I couldn't let that happen. I was in a panic. Someone was now trying to kill me, and worse, threatening to reveal my relationship with Fr. Tom. If this were to happen, there would be only one way to make it stop. I would need to kill myself.

Father Thomas Stanford and Sr. Martha (1980)

SURVIVOR INTAKE FORM

22(b). Were there anyone else that had knowledge of sexual abuse or assaults against you?

Fr. Frank Maione was Fr. Tom's lover, and **Sr. Martha** (I don't know her last name) was Tom's mentor, close friend, confidant, and bankroll. Sr. Martha was a Felician nun and principal of a school in Paramus, New Jersey. Sr. Martha was in love with Fr. Tom.

Sr. Martha did not like me.

One Saturday night Fr. Tom, Fr. Frank, Sr. Martha and I were hanging out in Tom's suite at the rectory. Sr. Martha was always dressed in her black habit.

There was music playing and the lights were low.

We were drinking red wine.

I remember Fr. Tom and Fr. Frank encouraged me to dance.

Fr. Tom turned up the volume on the record player.

Fr. Frank held his arms around me, pulling me close to his body. He was wearing his black cleric shirt, white collar, and black pants.

Fr. Tom and Sr. Martha looked on.

At one point I do remember Sr. Martha waiting for me outside of the bathroom when I came out.

She came up to me, contorted her mouth in an angry way and said, "You're not the only one."

Shortly after that night at the rectory, Fr. Frank invited me to sleep over his home in Cedar Grove. I remember Fr. Frank told me that he still had a bedroom at his parents' home.

He had been speaking to me after mass about the possibility of my entering the seminary and said he thought that I would make an excellent priest. There was a celebration mass at St. Paul's for some reason.

Fr. Frank took me out to dinner, and we spoke about the Seminary and what it was like being a priest. We also spoke about Tom. Tom had told me that he had left Fr. Frank for me because it was what God wanted of us.

I could tell that Fr. Frank and Fr. Tom had remained close in spite of their break-up.

That night at Fr. Frank's family home, Fr. Frank tucked me into bed.

He told me to have dreams about being a priest.

We chatted a little while he sat on the bed next to my side.

Fr. Frank kissed my forehead, turned out the nightlight, and went into another bedroom to sleep.

Fr. Bill Hatcher first knew when Fr. Tom brought me to a rented bungalow in Seaside Park, New Jersey that Hatcher and other priest friends had rented together, including Fr. Tom. I was approximately fifteen years old at that time. Fr. Tom invited me to stay the week with him. It was my very first summer vacation at the Jersey Shore. I believe Fr. Jim Lipnacki was there, also Fr. William Dowd. It was uncomfortable and the other priests all questioned why Fr. Tom would bring me. They thought it was inappropriate. I had slept over in a room with Fr. Tom. We slept in the same bed and had sex every night.

I felt worried and anxious having sex with Fr. Tom; so close to the other priests in the adjoining bedrooms. The walls were paneling and thin.

Fr. Tom had invited my parents and their best friends Lois and John to visit Seaside for the day when the other priests had gone on a day trip to Cape May.

Mom & Dad with friends Lois & John and Fr. Tom in Seaside Park, NJ. (1979)

Fr. Hatcher would see me frequently with Fr. Tom at retreats, homecomings (Search Weekends), and also in 1980 when Fr. Tom was transferred to Our Lady of Perpetual Help in Oakland, New Jersey where Fr. Hatcher was a Monsignor and Vicar. He would see me in Fr. Tom's bedroom which was directly across from his.

My 8X10 black and white headshot was on Fr. Tom's night table next to his bed in direct view of the hallway and passersby.

22. Was there anyone else that became aware of the sexual assaults against you?

Diane Robin: My friend. Married (separated) mother of two boys.

23. What was the date?: February 1980

24. What was their response?:

Love, understanding, and acceptance.

25. Who else did you tell?

No one.

26. Did you tell any family members?

My parents and brother.

27. Who else knows?

No one.

28. Is there any written or oral documentation (pictures) of the incident?

Yes – Photos and letters.

Chapter 19

My parents wanted to speak with Tom in the Keeping Room. They invited him over after dinner one night. They needed assurance that I was ok. My stomach was upset, and my fingertips ice cold, but Tom had assured me that he could handle them.

Tom arrived dressed as *"Fr. Tom."* He wore his black suit jacket and black priest shirt with the white collar, black gabardine dress pants, and black shoes. He looked like the perfect priest. He wore cologne and his favorite watch, and was perfectly groomed, as usual. Tom only wore his clerical outfit for mass, weddings, and funerals. This felt like a funeral.

The doorbell rang and my Dad went to let Fr. Tom in.

"Hi Bill." Fr. Tom said to Daddy, shaking his hand. Then Tom began shaking his head a little as if to say *"no,"* holding his arms open and drawing my father close to his chest like a moth to the flame, hugging him tightly. Father Tom's soft kiss to Dad's cheek sealed the deal.

"Co-let-te?" Fr. Tom said Mommy's name like he was asking her a question in a sing-songy way, and then he opened his arms moving closer to her.

Father Tom hugged Mom tightly, burrowing his head and collared neck, deep into Mommy's neck and shoulders, like a vampire ready to feed.

She was helpless.

Mom leaned in, her eyes soft, trusting, like she was offering herself to him. Then we all moved stiffly through the living room, like actors in a play no one had rehearsed, other than Tom and me.

My mother's face was tight with worry, my father unusually somber, and Tom, ever the orchestrator, had that serious priestly look he wore when preparing to deliver news that no one wanted to hear. As we took our places around the dining room table – the stage for every family decision, every reckoning, I waited for someone to acknowledge me. Instead, they began.

"Tom, we are just so worried about Keith. We needed to talk to you – to see you in person."

Tom nodded slowly, as if he had been summoned to some kind of intervention, and then he started talking.

"I completely understand, and I want you both to know that Keith means the world to me. He's like a little brother to me. We actually laugh when we are outside of the parish and people ask about our relationship and we joke and say that I am either his favorite uncle or older brother."

They spoke about me as if I wasn't really there, like I had left the room, or the world, and only my outline remained. Like a ghost. I could hear them shaping sentences around my name, packaging concern. Polishing it. Passing my spirit back and forth, like I was at my own seance.

"Well, Tom, you are more like a *son* to us, our *third* son." Mom said this to Tom, and I just sat there with my heart in my throat, suddenly pulled back into my body.

Mom reached out and touched Tom's hand squeezing it. Tom then delivered an Oscar Award winning monologue about the love we have for our children, complete with a memorized passage from the Bible.

"We trust you, Tom." Mom said with tears in her eyes. Both her and Dad tell Tom that they never doubted him. They believed every word he said. After that, Mom and Dad invited Tom to have dessert and coffee. We all sat around the table eating an Entenmann's cake, when all of a sudden, I felt Tom squeeze my knee with his hand.

"Colette, Bill, I was actually hoping to ask your permission for something and now seems like as good a time as any." My insides were contorted.

Just then, Tom, still dressed in his collar and jacket, pulls an envelope from his jacket pocket and hands me the envelope. I am in complete shock and have no idea what is going on. The last time this happened was on my sixteenth birthday and it was a trip to the Bahamas. As I am opening the envelope, Tom announces to my parents, "I'd love to take Keith on a trip to Disney World for his graduation! I stared at him pretending to be shocked like this was the first time I had heard this, but it wasn't. Mom gasped, clapping her hands together.

"DISNEY WORLD!" "Oh Tom!" "Keith, did you hear

that? DISNEY WORLD!"

I respond with just the correct amount of surprise in my voice.

"Are you serious?! That would be *amazing*!" I yell out.

Tom spreads his hands like a magician pulling off his final trick.

"I had just thought that he worked so hard on himself. Keith deserves something special."

Mom and Dad were thrilled. They had no idea that the trip had already been planned for months, and we already had the tickets for the Domenico Bus Tour to Orlando. It was part of Fr. Tom's performance, and he was perfect. The night was coming to an end and then the final scene.

Dad said, "Tom, why don't you just stay the night? It's already 10 p.m. You can sleep in Keith's room. Billy's away on a retreat, so there's an extra bed." I froze. Tom smiled like this was a wonderful idea. This was part of the plan.

"Colette, are you sure? I wouldn't want to impose." Tom said.

"Tom, we insist." My father chimes in. "I even have a new pair of pajamas that I think will fit you perfectly." Without hesitation Dad goes to his bedroom and returns, handing Tom a pair of his new, blue, plaid pajamas.

"Now don't stay up all night talking! Keith, you have school tomorrow." Dad says smiling ear to ear in *that* voice.

Tom chimes in, "I have to be up early myself Bill. Did Keith tell you both that I am his religion substitute teacher this week at Hudson Catholic?"

"Wow! That's wonderful!" Mom and Dad could not be happier.

"Tom, sleep well and we'll have breakfast in the morning."

Tom and I went into my bedroom and closed the accordion door, locking it with the magnetic closure. Tom grinned at me like *"I told you so,"* and then slipped his tongue into my mouth. We could still hear my parents' voices of admiration, their praise of Father Tom, as they made their way into their bedroom, closing their bedroom door behind them.

Mom and Dad would tell me the next day that they were impressed that Tom wore his black clergy shirt and white collar and that it showed a sign of respect and had meant a lot to them. Mom loved black and white. And she loved Tom's cologne. I knew that she found Tom attractive, she told me so.

Around this time, I began my career in the fashion industry working as a sales associate in a men's and boy's clothing store in Bayonne called M&M's. I was addicted to *Rush* and I was huffing every day. I would huff inside the bathroom stalls during the day at school in between classes and huff with my head in my locker with the liquid incense pushed into one nostril while holding the other nostril closed with my thumb. I would go to St. Aedan's after school to pray for a way out while huffing in the church pew. At M&M's, I would go into the dressing room, pull the fabric curtain closed, sit on the fitting room bench with my feet up, and inhale through one closed nostril, and then the other, as often as I could without passing out. You never met anyone who wanted to be more unconscious.

Meanwhile at home, a new alliance had been formed between Dad and I by the power of the Holy Spirit. After learning what had happened with Pecklers, Daddy dove more deeply into the Lord and religion, which made total sense. I introduced Dad to a Born Again Charismatic group that began meeting at St. Paul's School basement. Being Born Again and Charismatic emphasized the important work of the Holy Spirit and spiritual gifts, like the ones I had been receiving. Born Again Christians believe that these gifts are supernatural graces which Christian's need in order to fulfill the mission of the Church, which is to save as many people as possible from Armageddon. It was different than just being a Catholic. They wanted to save you, not kill you.

But there were only going to be 144,000 people taken by God during the rapture, and my father was going to make sure that he was one of them. In two weeks, Dad was speaking in tongues in the school basement squealing like a pig at a county fair. Actually, speaking a foreign language that he did not know. The only time I ever heard him speak differently was when he was trying to make an impression or say something important during one of our special event dinners, or introducing a new priest during our Sunday dinner, speaking that country-evangelical strange voice he used, certainly not like this. This was some African or Asian rhythmic-monotone-auctioneer chant of some sort. I was impressed. Maybe he did know morse code after all.

Dad was sure that he was part of the 144,000 – and that I was too, of course, for introducing him to his new Born Again faith. Unfortunately, he did not think that Mommy was going to be one of the 144,000 chosen people. In fact, he was *sure* that she was not going to be lifted up and told her so. Mommy was not on board and thought that it was weird and too extreme. But Daddy was barreling along. Saturday Night at the Fights had gotten weirder. Dad was constantly reading the bible now. Every Saturday it was his bible in one hand and Johnny Walker in the other, his version of the Holy Trinity. By 10 p.m. Dad would be yelling in tongues as he fought with Mommy. First low and under his breath, then shouting.

"Bashandalah! Eleyamah! The blood of Christ – HE IS HERE!

ELAH KANDARABASATAH!"

Daddy's words bounced off the walls, off the ceiling, and off of Mommy's last nerve. Her voice and tone, sharp as the snap of a wet towel, "Now cut that crap out, Bill! You don't know a single God-damn word of what you're saying!" Daddy turned, his eyes wide, his free hand pointing at her like she was the devil herself.

"You mock the *Lord* in our own house? You think you know better than the spirit of the *living God?*"

Mommy leaned forward in her chair, flicking the last ash of fake smoking into the ashtray.

"You're out of control with this religious crap and I DON'T LIKE IT! Did the Lord tell you to sit on your ass all day drinking beer and whiskey while I'm at work? And did the Lord tell you to hit me last night in your sleep again?"

"That was not my fault, and you know it, Colette! You know it's the nightmares!"

I can see through the five-inch opening of my accordion door that Daddy's red face is turning purple and the vein on the side of his neck is popping out.

Dad slammed his glass down on the table, some of it sloshing onto his bible. His voice dropped. Quiet and lethal.

"You better watch your mouth, Colette."

"Oh what are you going to do? Lay hands on me? And pray? Or are you just going to do what you always do and blame the war when you accidentally hit me in your sleep?"

Dad's face was twisted. Caught between fury and righteousness. He grabbed his bible and held it up like a weapon.

"You don't understand!" Dad screamed at her. Mom laughed. This time wildly and unhinged like Elizabeth Taylor in *"Who's Afraid of Virginia Woolf?* – a reminder of the night that he nearly strangled her. Dad's body could not be more tense. Gripping his bible like he might throw it at her, the fight on TV reached a crescendo and a knock-out punch sent the crowd roaring.

And then came Mommy's own knock-out punch, winning this brutal Saturday Night at the Fights by a unanimous decision.

"I should have left you years ago! Pop was right. I should have married *Leo*."

And there it was.

Mom said the worst thing ever heard in the Keeping Room, besides hearing my confession of how Pecklers had raped me. She turned and walked out of the kitchen, leaving Daddy alone with his bible, talking in tongue-like-gibberish, like a drunken sailor.

The crosses around our necks were getting bigger and bigger. Dad said that our faith needed to be visible, a tool that we could use to speak to other kids and adults to save them. They swung across our chests like they were weapons, shields, and signs that we were ready for a Holy War, ready for battle. Ready for the Rapture. Mom grew more despondent each day. Distant. She found solace in her counseling sessions with Tom. He was the keeper of all our family secrets and the keeper of our most personal confessions. We were all under Tom's spiritual guidance. All pouring our fears and our doubts into him. He knew exactly what to say, he knew every part of us. Fixing us. Saving us. Loving us.

Me and Dad, Seaside Heights, NJ (1977)

In one of Mom's counseling sessions, she confessed to Fr. Tom that she and my father no longer had sex. Things a son wasn't supposed to hear, but things that Tom told me anyway.

Honestly, it never crossed my mind. I had never seen a flash of passion between them. Not one stolen glance, not one teasing touch, not one kiss that lingered past politeness. What I had seen – reliably and rhythmically – was a kind of choreographed tension. Saturday mornings filled with Mom's cabaret singing and Dad's sharp, sometimes disapproving whistles slicing the air like warning shots.

They were always perfectly dressed, perfectly groomed, – hair set, shoes shined, lips lined, ties knotted. But all I ever saw in their precision was distance. They looked like a couple I didn't really know from a department store window. Styled together perfectly, posed together *Stepford*-ly, but sealed behind a sheet of glass. I had never seen a moment of passion between them, not one heated glance, not one playful touch, not one lingering kiss. Never desire. The only spark I had seen between them was the kind that lit the fuse on their Saturday night explosions. And Tom was there for them, like he was there for me. Like some sort of holy contractor, patching our cracked foundation with his steady voice and sacred connection. Keeping the walls from caving in. Holding us all in his hands. Guiding us toward something higher. Something of God.

Chapter 20

By the end of my freshman year at Hudson Catholic, Diane and I had faded out of each other's lives. There was no dramatic goodbye or final declaration. It was quieter than that. More painful somehow because of its silence. The calls that once came nightly after we had finished our classes at The Actors Prologue Theatre, became every other week. Then every three weeks, just to catch up. Then not at all. I told myself she had other responsibilities. Of course she did. She was married and raising two children. She had bills, schedules, a life outside of our short-lived friendship. But the truth was, not a single day passed that I didn't think of Diane. I would catch myself remembering her laugh during class or the time I was showing her a dance move and nearly tossed her out the open studio window. It wasn't just a crush. It wasn't just *puppy love*. Diane had been the first person to truly see me – and then just as quietly, she was gone.

Then one afternoon everything changed. It was the first week of my sophomore year.

I had just stepped out of school, my book bag slung over one shoulder heavy with textbooks, but not as heavy as the thoughts in my head. It was the same week that marked the anniversary of the nightmare with Pecklers – my internal calendar would never forget. I crossed the street to catch the Bergen Avenue bus home, trying to shake off the fog of that day.

Everything felt numb. The sky was cloudy. I had just left the church pew at St. Aedan's, where I had sat for what felt like hours – trying to feel *something*, trying to feel *anything*. I sat there crying, daydreaming of suicide, and praying for a miracle at the same time. But miracles don't announce themselves; if they did, they would have done so with trumpets and angels while I was on my knees in the empty church. Instead, they creep in when your head is down, and your heart has been beaten. I climbed on board the bus, tossed some change into the fare collector with barely a glance and looked up, and the world – my dark, dying world, had come alive.

There she was.

Diane.

Just as her eyes looked up to meet mine, Diane's face caught the sudden burst of sun through the dirty bus window like a halo. She hadn't changed – or maybe she had. Like me, maybe *everything had* changed. Our eyes, our souls, had locked again. Just as they did that night we first met at The Hotel Plaza. My sadness fell away. She was real. She was here.

My bright light.

My miracle.

My angel.

I don't even remember walking down the aisle. My body moved toward her like a magnet, like I was riding a cloud. Like we were being pulled by lifetimes towards each other –where we belonged. I slid into the empty seat beside her, stepping onto the pages of the story I had already written. Diane smiled and grabbed my hand, not the full-lipped firecracker grin I had remembered. This one was smaller and softer, as if life had taught her how to ration joy. Still, it was her. I'm sure she thought the same of me. We had been damaged, like parchment paper burnt around the edges. We sat for a moment just looking and staring into each other's eyes. And then she told me everything.

Diane's husband had left. Seven years married, two boys, a life, a marriage. A shore house bungalow that she earned selling hotdogs in a pushcart. Gone. Just like that. It happened on a Sunday in May. They had gone to her best friend's wedding that Friday and her sister's wedding that Saturday. Diane danced with her two boys to songs like *"Just the Way You Are," "Three Times a Lady,"* and *"Hopelessly Devoted to You."* Her boys and husband, dressed in beige and brown tuxedos, and Diane, the matron of honor for both, would be frozen in time. Lies trapped in wedding albums, filled with family, love, and commitment.

Sunday came and her husband said he was going to play basketball with his friends, and he never came home. No goodbye. No call – just the memory of Fettuccine Alfredo, the last meal they had ordered at an Italian restaurant a few weeks earlier at *The Lighthouse* on River Edge Road in Edgewater – having made the decision to try and work at saving their marriage. Then, just as Diane's Fettuccine Alredo was served, fork in hand, her husband of seven years and two kids said to her, "I don't think this is going to work out."

Diane put her fork down and said that she was going home.

Left with three dollars, two boys, and one pair of shoes, she had no idea what to do next. But then she remembered a guest at the wedding had told her how handsome her two boys were. "Are your boys models? They're so beautiful. They belong in magazines."

Diane laughed it off at first, but what else could she do? So, she took a chance and sent photos of her two boys to Ford, New York's premier modeling agency.

The miracle grew. Within months they were modeling, represented by the prestigious Ford Modeling Agency, rubbing shoulders with names no one knew yet, like Ricky Schroder, Jennifer Connelly, Yasmine Bleeth, and a twelve-year-old boy named Anderson Cooper. One of the adult female models that Diane's younger son was being photographed with, a model by the name of Janice Dickinson, had even complimented Diane on her boots while on a day-shoot in Connecticut.

Diane told me like it was nothing, but in reality, she had been handed a fairytale born from desperation. Diane explained that she needed something that allowed her to stay with her boys, something that paid an income to pay their bills, something that didn't require leaving them behind in daycare that she could not afford. She told me that she had been turned down by welfare for no good reason. And her younger boy hated the daycare. She knew it was important to be together with her boys as a family, and it allowed them to experience a part of life that they otherwise would not have. Modeling seemed like a magic door. Then, as the bus continued on Old Bergen Road, Diane dropped another bomb. She was seeing someone.

Asher was the neighbor across the street. She said it gently, but it hit me like a glass falling off a table. I felt shattered again. Everything inside me recoiled. Diane had started dating Asher two weeks after her husband left. I already knew that Diane had wanted to restart her life when she told me about her cancer scare the day we first met at the acting audition at The Hotel Plaza.

We didn't speak for the next few stops, just sat side-by-side as the rumble of the city echoed outside and beneath our feet. Even so, I couldn't believe my luck that the universe had let our paths cross again, if only seemingly for the length of the bus ride. But then the miracle deepened.

Before I had a chance to respond, Diane told me she had just signed up for a class that very week at Herbert Berghoff Studios, *HB Studios*. One of the most legendary acting schools in New York City, tucked into the cobblestone streets of Greenwich Village. She leaned in a little, like she was a kid sharing a secret.

"The class starts this Saturday. Michael Beckett is teaching it." She explained that few of the moms at Ford had known of him. "The price is eighty-five dollars for twelve weeks." She paused then added, "I'll write out a check to cover it for you. You can pay me back on Saturday when we meet. Registration is due tomorrow." I said yes with everything I had.

The bus was slowing, her stop approaching, but inside me, the world was speeding up. My whole life had just changed again in less than fifteen minutes.

Diane had opened a door for us to walk through –together. And I would not let her go this time. I would follow her to the ends of the earth.

I could already see the lights of the city and the wooden floorboards of a rehearsal room, and smell the scent of oak, dampness, and dreams. Saturday mornings at 11:00 a.m. for twelve weeks straight. We were meant to be together. I knew it in my bones. It wasn't a coincidence meeting Diane again on that bus, her extending this invitation – it was divine choreography. Cosmic course correction. The universe had spun me back into her world and I didn't even care how or why. All that mattered was that I was in it again. And within weeks, Tom's grip on me had loosened. Diane had stepped in like an angel and I let her in. She wasn't just a friend anymore. In my mind, she became my new obsession, the pulse under my skin, the fire I had been waiting to feel.

Asher had liked Diane from the time that her mother and father had moved onto Delmar Road. Diane, her husband and two boys lived in the upstairs apartment in her parents' home. He lived directly across the street in the apartment upstairs from his parents as well. Within a week or two, I had a pretty good picture of Asher that I couldn't get out of my head. Literally. I needed to know everything about him, just who my competition was. And Asher turned out to be a handful.

Asher Kimble was a circus sideshow act. For *real.* He rode his bicycle seventeen miles to work every day to the post office facility in Kearny, rode a unicycle around the neighborhood, ate fire, was able to walk a tightrope, scale trees, climb mountains, and – oh, least I forget, Asher was a part-time clown that sculpted animals out of balloons. Most upsetting was that Asher was a vegetarian. Diane knew that I had the palette of a five-year-old. I needed to actually get a look at him so I could see the man that had taken my heart away again for a second time. Diane pulled a photo from her wallet inside her pocketbook one Saturday for me to see.

Asher was caveman handsome – five-foot ten, with a full jawline, a perfect physique, an afro, a hairy chest, slightly neanderthal features, and pock-marked skin. It didn't help that he had his shirt off in the photo that Diane had shown me. He looked and sounded like a goddamn prehistoric *superhero,* and yet none of it mattered. Because sitting on that Path Train looking at Diane again, the only thing that mattered to me was that we had somehow found each other once again. I could work on the semantics. Asher could juggle flaming swords while balancing on a unicycle in a circus tent for all I cared. And he *had.* Diane and I were meant to be together. It was a miracle. And I knew it. Asher Smasher.

As Diane and I rekindled our friendship, she became my anchor in a storm that had been my life for far too long. I felt like I could finally breathe again – talk, laugh, dream out loud, and create again. And in that safety – within two weeks of late-night phone calls after the kids were asleep, and after Asher had left on his bicycle for his night shift, I began to tell Diane more of my story. Well not *everything*. I told her I was deeply involved with the church and that most of my free time was spent volunteering, singing in the folk group, and helping out at Search retreats. Then I told her about Fr. Tom, my best friend, my mentor, the priest who changed everything for me. Diane listened closely, never judging. She had already told me early in our friendship that she had never heard of a mother and son so close as me and my mother. I wanted Diane to know her better. As well as Fr. Tom.

I decided that I wanted Tom and Diane to meet. I thought maybe Tom would like her. Maybe to see that my world wasn't just stained-glass windows and Sunday mass. I guess a part of me also wanted to show Diane off to him – to prove that I had relationships too. That, I had other friends. After all, Tom had close friendships with Fr. Frank and Sr. Martha. My world didn't revolve solely around him anymore.

It was the first time I ever brought someone from the outside into the closed circle of St. Paul's that I shared with Fr. Tom. Up until then, it had always been just him and I and our sacred, secret friendship. One Saturday Diane asked me if he'd like to come with us to *The Roxy* in Manhattan for a roller disco afternoon session.

"It'll be fun," she said. "Besides, it's time for me to meet your priest friend."

I remember blinking, almost flinching. The words *"priest friend"* sounded wrong coming from her mouth. But I wanted her to meet him. She thought it would be fun – light and innocent – the three of us gliding under the mirror balls and neon lights. The following week I arranged for Tom to meet us in the city after we finished with our acting class.

It was a disaster.

Tom drove into the city and met Diane and I outside of The Roxy. We had just left acting class at HB. We could see him waiting outside, arms crossed and already looking uncomfortable. As we got closer, Tom's eyes were squinting behind his wire-framed glasses and the New York City noise. His face tried to smile, but it didn't fit right on his face. Diane extended her hand and Tom took it politely, but cautiously. He looked her up and down once-subtly, but not subtle enough. Her painted nails, the way her hair caught the light, her infectious smile and animated eyes.

"Nice to meet you," Tom said, the words slightly too formal. "I'm Father Tom."

I could see it in her – a quiet calculation.

"Oh, so you're the *famous Father Tom*," Diane responded. Her eyes flickering with mischief. Diane wasn't threatened; she was curious, *very curious*. His stiffness amused her, like a man wearing a suit at a beach party.

She didn't trust him. I could tell.

I stood between them, beaming and nervous, trying to bridge the gap. But even in that first handshake, I felt it. They were measuring each other up. Silently. Strategically.

One was a priest who'd never been challenged by a

woman like Diane. The other was a woman who was afraid of nothing and no one. A woman with a keen intuition.

Father Tom wasn't built for skating. Not even close. He wobbled like a newborn colt and clung to the walls as if his priesthood depended on it. Everything about it was wrong. I remember watching him – sweating and irritated – and realizing that he wasn't enjoying himself. He was tolerating Diane. And me. Tom had been polite when they met – pleasant, but distant. Diane on the other hand was intrigued about Fr. Tom. Her gut told her that something was off, but she couldn't put a finger on it. And of course, none of us could have. That veil had never been lifted.

We tried it again. Another night out. This time Diane invited her friend Janet to even the count. We went to The Bottom Line to see Robby Benson perform. Diane and I had seen *Ice Castles* together just weeks before. We were obsessed with the romantic film, quoting lines like kids practicing for a school play. But that night the magic didn't carry. Tom was more wound up than ever. When Robby launched into a quiet acoustic number, Diane leaned toward me and said with a little smile, "He kind of reminds me of you, Keith. That same sensitive thing going on." Tom didn't smile or act like he had heard her comment. He barely looked at her. He leaned into me. "I don't know what she means by *that,*" he said flatly. Diane, hearing him leaned in and said, "I just meant that Keith has that emotional depth that Robby has." Tom just turned his head back to the stage, and that was that for the rest of the evening. Tom checked his watch more than once.

Diane stopped asking questions, the silence between us started to speak louder than anything else. Still Diane's intuition stirred. She kept asking little questions about him and about our friendship, not pushy, just quietly alert. Looking back, maybe Diane wasn't curious. Maybe she was testing him. Testing us. Trying to get some answers. Maybe in time they would be able to become more friendly with each other. I was just happy that I got to spend every Saturday with Diane.

Every Saturday morning at 8 a.m. I took the bus from our apartment in Bayonne to Diane's apartment on Fulton Ave. in Jersey City. From there we would walk back up to Kennedy Boulevard, hop on the bus to Journal Square, and take the Path train over to Christopher Street. HB was a short walk from there.

The acting class was filled with very interesting people. There was Patricia, a beautiful redhead with translucent skin, bright blue eyes and a beautiful big white smile. Steve, a comedian with long hair, a Roman nose, who wore sneakers with no socks. An African woman, whose name I cannot recall, and then there was Rob Carrington.

Rob Carrington was the closest you could get to being next to a movie star. He was tall, had dark brown hair and chiseled features. He also had broad shoulders and good posture, both of which I did not have. Plus, he worked for *ABC News*. I had dark hair, but honestly, I had nothing else compared to Rob and I was very jealous of him. He was very nice to me and very likable. He was kind and looked *perfect* standing next to Diane. I wanted to hate him so much. I had pimples and no physique to speak of.

And there was Rob, looking like a *Jordache Jeans* model.

"He seems nice," Diane whispered during a break, nudging me with her elbow.

I narrowed my eyes at Rob, who was laughing with Patricia like he didn't know that he was better looking than all of the people in our class.

"Yeah," I snapped, "in a *Superman-meets-Tom Selleck* kind of way."

Diane laughed. "You're ridiculous."

"No, he's *ridiculous*. Look at his posture. He's standing straight up like a flagpole."

"Well maybe it would be a good idea for you to stand up straight as well." Diane said with a laugh.

"Not funny." I responded. "Oh great. Here he comes."

"Hi guys, where are you two from?" Rob said with his warm, perfect smile.

"Bayonne." I told Rob, half-looking at the floorboards.

"Bayonne?" Rob said with his same annoying smile, "Nice. My cousin lives in Bayonne."

"Great," I said, instantly regretting it. "We have a ShopRite."

I immediately wanted to go through a trap door in the floor. I sounded so stupid.

"Love ShopRite," he said, somehow making even *that* sound cool.

Still, he was nice. Like *maddeningly* nice. And likable. The worst kind of threat.

That second week, our acting assignment from Michael Beckett, was to act out a solo sensory exercise, with no words, just using our minds and bodies. Sensory exercises are acting using your five senses to recreate the reality of something. Real actors call it *Method Acting*. For example, you could work on trying to recreate eating a hot bowl of soup or drinking from a coffee cup, which is exactly what the African woman and the part-time comedian did. First you would concentrate on how the cup looks, color, shape, etc., and then feel the temperature of the cup in your mind, and how the coffee smells and tastes. You would also carefully concentrate on the sounds that you hear when you sip the coffee, or stir the coffee perhaps with a spoon, listening to the sound, the clinking of the spoon. Opening a packet of sugar and stirring it into the coffee. Diane had intuitively used method acting that first night that we had met while auditioning for The Actors Prologue Theatre. I knew that I needed to make a big splash, set the tone for my New York acting career, as well as show Rob Carrington and everyone else in our class that Diane belonged to me.

I prepared at home the entire week, acting out my scene on our living room floor. I was on my way again to Hollywood. That morning, I packed a bag with the necessary scene props, as well as a snack – Reese's Peanut Butter Cups, a bag of Wise Potato Chips, and a Coke. I paid no attention to anyone's scene. I was too upset. I had somehow managed to lose track of Diane at some point during our break, and with my ear to the bathroom door, I discovered that Diane was in the bathroom with Rob. And it sounded like they were kissing. With Reese's Peanut Butter Cups in hand, I burst into the bathroom and literally put my body and peanut butter cups between Diane and Rob. I told Diane to leave the bathroom with me immediately! Like she was under house arrest. Rob and Diane looked at each other but did what I had asked. They were clearly patronizing me, and Rob had a smirk on his male-model-stupid face. I couldn't just shout it out, but I made it clear to Rob – that Diane and I were meant to be together, and nothing would stop me from accomplishing our destiny. I was still dealing with Asher, and now this.

It was my turn to act in my scene. I went back into the bathroom to change, annoyed, but determined. I would be method acting out a sensory beach scene that I had practiced in our living room, laying on our green shag carpeting. *They'll see*, I thought to myself. Rob will be sorry.

I would be laying on a brightly colored yellow and white-striped terry-cloth beach towel that I had taken from the top shelf of my mom's linen closet. In addition, for my performance, I would be wearing my brother's red Speedo that I took from his top drawer – the Speedo he wore when winning medals while swimming in high school swim meets for Hudson Catholic. Approximately three or four minutes into my scene, I realized while laying on my beach towel, laid out on an imaginary beach, with imaginary sand between my toes, with imaginary sunglasses on, for all of my fellow thespians to see – that perhaps I had gone too far.

Sprawled out on the worn oak floor having been the stage

for thousands of actors since the 1940's, accomplished and aspiring thespians, playwrights, and directors such as *Jack Lemmon, Al Pacino, and Robert De Niro* – there was now me. About to be discovered.

I lay completely naked with the exception of Billy's red skimpy Speedo. I had wished that the sunglasses were real, so that I would not have to look anyone in their eyes. You see, the more disturbing issue at hand was that I had taken a large russet potato from my mother's vegetable basket that morning, and as I was changing into Billy's red spandex Speedo in the HB studio bathroom, I positioned the potato into the white mesh pouch sewn into the front of the swimsuit. It looked gigantic. It gave the appearance that I had a ten-inch potato penis. In all honesty I could have used a smaller potato, like a fingerling, but it was too late now. If I nixed the potato prop, I would look like the underdeveloped sixteen-year-old boy that I was. I had seriously considered penciling in hair under my arms and a line of dark brown pubic hair leading to my Speedo but was running short on time. I was all in. Until now.

The fact that I was six feet tall and had a twenty-seven-inch waist and protruding ribs over-accentuated my overstuffed starchy-Speedo. Everyone in the class was speechless. Diane's jaw was open. I could hear actual gasps in the studio.

Scanning the faces of my fellow thespians proved there was an overall consensus of disbelief and sheer astonishment. In retrospect, I had made myself look freakishly disproportionate. I began my scene sitting up on the towel and acted like I was applying suntan lotion onto my body. First applying lotion onto my long extending arms and gangly thin legs. Then I continued applying the imaginary suntan lotion to my thighs, stomach, and chest. I laid down on the beach towel on my back for a couple of moments and then positioned myself to arch up on my elbows as if I were facing the imaginary sun, crossing my legs out in front of me at my ankles, accentuating a ridiculously large red spandex-covered russet potato. To finish my scene, I just laid there in the imaginary sand, unable to move, paralyzed with not knowing what my reviews would be from my fellow actors. I slowly leaned back, bringing my knees up and into the air, bending them to burrow my feet into the imaginary sand. That was a big mistake.

    The potato fell from being secured in place in the white mesh Speedo-pouch, *slipping* out from the side of the flimsy, thin mesh, falling between the space where my butt met my thighs. It had now become a gigantic *potato-testicle* swinging in between my boney knees like a mini-hammock. I couldn't be any more humiliated. It was beyond embarrassing. I stood up slowly, praying that the potato would stay in place and not altogether fall out the narrow side of Billy's bikini and bounce across the hardwood floor of the studio. I tied the striped cabana towel around my waist and I walked semi-naked across the oak floor, trying to keep my thighs and legs pressed firmly against each other, grinding my boney knees together and trying to look cool, a slow swagger to the second row, but looking more like Mrs. Swiggins from *The Carol Burnett Show*, walking across Mr. Tudball's office in a tight skirt. By the grace of God, I made it to the back of the class without losing my potato and took my seat next to Diane.

Diane leaned over and whispered into my ear.

"Are you *serious?* What is *that?*"

"What is *what*?" I asked her, acting like I had no idea what she was referring to. I sat with my legs still pressed together, my hands planted on top of my lap to cover my potato until I had time to get rid of it and get dressed.

"What did you put in your bathing suit? Is that really your *penis*?" she asked, as her laughter began to escalate. I leaned in close to her and whispered in her ear so that Rob could not hear our conversation as he was seated in the metal folding chair on the other side of her.

"No. It's a potato."

"A *potato? A potato penis?*"

"No it's just a potato."

"But why would you do that?" Diane would not stop asking questions and laughing.

"Why would you do that?!"

We both laughed so loudly that Michael Beckett said that he would separate the two of us if we continued disturbing the class.

Why would I do that? I knew why.

"Because I wanted to impress the class with my big penis."

"But it's not a *big penis*! It's a *big potato*." Diane laughed hysterically, needing to put her head between her knees so Beckett could not see her.

"I know what it *is*." I answered Diane in a nasty tone and gathered up my jeans and tee shirt and dashed into the same bathroom that I had kicked her and Rob out of.

One Saturday while in New York, I bought *Backstage*, an entertainment industry newspaper for actors, and read that the producers of a new film were about to start production – *Saturday Night Fever*. The production company was looking for actors to star in it. Diane and I had our headshots taken, black and white 8X10 photos to send out to the casting directors. I wore my 14kt. gold Italian horn. We were going to be famous. We knew it.

Diane and I were never contacted for *Saturday Night Fever*, but we had our pictures ready to go for auditions and other films like *The Blue Lagoon*, but lost out again – this time to Brooke Shields and Christopher Atkins. I felt like we were getting closer. *Saturday Night Fever* starring John Travolta was opening in theaters on December 16th – Diane's birthday – 12:16. The exact time on the clock of St. Paul's steeple that I had sketched, was now being used as the cover of the church bulletin.

I wanted us to go see the film together, but Diane had already made plans to see it with a girlfriend. Instead, I thought of a better idea.

I had asked Tom to pick me up after school on the day of Diane's birthday and drive me to her apartment. I had already been inside briefly on Saturday mornings when we met to catch the bus to New York for acting class, but this time was different.

I had bought Diane a gold heart necklace from Macy's and had a "*D*" engraved on the front of it. I wasn't thinking about Asher. I wasn't thinking about how this would look. I didn't care. I was thinking about Diane – and her reaction. About the way her eyes would light up when she opened the box and saw what I had given her. I needed her to know that I loved her more than a friend, and her birthday was the perfect excuse. Besides, I needed to send a message to Asher. And it worked. At least in my mind.

"Asher, *come on.* Stop. Keith is just a kid. He's *sixteen!* He has a crush, that's all. Just a crush." Diane reassured Asher.

"Yeah, Well I don't like it," he said.

In my sixteen-year-old mind, Diane and Asher break up over me, and Diane and I live happily ever after. But that didn't happen. I ended up going to see *Saturday Night Fever* with Fr. Tom at Journal Square just two blocks from Hotel Plaza. Sitting in the darkness of the theater, I watched John Travolta transform into everything I dreamed of becoming. I longed to be Tony Manero – the Disco King of Brooklyn. A paint store clerk by day, and disco dancer by night. I was mesmerized. I watched the way he moved, the way he commanded the room, and the way every guy wanted to be him. I saw myself in Tony Manero. Obsessed with his hair. Struggling with his family's expectations. A brother who is a priest. And then Annette. Drunk. High. Saying yes – and then, no. Guys not stopping, when at that point she had wanted them to. I felt my stomach turn. My hand started to shake. I became hot and cold -all at once. A fever was spreading through me I wanted to run out of the theater, but I couldn't move. Fr.

Tom's hand found my shaking arm, pressing it lightly – keeping me anchored. He could see that something was wrong. Just as he always did. He knew exactly when I was most vulnerable. And he always helped me through it. But I couldn't look at him. I couldn't breathe. And then Bobby. Seeing him on the bridge. The Verrazano Narrows Bridge – the Devil teasing him, whispering similar words in his ear that He had said to me. Words like "Do it. Do it." And then he did. The bridge, the concrete, that river swallowed him whole. I felt like Bobby. I cried in my seat, my hands and body trembling. Tears running down my face. Bobby fell. Or jumped. I wasn't sure.

I wasn't sure who I felt like more – Annette or Bobby – but when Bobby fell off the bridge, I felt it in my gut like it was *me* falling off that bridge. Like I was on that railing looking down. The credits finally rolled. I didn't want to talk about it. I didn't want to think about it. So, Tom and I went back to the rectory to drink, to do drugs, and to forget.

Chapter 21

I was working at The Gallery now a few days a week as kitchen and banquet help and it sure had its perks. I was mostly running plates and dodging cigarette smoke or the occasional knife being thrown at my head from our crazy Satan worshiping cook in the kitchen. On weekends the catering hall transformed into a dance club – the pulse, the disco beat, and the scent of cologne strong enough to strip paint, it was the kind of place where everyone knew each other and the rules would be just lax enough for a sixteen-year-old kid like me to slip through. Besides Ronnie, the owner, didn't play by the rules, and I was the cute kid who occupied his girlfriend, Rachel, at the bar while Ronnie took his wife's phone calls in his office.

By now I had already mastered the art of being a shapeshifter, a chameleon – able to be what someone needed me to be. My face had thinned out and my confidence was manufactured but convincing, and no one ever asked for ID – at least not from me. Diane on the other hand wasn't as lucky. One night after acting class, a group of us decided to hit the rooftop lounge at Holiday Inn on Tunnel Avenue. If you wanted to drink without being bothered or proofed, this was the place to go. I knew that because Fr. Tom had checked us into a room at that Holiday Inn one afternoon when the rectory was too risky.

The Holiday Inn had a great DJ who knew exactly what to play to keep the floor moving. Diane and our five friends slid into a red leather circular booth and within minutes the waiter appeared. He barely glanced at me before taking my order, but when Diane ordered he hesitated, then asked for proof.

"Can I see some ID?"

Diane blinked, having been caught it seemed, then smiled.

"Oh, *come on*. I just turned twenty-seven." Diane went through her purse and handed over her license. And then the DJ played.

I ended up having too many drinks for a school night. But I wasn't thinking about school at that point. I had already been cheating since freshman year, just to get by. Who could concentrate or prepare for class? For tests? I was moving much too quickly for that. Besides, I was going to be famous lest you forget.

Diane casually mentioned to me that she had taken *Hustle* lessons with her husband.

"We never got to use them," she said, swirling her straw in her watered-down screwdriver.

"He left before we were able to dance."

"Oh really?" Diane's words hovered above our heads, just long enough for me to catch them. I extended my hand to her.

"What are you doing?" she said.

The DJ dropped "*More, More, More,*" and I felt that spark as I took her hand. The same spark I felt a year earlier at The Hotel Plaza when our fingers touched in the elevator.

"May I have this dance?" I looked Diane straight into the blue oceans of her eyes.

"You're kidding, right?" she said, amused.

"I'm not kidding you," I grinned. "I can dance."

"No, you *cannot*. Come *on*."

"Yes, I *can*," I said, pulling her out of the booth, "Come on."

She raised an eyebrow, but her smile was already forming.

"You better know what you are doing and better not throw me out the window like you almost did at The Hotel Plaza," she said while slipping her hand into mine.

The moment we got on the dance floor, the moment I placed my arm around her waist, something changed. Her body shifted to take the lead.

"Uh-uh," I said with a smirk, tightening my grip around her small waist just enough to make her pause. "Let me lead."

"Oh?" Her big eyes flashed, playfully.

"Okay, big shot. Show me what you got."

Diane's breath smelled faintly orange. Her lips, parted ever so slightly, curved into a dare. Her long lashes fluttered as she blinked slowly, seemingly comfortable in my arms like she belonged there. I leaned in, my mouth close to her ear.

"*You have no idea what you are in for.*" And then, I

showed her.

My body remembered every dance from every basement wedding, every communion party, every fiftieth surprise party at The Gallery, and every night I'd practiced in the mirror pretending to be Tony Manero. I spun Diane around and pulled her back into my chest, half-spinning her in-and-out of my arms. Her curls flew. Our legs crossed, hips snapped, sweat glistened on my forehead. People on the dance floor moved back forming a circle around us. When the chorus hit, Diane threw her head back and laughed.

"More, More, More!" she sang, shimmying on the dance floor.

That next Saturday night I invited Diane and Fr. Tom to see me dance in the first disco contest to be held at The Gallery. It was my very first dance contest. I had decided to wear my purple velvet suit with wide lapels, a white satin spread collar open shirt, my gold chain and Italian horn, and my navy and purple patchwork suede platform shoes. My hair was sprayed and coiffed perfectly like Tony Manero, and I walked down to Kennedy Boulevard at 7 p.m., with the same swagger John Travolta had walking in the opening scene of *Saturday Night Fever* to catch a bus to Jersey City. While waiting at the bus stop, a car full of teenage boys drove up to me, pulling up to the bus stop two feet away from where I was standing. They were laughing loudly and whistling as they drove closer and the two boys in the front seats lifted themselves over the top of their car, hanging out of the window. I was squinting and smiling at the same time, sure that I must have known them from school. They then proceeded to throw a quart of cold beer and a large cup of soda at me. The cardboard container with the beer hit me square on my forehead and bounced to the pavement. The cold beer covered my lacquered Tony Manero hairdo. Next another boy threw a full cup of soda and ice, hitting me directly in my face, dripping down into my hair forming a cavern of Aqua Net Extra Super Hold. The ice hid in spaces throughout the sticky clots of my hair, now glued to my face and neck. Some chunks of ice fell down into my shirt collar and slid down to my waist. My velvet suit was drenched and ruined, my patchwork platform shoes stained and wet with beer. The boys pulled away laughing wildly, calling me names that kept repeating in my head.

"FAG! QUEER!

Ha, ha, ha, ha, ha.

FAGGOT!!!

DOUCHE-BAG!!!"

Shaken and disorientated, but not deterred, I turned around and walked back up the block to go home and change. I was so angry I cried. By the time I got home I looked like an absolute disaster. Mommy gasped, *"What the hell happened?"* I just stood there, soggy, dripping, sticky, shaking with anger – ice cubes still falling from my head suddenly finding their way out from the lacquered caverns. Melted ice and cola sloshed around my waist. My white satin shirt was stained with Coca Cola. The color of poop. But it didn't stop me. I just walked past her, straight to my room, and pulled shut the accordion door.

I peeled off my beer-soaked purple-velvet suit, scrubbed my face, and changed into my steel blue quiana shirt and slate blue seamless bell bottom pants and navy leather platform shoes. I shampooed my hair, blew it dry, re-lacquered it, and put my 14kt. gold thin chain and gold Italian horn around my neck for the second time, calling on the strength of Tony Manero and Jesus to get me safely to The Gallery. Then I walked right back out the door. I was determined. I was going to win this dance contest.

I arrived at The Gallery twenty minutes before the dance contest was set to begin. The place was mobbed. Gone were the kitchen trays and slamming oven doors. Gone was the cigarette smoke and knives flying from our demonic chef. Tonight, the banquet hall where I usually bused tables had become a glittering disco palace. The music was already pounding when the side door opened and Tom walked in – looking nothing like a priest. No collar, no black shirt. Just dark gray slacks and a white button-down with the top few buttons undone and a gold chain with a crucifix catching the light as he walked in. He had a glass of red wine in one hand, eyes scanning the crowd like he was deciding who to stand next to. A moment later, Diane appeared from the opposite entrance. She wore black satin pants that tied at the ankles, high black heels, and a hot-pink silky blouse with the collar turned up. Diane made her way over to Tom with a glass of white wine in her hand. Her eyes found me instantly and a smile tugged at the corners of my mouth. Tom and Diane ended up side by side near the edge of the crowd front and center for my dance debut, like two judges at the Olympics. It was time.

The colored lights spun above my head. Strobe flashes breaking the night into moments I'd never forget, like frames of film being edited on the dance floor right then and there. I was suddenly starring in my own film. The mirror ball rotated slowly overhead scattering fractured stars across the walls and floor. My sweat slipped down my open chest, pooling in my bellybutton. The room pulsated with heat and heartbeat. The heady scent of cologne and perfume filled my head like *Rush*. I was now standing at my own altar – the dance floor. Suddenly my name was called and the dance floor cleared.

"Keith Brennan, please take the dance floor."

I took a deep breath and stepped out onto the dance floor. Then, as I moved into position – it happened. A Spanish guy from the kitchen, *Carlos* – who had been eyeing me all night, jealous of my outfit, my confidence, my hair – just *happened* to knock over his cocktail onto the middle of the dance floor. A dark sticky splash of sabotage. My foot hit the spill as soon as I moved to center stage, and I went down. Hard. There was a sharp gasp from the crowd, and then the laughter. Carlos and his crew couldn't hold it in, they howled like they just saw a clown fall on a banana peel. My cheeks burned, my leg ached. For a half-second, I almost gave in. I almost allowed myself to crawl off the dance floor and hide. But then, as I pushed myself up, my eyes connected with Diane's, and something rose up inside of me. A rage. A fire.

And then I danced.

Really danced.

All the hours spent in my bedroom rehearsing had paid off. The turns, the slides, the double-point-finger snaps. I had every step from *Saturday Night Fever's "You Should Be Dancing"* memorized like it was scripture. The crowd roared as I took the dance floor like it was mine. I slid, spun, dropped, and rose again. There were a few stumbles. My leg buckled once, but I played it off with a flourish like it was part of my routine.

When the chorus hit *"You should be dancing, yeah!"* I felt something exploding in me. All the uncertainty and all the mixed-up love I had for both of them watching me from the sidelines poured into my arms and legs and became something holy. Like I had been slain by the spirit. Like my feet were speaking in tongues. When the song ended, I dropped to one knee – with my right arm pointed to the heavens, and the entire place erupted with cheers, whistles, clapping, and stomping.

First prize.

Take that Carlos.

They called my name and handed me a glimmering gold trophy with a mirrored ball on top. It looked like it belonged in a carnival, but to me it may as well have been an Oscar.

I looked up and there they were.

Diane was clapping wide-eyed, laughing through her shock and amazement.

"Oh my God! *Oh my God!*" she said when I reached her, still catching her breath.

"Where the *hell* did *that* come from?"

"You never said you could move like *that*," Diane added,

her voice almost breathless.

"I tried to tell you," I grinned, sweating and exhilarated. Out of breath.

"You just didn't believe me."

Diane shook her head and gave me a quick kiss on the cheek. "You're dangerous, Brennan."

Then I turned to Fr. Tom.

He stared at me, wine glass still in hand, lips parted slightly, but his face was unreadable. Somewhere between impressed, annoyed, and something else.

"You were...*good*." He finally said. "A little *flashy*."

Diane looked between us, sensing the tension.

"Well," she said, raising her wine glass, *"To the King of Disco."*

I held up my trophy like it was The Academy Award for Best Movie.

"I'd like to thank the Academy," I continued, "and all of the support in making this dream come true. To my family and friends who are here tonight, thank you! Especially my spiritual mentor, Fr. Thomas Stanford and Miss Diane Robin who was there by my side through it all."

My eyes locked with Tom's just long enough for the message to land.

That's when he said it.

With Diane still glowing beside him, giddy from my performance, Tom took a slow sip of his wine and with a crooked little smirk, said, "Well, at least you dance better than you sing and play the guitar."

It was meant as a joke. Maybe. But the words sliced through me.

Diane stopped mid-laugh, glancing at him, and then me. Then back at Tom.

I felt my chest tighten, the heat rising into my face, not from the performance, but from the *sting* of that one sentence. Tom knew exactly what he was saying. He knew how much the folk group meant to me. How much he meant to me. And yet he said it anyway. Something mean disguised as a joke. It wasn't just a dig at my singing, it was a reminder, a power move. A twisted way of yanking me back down to earth after I had just soared.

But I forced a smile, held my trophy tighter, and looked him dead in the eye.

"Guess I'll just stick to what I'm good at," I said my voice *steady,* even if my heart wasn't. Diane caught on. She locked her arm around mine and pulled me a little closer.

"Don't listen to him," she whispered in my ear. "You were *amazing*. You *are* amazing. You're going to be famous someday."

And for the rest of that night, as the music throbbed and the lights spun, as people kept coming up to slap me on the back, I tried to hold on to her words. But Tom's lingered longer.

My 1978 Headshot

Chapter 22

Unfortunately, Mondays always rolled around too quickly. It was time for the King of Disco to return back to high school. I had just enrolled in a pottery elective. I was determined to prove my devotion to Fr. Tom and our Lord by making Fr. Tom's chalice for his ordination. Not *buy* him one. No, *make* him one with my own two hands.

There was only one other kid in the class, and he mostly came for the free kiln access so he could make bongs disguised as vases. This should have been my first sign that this was not a normal idea, but it left me plenty of alone time to huff *Rush* under the sculpting table when the feelings got too big, and plenty of time to shape my current obsession, from wet clay into a chalice. I poured myself into that vessel literally and figuratively. I sculpted open waves crashing around the cup's bowl and carved little seagulls and clouds into the stem, circling around the blood of Christ. A bright yellow sun beamed over it all because I thought it looked hopeful. And then on the bottom of the pedestal I carved three tiny letters in my tightest, most secret handwriting. I-L-Y. Not I love you. That would have been too obvious. Just

I-L-Y – the shorthand Fr. Tom and I used at times. A homage to Peter, Paul, and Mary's *Puff the Magic Dragon* that we would listen to alone in his room while getting high.

The chalice was beautiful in the way only something made by a trauma-bonded spiritually-obsessed teenager in an all-boys Catholic High-School pottery class could be. Fragile, cracked in places, and thick with meaning no one else would understand. It was my offering to Tom, my masterpiece – complete with my own blood poured into wet clay to hold His. It was actually a prick on my finger and five drops of blood, but it was still my own blood and a way that I could be a part of Tom's mass – part of *him,* even in the times that we were apart. Like I had tried to do for his thirtieth birthday. A milestone. The year that Jesus began his ministry, and when Fr. Tom conveniently got shipped to the absolute outer rim of the Newark Archdiocese, which might as well have been Alaska.

I, of course, took it personally. So naturally, I decided to express my devotion the only way that made sense at the time, by buying him a cockatiel. That's right – a bird. A living, screeching, seed-spraying, feather dusting cockatiel.

Mommy drove me to the pet store on Central Avenue. I didn't stop at the bird. Oh no. I bought the bird *everything.* A massive oval cage – big enough for me to practically sit in, swings, assorted perches, a mini bird bath. Mirrors. Lots of mirrors. And the book *How to Train Your Cockatiel to Talk: Because Sometimes Love Isn't Enough.* I had tried to teach the bird to talk for three entire days when the bird lived in my room.

"Say – KEITH. Where is KEITH? K-E-I-T-HHHHHH."

Nothing. Even after saying it at least a thousand times.

On the fourth day, Jess and I loaded the bird into the back seat of her car and made the long drive to Our Lady of Perpetual Help in Oakland. I had planned a grand unveiling. I knew that Tom was going to love the bird.

I had blindfolded Tom the moment we got to the rectory. He was surprisingly compliant. I sat him with Jess on the edge of his bed. He looked…uncomfortable. But that was part of the fun. I just knew that Tom was going to love the bird.

"Is it a cake?" he asked.

"No."

"Is it clothing?"

"Nope."

"…Is it alive?"

I didn't answer. I just whispered to both of them, "Wait here," and left the room.

I carried the cage in. Jess looked unsure. Tom looked nervous. I removed his blindfold and looked at his face. It was a very specific expression – a forced smile holding hands with horror.

"Ta-da!" I said. "It's a cockatiel! For your 30th! So you'll never forget me!"

Tom blinked. Slowly, like he was buffering what was about to come from his mouth.

"I thought…I thought that you could teach it to talk. And it would say my name. And whenever it did, you'd think of me."

"Say KEITH...SAY KEITH!" I shouted at the bird. "SAY KEEEIIITTHHHH"

There was dead silence. And then the bird suddenly let out the shrillest, most blood-curdling squawk I'd ever heard.

Tom winced. The bird flapped violently against the cage bars.

"I don't...really *do* birds," Tom finally said under his breath. "They are kind of unpredictable." That was funny, I thought coming from him.

I plopped onto the end of his bed devastated. Rejected.

It didn't help that the stupid bird chose that exact moment to go crazy and shit all over the cage. That week Tom had someone from the parish adopt it.

The day Tom had been ordained a priest should have been etched in my memory just like all of the other times we had spent together that remain so clear. But *that* day remains cloudy for me. I remember it in short scenes. Most of it with my part edited out. The Sacred Heart Cathedral in Newark. The heat of the incense curling toward the ceiling and twisting my insides. Tom, in his white vestments, the gold metallic threads catching his light in every step. The golden chalice in his hands? *Not mine.*

Not the one I had carved with my own hands – using my own blood, with the hope, that maybe, just maybe, he'd lift it above his head and think of *me.*

No, the one he held was *polished gold.* It was smooth and perfect. And it looked expensive.

No fingerprints. No part of me. No, I-L-Y secretly carved

into the base.

Just *Love, Martha and Frank* professionally inscribed on the base.

Mine sat backstage somewhere. Or in a box back at the rectory. I stared at him, waiting for his eyes to find mine. Waiting for some signal. Anything to show me I still mattered. But he never looked my way, not once. I felt invisible. Forgotten, like Mary Catherine's photo left hanging on the wall in Belleville.

Everyone else was glowing. Sister Martha cried into her white embroidered handkerchief like Tom was her firstborn and this was his coronation, not his ordination, weeping like he was getting crowned to become King. Fr. Frank, Tom's ex-theology professor, ex-partner, ex-*lover* – stood tall in his clerical robes, beaming like a proud big brother, doting father, or whatever their relationship was now. The boundaries had become unclear. In the days leading up to his ordination, I discovered that Tom and Frank were having a home built on a cul-de-sac in Manahawkin, New Jersey. Tom brought me there to check on the construction one day. Apparently one of the workers had shit in the tub. Tom cleaned it while I snooped around, finding some sort of lube that gets hot when you blow on it in Fr. Frank's bedroom nightstand. Clearly things were changing. Or maybe they hadn't changed all along.

I was finally seventeen and I thought maybe now, maybe soon, Tom and I would leave everything behind and start a new life together – in a new church, in a new place, a new country. But I began to feel like we were beginning to slip away from each other.

I needed to do something. I needed God in my life now more than ever. Tom and I needed to reconnect and Columbus Day Weekend was *just the answer*. The trip to the Catskills would be a getaway with family and friends, laughter, and nature. A kind of spiritual retreat, culminating with Tom saying mass at sunrise on Sunday, Columbus Day, our last day together as a group.

Tom and I arrived early Friday morning. I wanted to get in the full day, and besides, we needed to select the bedrooms and see where everyone would be sleeping, get the house organized with blankets and pillows and stock the fridge. Tom and I invited my mother and father, their best friends Lois and John, my sixteen-year-old steady girlfriend Becky, Sr. Martha, Jess, and Diane and Asher. I needed to meet Asher in person at this point and figured this was the perfect opportunity for us to get to know each other.

Dad brought a large tray of his famous mini-chicken drumsticks that he made every Christmas Eve and of course a gallon of red wine to wash it all down. Mom brought a large tray of Nanny's homemade lasagna and meat sauce. Everyone else brought wine, chips and dips, salads and desserts. We had plenty to eat and drink. Sr. Martha and Jess would share a room with two double beds. Mom and Dad drove up with Lois and John and shared a bedroom as well. I shared a room with Tom, and Becky slept on the couch. Diane and Asher, the last to arrive, had their own bedroom at the back of the cabin.

I baked frozen appetizers – pigs in the blanket, mini

quiche, and tater tots. I scoured the surrounding area around the cabin for kindling and wood to start a blazing fire – a warm welcome for our family and friends, the start of a long and beautiful weekend. And for me and Tom, hopefully a new beginning. It felt like God was beginning to slip away from our relationship.

Diane and I somehow convinced Becky to allow us to wash her hair in the sink and allow her hair to dry curly. We wrapped her head in a towel like she was royalty at a chic salon and did her make-up too. When Diane and I were done, Becky looked breath-taking, like Sandy at the end of *Grease*, right before the music kicks in and Danny Zuko forgets how to speak. Becky had that kind of beauty – bright, clean, Barbie-doll perfect. Effortless. All American. She was everything I thought a perfect girlfriend to be, and for a while, she played the part so well it almost convinced me I could too.

Becky came from a wonderful family. Her mother was warm and generous and treated me like I was already part of their lives. There was no edge, no suspicion, just acceptance. No need for me to drink liquor or get high. I could just be a normal seventeen-year-old kid. And if I had been born into a different boy's body, in a different life, she would've made the perfect wife.

Her godfather, her mother's brother, was the kind of man who did things in grand, sweeping gestures for his beloved goddaughter. For Becky's sixteenth birthday, he bought Becky and me front row orchestra seats to see Frank Langella in *Dracula* on Broadway. A limousine picked us up and floated us through Manhattan like we were celebrities. After the show, the driver took us to the Rainbow Room for dinner and dancing – polished floors, chandeliers, the skyline glittering around us like jewelry.

The next day, Saturday, was a great day. A Short hike. A campfire. Asher even entertained us all with fire-eating and a tight ropewalk that he hooked up across two trees. I have to admit, Asher had an impressive repertoire and his upside-down push-ups, bare-chested against the side of the cabin, was an impressive display of masculinity and strength. He was very charismatic. We all went to bed by midnight, having shared a great day together. We would need to be up at sunrise. Tom was going to say a sunrise mass with the chalice that I had created for him.

Sunday morning, Jess and I were situated in the living room already playing *"Be Not Afraid"* softly as background music for everyone to fall into the living room and take a place on the couch and surrounding floor. One by one, doors creaked, until the entire gang drifted in. With the drapes pulled back on the patio doors, we had a perfect view of the sunrise coming up over the lake and trees. The sun was rising in slow motion, bleeding orange and pink over the lake and lighting the trees like torches. We were all bathed in gold. It looked like the cover of a Catholic Retreat brochure, or maybe a Catholic Cemetery brochure.

And then he appeared. Fr. Tom, *officially Father Thomas Stanford.*

No cassock just slacks and a sweater under his stole. He

moved with deliberate slowness. Tom always had a theatrical flair. He stepped to the makeshift altar, a folding card table that Jess and I found, covered in a lace tablecloth. Halfway through the mass, Tom did what I was waiting for all weekend.

Father Tom raised *the chalice*.

Our chalice.

My chalice.

The one I had sculpted with my own hands. The waves, the birds, the tiny rays of sunshine radiating out of the yellow painted blob. The secret I-L-Y carved into the stem. Tom lifted it up and towards me. *Finally.*

Praise Be the Glory was mine.

All mine.

With calm reverence, Father Tom celebrated mass.

"This wine was brought to us this weekend by our *Brother Bill*." Daddy looked as if he was being canonized. Tucking his chin down into his chest, blushing, humbled by Father Tom's words. His *new* words, now that he was officially a full-fledged priest.

Tom lifted the milk pitcher we found under the sink to put the red wine into and then he proceeded to pour it into our chalice.

"Take this, all of you, and drink from it, for this is the chalice of my Blood, the Blood of the new and eternal covenant, which will be poured out for you and for many for the forgiveness of sins. Do this in memory of me."

I was in a trance. I had lived for nearly two years to get to this point. It literally took my blood, sweat, and tears, but I finally had my own priest, like Billy had.

During Tom's mass, my mother folded her hands with Dad at her side. Becky, who still signed her notes with hearts and arrows, scooted over to sit at my feet, her head gently on my knee. Diane and Asher were curled up together on the blanket sipping hot coffee. And Sister Martha, dressed in her habit-suit that she always wore, sat stiff in a chair near the corner of the room, her lips pressed into a line so tight it looked like her mouth had disappeared. She didn't clap. She didn't sing. She just sat there with that creepy tight-lipped smile she always had and that silly half-cap on her head.

After Tom said mass, Jess and I played guitar and sang as everyone had coffee, cake, and cookies, like a church social. Then everyone prepared to leave later that afternoon. Mom helped pack up Tupperware filled with Nanny's lasagna for Diane and Asher to take home. Eventually, everyone kissed and hugged and said goodbyes. Diane and Asher were the last to go. Asher used the time that Diane and I talked, reviewing the best parts of the weekend, to climb up the tree and make woodpecker sounds.

After Diane and I said our final goodbyes, I watched her as she walked down the dirt path, walking through gold and brown fall leaves that were beginning to decay and fall apart. The sun had set. I stood there, in the door jam, watching Diane get smaller and smaller as she and Asher started driving down the wooded gravel path.

By now the kitchen was dim. Washed in the last gray light of the day. I was still thinking of Diane. Wondering if she was thinking of me, the way I was thinking of her. Like maybe something had been left unsaid that weekend. That's when it happened.

Without warning, without a word, Tom shoved me up against the kitchen cabinets. His force knocked the wind from my lungs. Before I could make sense of what was happening, his mouth was on mine, his tongue was down my throat. His hands and his weight on me his breath reeking of cigarettes, wine, and bitter coffee. He then began kissing my neck.

And then I froze.

Time folded in on itself and began spinning like the start of every *Twilight Zone* episode – where the screen, black and white, starts spinning down a rabbit hole.

I had opened my eyes. Across the kitchen, just above the sink.

A window.

And in the window, she was there.

Diane.

Staring straight at me. Her eyes locked into mine. Wide. Unblinking. Like she had just witnessed a car crash and wasn't sure if I was alive. She didn't move. Not at first. And neither did I. Because suddenly, the gravity of what was happening cracked open both of our souls, like we had both been struck by lightning. Apparently, she had sensed something. She always had. Maybe it was intuition, or maybe it was love, but something pulled her back to me. She had shouted out to Asher to stop the car just as they had reached the end of the wooded path. She told Asher that she thought she had left her keys back in the cabin. She jumped out of the car and ran back up the gravel path and hoisted herself up onto an empty paint can beneath the kitchen window to look inside.

And now she *knew*.

I shoved Tom off of me – hard and bolted for the kitchen door. The cold hit me like a much-needed punch in the face, my voice cracking as I yelled into the night,

"Diane! Diane!"

But she was already running half-way down the path, having jumped down from the can of paint, landing hard on the leaves and gravel.

"Stop! Diane…STOP!" I shouted, stumbling over fallen branches, my legs shaking, my lungs burning. Finally, she froze, like a deer caught in headlights or something else too awful to face.

And then, slowly, cautiously – like she didn't fully know what she had walked into – she turned to me. We stood face to face five feet from each other. Breathless. Speechless. The world spun around us. I searched her face for a sign, any sign, – anger, understanding, or anything that would give me permission to speak. To somehow explain the unexplainable. But there was only silence. And her eyes. Still wide. Still holding me in place.

"Please, can I call you *later*?"

Diane shook her head *no*.

"Why don't we talk tomorrow? It's going to be a long ride home for me. The kids will be waiting." And with that, Diane turned and walked away.

Then I turned back toward the cabin. The door creaked behind me as I shut it. And I began the painful process of compartmentalizing. But this was too big to force into a box and shove to the back of my mind. I was beginning to run out of space. Let's face it, I needed to survive getting home, and that would take a cocktail of Stelazine, weed, *Rush,* and leftover wine/blood from this morning's mass. Because if I didn't *die* right in front of Diane right *then* and *there* on the gravel path in front of the cabin, I could more than likely, based on past experience, convince and self-medicate myself into believing that she saw *nothing*.

So, I stood in the kitchen, with my back up against the kitchen door, and immediately began working to seal this moment into some distant unreachable part of myself. I was masterful – yes – but this tested my very soul. *This* after all was *Diane.*

And she couldn't be fooled. Not like the police, or teachers, or other priests, or nuns, or parents, or friends, or doctors, or brothers, or girlfriends.

I had been *discovered* alright.

By *Diane.*

Chapter 23

Diane never once mentioned to me what she had seen in the Catskills. Not a word, not a knowing glance. Not even an off-hand comment. And so, like everything else – every awful, ugly, twisted, disgusting, sad, lonely, paralyzed, dirty, secretive, sneaky, and shameful thing that I had been a part of, I packed it all away and buried it somewhere that would never see the light of day. Location: UNKNOWN.

And that was that. Until it *wasn't*.

Later that month for Halloween, Diane and I decided to get tickets to the *Bill Boggs Show* which was filmed in New York City. It felt like a fun distraction, a way to shake off everything that had been building between us. I was Dracula of course, with my long velvet cape, slicked back hair, heavy eyeliner that smudged halfway through the Path ride there, and fake blood dripping from the corner of my mouth. Diane was *Cher* and she pulled it off perfectly. Long black wig, fake eyelashes, and glitter on her eyelids. Diane looked like she had just walked off the Vegas stage. Every head turned on Journal Square when we were getting on the Path train.

We managed somehow to score seats in the first row. Elizabeth Ashley was the guest.

Twenty minutes into the train ride home, Diane turned to me and said casually,

"I think Asher might be getting ready to propose."

"Marriage! What!?" My stomach immediately flipped, my throat tightened, my chest started pounding like I had run a mile.

"No, no, no, no, no, no. Are you serious?" I asked. Diane nodded.

I didn't say anything. I wanted to scream and throw something. I probably did slam my hand up against the Path window. It was the worst thing I had ever heard, but who was I to talk. *Who was I?* A seventeen-year-old kid. Fifteen when we met. A teenager who could provide her with nothing. No security. No stability. No future for her or her kids. No plan in sight. Just a heart bursting with love for her. But love didn't put food on the table. And besides, my life was in shambles.

One Sunday I drove up to visit Tom. It was my senior year, and I had my first car – a used Toyota Corolla that I paid $900 for, – nothing fancy, but to me it was freedom. I drove up to Our Lady of Perpetual Help in Oakland. It was the first time I'd ever been able to drive away from things.

Tom greeted me after mass, still beaming from his homily. People shook his hand like he was a local celebrity. He looked happy and fulfilled, and *distant.* Then Tom introduced me to someone.

"This is Ricky," he said.

Ricky was small. Pale. Braces. Freckles. Looked like he was twelve years old.

I shook his hand gingerly. I was shaking hands with a child. Ricky tried to give me a half-smile, but he looked down to the floor like he was intimidated. I felt something inside me twist. Something dropped. I didn't know what I was feeling, but it felt vaguely familiar. I didn't have the language for it. Over the next few visits, it became clearer. Not in words, but little things. Suddenly my 8X10 headshot was no longer on Tom's bedside nightstand as it had been since I gave it to him. Now, a wallet sized school photo of Ricky was half-tucked under his ashtray.

By February, I couldn't keep it together anymore. And then came the night that broke me. A group from vocal class that Diane and I had started taking, decided to go dancing in the city. Diane and I met at a friend's apartment on 29th street in Bayonne beforehand. Diane was able to borrow Asher's car. As soon as she pulled up in front of the apartment, I jumped into the front seat. Before Diane could even say hi, I collapsed into her arms.

"What happened?" she said, concerned. "Are you okay?"

I tried to speak. Nothing came out. My throat locked. My chest heaved. I covered my face with my hands and sobbed uncontrollably. Diane held my face up – snots and all.

"Keith," she said softly. "Talk to me." And I did. I told her everything.

Not in a polished well-groomed *Brennan* way – this came out unprepared and raw. Like pieces of broken glass – sharp, ragged, confusing, bleeding.

"I don't know what's happening," I said. "With me. With Tom. With all of it. He…he kissed me. A while back. In the kitchen. At the cabin. And I thought I imagined the scene in my mind. But I didn't."

"Diane, you *saw* it. I s*aw* you. That afternoon at the cabin."

Diane nodded, her face pale.

"He's with someone else now," I said, my voice breaking. "Some kid. Ricky. He looks twelve. I don't know what's happening."

"Did Tom hurt you, Keith?" she asked, barely audible.

I shook my head. "No, not like that. He never hurt me…I mean, he *loved* me. I loved *him*."

She didn't say anything for a long time. She just held my hand and kept repeating that everything was going to be alright. She whispered close to my ear.

"I'm not going to let you fall apart. You'll never be alone. We will get through this together." I looked at her grace, her knowing, her strength. And I knew from that moment on that everything had changed.

Feb. 16, 1980

Dearest Diane…

I want you when the shades of eve are falling
And purpling shadows drift across the land;
While sleepy birds to loving mates are calling –
I want the soothing softness of your hand.

I want you when the stars shine above me
And Heaven's flooded with the bright moonlight;
I want you with your arms and lips to love me
Throughout the wonder watches of the night.

I want you when in dreams I remember
The lingering of your kiss – for old time's sake –
With all your gentle ways, so sweetly tender,
I want you in the morning when I wake.

I want you when the day is at its noontime,
Sun-steeped and quiet, or drenched with sheets of rain;
I want you when the roses bloom in the June time;
I want you when the violets come again.

I want you when my soul is thrilled with passion;
I want you when I'm weary and depressed;
I want you when in lazy, slumberous fashion
My senses need the haven of your breast.

I want you when through field and wood I'm roaming;
I want you when I'm standing on the shore;
I want you when the summer birds are homing –
And when they've flown – I want you more and more.

I want you, dear, through every changing season;
I want you with a tear or with a smile;
I want you more than any rhyme or reason –
I want you, want you, want you – all the while.

~Arthur L. Gillom

Hello Diane,

"Set your course...follow your dream."

Within you I see such a beautiful person, one who is so special, so very talented and sensitive. I just want you to know that you have been such an important part of my life for the last few years and that I hold you close to my heart. You are the only person whom I may be "totally" myself with. The only one whom I may tell my doubts, my faults, my insecurities to.

I thank God for you often and I now realize that all things happen for a reason and that people should just sit back and let things take their course.

It's so nice knowing another "Romanticist." I love talking about the dreams we both share and how things will be "when we make it" (no pun intended). You have so much to offer and you are the best natural actress I've ever seen. Nothing pleases me more than when I see you acting. You're the best and Beckett and all the rest know it too.

I hope our special friendship continues forever. Let there always be openness and honesty in our relationship.

As you read this right now, I'm in bed thinking about you.

I want you – someday,

Keith

It was no secret to Diane that I was crazy in love with her. I never *said* those words. I wrote them. In letters and cards. In drawings, in scenes, in songs. The truth *was,* we were only friends. She was still with Asher, and I was still seventeen, balancing whatever relationship I still had with Fr. Tom and with Becky. I knew I had to end it with Becky. My dark world was no place to be for a girl like that to get tangled up. But with Diane, I couldn't hold back anymore, not after I had told her everything that cold winter night. Diane didn't push me away after my confession. If anything, she seemed to pull me in closer – as if somehow, she understood the weight of what I was carrying. That next month, the weight became much lighter.

It was March of 1980, one of those cool early spring nights. The smell of the air was beginning to get sweeter. Diane had invited me to accompany her to the Hotel Ansonia in New York City to support her friend Sandy's husband, Geoffrey, who was performing in an actor's showcase for agents and casting directors – a shot at the big time. Geoffrey was going to be famous too. We could all feel it. I wore the gray suit I had just worn two weeks earlier to a junior prom of another girl that I had begun to casually date. It still had the scent of Gucci on it. I checked myself out in the mirror before I left, unsure if I looked "*City enough.*"

I wasn't ready for what I saw when Diane opened the door to her apartment. I rang the bell and listened as heels clicked down all ten stairs that led to her front door – one by one. And when the door swung open, the world lit up. Diane looked like a movie star. Her hair, usually soft and casual, was pulled back on one side over her ear, which showed off her jawline and high cheekbones. She wore a long black trench coat that cinched at the waist and flared just slightly over her hips, and beneath it, I could see the shimmer of a deep sapphire blouse, something silky. Her earrings were simple gold hoops. I stood there stunned, my hands suddenly unsure of what to do with themselves. Diane smiled.

"You clean up well."

"I was just thinking the same thing about you," I laughed.

"You look like you're about to win an Oscar." I smiled, looking her up and down.

"Well, let's go. We have work to do."

Diane locked the door behind her, and we stepped out into the cool night, our breath forming small clouds as the city pulled us closer and closer. Diane linked her arm to mine without saying anything as we walked to her car. There was something about those moments, about her, about us, about the way we looked like a real couple walking towards something that made us forget all of the noise. All the confusion. All the heartbreak waiting in the wings. That night wasn't about the past. It was about possibility. Together, on our way into the city, Diane and I had never looked more like the future.

We were beginning to know the city like the back of our hands. Forty minutes and half a bottle of Rhine wine later, we were seated next to Sandy waiting for Geoffrey to perform. Geoffrey was Dick Van Dyke meets Matthew Broderick. A song and dance man – an animated comic actor with boyish charm and looks. During the intermission, Diane and I had another glass of wine. We were feeling very…let's say relaxed, and we then decided to check out the bathrooms. We made our way to the elevator.

When the elevator made its way to the lobby, we both stepped in. The doors slid closed with a soft thud, cutting off the faint hum of *"Rhinestone Cowboy"* that was playing in the lobby. The elevator lights made everything feel warmer, more intimate. The moment the elevator doors closed, it was like the world outside ceased to exist. Diane and I were alone and her signature perfume, *Tigress*, filled the small space instantly – an intoxicating blend of spice and heat. Diane's scent curled around me, making my pulse race. It sucked the oxygen out of the air and replaced it with something impossible to describe, something primal. The elevator became as hot as a sauna.

I played with the cuff of my suit jacket, trying to seem cool. She turned her head, her blue eyes catching mine as I turned to her, looking like she could see right through the nervous energy that I was trying so hard to hide. She took my breath away.

"You look very handsome tonight," she said, her voice low and smooth, holding up her hand to semi-block the side of her mouth as though she was letting me in on a secret.

"You look *amazing*." I said to Diane in return, feeling her presence beside me, her cobalt blue and black striped silk shirt shimmering subtly as we leaned back against the mirrored wall.

"Do I pass for glamorous?"

"Glamorous," I replied, *"is an understatement."*

I fidgeted. And started jerking. Shrugging.

"You okay?" Diane says, smiling. "Don't be nervous, I'm harmless."

I glanced at her again, this was the first time that I had seen Diane look like this. And act like this. But she wasn't acting – even though she looked as if the universe had cast her in a starring role. Gone was the casual, no-frills Diane I'd grown used to seeing at HB on Saturdays, where we would sit side by side in class, her hair tousled and her makeup minimal. More Earth Mother than Hollywood Star. This was Diane transformed.

Her hair, normally loose and natural, had been coaxed into perfect curls that framed her face like a halo, each strand catching the light of the mirrored walls. Her eyes, her incredible blue eyes, were framed by shades of shadow and liner, smoky but not overdone, as if she had borrowed the charcoal and purple dusk and painted it onto her eyelids. Her lashes were long and dark, curling upward in a way that made her movie-starlet-gaze feel even more piercing. But it was her lips that had stopped me in my tracks. They were painted a deep sultry rum raisin color, matted, like a dark cherry on top of a sundae. We couldn't stop staring at each other's reflection cast onto the mirrored walls of the elevator.

The elevator jolted slightly as it began to climb, and Diane shifted closer to me, her hand gently touching mine, reminding me of the only other time we had been in an elevator together – The Hotel Plaza, the night we met. The night we touched.

She tilted her head back, studying me through the

reflection. We undressed each other with our eyes. We scanned each other top to bottom, with Diane of course pointing out with her *naughty-angel second glance* look complete with an *eyebrow lift*, that I now appeared to have become aroused.

"Grey suits you," she said.

Before I could think of a reply, Diane turned toward me, gently pushed me against the elevator wall, studied my face for a beat, then leaned in, standing on her tippy toes, her hand sliding inside my suit jacket, her palm resting over my pounding heart, and then her lips found mine.

The first touch of our lips was soft – exploratory. The dark, rum raisin lipstick was warm and sticky, its sweetness mingling with the scent of her perfume. It was sensory overload. Then our tongues touched for the first time. Just the tips. I could taste her now. I could feel the heat of our bodies touch, my chest dripping with perspiration, as our tongues explored deep into each other's mouths. My hands found the curve of her waist through her silk shirt. The feel of her hips and ribcage, which protruded from her narrow waistline. The feel of the subtle shift of her muscles as her thin frame pressed closer against mine. The mirrored walls of the elevator reflected us into fragments, shimmering our souls into the light, like a scene out of some music video. Just then, the elevator chimed softly signaling our floor, and Diane pulled back, her cupid lips curling into a smile that felt like both a promise and a tease.

"Let's not keep the night waiting," she said, stepping back from me just enough to smooth out her lipstick with her pinky finger, savoring our very first kiss in this lifetime.

Diane smiled again, softer this time, her eyes gleaming. The elevator chimed, breaking the moment, but as the elevator doors opened, we knew that something had shifted between us. It wasn't just a kiss. It was the moment that had *rewired* everything.

Diane was my shock treatment.

We each went into our respective restrooms, wondering in our minds what on earth had just happened. I splashed cold water from the sink onto my flushed face and tried to pull myself together.

Diane and I made our way back down to the theater for the ending of Geoffrey's showcase and only spoke a few words to each other. We were processing what had just happened. After the show was over, we made our way onto the New York streets and began walking back to Diane's car, actually Asher's car.

The night was alive on the upper east side of Manhattan, but it was cloaked in a veil of cold misty rain. The city glimmered with reflected light from streetlamps, neon signs, and the occasional Yellow Cab zipping by – their tires slicing through shallow puddles on the slick asphalt. Diane loved the rain and looked forward to cloudy days because that's when she shined the brightest.

The rain tapped against the roof of the car like an erratic percussion, almost in time with the rhythmic pulse of the city's nightlife. Pedestrians rushed under umbrellas, some hailing cabs, others simply disappearing into the rainy haze, all of them blissfully unaware of the steamy chaos unfolding in our parked car.

The leather seats squeaked as I awkwardly shifted in my seat unsure of where to put my hands at first, unsure if my heart was racing because of Diane, or the fear of being caught. It wouldn't be my first time.

I pulled off my suit jacket, now wet with the frigid evening rain, and Diane removed her black sleek trench coat. Wet spots were scattered across Diane's cobalt blue and black stripped silk shirt which shimmered faintly under the dim interior light. It felt like a scene that belonged in a black and white Woody Allen film.

"This is…*not* subtle," Diane said with a grin, glancing at the windshield, now almost entirely opaque with steam. I fumbled my words, something about it being a scientific phenomenon or condensation, but the explanation was abandoned halfway through as Diane's lips found mine again, kissing me in a fogged-up car on the New York City streets.

"Shhhh…." Diane whispered three inches from my face. Just far enough to insert her pointer finger through the space between our lips. "Don't talk." I tried to keep my cool, but the nervous energy and heat radiating from me was undeniable. I felt like a radiator about to blow.

A passerby glanced at our car curiously, their head tilting as they saw the fogged-up windows. I froze, wide-eyed like a teenager caught red-handed. Diane laughed and tugged me back in.

"Relax. Come over here." She jerked me back close to her

body. *"I love you."* she whispered, her voice raspy.

"I love you too, Diane."

"What's New York without a little excitement?" she whispered just before we closed our eyes and allowed the heat to swallow us, disappearing into the steam.

The rain hammered harder against the roof over our heads and windshield, a pulsing rhythm that drowned out everything beyond our cocoon. The city could've been burning to the ground, and we wouldn't have noticed – we were already on fire, lost in the slow, delicious ache of wanting each other.

I bumped my elbow into the glove compartment at one point sending its content spilling onto the floor.

"Smooth," Diane teased, her eyes sparkling as she reached down between my legs to help gather the mess, and I stammered out an apology.

"Don't worry," she said, leaning in close again, her lips brushing my ear as she whispered, "I like awkward."

The rain continued its tap dance on the roof of the car and somewhere in the distance – a cab honked, a dog barked, and life on the Upper East Side went on as usual, completely unaware that, in one parked car, an unforgettable chapter of our lives was being written.

Two weeks before my eighteenth birthday, Diane invited me to her apartment to have dinner with her and the boys after acting class in the city. I was thrilled. It was supposed to be a normal night, but nothing in my life was normal. The boys were excited in the way little kids get when they're just happy to have somebody new at the table. I sat next to Diane, and we passed around plates of spaghetti, garlic bread, paper napkins folded in-half, ice-tea for the boys, and a glass of wine for her and me.

It should have been warm and safe. The feeling of happiness should have been enough. But somewhere between the laughter, the clink of forks, and the easy rhythm of belonging, something inside me snapped. The feelings were overwhelming and foreign. I don't remember deciding to get up during dinner and walk into the bathroom. I don't remember finding the scissors in her medicine cabinet and placing them on the edge of the sink and locking the door and I don't remember removing my shirt, but somehow, I was standing there, staring into the mirror like it had betrayed me. My chest was tight and my breath short. Panic wrapped around my heart and my brain like barbed wire, squeezing it. Something inside me was screaming to get out, and I didn't know what else to do. I grabbed a chunk of my hair in the front and started cutting. A thick brown strand hit the edge of the sink and slid down the side. Then another, and another. I was shaking, my face contorted in the mirror. I couldn't stop sobbing. I heard one of the boy's voices in the hallway.

"Mommy, your friend Keith is crying in the bathroom."

Then footsteps. Then a knock.

"Keith?" she called gently. "Are you okay in there?"

I couldn't answer. The scissors trembling in my hands. I kept cutting. Hair falling in waves. Floating to the tile floor. My heart beating like a drum.

"I have to get rid of it. I have to get rid of it. I have to get

rid of it."

"Keith," she said again softly, her voice pressing close to the door.

"Tell me. Get rid of *what*?"

My voice broke, guttural like it had come from somewhere deep in my soul.

"The monster inside me."

Silence.

Then the doorknob jiggled.

"Keith...*please*. Please open the door. Let's talk. I'm right here, okay? You're not alone."

I slid down the wall crying. Scissors still clutched in my fist. My eyes burned. My hair – uneven and ragged – hung in limp pieces around my face. My chest heaved and strands of clumped up wet hair glued themselves onto my hollowed cheeks. If I cut enough maybe the feelings would go away. Maybe I could cut away the part of me that felt dirty and wrong, like editing one of my films. I couldn't cut my wrist open. I couldn't slash my throat – not in front of the boys. I couldn't leave behind that kind of trauma.

I don't remember unlocking the door, but suddenly Diane was there. She stood in front of me without saying a word. She slowly reached for the scissors first and took them gently from my hand, setting them beside the sink. Then she pulled me into her sweatshirt. I buried my face there, breathing in fabric softener and freshly shampooed hair. Diane held me like I was something precious, not broken. Just lost. I cried so hard I could barely breathe. Diane rocked me back and forth.

"It's *okay*," she whispered. "*Shhhh*...Let it out. It's okay, let it all out."

"I'm sorry," I choked. "I don't know what's happening to me."

Diane and I slid gently down the tiled wall. Cradling the back of my head with one hand the other around my waist, she rocked me, slow and soft, back and forth. I whispered to her.

"I don't want to feel like this anymore."

"You're not a monster Keith. You're hurting."

"I feel like one."

"You're *not*. You're beautiful. You're good."

I nodded, sobbing again.

She pressed her forehead to mine, lifting my face up with her gentle hands that reminded me of Nanny's.

Diane kissed my cheek, then the corner of my mouth. Soft, like her breath.

"*I'm right here,*" she whispered. "I'm not going anywhere."

Her hands didn't rush. They just held me. We kissed again – gentle, not desperate. Just needing more. Not a hunger, but a knowing. Around us, the floor was scattered with strands of my cut hair and silver scissors, a reminder of the transformation that was taking place. The pink coral tile that once felt cold beneath my knees now radiated warmth. We didn't speak. We just moved closer, our breath synchronized, our skin touching in a rhythm that felt familiar – like we were remembering something so natural but took another lifetime to feel. We stayed like that for only minutes, but it felt like an eternity. The only sounds were our breathing, steady and slow, and the quiet staggering beat of something inside of us telling us that we had finally come home. We were exactly where we were meant to be. This is what love felt like.

And then a knock on the door.

"Mommy? How's Keith? Is he feeling better? Are you coming out soon?"

Diane and I covered our mouths because we burst into laughter. The tears flew out of my eyes again, this time from happiness.

"Yes, Honey. Keith is feeling better. We'll be out in a minute." And in that moment, I knew that we were going to be a family.

We kept our relationship a secret for a few months, after all I was still in high school and was set to graduate in June. Diane would come visit me while I was in school. She would stand in front of the PIX Theatre directly across from my class. I was seated next to the window where I could see her, and we would look at each other from across the street until class was dismissed and we could be together. We would walk to Boulevard Drinks for hot dogs or Myers Luncheonette and have an hour together. Kids at school wanted to know who my girlfriend was. I told them that I was dating Diane, an older woman, separated from her husband, with two kids. They all just looked at each other,

laughed and said,

"No Fucking way! You're crazy!"

They would see. They would *all* see.

I wanted to take Diane to my prom. God, I wanted that more than anything. I had just turned eighteen. But it was out of the question – too taboo, too many eyes, too many whispers behind cupped hands, like Diane would do when she was talking 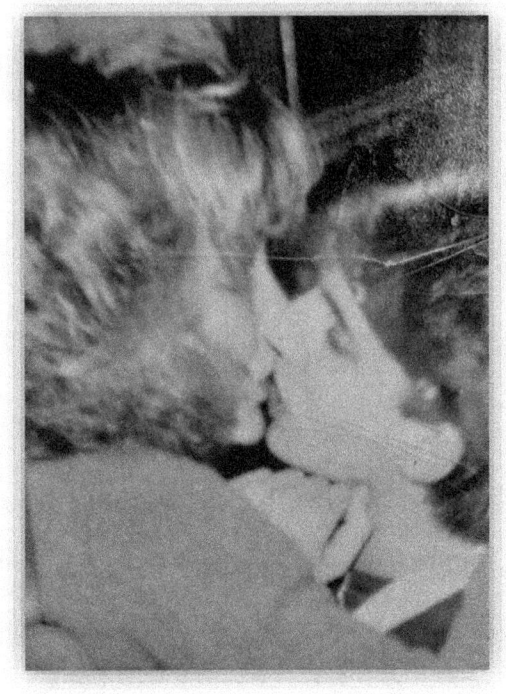 about someone. Besides, she was still technically with Asher, still technically married. I was still technically with Becky, and of course there was Fr. Tom still spinning in orbit around our lives. It seemed complicated, but the truth was Diane and I knew what we were to each other. It would just take some time to leave everyone all in one piece.

I graduated from Hudson Catholic that June. Diane couldn't be there, but Diane being *Diane* found a way. She always did. Just before the ceremony, she met me at the side door of the school. I slipped out the door in my graduation gown, and there she was just as we had planned it – leaning against the brick wall like some glamorous starlet. We may as well have been Bonnie and Clyde making a break for it. We laughed, breathless, and ran to the corner, where no one else could see, and kissed. And for those few seconds, everything disappeared, including St. Aedan's Church, which sat directly across from us. We pulled apart for a moment, still out of breath, with only our foreheads touching.

"You smell like Aqua Net," Diane said to me laughing.

"Oh yeah?" I snapped back, "Well you smell like *Tigress,* and you know how that makes me go crazy."

"You are crazy! Now get back into high school and get yourself graduated!" We laughed, holding hands until we made our way to the side door.

"I love you, Diane. I'll always love you."

"I love you too."

Six months after graduating high school, on October 4th, 1980, the world as Diane and I knew it would be changed forever, right there on Fleet Street in Jersey City. The Ukrainian Center was bursting at the seams that night, packed wall to wall with an audience that had no idea what they were about to witness. The occasion? A double-billed workshop concert titled *Miniature Fame* directed by our vocal coach Jim Stathis, whose vocal studio sat above the State Theater on Journal Square. It was a homage to the movie *Fame* that had recently come out. Diane and I had been studying voice there for months, pouring our love story into every note, every breath, every lyric. But this night, this Saturday night wasn't just about vocal technique. It was about revelation.

Diane's sons were in the audience that night, and her older boy, just nine, a fitting model for Ralph Lauren, was in the wings helping the female performers on and off the stage. Which meant, of course, that Diane's soon-to-be ex-husband was in the house- along with his mother. But Diane didn't stop there. She invited everyone – her parents, her sister and her brother-in-law, and even Asher. And me? My parents, my grandparents, my Aunt Marie and Uncle Bob, my parents' closest friends Lois and John, my girlfriend Becky, her mother Phyllis, and Fr. Tom. All sitting side by side in one long row of folding chairs. So many layers. It was like hosting a wedding, a family reunion, a funeral, and a Broadway debut all in one night, except no one knew the script but us. We were about to do the unthinkable.

When the lights dimmed that night at the Ukrainian Center, the entire room fell silent. And then – boom. A spotlight hit the stage.

There we were. The entire voice class standing side by side in a line across the stage, swaying and singing our hearts out like we were on Broadway in *A Chorus Line*. But from the moment the music started, all I could think about was what was coming – *my* moment, *our* moment. And then when the other performers had faded into the background, the cue I had been waiting for. A thick cloud of stage smoke billowed out, and through it, I emerged.

I wore a black tuxedo, with my sleeves pushed up, a white tuxedo shirt, my black bowtie, and white Capezios. And then I saw her.

Diane sat perched at the edge of the stage, one leg crossed over the other. Her black fishnet stockings and heels dangled in rhythm and anticipation. She was dressed in a black bodysuit with rhinestone stars sparkling across her chest, two of them positioned directly over her heart. Her tuxedo jacket hit right above her hips, synched at the waist with a single rhinestone button that caught the light every time she moved.

Then I began to sing.

"Take my hand...take my whole life too..."

It was Elvis' *"Can't Help falling in Love,"* but I wasn't impersonating him, I was channeling something deeper. I was singing to Diane. And only Diane.

"Because I can't help...falling in love with you."

And the room changed. We immediately saw the reactions ripple through the audience. The bodies of our family began to sway, like a wave. Bodies separating from each other in their seats. One leaned left, then two leaned right. Like they had boarded a runaway train that had run off its track. Everyone could feel it, like a natural disaster was happening. And there were about to be a few more aftershocks.

Next, I sang *"Don't Cry for Me Argentina."* I belted it out and every word was again directed to Diane. And then that's when our row started to come completely apart. It looked like the parting of the Red Sea at one point. People were leaning away from each other, folding their arms, whispering to each other in stunned tones and expressions, looking at each other like *Did you know? Did you see this coming?* They weren't even cupping their hands over their mouths.

And then – Diane stood. She walked slowly to center stage as the opening chords of *The Rose* began to play. And I, still glowing under the hot lights and sweat-slicked adrenaline, sat cross-legged at the edge of the stage and stared up at her.

Diane sang to me.

"Some say love, it is a river..."

I sat there, watching her pour her soul into every syllable, every note wrapped in her love for me. By the time she reached the final note, there wasn't a single person left who could pretend they didn't know what was happening. We didn't hold hands. We didn't kiss. We didn't say anything at all. We sang.

Diane sang the final notes of *The Rose,* hanging in the air as the velvet curtain dropped and the applause and whatever strange sound the audience made began to ripple through the hall. It wasn't just clapping. It was a chorus of confusion, gasps, whistling, and half-hearted bravos. Backstage it was chaos. The other performers rushed around in a frenzy of costume changes and cigarette breaks. A few high-fived us, others hugged us. One girl said, "That was...bold."

Diane and I ducked behind the thick velvet curtains, laughing, kissing, *buzzing*. Not from nerves any longer, but from release. From *truth*. We weren't trying to shock anyone. We weren't trying to hurt anyone. We were just trying to *show* them who we were. Who we had *become*. What we meant to each other.

Diane and I would deal with the fallout later. But for those two shows, on stage, we were nothing but fearless. And we were in love. "That's it," Diane whispered breathlessly in my ear, her rhinestone stars glittering like fireworks. "That's the last time we play it safe." I kissed her cheek. And then came the gauntlet.

We emerged into the hallway after the final curtain, where our families were bottlenecked outside the main doors, some trying to leave, others waiting for us with crossed arms, eyes wide, and confused expressions. My mother and father thought we were fabulous and were full of compliments, still painfully unaware. Aunt Marie, one of my biggest fans, grabbed my arm and planted a big kiss on my cheek.

"You're both going to end up in Hollywood. You look like movie-stars."

Lois leaned in and whispered, "John thinks you two just hijacked *Evita,* but I thought you and Diane were absolutely fabulous!"

And then came Becky.

Her face was a frozen mask of disbelief. I hugged her and said that we would talk. I spun around to leave, but before I could grab Diane, Fr. Tom appeared like an apparition. He wasn't dressed in clericals that night, just a brown corduroy blazer and black turtleneck, trying to look cool but failing miserably. His jaw was tight, his eyes narrowed through his glasses, arms folded like a disappointed drama teacher.

"Well," he said. "That was certainly...*dramatic.*"

"Tom," I said. "It's called *Miniature Fame.* What'd you expect?"

He didn't laugh. He looked at Diane with a sharp, critical gaze.

"You look...very...*underdressed.*" Tom said to Diane.

"Well," Diane answered, "we're off to the city to go dancing. This is what I look like when I'm dancing."

"We should talk," Tom muttered to me.

"Not tonight," I said, already stepping backward, tugging Diane's hand. "We're off to dance the night away."

From the corner, I could see that Asher was leaning against the bar, arms folded, a grin stretched across his face like a man who knew all along. A man who knew that a sixteen-year-old was more than infatuated with his girlfriend. A man who knew it was much more than *"puppy love."* A man who knew that I planned to be with her forever. My mind flashed to the memory of Asher when he came bare-chested into the Bayonne restaurant I was waitering at clutching a book – *Jonathan Livingston Seagull* – and went off on a rant about how Jonathan, a seagull, obsessed with flying – faster, higher, more beautifully, eventually discovers unconditional love. *"May the better man win."* Asher said to me before leaving me standing in the middle of the restaurant with my heart in my throat.

"You two really blew the roof off," he said. "I didn't know you could sing like that Diane." They hugged goodbye, Asher and I shook hands, a strong handshake, harder than it typically would be, and then Diane and I ran out the door and burst onto Fleet Street where I had parked my car.

We were heading to New York. To dance. To drink. To

let the city swallow us in all of our glittery glory. We hadn't become famous that night, but something much bigger happened. We had revealed ourselves. Fully. Without apology.

Diane & Keith, Miniature Fame, Jersey City (1980)

Chapter 24

SURVIVOR INTAKE FORM

29. Where is your abuser now, if known:

Fr. Keith Pecklers is in Rome, Italy. He is the professor of Theology at The Pontifical Gregorian University. He is the author of six books and considered to be the world's expert on the Liturgy. Pecklers is also the ABC News Correspondent for Vatican Affairs.

Fr. Tom left the priesthood and is the musical director of Holy Cross Church in Wayne, New Jersey. He is also Holy Cross' CCD teacher.

Fr. Keith Pecklers

30. When did you first tell someone about the incident(s)?

Diane found out during Columbus Day Weekend.

Fr. Tom and I had rented a house in the Catskills for Columbus Day Weekend in 1979. Tom said that I could invite friends to stay over. He invited Sr. Martha and Jess, my parents, their best friends, Lois and John Conners (now deceased), my fifteen-year-old girlfriend Becky, and Diane and her boyfriend Asher. All came up on a Saturday and stayed over. I shared a room with Fr. Tom. He said mass at sunrise Sunday morning, and I sang and played my guitar.

Later that day, everyone started to leave. My good friend Diane and her boyfriend Asher were the last to leave. As soon as their car pulled away, Fr. Tom wasted no time and pushed me up against the kitchen cabinets, kissing and fondling me.

Diane had thought that she had left her keys. Asher stopped the car, and Diane ran up the dirt path to the kitchen window. She lifted herself up to the kitchen window. She saw Fr. Tom kissing and molesting me. I opened my eyes and saw Diane looking at us; our eyes then connecting. I pulled away from Fr. Tom and ran out of the kitchen and down the dirt path to get to her before she reached the car. She didn't mention to me what she had just witnessed and made up an excuse about misplacing her keys. She pulled away shaken. I was devastated but went into denial mode and blocked it out.

Fr. Tom, towards the end of our abusive relationship, told me that Fr. Bill, Pastor of Our Lady of Perpetual Help, did not want me in his bedroom with the door closed any longer. Fr. Tom and Fr. Bill shared an adjoining bathroom that connected their bedrooms. Fr. Tom had sex with me in this bathroom.

When I was strong enough, I went up to Our Lady of Perpetual Help in Oakland and met with Tom in his room at the rectory. He left the door open, and we ended our relationship. I told Fr. Tom that I was in love with Diane. Fr. Tom told me that we would remain close friends and that one day he would officiate my wedding when I find that special girl.

Fr. Tom put his hands on my shoulders, looked me in the eyes and said,

"Just know that I will be there to pick up the pieces of your broken dreams."

Before I left, he told me to look outside his bedroom window onto the rectory courtyard. He told me that the copper Mazda RX7 parked there was his, that Sr. Martha had bought it for him and that I could borrow it whenever I wanted to. I left and never looked back.

PLEASE TAKE AS MUCH TIME AS NEEDED

It was over, everyone was out of the picture, including Tom, Asher, and Becky. It was time to tell my parents everything. I didn't plan it out. I didn't rehearse what I was going to say. There was no speech, no practice run in the mirror. I needed everything to be out in the open. I was done keeping secrets. I didn't even write down on the back of a napkin what I was going to say in case I chickened out. I just knew tonight was the night.

It was a Friday at The Sunrise, our Brennan weekly tradition for the last few years. Two large pies, antipasto, and a *side of French*. A pitcher of Coke, and a pitcher of Budweiser for Dad. The waitress, Lorraine, already knew our usual. She didn't even bring menus. She greeted us with a "Hey, Brennans" and a stack of paper plates, and disappeared into the kitchen like she was part of the family.

We slid into our usual red vinyl booth, the type where the cushions stuck to the back of your thighs like duct tape in the summer. The jukebox was playing REO Speedwagon "*Take It on the Road.*" Mom had already started organizing the parmesan, red pepper, oregano, and garlic dispensers like it was her restaurant.

And me – I was buzzing. *Manic*. And I hadn't huffed *Rush* since leaving Tom.

I just blurted it out.

"So…I need to tell you both *something*."

"*Oh, good God,*" Mom paused, mid-sip of her Coke. Dad had one of those little pepperoni cups hanging out of his mouth like a tongue.

I took a deep breath.

"I'm eighteen now. And...I need to be honest."

"Oh *Lord*. We thought we had heard it *all*." Mom said tugging at her shirt like she had just gotten a hot flash.

"First off...I broke it off with Becky this week."

"Oh, *Honey*." Mom said immediately. "I'm so sorry..."

I cut Mom off at the first cough.

"And Fr. Tom and I...we were more than *friends*."

"We were in a *relationship* together for the past three years...after Pecklers."

"And *now*...I'm with Diane."

"*I'm in love with Diane,*" I continued. "I *always have been*...*since* the day we met."

"Diane is getting a divorce."

"It has nothing to do with me."

"We were just friends until I turned eighteen. We're *together*. That's it. That's *everything*."

Silence.

Mom had a forkful of antipasto hanging half-way between her mouth and her plate, like she had been flash frozen. A slice of salami as big as a sliced almond, drooped tragically from half-a-black olive. Her eyes locked on me like she was trying to determine if I had joined a cult or maybe I was speaking in tongues like Daddy now.

Then Dad slowly pulled a stretch of mozzarella out from between his lips stretching it out with his fingers like it was dental floss. Finally, Dad cleared his throat, looked down into his slice, then up at me.

"Let me get this straight. You're with *Diane?*" Dad was squinting at me like Clint Eastwood in *Bronco Billy*. Squinting like he was trying to remember *which* Diane.

"You mean *Diane* from the folk group in *Union City?* Where those *two strange albino* German brothers sing and put on plays? That *ditsy* blonde that slept over our house and came out to watch TV in a black lace *negligee?* A *Teddy?*

Is *that* what it's called *Colette?*" Dad was speaking in his country voice again.

"No Dad." I sighed, "That was *Kathy*. And Lucas and Noah are not albino. They're just pale."

"Kathy with a *K?* Right Keith? Wasn't it Kathy with a *K?*" Mom chimed in.

"And she was very nice. Very *warm*. She was a *hot little number*." Mom went on.

"Didn't she give you that gold Amethyst ring?" I quickly responded yes – not that *Kathy* mattered at this point.

Then Mom shot out, "Keith, do you mean *Diane?* – *Diane?*" I nod yes.

"Mom, there is only *one* Diane."

Mom leaned in. *"Diane – Diane – Acting – Diane? Singing – Diane?"*

"MARRIED – DIANE???"

"DIANE with the two boys?"

I nodded and continued. "Well, she's not going to be married much longer. She's getting a divorce. She's already legally separated."

Then Mom did a quick sip–cough–sip–triple cough–sip *combo* with her Coke.

No one moved.

No one blinked.

Finally, Dad cleared his throat.

"WE LOVE DIANE!"

I stared in disbelief. But then compared to running away with a priest to Thailand, joining a cult, or being found face down in a ditch with a needle in my arm, this was a parental dream come true.

"She's beautiful," Mom said, *"The face of an angel."*

"And her boys are adorable." Dad added. "They're welcome at our house any day of the week!"

I sat there in shock.

"That's it?" I asked.

"That's it, son." Dad said to me. "Why not have them all over for dinner next Sunday?"

"Sounds great to me," Mom added.

"I figured you were going to tell your mom and me that you were becoming a monk or moving to Hollywood to become an actor."

"No Dad. I'm going to stay local so that I can act and maybe model in the city."

"And you're going to make it sweetheart." Mom added. "Especially with a beautiful, smart girl like Diane at your side."

Diane and the kids became a part of Sunday dinners and

holidays. Mom and Dad referred to the boys as their grandkids. Poppy would inhale two cigarettes through his nostrils at one time and then blow smoke rings across the dining table. Everyone was so warm and welcoming.

Except Billy.

"Next, she'll be *sleeping in the tub*. You wait and see!" He yelled at Mom and Dad.

It was the first time in my life that maybe I had something that Billy didn't.

I left college that October after finally ending my relationship with Tom, with a dime bag of weed and a puppy – Charlie. He had been roaming around campus looking for someone to save him. I decided to surprise the boys. Ramapo was a dumb idea for me because I had no interest in school, or reading, or studying, or any of it. Charlie turned out to be a poor choice too. Diane was not allowed to have a dog in her apartment.

You see, I had already signed up for Ramapo College earlier in the year to be closer to Tom in Oakland. I lived in the townhouse dorms on campus. Somehow, I ended up rooming with the entire black basketball team. I had taken out a student loan of twenty-five hundred dollars that was nearly depleted. I shredded all of the songs and scripts I had written while at college, then set my journals – my writings, my thoughts – on fire. I wanted to erase all of it like it had never happened. Mom had already taken down my bed and given it to the Goodwill, so I was sleeping on their early American Ethan Allen couch in the living room. I would stay up late and write Diane letters.

Sunday, Oct. 26, 1980

Dear Diane...

It's 11:30 p.m. and once again I know that I'm going to have great difficulty sleeping. I feel very mellow. I'm not depressed or confused – just feel reflective & pensive.

First let me start by saying I had a really great time Saturday evening. You looked so beautiful, as usual. While sitting in the Howard Johnsons across from you, flashes of the Sheridan Square Restaurant scenes entered my mind. We have both come such a long, long, way.

I pictured you as you were in the Hotel Plaza days and then how you looked Saturday night and could see all the remarkable changes in you. You were pretty then, but now, well now, you're really very beautiful.

I remember my mother and I were sitting in the old beat-up black torn loveseat in the lobby, and You walked in. You were wearing denim. I said to myself, "Now there's a nice girl for you." I had you pegged as being 15 or 16 yrs. old. It was all mapped out already. Then, wham! At 9:30 p.m. your "husband" and two children came strolling in to escort you home. Oh God! She can't be married I thought.

I remember the Tuesday nights when you and your husband would drop me off at the city line and those very special times when you would drive me all the way home.

I remember when we would look out the Hotel Plaza at New York and say how we would be there someday. Silently in our own minds we both knew it would be together too.

We've come a long way. So here I am in my living room. Diane, whatever I'm going through, I hope it gets to the point real soon. I'm growing tired, so tired of going from one mood to another. It's been so long, actually it's been "never" since I've been happy. I'll even settle for being content. I'm praying to the Lord for the extra strength I need because too many times lately I want to chuck in the towel and call it quits.

I feel so lonely these days, so lonely my whole life. I've always been missing something, but I can't figure out that missing link. So many times I prayed as a child that God would let me die during the night. I know the love you have for me is real and true, and a very deep love. Its kept me going for quite a while. Without you I'd be nothing. I would be lost.

Sometimes I feel like my head will explode or something. (I'm just putting down whatever comes into my head now.) Sometimes guilt becomes unbearable, sometimes I feel like a total failure. What is it that I hate about myself? I have to find out. Why do I feel so ugly so often? I feel like I'm not making any progress in spite of the fact that I know I've changed a lot since a year ago. Diane, why did I have to go through all the shit I did? Why would I choose such situations? Why didn't anyone notice how messed up I was at 13? Why did my family give me so much freedom as a kid? I'm angry now.

My brother is home from work. Why doesn't he love me? I remember as a kid I looked up to him. I thought he did everything right. I thought he was good looking I would look into the mirror and cry and cry, and I would ask God why I was so ugly and why Billy was so good looking.

I always wanted a brother. I wanted someone to laugh with, to cry with, and there was no one. I wanted him to take me places and to introduce me as his brother, but he never did. I wanted him to be proud of me. I wanted him to talk to me about what I was going through, but he never did. I needed someone to tell me that I would be alright, but he would just tell me how messed up I was.

I used to dream about what it would be like when I was 18 and he was 22 I thought about how nice it would be to go *drinking together or something. Colleen told me I look like an only child. I am, in a sense.*

Maybe it's not right to blame him. Maybe it's been me. Maybe I did something to hurt him.

I'm praying that something happens soon to give me confidence. Anything. I need a sign from God that I should keep going towards my goals. Life is so hard I hope I get through this.

I want to be famous someday. I'm tired now. I love you so much and I pray every night that God keeps us together forever – in this life and in...Paradise.

Best of my love always,

Keith

Within a week or two of job hunting, I found a job in Manhattan, working at Windows on The World at The World Trade Center as a banquet waiter. I didn't know what else to do. My experience up to then had been only restaurants and retail.

It was my very first day on the job – 6:45 a.m. and the sun was just breaking through the clouds over Manhattan. In less than an hour, the place would look like God's own boardroom – crystal glasses sparkling, white linen draped over long tables, two-hundred Wall Street power players buzzing about mergers and money over muffins and omelets. I was standing there in a starched white jacket three sizes too big, a black clip-on bow tie slowly strangling me, with what looks like the entire sugar supply of the restaurant, in a big white plastic bin.

"Hey, rookie, fill the sugar bowls. Fast. The wolves come in at seven." The head waiter, *Steven,* shouted across the hall.

"Copy that. Sugar it is."

I grab the bin of sugar, and I go down the line of sugar

bowls like a madman playing The Nutcracker with the teaspoon.

By 7:10 a.m. the first wave of coffee sips hit.

Morgan Stanley Executive #1:

"What in *God's* name?" His face is twisted, his eyes squinting tightly, forming deep lines on his tanned, well-groomed face.

Cantor Fitzgerald Guy:

"My tongue! My tongue! Jesus Fucking Christ! Did they make this with *seawater*?"

Then cups were being dropped. Crashing to the tables, splattering coffee on their thousand-dollar Zegna suits.

Something was amiss I thought. Someone at table #17 began dry heaving. I was still not sure what the problem was. Then, I ran back to the waiter's station just outside the banquet room where I had grabbed the bin of sugar. Except I had grabbed the wrong bin. *Salt* it read. Pure *salt*. Then Mr. Barcelona, the Banquet Captain from Hell – part mafia-don, part Disney villain – came storming in screaming each of his words separately, even more loudly once he got to bowls.

"WHO. FILLED. THE. SUGAR. BOWLS!?"

Mr. Barcelona paced in front of us like a drill sergeant. He narrowed his eyes.

"If someone doesn't confess, I will personally have all of your fingerprints lifted off of those sugar bowls, and have HR compare them to your social security numbers and find out who you are!"

Even though I knew that your fingerprints had nothing to

do with your social security number, I was still twitching but no one ratted me out.

Then came Disaster #2.

An hour later, I was hauling a cart stacked with one hundred *monkey dishes* (the little, tiny white ceramic bowls – not actually sure what they have to do with monkeys) down the hall to banquet room number two.

I hit a bump in the hallway floor.

NOOOOOOOOO I closed my eyes. *Oh my God.*

CRASH.

It sounded like two Lincoln Continentals in a head-on collision. And then Mr. Barcelona materialized out of nowhere. Again. I braced for it. This is it. *Fired.* Done. Back to Jersey. Instead, he sighed deeply, like a man who realized his world was doomed, and walked away mumbling under his breath in Spanish. And then, somehow…I *survived.* I also made some really nice friends. We had a great time during our shifts. Later that week, we were forced to attend *Master Wine School* – hosted by *Kevin Zraly*, the *sommelier* at Windows on the World.

"Today, and every Wednesday this month, we'll taste fifteen wines before 2 p.m. Remember – sip, swirl, spit. Don't swallow." Steven poked me in the side-laughing.

"We sip. We swirl. We do not spit." Steven covered his mouth laughing.

Steven and I laughed. He was my first real gay friend, excluding Fr. Tom.

One week I waited on John Denver and his wife Annie,

who argued at the table, and then at the end of January, the freed American hostages from the Iran Hostage Crisis, who were released by Ronald Reagan, with the help of our Canada ally just minutes after Reagan was sworn into office. I still have the menu from that night, along with a rose corsage and a packet of sugar.

This would be my job until I could figure something else out.

After seeing the success Diane's boys were having as models, I thought that I could possibly give modeling a shot myself. I started to think – why not me? I had the look. I had the attitude. I had the walk. I had the wardrobe. And I certainly had the dream. Some of my favorite days were spent tagging along with Diane and the boys on photo shoots in the city, especially during the holidays.

That Christmas, Diane and a few of the Ford moms and their kids decided on an outing to Rockefeller Center for ice skating, followed by burgers at P.J. Clarke's. We were a whole little model caravan – four child models and their moms, Diane, and me.

One of the girls was a soft-spoken, porcelain-skinned beauty named Jennifer Connelly. She couldn't have been more than eleven, and she seemed sweet on Diane's older boy – a fitting model for Ralph Lauren. It was adorable, like a scene out of *The Princess Bride*. He was definitely *sweet* on Jennifer!

At the table, between mouthfuls of burgers and swigs of Coke, Jennifer's mom, Eileen, kept bumming drags off my cigarette. She was friendly, but a little jittery and pushy.

"Do you think Jenny has a shot?" she asked Diane. "I mean, *really* has a shot?"

Diane assured her she did. Jenny had something about her that seemed destined for stardom.

And that was it. The moment. That flicker of realization – if they could do it, why not me?

A week later Diane got us both invited to *The Face of the '80s* – a Ford Agency event at the Beacon Theater, hosted by none other than the queen of the modeling world herself, Eileen Ford. The room would be packed with fashion royalty, stylists, photographers, and agents. It was the place to be *seen,* and I planned on being *seen.* I would dress as *The Rockstar,* one of the model looks I had been working on in my bedroom. I wore tight leather pants, a long black satin trench coat, opened up, shirtless, with short black leather gloves, a spiked belt that I got on St. Marks Place, and pointy cock-a-roach killers from Canal Jeans. A spritz of Gucci, and I was ready to be discovered.

The Beacon Theater was a glamor-fueled circus of models in sequins with hair sprayed into architecture and photographers in turtlenecks . And there in the center of all, was Eileen Ford herself. White blouse, wide smile, dancing the Jitterbug.

Diane nudged me. "Go talk to her."

I choked on my drink. "*Now?*"

She raised her eyebrow. "NOW."

Two Seven & Sevens in, I was brave enough – rigid enough – to believe that I had nothing to lose.

"If you don't ask," Diane would say, "the answer is already *no.*"

I weaved my way through the crowd, heart pounding in my naked chest, and I tapped the Queen of Models lightly on the elbow.

"Excuse me, Mrs. Ford?"

She didn't hear me.

I tried again, this time a little firmer on the shoulder. She twirled around mid-jitterbug and stared me up and down with those regal, piercing eyes that could determine your marketability in under three seconds.

"Yes?"

"I just left college, and more than anything…I want to be a Ford model."

"What should I do?"

There was a pause.

Then, without skipping a beat, she said, "Well, I'd love to help you, but I only run the Ford Women's division. You need to speak to Joe Turin."

Then she took my hand into hers, and we finished dancing the jitterbug. It was truly so sweet and generous of her.

That Monday I went to the Ford Modeling Agency and spoke to a woman that Diane knew from the children's division,

Patti, who told me that business was very slow, and that they will not even see you without a portfolio. After looking me up and down, Patti then had second thoughts and called Jillian, who worked in the Men's division and was located one floor down. After Patti spoke on the phone with Jillian – a side-mumble complete with a cupped hand – a dead give-away that Patti was describing me over the phone which I immediately believed that it was a good sign – Jillian told Patti that I should come down to talk to her! I was so excited!

I opened the wooden door to the Men's division, nervous and fidgety. I approached the receptionist, who visibly raised an eyebrow as she looked me up and down, head to toe. I was extra tall that day, probably six foot three or four, because I was wearing my cowboy boots.

Dressed in my best Cowboy look, I wore Calvin Klein tight jeans tucked into my black cowboy boots with the white stitching and three-inch block heels, paired with a chambray denim shirt tucked into my jeans and finished the outfit with a black leather belt with a big black and silver trimmed western buckle. I also wore a red bandana tied around my neck, but not rolled up, more like an ascot, or a bank robber.

I also had eye make-up on. And some foundation. And

some blush to give me color.

My hair was encased in Aqua Net. I needed to look the part.

I would bite down hard on my bottom lip to make it fuller and give it color. I also brought a piece of wheat to use as a prop to show them exactly how I could appear on a shooting. Afterall, I had years of practice with Mommy and Billy, so I knew how to model. I was so excited. Patti must have seen something in me that she wanted Jillian from the men's division to see.

"Can I help you?"

"Uh, yeah, I have an appointment with Jillian."

"Oh, yes, are you Keith?"

I was so excited. Patti must have seen something in me that she wanted Jillian from the men's division to see.

"Yes!"

"Ok have a seat and Jillian will be right with you."

I nodded my head, my heart pounding as I checked the wooden seat part with my hand first to make sure that I sat in the seat and didn't fall on the floor. It's happened before. Moments later, the office door opened, and Jillian welcomed me into her office with a puzzled look on her face.

I stood up quickly and walked into her office, my cowboy boot heels clicking and clunking on the hardwood floor like a Clydesdale horse. I stood as tall and straight as possible. The spasms in my neck and shoulders from my obsessive shrugging and jerking making it difficult to have good posture. I hear Poppy in my ear. *"Be rigid. Be rigid."*

Jillian gestures to my cowboy attire, struggling to find the right words.

"I wasn't…expecting this."

"Oh! Yeah, Um…I thought it would be a good idea to, um…you know, um, come dressed as one of my modeling looks."

My anxiety was through the roof at this point, I felt as if I was actually having a mild stroke.

I already knew that I had to be extra confident and show them what I was made of. Never once did I think I was wrong in my wardrobing decision. I stayed rigid.

"Well, I've always been interested in modeling and acting, and I think that Ford would be a great fit for me. I'm willing to work hard and…"

As I'm speaking to Jillian, I couldn't help but notice Jillian's eyes betray her straight face and her shifting pupils still trying to take in all of the nuances of my presentation. I stopped talking at that point. I realized that I was sounding like Daddy speaking in his country-evangelical-Butler, New Jersey-speaking voice.

Jillian continued to slowly scan every part of me, from the outline of my Aqua Net lacquered hair, shifting across my face, tracing my lined and mascara coated eyelashes, drawn in eyebrows, down to my swollen bitten bottom lip, down to what could have been the start of a drawn-in cleft chin (but something told me not to). Then, to my red bandana-bank-robber/ascot, and open shirt, which was unbuttoned to the button just above my navel. Finally, to my lanky denim legs and ending at the pointy toed tips of my black polished cowboy boots. I thought The Cowboy was a good choice for the interview, but I'm glad that I decided to leave the cowboy hat home. It would have been too much.

Jillian then told me that in order to transition from the rodeo to the runway, that I would need to be able to have *many looks*, and that I should come back in a few months with a portfolio. I already had the looks, I would just need to have them shot professionally.

I thanked Jillian and then left her office and Ford, and started my trip back to Jersey, excited to tell Diane what had happened and anxious to find a New York City photographer!

Chapter 25

Lucky for me, I was able to find a photographer in the city. I had taken the bus into The Port of Authority and then I was off to 42nd Street to begin my career as a model. That was if I didn't get killed first on the way to the studio. The air smelled like hot pretzels and semen. Porn theatres lined the streets and every marquee screamed something obscene in flickering red bulbs. Every other doorway was either a sex shop, a psychic with no teeth, or a guy trying to sell you drugs or a broken Walkman. And somewhere in the middle of all of this chaos was me – a Catholic boy from Jersey City, nineteen years old, stepping into Times Square with a dream and a black duffle bag full of wardrobe changes.

I found the ad in *Backstage* and couldn't believe my luck, the photographer also specialized in full body shots. Diane made me feel like anything was possible. She loved me so much. She believed in me. And when someone loves you like that, you start to believe in yourself. But I still had to make it to the studio alive.

"Hey pretty boy! A wild-eyed skeleton in a ripped tank-top, with a shoelace as a belt and a glittery eye patch, had begun screaming and chasing me. I ran as fast as I could. I clutched my duffle bag and bolted through the traffic, dodging cabs, pimps, Hare Krishnas, and a man in a gorilla suit handing out flyers for a sex dungeon.

Finally, miraculously I spotted the address. I made it to the studio. A second floor-walk-up above The Sticky Ritz Theatre. Safe at last.

Inside, the studio was surprisingly legit. A backdrop. A giant mirror. Industrial lights. A hair fan. A wardrobe rack, and most surprisingly, a make-up artist. I knew that I was on my way. I tried to act out each pose, each character, as I had practiced in my bedroom.

First up: **James Bond.** Cigarette dangling. Suit jacket askew. One eyebrow arched like I knew a secret or had just assassinated a dignitary.

Then: **Stretch Armstrong.** I wrapped a bicycle inner tube around my head, neck, and shoulders. Art, I thought. Something you would see in Italian Vogue. This proof sheet mysteriously disappeared. It was very Avant-garde anyway.

Then: **The Cowboy.** A personal favorite. This is how I looked when I showed up at Ford Models Men's Division. I had to shimmy into my size 28 Calvins by laying on the studio floor for this shot. I topped it off with a cowboy hat. Note the piece of wheat. I knew it was important to commit to the work.

Then: **The Sexy Bathrobe/Apple Guy.** Don't ask. Just know that it involved strategic robe placement and an apple.

And finally, **The Rock Star.** This was the *one*. The look I felt most comfortable in next to The Cowboy. The look that made Eileen Ford stop mid-jitterbug for closer inspection. This was the look that would make me famous.

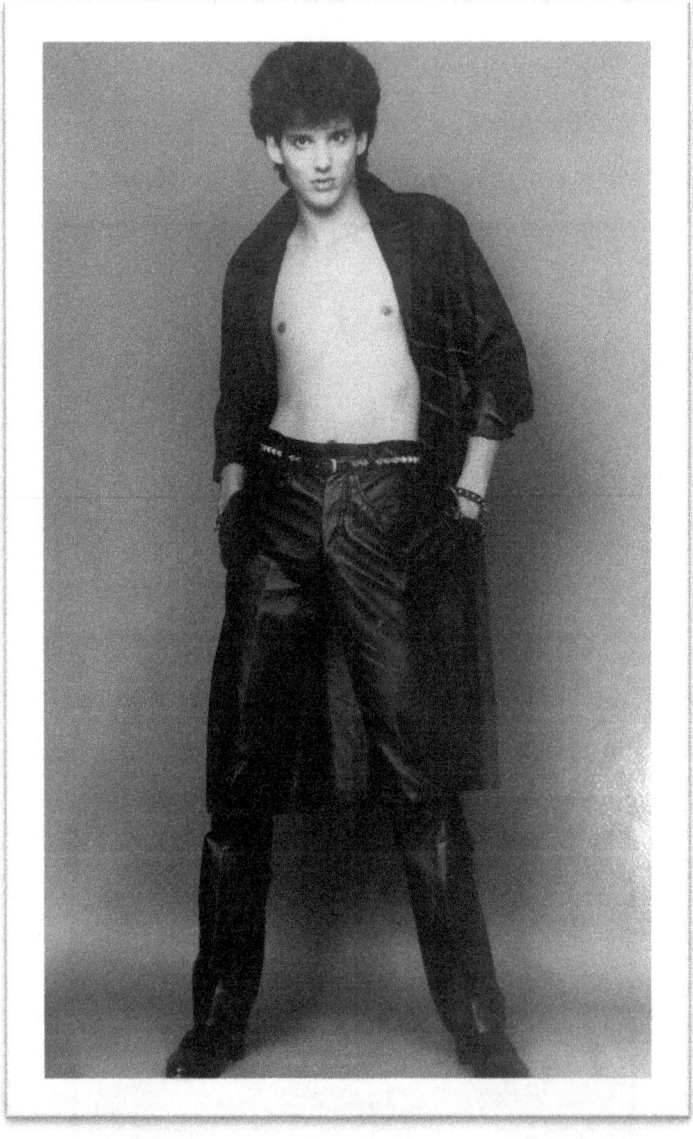

Once I had my portfolio, I began to send my head and body shots out to open auditions that I found in *Backstage*, but I started getting strange messages on my answering machine.

"Hi, yes, we're looking for *'sexy leather guy.'* Is that you?"

"Hello, uh, this is...let's just say a *collector*...I saw your cowboy photos, and I have a barn in upstate New York I would like to shoot you in."

One guy just breathed for 47 seconds into the phone receiver and then hung up.

Meanwhile, I continued working at Windows on The World.

March 10, 1981 was the anniversary of our first kiss. One year since that magical night in the elevator on our way to Geoffrey's showcase. Geoffrey still wasn't famous, but that night had meant everything. It was the moment my life had truly begun. I wanted to do something special for Diane. Something that would surprise her. Something that would show her just how deeply I loved her. So, with a mix of inspiration and something close to divine intervention, I created a gift for her. Something that never existed. I decided to create a design for Diane that she could wear.

The sweatshirt had started off as a plain white canvas but with my mom's sauce pot, a box of green fabric dye, and a burst of creativity, I transformed it into my original design. The final color wasn't the deep emerald I had imagined, but a soft olive green. Warm pistachio and unexpected. Then as if the idea had been placed into my eyes and hands, I painted metallic gold grapes onto the fabric. Still, it needed something more. I found green silk leaves and stitched them on by hand, like Nan had taught me, onto the fabric, layering them over the golden grapes.

That weekend I stayed at Diane's house, and we celebrated in the way that only we could. Lots of laughing, music, and talking. Diane's soon-to-be-ex-husband had the kids at his mother's house for an overnight visit. Diane made French bread pizza and chocolate brownie sundaes.

I reached over to the nightstand and pulled Diane's gift into my lap. I had wrapped it at home in tissue paper and red ribbon and snuck it under her bed earlier that evening.

"I have something for you."

"You do?"

Diane sat up slightly and took the gift with both hands. Her fingers worked through the red ribbon. After she untied it, she took the ribbon and gently rubbed the frame of her lips, starting at her cupid's bow, staring at the gift as if she was in a meditation – slowly savoring the moment. Diane had told me about the Christmas when her husband didn't buy anything for her. Didn't give her a Christmas present. It was the saddest thing I had ever heard, and I had promised that would never happen again.

When she lifted the sweatshirt from the box her lips parted, and for a second, she just stared at it, her breath caught somewhere between shock and wonder.

"I made this for you."

"You made *this*? For *me*?" she whispered.

"Yes." I swallowed, suddenly nervous.

Diane lifted the shirt from the box and ran her fingers and hands over the body of the shirt, her fingers gently lifting each of the silk leaves, then making her way down, feeling the surface of the gold metallic paint I had used for the grapes. She continued to trace each detail with her fingers.

"It's beautiful," she said, her voice thick with emotion. "I had no idea you could do this." Diane couldn't stop shaking her head.

"I had no idea either. Until I did it." She pressed the sweatshirt to her chest then turned back to me, her eyes glistening with tears.

"This is the most beautiful thing anyone has ever given me."

"Well, I wanted to give you something that no one else in the world would have."

Diane smiled, and then she leaned into me, her lips brushing against mine. When she pulled away, she placed her forehead against mine, her hands still holding onto the sweatshirt like she never wanted to let go.

"I love you," she whispered in my ear. The words settled into my bones and into the deepest parts of me. Diane had cured me. She had healed the diseased part of me. The part that lived deep in my marrow. I ran my hand down her back.

"I love you too, Diane." She curled back into the headboard, still holding the shirt against her heart.

"I'm wearing it the next time I go into the city. This is something special."

A few days later, Diane wore the shirt to a shooting in NYC with the boys. The art director and everyone on the set wanted to know where she got it and who the designer was. She told them that her boyfriend had designed it. They told her that I could easily sell them. That it was special.

Coming back to Jersey City on her way home, Diane stopped at a men's store on Journal Square to see if the owner would comment on it, and sure enough, the owner of the boutique wanted to know where she got it. Diane went directly to the phone booth on Journal Square and called me at home and told me that I was now a fashion designer!

I had just begun sending out my headshots to try to get my modeling and acting career started, but Diane gave me the idea of designing a few more clothes. Besides, the calls I was getting from my photos were weird and didn't sound legitimate.

The first two-piece outfit I designed was a black sweatsuit with metallic gold high heel shoes painted on the front with olive green satin bows stitched on the toe with a small oval pearl. I then hand stitched fur around the neckline, shirt cuffs, and around the legs.

I also made Diane a fur headband. I designed a fur trimmed jacket as well. Diane was my muse. For my birthday, my parents bought me a sewing machine at Sears. I had to start making patterns and sewing the fashions myself. The sales associate was instructing Diane how to thread the sewing machine. I told the sales associate that it was for me. He offered lessons that Sears was giving, but I told the man that I didn't have time for that and that I would teach myself how to sew. I took the last $100 from my student loan and did exactly what any financially responsible inexperienced designer would do. I bought a dozen sweatshirts and trimmings and began making clothes. This was the beginning of something big.

Diane and I had an unexpected fairy-godmother, Madeline, Nanny's upstairs neighbor, the angel who knitted my blue birthday vest. I had known Madeline since I was a young boy. I would stop by to say hello with Nanny every so often. Madeline was in her sixties, blonde and overweight. She mostly sat in her kitchen, like Nanny did. Madeline invited Diane and I over to visit her one afternoon, leading us into her tiny apartment like she was about to reveal some great family secret. She pulled out a dusty old wooden box, her hand shaking lightly as she lifted the lid. Inside a treasure trove. Buttons, satin ribbons, jewels, ribbon flowers, lace. Fifty years' worth of sewing treasures collected and tucked away, like she had been waiting for that exact moment to pass them on.

"Make beautiful clothes." Madeline said, pulling us in

toward her large bosom to kiss us both. "Make something beautiful." I kissed her on the cheek, and just like that we were in business.

My parents were beyond supportive. They allowed me to turn their entire Early American dining room into my daytime design studio. Mom and Dad left for work at 8 a.m. sharp and Diane came over at 9 or 10 in the morning and we'd get to work.

I would cut the fabric, drape it over Diane, and sew it together on my Kenmore sewing machine, which fit perfectly in their Early American dry sink. It was the easiest thing in the world. We ate lamb chops and veal cutlets straight out of my mother's fridge and stopped every day at exactly 12:30 p.m. to watch *The Young and the Restless*. Mom and Dad didn't care that we were eating them out of house and home, they were just so happy that we were together.

Within two weeks, I had designed enough clothes to be considered a collection and began selling my designs to local boutiques in Bayonne and Jersey City. In three months, I was able to leave Windows on the World and move full speed ahead into fashion.

Within a year we were supplying boutiques all over the

tri-state area. It happened so fast we barely had time to breathe. I couldn't make our clothes fast enough. I rented a small studio down the street from my parent's apartment, paying $150 a month for a windowless shoe box of a workspace. I couldn't afford a phone, so I spent my days running up and down the block to check my phone messages. The studio was right next to a mechanic's garage and the fumes from the exhaust seeped through the walls filling the studio with the steady stream of industrial strength carcinogens.

Nanny took over sewing jewels and beads once we were in a handful of boutiques. Diane and I couldn't keep up with the orders. Nanny was sewing hundreds of trimmings by hand. I had changed my label name a number of times until I settled on my grandparent's name "Rennar." It was a piece of my history woven into the future I was creating, and it sounded "Frenchie" as Poppy would say. It was perfect.

Rennar Designs was born. We felt so free. I worked at our studio day and night. Some nights I never went home. Soon we started to get the attention of local media and newspapers.

Diane and I would get dressed up to the nines in my wild, Avant-garde designs – cut-up, patched-together, painted and studded rockstar-couture. Our looks weren't just bold, they were loud. Picture us in neon colors, with slashes of fabric and leather layered and sewn in, like a 1980s music video. And we played the part to the hilt. We'd load up my baby blue Toyota Corolla – the star of its own show, and drive around New Jersey looking for potential business.

That car was a rolling masterpiece of performance art. After I moved back home from college, I painted a 10-inch glossy black stripe straight down the center from the hood to the trunk. The head rests were covered with black faux fur. The dashboard, a shrine to Smurfs, had blue figures hot-glued in place because my Toyota was a stick shift. There was always a patchouli incense stick burning, and at night I'd light a candle in the cup holder. The car was fully decorated, and I was ready to roll into the fashion world with Diane by my side.

I would load up the car with our 6 foot. long silver rolling rack and stuff all of my creations into the trunk. We weren't just selling clothes, we were selling *us,* the dream. Diane would say to the press that we were selling *"Fantasy Wear."*

The 1980s soundtrack blared from the car speakers. *Blondie, The Clash,* and *Madonna,* setting the mood as we cruised into rich manicured towns – Fort Lee, Ridgewood, and Short Hills. The kinds of places where women toted designer bags that cost more than my car. We'd pull in front of these posh women's boutiques and jump out onto the sidewalk looking like rock stars on tour. We'd pop the trunk. Out came the rolling rack. We'd set it up right there on the sidewalk pretending this was a totally normal thing to do, like, "Oh doesn't everyone just pull up and start their own trunk show unannounced?"

Then came the moment of pure chaos. Diane and I would grab the rack and without so much as knocking, drag it right through the boutique's front door. The sound of metal clanking against the tile floor was *loud*, and heads would whip around. The saleswomen, the customers, everyone would just *stare*.

"HEY, HEY, HEY! WAIT A MINUTE! WHO THE HELL ARE YOU?" came the voice of Lynn Hoffstein the owner of a Corner Collection Boutique in Fort Lee. She looked at us like we had just rolled in from another planet. Which honestly, we sort of had.

"YOU CAN'T JUST ROLL IN HERE WITHOUT AN APPOINTMENT!"

"IT'S NOT HOW THIS IS DONE!!!"

"YOU HAVE A LOT OF CHUTZPAH!!!"

"YOU DON'T JUST SCHLEP A RACK OF GOODS INTO MY STORE WITHOUT AN APPOINTMENT!!!" Lynn Hoffstein continued yelling.

"Oh, hi!" I said, as if this was totally fine.

"We're here to show you some original designs from our *collection*." I said this like I was Calvin Klein, with a hint of patchouli incense in my hair. Diane backed me up with total confidence like I was about to change this woman's life. We didn't flinch. We'd start selling the clothes right then and there, with Diane making quick changes in the dressing room in and out of my designs. We didn't take no for an answer. It wasn't in our thinking.

The thing was, we *did* look like stars, our hair teased to

the heavens, makeup bold enough to be seen from space, and my designs? People stopped us all the time on the street, asking, *"Are you two in a band?"* or *"Are you famous?"* And Diane and I would always smile and say, *"Not yet."*

And the best part? It worked. Boutique owners would go from *"Who the hell are you?"* to *"Wait...this is amazing. How much for wholesale?"*

Keith and Diane (1982)

We would put on a complete show, and the boutique owners and clients loved us. We'd walk out two hours later with checks and orders in hand, strutting like we'd just closed a million-dollar deal. In those moments, we felt unstoppable. One day, everyone would be dressing in my designs.

Chapter 26

From the very first time I heard about Studio 54, I wanted to be there. Not just inside – I wanted to belong. To dance with Liza and Halston, to laugh beside Mick and Bianca, to brush past Farrah and Cher in a cloud of cigarette smoke and strobe lights. It was the '80s after all, and anything felt possible, but by the time I was finally old enough to get in, the original dream was already fading. The club's owners, Steve Rubell and Ian Schrager, had been arrested for tax evasion, and their golden age was over. A scaled-back version remained – new owners, new crowd. Still glittering, still glamorous, still full of the kinds of people I wanted to be near or be. I had an idea that if I could just get one of my designs onto someone famous, I could leapfrog the long, winding path to success. And who better than Cher.

Cher was starring on Broadway in *Come Back to the 5 and Dime, Jimmy Dean, Jimmy Dean*. I decided to make her a dress as a gift and then wait for her at the stage door for her to come out. It was a brilliant idea. The design was similar to something that I had designed for Diane. A fitted white tunic jersey dress, hand-painted with Japanese calligraphy, delicate silk leaves fluttering along a branch, and a white jersey cummerbund tied at the waist. Elegant. Eye-catching. Diane wrapped the dress in a beautiful box with a wide red ribbon and a handwritten card addressed to Cher explaining who I was.

It was perfect.

That night, Diane and I drove to the theatre and parked near the stage door. We waited in the car, engine off, prayers on. Around 10:30 p.m., the theatre stage door finally opened.

Cher stepped out.

Fans swarmed – autographs, flashbulbs, chaos.

I was lost in the shuffle, and Cher was quickly ushered into a waiting limousine.

"Go! Go!" Diane shouted out of her car window. "GO!"

I jumped out of the circle of fans and raced toward her limo with her gift in my hands.

"Whoa! Whoa! Where do you think you are going? Get back!"

"Please, I'm a fashion designer. I made a dress for Cher. I just want to give it to her."

And then, like something out of a movie, the tinted window of the limousine began to lower.

There she was.

Cher.

No stage make-up. Her hair pushed back. She looked different – real. Still beautiful, but human.

"Hi," I said, catching my breath, "I'm an up-and-coming fashion designer. I made this for you. I hope you like it."

Cher smiled.

She thanked me.

And then the window rolled back up and the limo pulled away.

It was short, but it was sweet, and I accomplished my goal. Now I would wait.

And I waited. And waited. And waited.

Cher never called.

But that didn't deter me.

It was Diane's birthday that December, and I decided to surprise her with a beautiful outfit and a night to remember.

The snow was beginning to fall in thick heavy flakes coating New York City. Diane and I had miraculously parked the car right on the street a few steps away from Studio 54. A sure sign that Studio 54 would be ours tonight. Diane stood next to me shivering in the outfit I had designed as part of her birthday surprise. A white sweatshirt hot-pants ensemble with cascading black-lace ruffles, hand pleated and gathered, framing her face and decolletage. All beneath three-inch thick shoulder pads. On top of that, a white sweatshirt material-long coat I created with more black-lace ruffles sewn around the wrist and hemline. Diane wore white opaque tights, and her black boots that I had adorned with ruffled cuffs at the ankles. I was definitely a maximalist.

I was dressed for Studio 54 in my Rock Star modeling character outfit. Leather pants, pointy black shoes, black trench coat, short black gloves, spiked belt – completely shirtless, my chest and stomach covered in snow. We slid our way towards the entrance. Studio 54's neon lights hummed above us, the base from inside pulsated through the walls. The heartbeat of glamor and fame just on the opposite side of us. Soon we would be dancing among them.

The line moved inch-by-inch as the doorman, a tall thin bald black man in a black pea coat, surveyed the crowd plucking chosen ones from obscurity and granting them entry. My heart pounded. I nudged Diane closer. The snow swirled around us, turning our breath into a misty soft hail. He looked at us. And then nothing.

His eyes swept over us as if we were ghosts. Invisible. I swallowed hard, shifting on my frozen feet, pulling the wet trench coat over my iced nipples. Maybe he hadn't seen us. Maybe he would come back, do his second scan and realize he made a mistake by not letting us in. The line moved again and we didn't. The red velvet rope never lifted. I turned to Diane, my chest tight with disbelief and frostbite.

"I think we should leave."

"I thought we should have left thirty-minutes ago." Diane shrugged, her lace-ruffles floppy with ice. "Let's just go get something to eat." She was *completely* unfazed. I was devastated.

I exhaled a long-slow breath of defeat, and we skated our way to the car, holding each other up. My dream becoming footprints and disappearing under fresh layers of snow.

Studio 54 glowed behind us like a fantasy we had almost touched. We ended up at Umberto's on Mulberry Street, had pasta and a bottle of red wine, and called it a night.

I still held on to my dream of one day being at Studio 54.

In the meantime, my designs were selling out in boutiques across the tri-state area and the local press was beginning to take notice.

THE JERSEY JOURNAL, TUESDAY, JUNE 8, 1982

A SUCCESS AT AGE 20

By Maureen Nolan

If the life story of Keith Rennar ever makes it to a Broadway stage or movie screen critics may be tempted to doubt its authenticity.

But they would be wrong.

However improbable the saga of Keith's life may sound, it's nothing but the truth.

The scenario goes like this:

As a young boy, Keith vows to "make good" by his 20th

birthday.

He graduates from high school, attends college for a while, drifts into an odd assortment of jobs. He takes acting lessons, performs community theater, and tries modeling. He designs some shirts, hand painting them in eye-catching colors. Finally, a waiter at the Windows on the World, he grows more and more dispirited as he serves the rich and famous their gourmet meals and vintage wines.

He is almost 20.

Within nine months, his glamorous fashion designs are in such demand that he is often up working until the wee hours of the morning, supplying dozens of clothing stores throughout New York and New Jersey, including Mademoiselle and Variations in Bayonne and Sherri-Anne in Jersey City.

He has just turned 20.

Keith, a native of Jersey City, is now living and working in Bayonne, his fashion business successfully launched and his future rosey.

"I have never worked so hard in my life." Keith admits. "It's great getting paid for something that you really love to do."

Always artistically inclined, Keith spent hours making costumes and clothes when he was a youngster, but never considered fashion design as a serious career possibility until last September.

It was then that his lucky break came when friend Diane Robin wore one of his hand painted shirts to a modeling session where it drew raves from the photographer and the other models.

"Everyone wanted to know who designed it," Keith remembers. "Diane explained that I did it, and they wanted to know if they could get one. On her way home, she stopped at a boutique to see the owner's reaction and he liked it, too. When she saw me later she told me, "Keith, you're a designer."

Encouraged, he decided to "take a chance."

He quit his job, withdrew his last $100 from the bank, and worked day and night on his designs.

"I took some shirts over to Mademoiselle in Bayonne," he recalls. "They bought about 20 of them and it took off from there."

Keith's business is basically a one-man operation. He sketches the clothes, paints and decorates them and sells the finished products. The only outside assistance he relies upon are the Jersey City company that manufactures the clothes and the models he uses for his fashion shows.

At first, he admits, store owners were a little wary of his youth.

"They look at me and think I'm too young," he says. "But once they see my clothes, they like them. And they buy them."

And what is the secret to his success?

All his clothes – evening wear, fun wear, sweat suits, shirts, and tunics – possess the knockout combination of glamor and fantasy.

A pink flamingo adorns one shirt, a fanciful unicorn another. Antique lace adds elegance to a pretty top. Tunics sport gold beads and a mini-dress a row of silk leaves.

"My clothes are for the woman of the '80s who wants to look a little daring, a little sexy and provocative," Keith says. "A woman wearing one of my originals is guaranteed to be looked at when she enters a room."

"His clothes make you feel special," Diane Robin says. "The beads, the sequins, the rhinestones, the colors make you sparkle. They brighten your face."

Believing fashion to be "the whole look" and not simply the clothes, Keith also hand paints a variety of wooden jewelry, including bracelets and hair combs.

"Fashion isn't just the outfit," he feels. "It's the accessories, the hairstyle, the cosmetics, the whole way you project yourself."

In a Rennar original, he believes, it is easy to project a confident, attractive image.

"You feel glamorous in his clothes," Diane Robin adds. "You know the person who made them took time over them. It's really fantasywear."

But Keith also adds, his clothes are also an investment and not really so casual.

"Many of my designs are pretty conservative," he says. "The tunics, for instance, or some of my shirts. And it's easy to match things up. My Japanese kimono, for example, could be worn with black silk pants and a black camisole for a great evening look."

Many of Keith's styles, including the kimonos and Japanese sweat suits, show the Oriental influence of his two favorite designers, Kenzo and Kensai Yasamodo, but his ideas are strictly his own.

"They just come out of my head," he says. "And sometimes, if a customer requests a special design, I'll sit down with her and discuss it. Then I do some research. One woman had a ceramic unicorn and she wanted it painted on a shirt. So I read up on unicorns to know how to paint one."

The finished product was a grand success and inspired Keith to make an additional half-a-dozen.

Keith's clothes, all machine and hand washable (never dry clean them he warns) appeal to females of all ages, from 12 to 70.

"My own grandmother has a Japanese sweat suit she wouldn't part with for the world," he says. "She even wears it to go shopping."

In addition to his designing, Keith also collaborates with stores to present fashion shows featuring his designs, using models Diane, Mary Frances Caloro, and Pat Scord.

But even as his business takes off, Keith is looking towards the future and designing plays no part in it.

"This is just the stepping stone to bigger and better things," he says. "I've gotten offers to open a boutique but I don't want to be tied down. I want to expand and have my name become well known so that I can move on into different areas. I've always felt that you only live once, so give it your all."

In the meantime, he's working on his fall and winter lines as well as adding beachwear to his summer collection.

Will the small town boy become even more of a success?

Stay tuned.

Two months after this article was published, I read a story about political, social activist, and anti-war leader Jerry Rubin, and how he had recently started networking salons in New York City at Studio 54.

Studio 54 – the dance club – had closed.

"Good!" I thought when I read in *The New York Post*. My voodoo spell had worked! It was the end of Sodom and Gomorrah. Enter Jerry Rubin.

Jerry Rubin became a successful businessman in the 1970s. I remembered seeing him on *The Mike Douglas Show* with John Lennon and Yoko Ono. I originally thought he was Charles Manson because he resembled him, his behavior was erratic, and he looked crazy. I later learned that Jerry Rubin was a member of The Chicago Seven during his political activism heyday, had been arrested a number of times leading opposition against the Vietnam War, supporting Black Power, and the legalization of marijuana. Now, Jerry was producing *networking parties* at the now-defunct Studio 54.

I had a new idea. Diane and I arrived at Studio 54, prepared with one-hundred business cards in my pockets and in Diane's purse. I was not one to give up easily. Diane and I weren't just there to be noticed – we came with a purpose. We were there to make connections, to shake hands, to make sure we weren't invisible this time. Most importantly I had one mission – to find Jerry Rubin in a crowd of hundreds at Studio 54.

Diane wore one of my creations, a dress stitched together

with confidence and sheer determination. We forced ourselves through the crowd. Studio 54 was electric, buzzing with the pulse of possibility. No longer a nightclub, it had become a place of power where the right introduction could change your life. I could get discovered in a place like this.

> *At these Networking Salons "... relationships are started, business opportunities expanded, deals are seeded, exciting adventures launched, lives changed, and romances tempted as people meet one another...'*
>
> — Jerry Rubin
>
> **Program**
>
> 5:00 to 10:00 p.m. - Networking
> 10:00 p.m. on - Dancing and Entertainment
>
> Buffet dinner available.
> For your dancing pleasure, we invite you to remain for the party from 10:00 on.
>
> Admission is $6* with this Salon Card and a business card.
>
> *Part of the proceeds will be contributed to a different charity every week.

And just then...there he was, Jerry Rubin. Not *Jerry Hall*, but still a guest on *The Mike Douglas Show*. A semi-legend of a man who had once been arrested for inciting riots was now wearing a blazer and shaking hands like a Wall Street executive. I inhaled deeply, steadied my voice, and stepped forward with Diane at my side.

"Hi, I'm a fashion designer and this is Diane, my model.

Jerry looked at me. Then Diane – *up and down*.

"Did you design this?" Jerry asks. Diane was drop-dead

gorgeous.

I made her a dress – a turquoise silk wrap kimono with hand painted Japanese letters down the side, embellished with seeded beadwork and hand-made silk rosettes. It was the same dress photographed for The Jersey Journal only two weeks prior.

Intrigued, Jerry continued.

"In two weeks, I'm producing a fashion industry party," Jerry continued. "Are you interested in showing your collection? How about you and your angel put on a little fashion show."

"Nothing too elaborate," he continued, "Just your *elevator pitch* to the industry. You get your fifteen minutes of fame in Studio 54."

I had that feeling again. That same feeling that had followed me everywhere. And now that feeling was staring me straight into my eyes again. Similar enough looking eyeballs, yet the souls behind them presented me with different choices that came with different outcomes.

I could barely move.

The voice in my head said, *"Yes, thank you."*

But I still couldn't move.

"Yes. We'd love to." Diane leaped up onto her toes, her black ankle straps and seamed stockings revealing themselves, as she reached up to kiss my cheek.

And it was that elevator kind-of-feeling in me. This was really happening to me. To *us*. This is what love had done. I had no time to be nostalgic. I had a fashion show to design.

A fashion show at Studio 54. And it was in two weeks.

I knew that it had to be a revelation of some sort. What I came up with was part performance art and part runway. I needed to show all of my skills at once, and I had fifteen minutes to get it all in. I would sing. I would dance. I would design clothes. But we needed a name for our show....hmmm. Diane came up with *"Saints and Sinners"* and I loved it! It invoked the hints of moral ambiguity and playfulness, and at Studio 54, everyone had been a little of both. The sacred vs. the profane. It was perfect.

Seven of our friends, plus Diane, agreed to model. I designed nun costumes for each of them, full-length habits in black satin, with pristine white sashes cinched at their waists. Around their necks, white collars and then the *piece de resistance* – the Flying Nun hats that I created from cake boxes from a local bakery. An homage to Sally Field as *The Flying Nun*. It was oversized, theatrical, ridiculous, and irreverent. We weren't just walking into Studio 54, we were processioning, like saints entering a cathedral of sinners.

The lights dimmed. The music paused. The crowd buzzed with curiosity.

Then the doors opened – and we entered.

One by one the "Nuns" glided to the stage, their rhinestone encrusted cat-eye sunglasses glimmering under the spinning disco ball. Their hands held together in prayer. The club's spotlights bathed us in white light, as if we were making our way to Heaven. *And we were.* People turned and stared. Then immediately followed with laughter, confusion, and awe. It all mixed into this electric, unexpected vision. These were *"Nuns by*

Rennar" I announced, grabbing the mic from its stand. *"Nuns on a mission."* I continued speaking among rounds of applause and laughter.

Once we were all on stage, Diane center stage, me to her

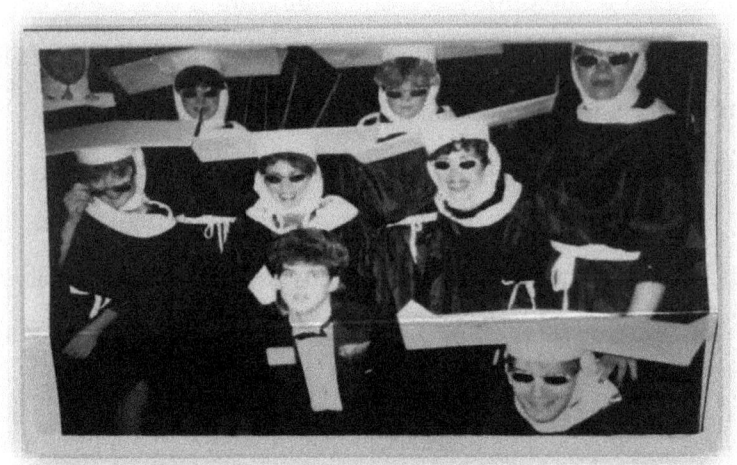

Nuns by Rennar (1982)

left side, I began to sing.

"Heaven...I'm in heaven...
And my heart beats so that I can
hardly speak..."

The spotlight found me, dressed in a black tuxedo.

"...And I seem to find the happiness that I seek
When we're out together dancing
Cheek to cheek."

The crowd hushed. The audience of sinners leaned in.

"Dance with me, I want my arms about you
The charms about you will carry me
through..."

And then, right on cue

It happened.

Each nun reached down and yanked their white sash. The robes fell away like feathers drifting to the stage.

Gasps. Applause. Screams. Two-finger whistling from the male sinners in the audience.

Each nun modeled a unique design that I had created. Tailored, sensual, defiant. Satin, mesh, black lace, cutouts, metallics. *Rennar Nuns* were fun and sexy. Not miserable like Sr. Martha. In the center of it all stood Diane at my side, wearing the dress that I had designed just for her – *The Funeral Party Dress*. A homage to designer Betsey Johnson. Blood red. Structured black lace bodice that laced up in the back. Black lace ruffles draped around the neckline, sleeves, and hem. It was drama. It was sorrow. It was resurrection.

Diane and Keith –Studio 54 (1982)

And then the room erupted in applause.

And Jerry Rubin, standing stage center in the audience – beaming. Jerry pushed his way through the crowd with Mimi Leonard, his girlfriend, her mouth open in awe. They made their way to us just as the lights faded, and the last note of *"Cheek to Cheek"* still hovered in the air like smoke. He reached for my hand to shake it.

"That," he said, "*was spectacular.*"

Mimi nodded, her big eyes sparkling.

"I've never seen anything like it. Is there anything you *can't* do?"

Jerry pulled a card from his jacket pocket and pressed it into my palm.

"I'm calling you tomorrow. Expect my call. We need to talk. There's something here. You're onto something."

The Next Day Jerry Rubin called me as he promised. Diane and I had been praying for a miracle. *As usual.* And now here it was. Jerry wanted to talk about a project, something we could collaborate on. He invited me to brunch at his loft in Tribeca.

I barely slept the night before. The thought of sitting across from Jerry Rubin discussing ideas with him and Mimi, was too much to wrap my head around. I parked in the garage around the corner. It was a sunny day to make matters worse. I had carried negativity on my sunken shoulders for twenty-one years now. Even with Diane at my side, some days I still felt like I was walking through life with my cement-colored leisure suit still on. I took a deep breath, a quick shrug and jerk, and rang their buzzer.

Mimi Leonard, his girlfriend, answered the door.

"Hi Rennard." Mimi said.

"Um…um. I'm sorry…It's Rennar. REN-ARE" spelling out each letter. It was hard enough trying to come up with my professional name.

Keith Brennan was straight on out. No chance. *Keith*

Brennino was in the top three, followed by *Keith Rennar* and lastly, just *Rennar*. Pronounced the way Poppy did, with two syllables – "REN-ARE," each spoken slowly, like he was ordering a side of *French*. It was difficult enough for me and Diane to come up with a name to begin with. I no longer wanted to share a name with Pecklers. Especially with something that I was creating, born from my soul.

Mimi giggled, like she was still drinking or perhaps had not yet gone to bed from the night before. I stepped inside and my breath got caught in my throat. A king size mattress was in the middle of the floor, white sheets tangled from it and around it looked like the aftermath of some bohemian fever dream, and there was Jerry, half draped on one side of the bed, lounging like an emperor. A dirty white tee shirt on top and only God knows what on the bottom. In the middle of the mattress were plastic containers of cream cheese and butter, four bagels, a quarter-full plastic container of Tropicana, and three mismatched coffee mugs.

Jerry looked up at me grinning.

"Take off your shoes." He said, "Make yourself comfy and join us."

My mother and father's faces immediately popped into my mind. If they ever knew I was about to get into bed with a 60's political activist and his girlfriend, they would collapse and die on the spot. After all, I had already put them through a lot. This was the antithesis of my world as a Brennan. Yet here I was, in a possible situation.

I swallowed hard and then I took off my shoes and I stepped onto the mattress – gingerly, like I was stepping on marshmallows. I found a more isolated corner and folded myself up to half-lay and half-sit on it. I reached for a bagel. I had no idea where this was going.

I was my usual overdressed self, but at least I had chosen the right kind of *overdress*. Black jeans, black button down – open just passed my chest, and my pointy black cockroach killers. My clothes and hair felt like armor to me. Especially in the setting where the rules of my world didn't seem to apply.

Jerry stretched out on the mattress with an everything bagel in hand, completely at ease.

He got right to the point.

Gulp.

"Would you be interested in designing costumes for my weekly themes at my salon at Studio 54?" Jerry asked casually, dropping it as he licked cream cheese off the side of his bagel.

"Every week, different themes. Finance, beauty, fashion, medical, television. The ideas and creations will be all your own. The exposure would be incredible for your label. You'd meet angel investors, backers, and the right people."

And then there was the catch. There was always a catch.

"I can't *pay* you. You have to cover the cost of the designs yourself." Jerry glanced at me and then to the container of smoked salmon, raising the container to his nose all in one swift move "Is this fresh?" he says, turning to Mimi. Then back to me.

I listen like I'm at a legitimate meeting. I clumsily

positioned myself up on one elbow, with a dirty mug of Tropicana

in my hands. If I had been a different person in a different life, like the one before Diane, I would have said yes on the spot and probably would have been sleeping with both of them to boot. But something in me hesitated. Even though I would be throwing myself into a world where each week brought a new opportunity, where my work would be draped over bodies dancing under the mirrored lights of Studio 54, I told him I'll have to sleep on it. At home. In my own bed. By myself.

All of us laughed and Jerry raised his dirty coffee mug in an unspoken toast to my hesitation. In the end, I decided against it. It would take too much time away from fulfilling store orders, the real tangible work that we were already building on. And besides, Diane and I had already met a backer by the name of Milton Featherstone, a businessman and investor, the night of our fashion show. A man with a rooftop terrace on the Upper East Side. He generously invited Diane and I to use his apartment and terrace for a fashion shoot. Mr. Featherstone had me at shooting.

When we arrived at his apartment everything seemed above board. Classic upper east side taste, expensive, at least by the look of it. It was only the second east side apartment that I had ever been to, but the place smelled like money. Mr. Featherstone led us through his apartment speaking about his wise investments that had gotten him to this point, and how he was looking to be in the *"fashion space."* He looked like Mr. Whipple from the *Charmin* toilet paper commercials, only a few years younger. It all sounded promising, until we had to walk through his bedroom to get to the terrace, and that's when I saw the multicolored condoms sitting on his bedside table arranged in a supersized clear glass candy dish. There had to be at least fifty or sixty condoms – orange, red, blue, yellow, black, white, purple, green.

Diane and I exchanged a glance, one of those silent 'are you seeing this' moments, complete with eye contortion and head tilting. Mr. Featherstone, completely unfazed, gestured toward the terrace.

"Call me *Milton*" stood on the side of his terrace watching us like he was a Hollywood mogul who had just captured his latest prey. I hurried through taking photos of Diane, and honestly, they looked amazing. We decided right then and there – no investors. No creepy businessman with bowls of colored condoms.

Diane on Milton's terrace

At least we were able to add to our portfolio of photos.

Things started happening so fast it felt like I had stepped onto a runaway train. One moment Diane and I were grinding away, hand delivering merchandise, praying for miracles, and the next, doors were flying open in front of us. It started with meeting another fairy Godmother, who would point me in the next direction. *Connie Anton,* the owner of a boutique in Nutley, New Jersey. Connie had taken a liking to me and Diane – our energy, our designs, our drive. One afternoon after I dropped off a rack of designs at her store, she did something that took my breath away. She pulled out her checkbook and with a single flick of her pen, wrote out a check for twenty-eight hundred dollars. I stared at it, completely confused.

"What is this for?" I asked Connie. She had already paid for the rack I had just delivered.

"You're going to rent a space at the New York Coliseum Boutique Show." She said matter of factly.

I had no idea what she was talking about. Somehow, two weeks later, Diane and I found ourselves in the middle of the New York Coliseum Boutique Show, a massive trade event where boutique owners and buyers from around the world place orders for their goods.

We had rented the smallest possible booth space available. Just enough space to squeeze in Diane, me, and a rolling rack of my designs. Diane, always thinking, brought fresh strawberries to give out. Customers thought this was a cute touch. What we didn't anticipate was that there would be thousands and thousands of people streaming through the show. We had no idea what we had gotten ourselves into. And then *Cosmopolitan Magazine* stopped by, and the editor picked up one of my dresses, held it up to the light, and smiled.

"Can you bring this to Cosmo on Monday?" I nodded, barely breathing.

"Helen is going to love this."

We ended the weekend with over $50,000 in orders! It didn't seem real.

Monday morning, I arrived at the office of *Cosmopolitan Magazine* with my dress in hand. I sat outside of Helen Gurley Brown's office while she inspected it. My dress was photographed for the Christmas issue of *Cosmopolitan*, with Brooke Shields on the cover. If that wasn't enough, the costume designer for *Dynasty*, one of the biggest shows on television ever, fell in love with our line at the show. She placed an order for six outfits for Heather Locklear's character *Sammy Jo*. I was soaring. My designs were about to be on *Dynasty! Dynasty* and *Knots Landing* were my favorite shows. Everything we had worked so hard and dreamt of was materializing right in front of us.

And then one of the biggest regrets of my life. I was *one* week late with the *Dynasty* order and the production department refused it, stamping the box with a big red REJECTED.

I remember opening the box when it arrived, staring at the pieces that were supposed to be on television. On one of the most *watched* television shows of all time. I couldn't make the clothes fast enough. That was the moment I realized I couldn't do it alone anymore.

Rennar Designs (1983)

Chapter 27

Our business exploded. What started as Diane and I working elbow to elbow in my parent's dining room, threading needles and hand-painting on their dining room table, had grown into a full-fledged business. Within six months we had outgrown the $150 studio I had rented down the street, and we leased a proper factory space. Bayonne still had two or three old sewing factories left; it had always been a working town. We hired five Italian seamstresses from a local factory where the owner was a Gestapo and walked the aisles in between the seamstresses with his German Shepard. Diane and I treated our employees like they were our family. We personally served them assorted chocolates at 3 p.m. each day. Each one was a master – Philomena, Rose, Elizabeth, Fannie, and Marianna. These women became my professors, my mentors, my fairy God-seamstresses. We worked shoulder to shoulder bedazzling and stitching our way through thousands of designs. I had my brilliant assistant, Kelly, by my side, who started at 16 and stayed for nearly 20 years.

    I would get a design idea, make a pattern, then cut it out of cloth and sew it together. Next, fittings with Diane, and then to Philomena and Elizabeth for the finished garment. We had showrooms on Seventh Avenue, Miami, Chicago, LA, and Dallas. We were ordering sixteen wheelers full of fabric. Diane and I traveled on weekends producing our fashion shows. The press caught on – local newspaper and cable television shows. Our story was everywhere. It was thrilling. Exhilarating.

After years of grinding, Diane and the boys and I bought our own home together. It was a milestone – a dream we had envisioned, and now it was a reality. It was around this time that Diane's younger son landed a role that would put him into the world of Hollywood, as the photo double for Tom Hanks' young friend in *Big* directed by Penny Marshall. In the film, the scene where Tom Hanks and Billy, his best friend, walk down the street together, he had to perfectly mimic Billy's movements. Penny recorded Tom coaching the scene on VHS tape so that they could take it home and study it on our VCR. He spent hours hanging out with Colin Hanks, Tom's son, who had been brought on to the set to tag along with his dad. At one point, Diane asked Tom Hanks if they could take Colin to get something to eat, which Tom in his usual easy-going way, said sure. So off they went and grabbed lunch together like it was the most normal thing in the world. Somewhere in the middle of their outing, Colin found a pair of sunglasses he wanted, and Diane bought them for him. Colin promised that his dad would pay her back, except Diane is still waiting.

Tom Hanks – You owe Diane five bucks.

By Christmas 1987, Diane and I had known each other for

10 years and yet we had never once spoken about marriage. Not because we weren't committed, we already knew we were bound together for life, but I wanted Diane to have the big wedding she never had. I wanted the world to see what we already knew – that we were *forever*.

I proposed to Diane Christmas Morning. She was shocked.

At first, we thought we'd get married in the Catholic Church – St. Paul's, where we both were raised. That was until the priest told Diane and I that she would need to get her previous marriage, which lasted seven years, annulled. "And what about my boys?" Diane said. "They don't exist?" Then the priest continued with a list of filing fees, investigation fees, decision fees, and possible psychological evaluation fees. Fees, fees, and fees. We looked at each other, knowing exactly what the other was thinking. Absolutely not. Instead, we found a gorgeous venue at The Manor in West Orange, New Jersey, where we could create the wedding we wanted, with no hoops to jump through. The Manor provided a minister, and we booked the date.

Two weeks before the wedding when we arrived for our rehearsal, the event planner greeted us with a smile and said, "Oh, by the way, your minister dropped dead of a heart attack this morning." We stood there looking at each other. "But don't worry," she said cheerfully, "we have a replacement minister you can use."

In the end, it was perfect. I wanted to have the most beautiful wedding possible, so I designed everything. Diane's wedding gown, six hand-painted bridesmaid's gowns with hand painted podesua heels. I even designed a gown for Diane's mother. The only gown that I did *not* design was *my* mother's dress. I offered, but Mom commissioned a gown from another designer in Montclair. She wore a hand-painted silk gown that looked incredibly close to the bridesmaids' dresses and Diane's mother's gown that I had created.

My Mother lost her voice the day of our wedding. She couldn't say a word.

Our wedding was outside in the rose garden, and we walked through arches of white roses as a harpist played in the background. I stood under the gazebo as her two handsome sons, now thirteen and seventeen, walked their mother down the paved aisle.

Everything was perfect. Our wedding photo and story was published in New Jersey Bride magazine.

But I still had an itch.

A month earlier I had written a letter to Bill Bell, the television producer and writer for *The Young and the Restless* soap opera. Diane and I had been watching every day for years. I had still been interested in an acting or film career of some sort. In the letter to Bill Bell, I wrote a character that I could play for him to consider. I had been told for years that I resembled Michael Damian, who played Danny Romalotti on the show. Danny was a rock star and, in my storyline, his cousin *Rennar,* a fashion designer from Paris, suddenly appears in Genoa City, the fictional town where Y&R is set, to shake things up, possibly steal Cricket, the producer of the soap's real-life daughter and Danny Romalotti's love interest. A few weeks after sending my letter, I received a reply.

It was from the casting director. She suggested that I continue studying acting, even though I had told her that I was a natural and suggested that when I plan a trip to Los Angeles, that I should contact her office and that perhaps we could set up a meeting with her and Bill! It was very encouraging. The timing wasn't right, but it didn't matter. It was encouraging. It was something. For me it was a sign that Hollywood *wasn't* out of the question. It just was not the right time.

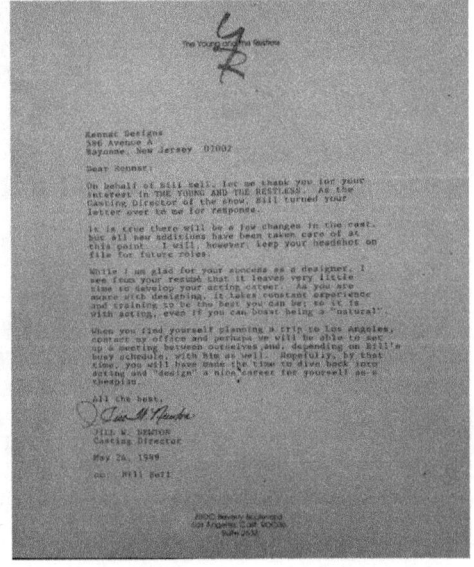

Dear Rennar:

On behalf of Bill Bell, let me thank you for your interest in THE YOUNG AND THE RESTLESS. As the Casting Director of the show, Bill turned your letter over to me. for response.

It is true there will be a few changes in the cast, but all new additions have been taken care of at this point. I will, however, keep your headshot on file for future roles.

While I am glad for your success as a designer, I see from your resume that it leaves little time to develop your acting career. As you are aware with designing, it takes constant experience and training to be the best you can be; so it is with acting, even if you can boast being a "natural."

When you find yourself planning a trip to Los Angeles, contact my office and perhaps we will be able to set up a meeting between ourselves and, depending on Bill's busy schedule, with him as well. Hopefully, by that time, you will have made the time to dive back into acting and "design" a nice career for yourself as a thespian.

All the best,

Jill W. Newton
Casting Director
May 24, 1989

For the time being, I would keep designing clothes. The business was evolving. Our designs began to reach more boutiques. Something unexpected happened, something that would end up being the most meaningful part of my entire fashion career. Boutique owners started to ask me if I could make my designs in sizes 1X through 3X. I thought, why not? It was an underserved market. A new challenge. An invitation to create something more inclusive. Within months, I became known not only for my signature styles, but for plus size fashion as well. Eventually I was designing sportswear, dresses, and evening gowns up to size 8X, because every woman deserved to feel beautiful. And then came Rosemary.

When I first met Rosemary, I realized I needed two tape measures stapled together in order to take her measurements. Her hips measured 108 inches, and when I walked completely around her, in a large circle, she didn't flinch. She laughed. So, I laughed.

We were just two people in the room making something happen together. Brought together for a reason. I designed several custom pieces for Rosemary including the dress she was eventually buried in. She was one of the kindest, warmest people I had ever met, and she taught me something I hadn't fully understood until then – fashion wasn't just about clothes, it was about *belonging*. About *seeing* someone and helping them see themselves as beautiful.

I felt a deep kinship with my plus size clients. A realization that I had spent years trying to fit into a world that didn't make *space for me*. So, I knew how they felt. They felt *unseen*. They were never *chosen*. We understood each other in a language that didn't always need words or interpretation. They made me feel special, and I made them feel special. We made each other feel normal and loved. It was an exchange of radiant self-worth.

Diane and I began traveling on the weekends producing fashion shows in hotel ballrooms and convention centers out of state and all over the East Coast. I would take their measurements, sketch custom designs, drape fabric over their bodies, and we would ship orders within two to three weeks. I remembered every woman's name, every color they asked for, every smile they gave me when they saw themselves in the mirror. These women embraced me. They welcomed Diane and me like family. There were hugs and lots of tears, homemade gifts, stories whispered in the dressing rooms – some joyful, some heartbreaking, but always *honest,* always *real.* And then one year at a national plus-size convention they honored me with "Designer of The Year." I stood in front of the ballroom holding a sculpted glass award and accepted this heart-felt award in front of a room full of beautiful, glowing, unapologetic women. And I cried. Not because I had made it in fashion, but because I had created something that mattered. It wasn't a dress for a celebrity, it wasn't a red-carpet moment, this was deeper, this was healing.

I was designing full-time, sketching and sewing and overseeing production. Orders were coming in, dresses were going out, but something in me was still hiding. The thinner I got, the bigger my hair became, like I was trying to balance myself out through volume and artifice. I had gotten to the point where I could no longer finish half of a sandwich. My appetite had all but vanished, swallowed by the pressure, the pace, and the quiet panic I kept hidden. Lucky for me, a clinical hypnotherapist

(1989)

had an office right across the street from our factory. I didn't even know what hypnotherapy was, but I walked in desperately in need of help. After three sessions something clicked. I could eat again. Not much, but enough to keep going.

Diane and I kept praying for miracles. We would light candles and talk to the ceiling, the heavens, whispering hopes into the space above our heads late at night when the cash flow was tight and the phone calls from boutiques grew colder. Every time we felt like giving up, some small miracle would come our way.

The early '90s had an energy, a buzz that made everything feel possible, but the recession that started in '89 hit us hard. Home interest rates were nearly 14%. Boutiques began taking longer and longer to pay. Ninety days. Sometimes more. Sometimes never.

After ten years of designing and manufacturing for stores that couldn't – or wouldn't pay on time, we made a bold decision that we would open our own boutiques. One in Bayonne, and one down in Manalapan. This way we could cut out the middleman and sell directly to our own customers and produce what was needed on our own terms.

Rennar Boutique – Bayonne, NJ (1993)

One afternoon Diane was getting a manicure at a local nail salon in Bayonne, just a regular weekday indulgence, when she overheard a small group of people talking about a film that was going to be shot in town. Instantly Diane could tell they weren't from the neighborhood, their tone, their energy was different, curious. Industry people. Her manicurist leaned in and whispered, "It's a movie with Demi Moore, Bruce Willis and Harvey Keitel. It's called *Mortal Thoughts*. Can you believe it? They are shooting right here in town."

Demi Moore. This was right after *Ghost* – she was America's obsession. And Bruce Willis? Still at the top of his *Die Hard* fame. Diane, never one to let an opportunity walk past her, turned to the group and introduced herself with grace and confidence. "I own a clothing company, and my husband is a clothing designer," she said. "Can I show you our line?" As fate would have it, she wasn't talking to just anyone – she was speaking directly to the location scout and the costume designer. Diane called me from the salon with urgency in her voice. "Get over here *now*. Bring two garment bags filled with your best designs. They want to see them ASAP."

I threw the bags together and hand delivered them to the salon. The next day, the phone rang. It was the costume designer.

"Demi loved your designs," she said. "We're looking for a real Bayonne feel, and you nailed it."

That was the beginning.

Rennar Designs ended up creating many of the specialized wardrobe pieces for the film, including the shirt that Demi's character wears when she murders Bruce Willis' character in the film. Diane and I were even invited, along with our two boys, her cousin, and a few people from our team, to be extras. There we were on a real film set, watching scenes unfold between Demi Moore and her real-life husband, Bruce Willis, wearing our designs.

During one break in filming, I saw a father approach Bruce Willis with his young son of maybe six or seven, an extra for the film. "He's a big fan," the father said. "Would you mind signing an autograph for him?" Bruce, deep in conversation, or still deep into character, barely looked at them and replied simply, "No," then, turned his back to finish his conversation. The man and his young son walked away. I remember thinking that maybe he was just staying in character.

Meanwhile, Diane was working behind the scenes in her own way. She had become Demi's secret fitting model. I would fit all of Demi's clothing to Diane's body first before bringing them to the set. We were in our glory. Demi Moore was kind, radiant, and gracious. She talked to us a few times on the set. Her character was pregnant in certain scenes in the film, and I created a maternity outfit for her that ended up in *The National Enquirer.* I even designed a custom mother-daughter look for Demi and her baby *Scout,* who she had given birth to a few months before filming.

So many magical exciting things were beginning to happen. One afternoon while I was in the Bayonne factory, the phone rang. A woman on the other end introduced herself saying she had just been to the Manalapan boutique and had fallen in love with a black velvet dress. The one with the gold metallic patches of the sun, moon, and stars. She wanted to know if I designed custom orders and if I could make a matching mother-daughter dress with a matching velvet hat for her daughter-in-law and her two-year-old granddaughter.

"Of course," I said. "Tell me more."

She went on to explain that her son adored celestial symbols. He loved the sun, the moon, and the stars. They're special to him," she said.

I thought to myself, that's nice.

She wanted the dresses in time for their family Thanksgiving dinner, for her daughter-in-law, *Dorothea* and her two-year-old granddaughter, *Stephanie*.

Something memorable. Something magical.

As I began to fill out our order form, I asked her name.

"Carol," she said. "Carol Bon Jovi."

I laughed, thinking I was clever. "Oh! So, I guess you're related to *the* Jon Bon Jovi?"

"Yes," she replied matter-of-factly. *"I'm his mother."*

I nearly fell off my desk chair.

She chuckled and then said, "When the dresses are finished, would you mind delivering them to Jon's private office in Fords, New Jersey?"

"There's no signage," she added quickly. "It's unmarked. Secret. I trust you won't share the location. We don't need a bunch of groupies showing up."

"Of course," I said. She had no way of knowing that I was good at keeping secrets. "Not a word."

But as soon as I hung up, I screamed for Diane.

We danced around the factory floor like kids who had just won the lottery. We couldn't believe it. This was one of those magical moments. A tiny miracle. The ones that were always wished for in moments of desperation. The universe was always listening to us.

A week later, Diane and I drove to Fords, New Jersey, hearts pounding like teenagers sneaking backstage. We had the velvet dresses hanging from the hook in the back seat. All we had was an address scribbled on a note, and the promise that there'd be no sign and no address on the door.

The building was tucked away in an ordinary neighborhood. We got out of the car and stood in front of what looked like nothing at all. Certainly not a place that Jon Bon Jovi would be working out of. It looked like an ordinary two-family house. No number, no name. Just a door. And so, like some fashion-fairy tale, we gave the secret *knock-knock*.

Just then, the door creaked open.

Standing there was Carol Bon Jovi herself.

She greeted us like old friends, ushering us inside, first checking that no one had followed us.

The year was 1995, and the music world was reeling in the headlines. Michael Jackson had been accused of child sexual abuse, and Carol didn't mince words. "I *absolutely* think he did it," she said without hesitation, her voice thick with conviction. "Of course he did it." Diane glanced at me, eyes wide. Carol Bon Jovi was outspoken, no question about it.

At some point, Diane asked her the question that anyone would ask the mother of a rock icon. "Did you always know your son was going to be famous?"

Carol didn't blink.

"I knew it in the womb." We believed her.

Then, somewhere between the laughter and stories, she shifted into business mode. She told us that Jon and his drummer, Tico Torres, were planning to launch a baby clothing line for their fan base. They already had a name – *Rock Baby*. They wanted something cool and edgy. "Would you be interested," she asked, "Designing and manufacturing the line?"

It was tempting.

After thinking it over for a few days, I declined the offer. I wasn't passionate about designing and manufacturing children's clothes. Carol gave us passes to see Jon perform at *The Supper Club* in Manhattan. I made a blanket coat to give to Jon's wife, Dorothea, that night. I'm not sure if she ever received it. It would not have been the first time we gifted a coat to a rock star's wife. In 1993, we made a blanket coat with piano keys on it and gave it to Christie Brinkley at Billy Joel's *River of Dreams Tour* concert at Madison Square Garden. We never heard from Christie Brinkley either.

A few years after the film, the miracles kept rolling in. The costume designer from *Mortal Thoughts* had a friend who happened to be the costume designer working on a new HBO show that no one could stop talking about – *The Sopranos*. She selected a few of our designs for the show including a two-piece plus-size outfit for Ginny Sack to wear during the funeral scene for her husband Johnny Sack. But then there was more.

One afternoon, another one of those magical phone calls came into our Bayonne factory. The line was crackly, the voice faint and rushed, almost breaking up entirely. A young Italian woman was speaking in broken English, clearly nervous and trying her best to communicate something extraordinary. From what I could piece together, she had heard about our plus size designs. Word had traveled overseas, and she was calling to invite us to Northern Italy to produce a fashion show for plus-sized women. She explained that the event was called the *International Grassoni* and it had become something of a legend. Her grandfather, their famously portly, charismatic restaurateur, owned a renowned establishment in the village of Cavour, where he hosted an outrageous tradition – a twenty-course feast for guests that had come across Italy and countries near and far. And then, this is true – after dessert, he would weigh everyone on the giant meat scale set up in the middle of the piazza. The man and woman who gained the most weight during the meal would be crowned *Mr. and Miss International Grassoni*. It was surreal. It was like producing my own film. Part John Waters. Part Fellini.

They flew all eight of us, Diane, me and our team of full-figured models, along with racks of our best designs, across the Atlantic. We were put up in a *villa-style hotel* with balconies that overlooked the manicured gardens of Piemonte.

The show was to take place in the heart of the piazza, and by the time we arrived, word had spread. The entire town was buzzing. Hundreds of Italians filled the piazza shoulder to shoulder, umbrellas in hand because it was pouring rain. The funny thing was, I had recorded the soundtrack for the fashion show, and the opening song was *"It's Raining Men by The Weather Girls."* The music began when the first model stepped onto the runway. Diane had attached silver tinsel-streamers to

black umbrellas as the models took to the runway. It was magical. One of the top plus-sized models in the States was a friend of ours named Nancy Goddess. I had designed Nancy a special outfit to wear. It was a Navy Blue two-piece slinky pant suit, with the word FAT across her chest in red, white, and blue sequins. The crowd went wild. But the finale was the best part. During one of the Boutique Shows in Manhattan at Jacob Javits, Diane bartered with a company from LA that made six-foot *angel wings* that you strap on with velcro. They were *magnificent*. Diane had found a perfect place for them, half-way around the world, in Northern Italy, having gotten them through customs in a twin-size mattress box for the finale of our show.

The sun cut through the gray clouds like a spotlight, pouring down in warm golden beams. The umbrellas came down. Cue the music – Enya's *Caribbean Blue*. Patricia, our beautiful African American plus-sized model was our finale. In a gold lamé gown with long exaggerated fluted sleeves. Pat – six feet tall – was a bona fide miracle walking out onto the stage with the angel wings strapped onto her shoulders. The crowd started cheering. Some threw their hands up in the air and clapped wildly, some cried as if they had witnessed a miracle. We knew that it was exactly *that*.

There we were, in the middle of a medieval town in Italy, showing our boldest, most joyful, most unapologetic designs on radiant plus-sized women who were told their whole lives they weren't allowed to shine. The show was a wild success. It was covered by *RAI International* and *Marie Claire*. From Bayonne to Cavour, we had brought our vision to life. And then...9/11, when everything changed – again.

The economy took another hit, and we felt it immediately. Business abruptly stopped. Weddings were postponed. Luxury spending had dried up. It became clear that we could no longer sustain the factory space we had once filled with so much fabric and ambition. So, we made the difficult decision to downsize, this time with the quiet understanding that I was intentionally working my way *out of business*.

We moved for our sixth and final time into a small design studio in Bayonne. I modeled it after a charming boutique Diane and I had seen years earlier on a trip to Rome – simple, but elegant. A couture shop. This time, I focused on what I loved most – gowns and evening wear for all sizes, for real women with stories and shapes worth celebrating.

And then, just when we thought the story was winding down, magic walked through our door once again. Literally. We never even had to leave Bayonne. The magic always found us. One afternoon, the producers of *MTV'S "True Life"* reality television show strolled into our boutique. The producer said that they were filming a new episode, a two-hour special called *"I'm a High School Senior,"* following two teenagers, one from Queens, and one from Bayonne High School, as they navigate the road to prom. The producers asked if I would design the gown for the Bayonne girl. Of course, I said yes.

What none of us expected was that the episode would turn out to be one of the top five funniest *True Life* episodes that year. It had everything – fashion, drama, teenage angst, big dreams, and even bigger personalities. Enter the angry father that marched with his family and *Promzilla* daughter to our boutique to beat me up because he disapproved of his daughter's less than appropriate prom dress. I gave her the gown of her dreams and gave MTV plenty of quotable moments. And then suddenly, I was famous. With teenagers.

Everywhere I went, they recognized me.

One weekend, Diane and I were down the Jersey Shore. I stopped into a liquor store to grab a bottle of wine for dinner, and as I walked out, I noticed a group of teenage boys and girls on the corner, whispering, pointing, laughing, not in a mean way, but in a *"You're someone"* kind of way.

At first, I panicked.

Did I sit in something? Was my shirt inside out?

But when I got to the corner, one of them blurted out, "Yo! You're the designer from *MTV True Life!*"

Another kid yelled, "Oh my God, can I have your autograph?"

There I was, standing outside a liquor store, pen in hand, signing napkins and pieces of paper like I was Tom Ford. It was absolutely hilarious. And once again, the universe changed the business, and it had reshaped itself. We had an incredible prom business for the next few years. But then came 2002, and everything I thought I had buried, had begun to unexpectedly rise to the surface.

Chapter 28

I was sitting on my couch, remote in hand, channel surfing when the news broke.

The Boston Globe had just published an explosive investigation exposing decades of child sexual abuse by Roman Catholic Priests, covered up by the highest ranks of the Church. The screen was filled with footage of press conferences, shattered families, yellowed yearbook photos of boys who had been sexually abused.

I froze.

I stared at the television, not blinking, barely breathing, as a strange dizzying panic rose in my chest. How could this be possible? For twenty-six years, I had convinced myself that what happened to me was isolated. A one-time tragedy, a one-time story that I had built my entire survival around. That I was the *only* one.

And now this?

There had been others?

The reports kept coming. The victim stories. The patterns. The timelines. The names of priests, dioceses, bishops – all confirming what I had spent a lifetime refusing to name. I couldn't believe what I was seeing and hearing. I had managed to compartmentalize what had happened with Keith Pecklers and Fr. Tom, filing it away in some dark, silent drawer inside of me. I had never fully acknowledged it – not to myself, not to anyone. I had never called it what it was because I was not ever sure of what it was. Not until now.

Now, with every word that flashed across the screen, it was unavoidable. Unforgiving. Undeniable. I wasn't alone. And somehow, that realization – that I was just one of many – was almost as devastating as the abuse itself. I wasn't special after all. I was just Keith Brennan, a boy with a secret that was no longer just his own. One voice in a growing chorus of boys who had been silenced. One name among a growing wreckage.

Later that afternoon, the phone rang. It was my father. His voice was heavy, unsteady, as if he wasn't sure he should say what he was about to say.

"Did you…see the news?" he asked softly

I didn't answer right away.

"Yes." I couldn't speak beyond that.

Dad stayed on the phone with me as we both listened to the breaking story on the television.

The news cycle hadn't let up since that morning. It was breaking news all day on every channel. And then every newspaper and magazine cover. It was all there. The veil had been ripped away.

The Vatican knew.

The Pope knew.

They had covered it up.

For decades.

And I sat there, watching it all unfold from my couch – alone.

Numb.

I kept waiting for the shock to wear off, for the ache in my chest to announce itself with a name. But it didn't. It lingered, heavy and invisible. Twenty-six years ago, I had managed to lock it all away. I had sealed it behind layers of success, creativity, and careful forgetting. For years I had told myself what happened with Fr. Tom wasn't abuse, it was a relationship. He loved me. That's what I clung to. That was the story that I told myself in my own mind in order to survive. But the news was unrelenting. And with every new detail, the lie I had lived, began to rise to the surface.

It was not love.

Not a relationship.

It was abuse.

Suddenly, what Sister Martha had said to me decades earlier began to make perfect, terrifying sense. I was *triggered* – there was now a name for it. My mind dragged me back, uninvited, to that night in Fr. Tom's suite at the rectory. It had been the four of us – Fr. Tom, Fr. Frank, Sr. Martha, and me. The room smelled of Tom's cologne, cigarettes, and red wine. I was important. Special. Tom had put on a record, and I remembered feeling chosen to be with the three of them. Like I had earned my place in their circle. Their coven.

I drank what they handed me. Tom and Fr. Frank taking turns making me drinks. I smoked what they lit. And I danced for them.

The sweat rolled off my forehead and neck down to my chest, my shirt – unbuttoned to my navel. Tom leaned back with his drink. Fr. Frank pulled me in. They smiled, nodded, and pulled me closer. I told myself that it was okay. That I was in control. That I was lucky to be there. Fr. Frank's black clergy shirt was half-unbuttoned, the white tab-collar slipped out and dangling. Beneath it, a thin white wife-beater that clung to his chest, his black curly chest hair sprouting from the top of his tank top. He reminded me of James Caan with darker hair. He pulled me in by my belt strap to dance on his lap. I could feel him through his black trousers. The room was hot. And spinning.

I wanted Fr. Frank and Sr. Martha to like me. I wanted their approval. I would have danced for Sr. Martha if she had wanted me to. I wanted to please them. So, I danced.

At one point I made my way to Tom's bathroom and pulled the vial of *Rush* from the front pocket of my jeans. I huffed the liquid gold incense – one nostril, then the other. In two seconds, the high hit and I was right where I needed to be. My brain fizzled and my vision blurred at the edges. I peed, then rinsed my hands, gripping the porcelain sink to steady myself. My breathing came in short, heavy bursts, like my heart was pumping overtime – too much for a fifteen-year-old. I reached for my aluminum comb and slicked back my hair, glancing at my reflection in the mirror.

I looked like a ghost in a boy's body.

My face was flushed and sweaty. My eyes were sunken and dark-ringed. Pimples flared across my chin. My white button-down was damp, clinging to me, unbuttoned all the way down to my concave stomach. Sweat rolled down the middle of my chest. I opened the bathroom door and Sr. Martha was waiting in the doorway.

She startled me.

She blocked the doorway with her stocky frame, arms folded tight across her broad chest and back. Her eyes studied me with disgust.

"Sister," I slurred. "Do you need to use the bathroom?"

She didn't answer me.

I stood in the door jam, doped and dripping sweat.

Instead, she smirked like she knew something I didn't and said, *"You're not the only one."*

Her voice was calm and detached. Not kind.

I stood frozen. Everything about her – her stance, her tone – suddenly reminded me of the weekend away at the cabin. The way she barely tolerated me. The way she spoke to me through clenched teeth. It all made sense.

Sr. Martha reminded me of Lucas and Noah's mother, the German twins from Union City, who once served me boiled hot dogs, watery beans, and gray boiled potatoes with such visible contempt I couldn't eat. She hated me. Sr. Martha had that same energy. That same cold, clipped judgement. Like a prison warden from a movie set in East Berlin.

It didn't fully register – not until now, decades later, standing in front of my TV, watching this horror unfold. Her message to me suddenly reverberated in my head.

"You are not the only one. You are not the only one."

And then, like a light switching on in a pitch-black room another face came rushing into my mind.

Ricky.

His twelve-year-old frail pre-pubescent body standing in front of me at Our Lady of Perpetual Help, with Tom's arm around his small shoulders. His freckles. His braces.

The puzzle pieces were clicking into place. And what they were showing me was far worse than anything I had let myself believe. I *wasn't* alone. And none of us were special. We were used for sexual gratification. It would take another five years. Five long, disorientating years of silence, confusion, and screaming headlines before I found the courage to use my own voice. It happened by accident.

I was flipping through channels, not looking for anything in particular, when suddenly – there he was. Fr. Keith Pecklers. His face filled the screen. He wore his priest collar, his hair perfectly groomed, his expression calm and calculated. He was being interviewed by Dan Harris on *ABC News,* introduced as an expert on Vatican Affairs. I froze. The remote slipped from my hand.

Pecklers was speaking about the Pope's visit. About

"*moving on*" from the sexual abuse crisis. He called it a scandal. They were still calling it a *crisis*. Like it was some financial white-collar crime, a bad PR moment. *"Moving on?"* This was the systematic rape of children – and no one was saying it, calling it out for what it was. And he – Fr. Keith Pecklers, having become the world's foremost authority on the liturgy, a theology scholar, was sitting on national television, cloaked in false authority, pretending.

Pretending that he was above it.

Pretending to be clean.

Pretending to speak from some place of moral clarity and authority. When in fact, he was the very thing they were all pretending to condemn.

I couldn't breathe.

I could feel my stomach turn, acid rising in my throat. My hands clutched the arm of the chair so tightly. I wanted to throw something through the TV. I wanted to scream. I wanted to reach through the screen and choke him. I wanted to scream that I knew what he had done to me. That I remembered every detail.

By 2005, I was done waiting for justice to come on its own. I had to make it happen. I decided to close *Rennar Designs* – twenty-five years was long enough. The kids were grown, and I was truly done with designing clothes. What had once thrilled me, now felt like a weight I no longer wanted to carry. The industry had changed. Fast fashion and cheap overseas productions were flooding the market. It became clear the Golden Age of our brand had passed. And then there were the wedding parties. The endless parade of young women I designed for – glowing, demanding, starry-eyed – only to get the call two months later – "I'm pregnant." And there I was, starting the gown all over again, like we were living in a custom couture version of *Groundhog Day*. People began bargaining with me like I was running a flea market booth. "I only need it for one night," they'd say. "Can you make it for $150?" To which I'd smile and say, "Well I'm only designing it once." I had reached my limit. It was time to listen to that voice that had been growing louder inside me telling me I was meant to do something else, something that mattered more.

I had discussed with Billy that I wanted to bring charges against Keith Pecklers and Fr. Tom Stanford. I wanted to hold them accountable, not just them – but the church that protected them. That made room for what they did to me. Billy looked at me, quiet for a moment, then said gently, "Keith, the statute of limitations ran out over thirty-years ago. They will laugh you out of the room." Still, he promised to look into it. I told him I needed to speak with an attorney who handled this kind of thing. I didn't even fully know what *this kind of thing* was. I still believed, in some distant bruised part of me, that fifteen-year-old part of me, that Fr. Tom had loved me. That maybe I had been complicit. Maybe I had asked for it. Maybe I misunderstood everything. The shame hadn't loosened its grip yet. But something inside me had shifted just enough to speak the words out loud, and once I did, I couldn't un-say them.

Chapter 29

After closing Rennar Designs, I took six months off to decompress from running a fashion business for twenty-five years, and then was prompted by Diane's Aunt Cookie, who worked at Neiman Marcus in Short Hills, to apply for a position in their couture department. In 2005, I had no idea what Neiman Marcus was, I just knew that it was expensive. Neiman Marcus was my first adult job at forty-two years old. I also decided once and for all to use Rennar as my first name, having always felt detached from my first name because of Keith Pecklers. My own name was a trigger. I was hired at Neiman Marcus in Short Hills as a specialist for a German couture label.

One day Billy called me at work – and I knew it must be important. I had asked Billy a few weeks earlier to help find me an attorney to talk to about bringing Pecklers and Stanford to justice. Billy explained what he knew the law to be, after all, Billy had become a successful trial attorney. He reminded me of the cold, hard, truth of the matter.

"They are just going to laugh at you. You have no case. The statute of limitations ran out over thirty years ago."

"I understand what you are telling me Billy, but I need to just find someone that I can tell my story to. I want them to know that I have not forgotten a single day."

Billy was calling me to follow through on his promise. He was able to set up a meeting with an attorney named Stephen Rubino, located in Margate, New Jersey. I remember thinking that Margate hardly sounded like the place a successful child sex abuse attorney would have his office.

The ride to Margate would be the most amount of time that Billy and I had ever spent alone together. Over the years, Billy and I grew to have an understanding of what had happened to us growing up. The clergy abuse was the icing on the cake. We realized that our parents had pitted us against each other and that we didn't stand a chance of ever having a close relationship. Once we realized the family dynamic we had grown up in, and realized that we were not to blame as to how we felt about each other, we began to like each other and learn about who we were. We had even vacationed together with our wives.

To meet the attorney in Margate, I wore a navy blue on blue striped suit with a white button-down French-cuff dress shirt. My tie was red, cobalt blue, and black, with a wide chunky diamond pattern. My cufflinks were silver brushed nickel rectangles with half-circle polished nickel shapes, and my shoes were polished. I was perfectly groomed as usual. The ride was long from Bayonne, but it gave Billy and I a chance to discuss what I should expect from the meeting.

The attorney introduced himself to me and Billy and told

us that he represented victims of clergy sexual abuse. He asked me to tell him my story. I was prepared. I was a Brennan. I had lived it over and over for the past thirty-two years. I remembered every detail. When I was done telling Mr. Rubino what had happened to me at the hands of Keith Pecklers and Fr. Tom, he looked at me and said, "That's one of the worst cases I've heard."

For a second, I thought he was just trying to make me feel special, but deep down, I knew he wasn't. He was telling the truth. And for the first time in my life, someone else had named it as *clergy sexual abuse of a minor.*

It was the second time Billy had heard some of the details of what had happened to me. The first time was in the Keeping Room when I had confessed what Pecklers had done to me, but this was the first time anyone had ever heard me speak out loud about the things that Fr. Tom had done to me. At the end of our forty-five minute meeting, Steve handed me a stack of papers held together by a black binder clip. It looked serious. He explained that it was a client intake form for survivors of childhood sexual abuse. Steve asked me to have it back to him in a week.

INTAKE FORM CONTINUED

31. Why are you talking about the abuse now?

I am talking now because it has taken 30 years to become mentally, emotionally, physically, and spiritually strong enough to do so. Also, I owned my own business and was a public figure within our community. I needed to stay focused and raise our two sons and take care of my family. I've only realized within the past 2 years the full extent of my injury. The first 10 years I blocked it out and shelved it somewhere. The second decade I thought I was equally responsible for what had happened to me. It took 25 years to realize that my abusers were adults and that I was a child. The last 2 years I've come to realize all that was taken from my life that can never be replaced. After I closed my business in 2005, everything began to rise to the surface.

PART III – SUPPORTIVE EVIDENCE

32. Do you have supportive evidence, please describe that evidence.

Letters, photos.

Keith Pecklers: Pecklers has a distinguishing physical characteristic to his penis. Besides being ▬▬▬▬▬▬, his erect penis has a severe bend half-way up. I remember being shocked. It seemed abnormal and grotesque.

PART IV - DAMAGES

33. What effect has the abuse you suffered from had upon:

(a) Your educational performance and the academic qualifications you have obtained.

The important formative years in high school that I should have been preparing for college were taken away from me. They cannot be replaced. The sexual abuse at the hands of Pecklers and Fr. Tom Stanford crippled me physically and emotionally. I could not concentrate on high school and resorted to cheating in order to pass my grades. I was a bright kid, charismatic and intelligent. I should be very successful at this point in my life. They were like a disease, and their abuse nearly killed me. I chose to rely on the only thing I had before the abuse began. I was a creative child and after my abuse, with no education or training, I started my own business with $100 blood, sweat, and tears, and became a fashion designer. Moderately successful, I produced my own label, RENNAR, which is my mother's maiden name. At 20 years old, I changed my name to Rennar. It had always upset me that my first abuser and I shared the same name. I felt triggered every time someone called me Keith. For the past 25 years I have been called Rennar.

(b) Your Employment history and career success.

My business and career has always been a struggle. I've worked with celebrities, film, and television shows and produced fashion shows in Italy, but after 9/11 I could not recover. I had to downsize. In 2005 I closed our business after 25years

(c) Your personal relationships, including friendships, intimate relations, and family relations.

I've never had any male friends since childhood. I am basically a loner and spend free time with my wife and family. I had trust issues with men. I see my parents and brother infrequently at best. I speak with my parents often by phone and have recently become closer with my brother.

(d) Your medical and psychological health, and your prospects in this regard for the future.

I went through many years of suicidal thoughts. I developed an eating disorder and anorexia. I have photos. I did not seek any medical treatment. My strong faith in God and the support of my wife Diane have enabled me to survive in spite of such evil that enveloped my life for years. I believed that Fr. Pecklers and Fr. Tom had given me AIDS. For 10 years I lived in fear, too afraid to get tested, embarrassed. This was at the beginning of when the world began to hear about AIDS. There were reports that the incubation period could be up to 10 years. I also suffered sexual intimacy issues and sexual dysfunction. I am completely fine now. I have suffered severe anxiety and depression. I self-mutilated during the abuse and used drugs.

34. **Treatment:** Have you received medical, psychiatric and/or psychological treatment for the abuse?

I went to a Hypnotherapist for my eating disorder. She was able to help me relax enough so that I could eventually eat half a sandwich.

In 1980, after the abuse ended, I went twice to a psychologist. She was located near Ramapo College. I never brought up the abuse. I spoke about my anxiety and depression.

PLEASE RETURN WHEN COMPLETE

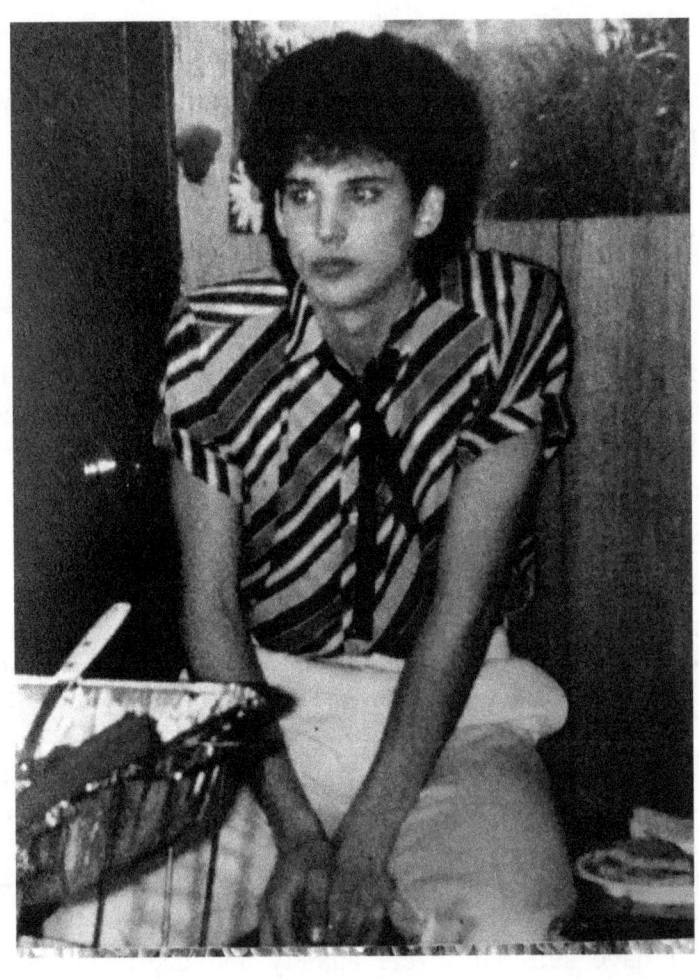

I found that once I began writing, that I could not stop. I could not put my pen down. It felt less like I was composing and more like I was channeling something that had been locked away for years. Thankfully, my mother had kept a few of my letters that I had written to her during the years I was being abused by Tom. Reading through letters and photos that were decades old felt as if I was peering into a time capsule – at a version of myself that I barely recognized. They turned out to be invaluable to me. Not because they were poetic or profound, just the opposite. They were pathetic, embarrassing, raw and painfully honest. They show someone who has survived horrific abuse. Someone who had been struggling to make sense of the impossible. Someone who was vulnerable, confused, exposed, and desperate for love. Desperate for escape. The letters were eye-opening. Disturbing. The authenticity and documentation of a boy, me, in odious words that scream pain and conflict. I can now read through the blurred lines of love and manipulation. I can see a boy who thought that he had everything in control but had been *"controlled"* all along. I see the indoctrination, the trauma, the need to be chosen. The need to be loved. I see the confusion, the panic, the sadness of misplaced devotion. The overwhelming weight of shame. And yet I see resilience, and the beginning of survival. I see a boy who refused to completely disappear, no matter how much evil was sent his way. These writings were proof. Proof that I had survived, proof of my own unfiltered voice from a past that I was no longer hiding. A voice that was becoming stronger.

12/27/79
Dearest Mom,

"If I can lend a helping hand to you my friend, and understand your need, and give it to you – a surety of friendship true,

I'll be content.

If I can share with you a grief, and help you see it at its brief; If I can hold your hand in mine through moments of a testing time,

I'll be content.

If I can guide you to the place of prayer, where by his matchless grace your soul will be restored and blessed, where God can do for you the rest,

I'll be content"

~Roselyn C. Steere

I'm writing in the living room and just thought that I would write you a few words, a few feelings. You know Mom I think about you often; sometimes I wonder if a little too much, but I guess one can never think about one's mother too much. I'm not sure exactly what the direction that this letter is going, but I'll just keep writing, ok?

I remember one Saturday afternoon in New York with Diane. We were sitting outside at a cafe drinking soda and we were talking about parents, and more specifically about mothers. I began to talk to her about you and our relationship, our "friendship." I told her that we discuss many problems and needs we have, and that we often go shopping together, out to lunch, and even go to movies together. When I was done, she said, "You sure have a strange relationship with your mother. Not many kids go to lunch, shopping, and movies like you do." Not many kids can say that they're friends with their mothers, but I can. Can you believe that I had to actually explain to Diane that I wasn't ashamed to admit it either? Don't get me wrong, she likes you and knows what a good concerned parent you are, but she found it hard to understand our relationship.

What it comes down to is that I guess good relationships are hard to understand because not too many people have them with their friends or even their "mothers."

So, it seems I have two relationships that no one seems to understand; you and Fr. Tom. You know that even Daddy has trouble understanding our relationship at times I think. I know that you do not like Fr. Tom spending money on me, but the way I look at it is that I try to give him things that money can't buy; like hope, discussing his problems that he sometimes has in his ministry. I try to be a good friend to him. His way of reciprocating is often to take me out to dinner and go out. He enjoys it and likes to be with me because I like to keep going out and having fun, like going to New York and stuff.

Fr. Tom is a fantastic person and one great friend who would never try to hurt me.

Back to you Mom, I worry about you very much. You're very important in my life and I like seeing you happy. We have a unique relationship too. Don't we? It's not so strange, is it? Things will work out with Dad. Don't be so hard on him. He's a good father and provider.

Read what Tom gave you, accept his good and his bad.

I have to go now, but remember Mom, I need you, and I hope that you always need me.

And remember, I'm always there for my "friends"

Love your son,

Keith

I continued writing until all thirty-six questions were answered to the best of my ability. I knew I had to release the client intake form, but only after I re-read it a hundred times.

Two weeks later, I met Billy in the parking lot of the mall. I was working, but I had something to show him. I got into his new burgundy Cadillac, breathed in the new car smell of leather, and handed him the letter that Stephen Rubino had drafted based on my client intake form. This letter, when complete, would officially put the Archdiocese of Newark and The Society of Jesus on notice.

Billy took it from my hand and read it through in silence, his face giving nothing away, and then, after a long pause, said "I thought it was going to be worse."

"*Worse?* How could it possibly have been *worse?*" I responded while trying to restrain myself from jumping through the windshield.

"Well, at least it wasn't anal." Billy said this matter of factly, like he was talking to Star Jones while working on a sex crime case at the Brooklyn D.A.'s office. "Billy Boy, you sure look sharp today." Star would say.

Billy had heard it all while working as Brooklyn's Assistant District Attorney in his earlier career days before making partner at his law firm. He prosecuted sex crimes. I was more interested that he had worked with Star Jones. *The View* was one of my favorite shows.

The air inside Billy's Cadillac felt thick like a vacuum now. The oxygen had been sucked out of it. I could feel my pulse in my throat. My first instinct was to agree with Billy like he had a valid point, but then I came to my senses.

"Well, it's still pretty fucking bad." I manage to respond while frantically rereading the letter, my eyes darting to certain parts, to horrific paragraphs, to words that never should have been written in the same sentence as *fourteen-year-old boy*. Words that I had become desensitized to. Seeing them in print was another story. The words Steve used described the acts of monsters.

I could feel my hands shaking, my body tight and tense. I wanted Pecklers and Stanford to experience the last gift of the Holy Ghost – *The Fear of the Lord*. Because, if they hadn't feared Him before, they were going to *now* if I had anything to do with it. I wanted revenge. An eye for an eye. A tooth for a tooth.

Billy looked me straight into my eyes. "I know that I have already told you this, but I want you to know that if something like this had happened to me as well, I would have told you. I would never have wanted you to go through this alone." I tell Billy that I know this, I believe him. He handed me back the eight-paragraph letter that changed everything in my mind, a mind, which in many cliche ways, had remained that of the fourteen-year-old boy. It was as though I was holding my eighth-grade writing project – *It Happened Like This: Creation according to Keith*. Well, now I've done it. I have exposed myself completely on paper – with my words. I purposely kept the client intake form from Diane. It was graphic, and we had never spoken about the details of what they had done to me. Diane never asked and I never offered. I read Stephen Rubino's letter more than a hundred times, nearly the number of times that I had been abused by Fr. Tom and Keith Pecklers. How could a teenage boy survive this without becoming a drug addict or killing himself? It was a miracle that I was alive.

Stephen C. Rubino LLC
Attorney at Law

2302 Atlantic Avenue
Margate, New Jersey 08402

(609) 555-0473
FAX (609) 555-6229

April 18, 2008

Most Reverend John J. Meyers, J.C.D., D.D.
Archbishop of Newark
Archdiocesan Center
171 Clifton Avenue
P.O Box 9500
Newark, N.J. 07104-9500

Superior General, Father Adolfo Nicolas, S.J.
% New York Providence of the Society of Jesus
39 East 83rd Street
New York, N.Y. 10028

Reverend David S. Ciancimino, S.J.
Provincial of New York Province of the Society of Jesus
39 East 83rd Street
New York, N.Y. 10028

Dear Archbishop Myers, Father General Nicolas and Reverend Ciancimino:

I represent Keith Brennan with regard to a sexual assault committed against him by Father Keith Pecklers, S.J. and Father Thomas A. Stanford. The sexual assaults committed by both of these men occurred during 1976-1980. At the time of the assault in 1976, Keith Brennan was 14 years old. Father Pecklers committed his sexual assault against Mr. Brennan during 1976-1977 while he was a lay music director at St. Paul's Parish in Jersey City, New Jersey. Thereafter, Father Stanford as both a deacon and an ordained priest committed a variety of sexual assaults against Mr. Brennan from 1977 through 1980.

The locations of the sexual assaults were varied and included St. Paul's Parish, Our Lady of Perpetual Help, the Brennan's family home, Father Pecklers' home and the home of Father Stanford and Father Frank Maione.

All sexual assaults are odious however sexual assaults against children bring a different level of depravity into the equation. Father Pecklers coerced Keith Brennan into the initial abuse by falsely indicating that his older brother William was also sexually involved with other males. Father Pecklers used force and on several occasions pushed Keith to his knees and held him down in order to have Keith masturbate Father Pecklers whereupon Father Pecklers would ████████████ ████████████████████████████████. The number of these assaults exceeded 50 incidents.

Frequently when perpetrators receive communication like this one, their initial reaction is denial. In order to bring some clarity on the veracity of the allegations contained herein, Mr. Brennan would be happy to discuss in person certain anatomical anomalies with regard to Father Pecklers' penis in the event that he offers such a denial due to his standing and accomplishments as a theologian and scholar.

Father Thomas Stanford's sexual and emotional abuse achieved yet another level of vulgarity. Father Stanford convinced a young teenager that the most significant gift anyone could give God was by making love to another human being and when sex occurred with a priest, Keith Brennan was making love to God Himself. Keith Brennan was made to feel special and blessed in this most exclusive union with Father Tom and His Lord. This grooming was the result of a dark and twisted mind causing lifelong damages. Father Stanford at the time was a resident of St. Paul's Parish as both a deacon and as a curate with the abuse lasting approximately three years.

Sexual abuse included oral sodomy, masturbation, ██ and with Father Stanford's ████████. Father Stanford would ████████████████████ ████████████████████████ Keith Brennan's ████████████████████, onto his body and would force Keith to do the same to Father Stanford.

During one specific incident Father Stanford took Keith Brennan to a shore house in Seaside Park, New Jersey with other priests. Father William Hatcher, Father Thomas Reading and Father William Dowd all questioned Father Stanford as to Mr. Brennan's presence and all of them knew full well that Keith Brennan as a 15 year old teenager was sleeping with Father Stanford in his room.

As you can imagine there is much more detail that Mr. Brennan is prepared to share with regard to the allegations contained in this letter. Keith Brennan's spiritual and emotional devastation over the last 32 years must by laid squarely at the feet of Father Pecklers and Father Stanford and the system which facilitated the seduction and the sexual abuse of a minor. These men used guile, undue influence and manipulation of Keith's emotions to gratify their own sexual needs.

The cost to Keith Brennan has been high including serious emotional and physical sequelae as a result of the abuse, lost education and career opportunities and a wholesale disruption of normal teenage development. While many of these losses are subject to precise statements, the true damages can only be assessed by his tenacious commitment to therapy and healing. Assault of the individual psyche under these circumstances is an issue that we unfortunately continuously have to deal with. Evaluation is always difficult, but not impossible. What is clear however, is the exploitation of a child/parishioner by a person who stands before them in a pastoral role invested with significant authority is a crime of immense proportion. It is an attempt to destroy another life for personal gratification.

Our request is actually quite simple. We wish to meet personally at a convenient location with Father Pecklers and Thomas Stanford, along with their superiors at the time of these abuses. We have no interest in any church entity funding therapy as that has been addressed personally by Mr. Brennan. The legal landscape in New Jersey has indeed changed but our preference at this juncture is to dialog. We do have interest in specifically enumerating both sexual assaults and the impact this has had on Mr. Brennan and his family in order to achieve an economic settlement for these abuse of acts. Over my career many cases at this critical mass seem virtually impossible to amicably resolve. However, over time it has been repeatedly demonstrated that when people confront difficult issues with candor and good faith, resolution can occur. Recently, the archdiocese and I engaged the services of retired Superior Judge Judson Hamlin in resolving another high profile case. We would certainly be willing to undertake a similar process in this case.

Sincerely yours,

Stephen C. Rubino

During the time that Steve was drafting my letter to the Archdiocese and The Society of Jesus, he suggested that we film a video to send to the Archdiocese and Jesuits to accompany the letter. I was excited to make a film. It sounded like it was going to be a real documentary. It also had the air of a horror movie. The drafting of the letter took a couple of weeks, and the filming was arranged by Steve's amazingly empathetic and comforting assistant/paralegal and film guy.

Mommy, Daddy, and Billy would be shot up against the sage-painted paneling in their living room, positioned on their Early American custom upholstered loveseat against Mom's white plantation shutters and slate blue sheared custom made balloon curtains that I hung and stuffed with tissue paper the week they moved in. After fifty years together, Mom and Dad had finally purchased their own home in an adult community My mother had everything that she ever wanted, a happy marriage and second career at the age of sixty-five, in addition to custom made plantation shutters, canvas awnings, seasonal flag poles, and as many goose-egg stones that could surround their double-width mobile home. Mom now kept her personalized note cards and bows carefully coiled and assorted by colors and occasions, tucked into the same antique dry sink where I used to keep my sewing machine back when I was just starting out as a fashion designer, drafting patterns and praying for ideas in the corner of their dining room. That dry sink now also housed her Bose, along with her Il Divo and Andrea Bocelli CDs, stacked perfectly in threes and draped in strands of spring garland. Forty-six years of my life, my dreams and my breakdowns, were about to be reduced to a fifteen-minute interview in a double-wide mobile home in an adult community in Spotswood, New Jersey.

As soon as the camera guy was set up, I could hear Steve's assistant preparing my parents and Billy on what was about to happen. How she will ask a question off-camera and then they are to answer it as best they can. I crept out of Mom and Dad's early American bedroom, adjusting the doll that lived on their bed. I can't remember the doll's name.

At least they were not sleeping on railroad tracks any longer. After sixty years together, they were finally able to work it out. Apparently, they were only miserable raising me and Billy.

I snuck down the 8X4 picture gallery hallway, adorned with at least thirty to forty family photos, custom-framed, with non-glare glass, careful not to alert anyone that I planned on eavesdropping. I was careful not to trip over the woven basket filled with magazines next to Mom's recliner, as I crept into the kitchen. *The Keeping Room* sign was now replaced with *Country Kitchen*. No fighting, crying, screaming, cigarette smoking, cursing, or groping in the Country Kitchen.

But I hid in their kitchen again, nevertheless, like I did when I was four and Mommy was chasing seven-year-old Billy around our apartment dressed as Harpo Marx. Only this time she is chasing a ghost from 1976. The only thing missing is my Dracula cape. This time, I am crouched behind the kitchen wall, up against the counter, under the *Country Kitchen* sign that is hanging six inches above my head. Gone is the whiskey bottle with the pencil drawn line to measure Daddy's Saturday drinking. Gone is the Zenith radio in the walnut wooden box as big as a bread box that played *"More Than the Greatest Love"* sung by Mom and Bobby Darin during our Saturday morning breakfasts that led inevitably to nights of unspeakable terror. Mom and Dad left the Catholic Church after I had told them everything, and a year or so after moving to Spotswood, Mom and Dad became Christians, complete with being baptized by the spirit – in a community pool.

Billy had called me a week before filming to tell me that he did not think that Mom would be able to do it. She had double knee replacement – two months earlier, and her nurse practitioner was still trying to tweak her medication. She had suddenly become depressed.

"Oh she's going to do it." I snapped at him. I needed to have her sit there on her Ethan Allen loveseat, with her hair and make-up perfectly done, and say what had happened to me – out loud and not look away. "I need all of you to do this for me."

Mom turned out to just be passable in her interview. She had no energy behind her words. At least she had words. It triggered me to think about the day of my wedding when Mom lost her voice and could not say a single word. Eventually they all got through the filming. Steve would have the film ready to go out together with his letter in two weeks.

I waited and then got the call that the DVD was ready. Diane and I went to Steve's office to pick it up. He handed me a copy.

"It's gone to their attorneys, to The Society of Jesus, the Jesuits, and to The Archdiocese of Newark." I had read recently that all cases eventually go to Rome and that the Pope was made aware of every case.

I stood there, the DVD in my hand, trying to wrap my head around the fact that my parents' testimony, on a loveseat, shot against the shutters, could now be echoing through the halls of the Holy See. It was unreal.

When the documentary began, I didn't know what to expect. I hadn't seen the edit. I hadn't heard the narration. I didn't even know Steve planned to open the film with a monologue. Fifteen minutes. That's all it was. A tight, concise, gutting sequence of words and decades of old memories, of me, my wife, and family, saying the unsayable. The unthinkable.

My mother's voice, careful and composed despite the uncomfortableness of having to speak the truth. My father's raw quiver. Billy – clear-eyed and heart-heavy. Diane, speaking the truth she had lived alongside me. And me – speaking out loud, in front of a camera, on film, what I had never wanted to believe had happened to the boy I once was. I sat down next to Diane as soon as we returned home, just the two of us, close together, and pressed play on the DVD.

The moment Steve's voice filled the room, I felt a calmness come over me. Steve was a seasoned storyteller, with a compelling tenor. It was as if Richard Dreyfuss or Morgan Freeman had taken the chair beside us, narrating the prologue to a life that had nearly slipped away. There was that same gravity, that same vocal recognition of quiet authority. It was a voice of inescapable truth.

Steve speaks as the camera scans a photograph of St. Paul's Church, from the steeple that I had nearly hung myself in, down to the church grounds, then scanning to the rectory where Tom and Pecklers had abused me. Sacred grounds that felt both cinematic and intimate. There was a secret in Greenville that no one knew about. An evil that had infiltrated the church during the years that I had been abused, and now my voice was going to be heard. I was going to tell my story.

Steve's narration bookended the film like it was a prayer. An invocation at the start, and a benediction at the end. He gave my story a dignity it had never been allowed to have. For thirty-two years I was voiceless. For decades I was on the outside of my own life looking in. But now Steve was giving it shape. Structure. Gravitas. Steve believed that it was worthy of being heard. It was the first time I had ever heard anyone speak the truth of what had happened to me out loud.

Steve: *"Many of us watching this video will have no reference point to the tragedy of early childhood sexual abuse, and in light of that fact, we are handicapped in discussing value. Evaluation is always difficult, sometimes contentious, but never impossible. What is certain, is that the turmoil of this sexual abuse scandal, have left parties teetering between crisis and opportunity. Without consequences, abuses of power are left to fester, putting future generations at risk. Without justice, there can be no accountability. Without accountability, there will never* *be reconciliation with the children of God.*

Recently, Keith Brennan, and members of his family, spoke of his abuse, and its impact to their lives."

Listening to Steve tell the opening of my story was surreal. Almost out-of-body, like he was describing someone else. A case study. A story about a boy I used to know.

Diane reached over and took my hand as we watched the film and I sat there, not moving, just letting it wash over me. All of it. I had only caught glimpses, and heard fragments, bits and pieces of my family's interview as I was hiding in the Country Kitchen while they were being filmed. Seeing it edited, on screen, was something entirely different. And then, the next scene began. The camera shifted from St. Paul's to my mother, her white plantation shutters, her voice gentle, uncertain, but trying to get through this for me.

Mom*: "Keith, as a little boy, he was like short and stubby, and he was just a really enjoyable baby. Keith, as he grew up, made us so proud. He was very creative. Very talented. He sang. He played the guitar. He excelled at everything he did as a young child."*

It hit me in the gut. Where most of my feelings lived. My mother, on tape, talking about the little boy I used to be. The boy *before*.

Then came Daddy, in his Butler, New Jersey country-voice, wrapping around each word in a kind of grief and disbelief.

Dad: *"And this was the way Keith was. When he was growing up, he always had something good to say and enjoyed* life. He had a great talent for music."

It sounded like they were speaking about someone who either had a terrible accident or was dead.

And then Billy.

Billy: *"He was making movies at a very young age. He would always have the kids in the neighborhood dress up in costumes and he would film them, and then we would run back and watch the movies. So, he was always extremely creative. Very fun-loving."*

And there it was – my movies. Billy remembered the movies I made, the costumes, my 8mm films edited in my playroom and then projected against a sheet in Susan's basement with the neighborhood kids. Maybe that's proof, I thought, that I had always wanted to be a filmmaker. I had been searching for decades for who I was meant to be. I felt close to Billy hearing him speak about me like this. It was a miracle that we had been able to heal our relationship.

And then my interview began. I took a deep breath.

Keith: *"The abuse ate away at my soul. I found it difficult to concentrate on anything else. The abuse was the first thing I thought about when I opened my eyes in the morning, and it was the last thing I thought of when I went to sleep. Everything else during my day was just, really just trying to get by. I lived my life like, not that I was in a bubble, but the world was in a bubble, and I was on the outside looking in. I never felt connected to my life once the abuse happened. And once it ended, even more so. I just felt totally disconnected with the world."*

Watching this, as the words leave my mouth, I notice the raw vulnerability etched across my face. I am vulnerable but not weak. I look strong and my voice is more steady than I had imagined it. I am rigid. Thanks Poppy.

Billy: *"He grew very withdrawn, and very quiet. It totally affected my relationship with him. I had no idea what was going on at that time, but he definitely became more distant, more withdrawn, quiet, and... didn't really... (sigh), alright I'll just say it – he really didn't live up to expectations that I think people had, going from this very creative, energetic kid, to this very withdrawn kid. I mean, he – he tried college for a very short period of time and then dropped out of college. He kind of floundered to a certain extent."*

I didn't move. I barely breathed. Billy wasn't wrong, but he didn't know. He couldn't. And I didn't know whether I wanted to cry, or run from the room that Diane and I were watching in. I wished someone could have warned that kid that Billy was talking about – the kid who used to direct and make films in the backyard and write music and books and make elaborate costumes – that something monstrous was about to crawl into his life and make a home.

Billy said I *floundered*. Like it was a flaw.

But *floundering* was how I survived.

What did they expect? That I would bounce right back like a rubber ball?

Floundering wasn't a failure; it was my flotation device.

It was the thrashing that kept me from going under.

It was not-dying.

I didn't have a roadmap for what I had lived through. I didn't even have language for it back then. Hell, I've only just now been able to speak about it. I only had feelings that didn't belong in my body. I was a hundred versions of myself pretending I was okay while quietly unravelling in church pews. You think that I dropped out of college because I didn't care? I dropped out because I couldn't sit still in a room with people talking about the future when I was stuck in the past, in the abuse. I *floundered* because there was no one there to show me how to stand. So yes, I floundered. Through jobs. Through bad ideas. Through the nights that I could not sleep. Through every silent scream. I didn't know that healing was possible then. I had to find true love, my angel, to save me.

Mom was up next.

Mom: *"We noticed a change in him, but you know, we couldn't comprehend what was going on, but he started having these pains in his chest, and feeling sick, and my husband and I discussed it, and he was losing weight and withdrawn looking, and we took him to the doctor and the doctor said, "Oh you know, he is just growing up. These are growing-up pains. He'll be fine. We'll give him some medication and he'll be ok."*

I remember hearing these words while I was eavesdropping during filming. I gripped the edge of the countertop so hard my knuckles went white.

Growing up pains?

Is that what it was called back then, when a boy's body

collapses under the weight of a secret he can't say out loud? When the soul starts shutting off the lights room by room in a house that is no longer safe?

The pills they gave me made me tired. Made me hollow. I remember laying in my bed at night thinking that maybe they were right, maybe this is just what growing up feels like. I mean, at least I wasn't beaten like Billy. Maybe those beatings were Billy's growing up pains. Maybe it was normal. Listening to Mom, I felt somewhat sorry for her that she was in her last chapter of life recounting decades of living in the abstinence of truth. But they didn't know any better. The world we lived in didn't hand parents a handbook on how to recognize the signs of a child being preyed upon. It handed them bottles of pills and told them that boys *"go through growing pains."* They believed that they were doing the right thing. If a doctor or a priest told you something, you believed them. Some things broken inside are difficult to detect.

Keith: *"We were a devout Catholic family. We were taught, basically, to never have sex before marriage, and for something like this to happen, to me, just seemed unbelievable, and it was totally shameful, and there was nobody that I could talk to, and the one person that I did go to confide in was Father Stanford and he talked to Pecklers and got him to stop, or whatever he said to him, only for him to in-turn take over, which to me, was incomprehensible that it could happen.*

The abuse started right as I graduated grammar school, so when I entered high school, that's when the abuse started with

Keith Pecklers. My entire four years at high school were spent in this enormous vacuum of abuse between Pecklers and Stanford. I couldn't concentrate on school at all. I went from being an A-B student to a B-C, and that was with cheating. I had to literally cheat my way through high school, because I just could not function and think. The years that I should have been thinking about my future and thinking about what college that I wanted to go to, and normal things that a kid fifteen, sixteen, and seventeen should be thinking about, were taken away from me. So, by the time that I graduated high school, I was such an emotional wreck that I had no idea what my future was going to be."

I sat beside Diane in the living room. I felt like I was watching a stranger narrate a tragedy. Like something you would see on *20/20* or *Dateline*. Only *I* was the tragedy.

I realized that I wasn't performing. There were no second takes. There wasn't a script or a cape to hide behind. These were my words, and I was surprised that I sound so well spoken, so eloquent. What struck me most wasn't the trauma itself, but how clinical and composed I sounded. There was no sobbing. No theatrics. Just a complete soul-baring. I thought to myself – this is what survival looks like. This is how it sounds. For the first time, I saw my teenage-self, not as damaged or lost, but as someone who had been buried alive – and was able to dig his way back out.

And then Diane appeared on screen again. Her voice was steady, but her eyes had carried the weight of two decades of pain.

Diane: *"You wonder where he would be. We are married*

for nineteen years.

When I first met him, he couldn't talk on the telephone to people. He was very shy and very inhibited about speaking to people at all. He's never had a male friend in all of the years that I have been with him. He has a lot of female friends; he does very well with women. His body language, when we would be with men, he would retreat, he wouldn't really be able to have a conversation or talk to them. I was always the one who was the stronger one, who would always orchestrate the way things were and lead him through.

Before we were physically intimate, he was afraid to have sex. I recall a time, it was rather peculiar, he was constantly, constantly, combing his hair, and cutting his hair. Constantly. He would go off into the bathroom and I would have to go in and say, what are you doing? Are you ok? And he would have scissors and keep saying 'I have to get rid of it! I have to get rid of it!' And he would literally cut his hair. Constantly. He had this metal comb, and he would comb his hair for an hour at a time. It was just unusual. There was time in one of the apartments that I was in, he was in the bathroom and he was just crying and carrying on, in front of the mirror, and I embraced him and said "Tell me what is wrong! What is wrong?" And he just fell to the floor and kept telling me how worthless he was, and that he didn't know what was going to happen.

He was extremely depressed. Extremely depressed and distraught, saying that he was worthless."

Diane's words kept coming. They were truthful. You only

get the truth from Diane. I heard things that I had buried, things I forgot that she had noticed. How I never had a long-term male friend. How she had to guide me, speak for me, protect me from a world that I didn't know how to move through. *"You wonder where he would be"* kept reverberating in my head. Diane's eyes met mine in every frame that I watched of her. I was reminded of the fact that she was all I ever wanted. All I ever dreamed of since meeting her at The Hotel Plaza. And even though I was so immensely damaged, I was clear in my sight, clear in my vision, that she would be the only woman that I would give myself completely to.

Keith: *"I had always thought about suicide. I always thought that, not so much that I would have the nerve to do it myself, nor did I think that it would be something that God would want me to do, but I would pray that I would die. I would pray that something would happen to me. I would pray that it would be taken out of my hands and that I would be killed or just not wake up."*

My words hung on the screen. Still, heavy, sobering. I had said it. Out loud. On film. Not just in pleadings to God while sitting at St. Aedan's – in a dark church, crying in a pew. I said it on camera. I had a profound aching for that boy, that teenager. That fourteen-year-old who spent night after night bartering with God like a desperate child. Promising to be better, more loving, more accepting of what God was asking of him. I didn't want to die because I hated life, but because I couldn't imagine a version of it where I wasn't in pain. Watching and listening to the story of my younger self, I wanted to reach through the screen and hug that version of me. I wanted to tell him that – you make it. And not just live, but love. You will meet the love of your life. You will live in a life of creativity, and most of all, you will find purpose in the very thing that almost killed you. That boy who begged to die became a man who chose to speak out about it.

Diane: *"He just seemed like he was so broken. His skin - he had very bad skin. Very bad skin. He constantly went to doctors to try to clear up his acne. He was so skinny. He couldn't eat anything. He had food phobias, and he does until this day, though he is getting better. So, so thin. Sickly looking. Very, very dark circles under his eyes. He would wear coverup, that is how black his dark circles were."*

I blink slowly, watching Diane describe me on film, watching her remember. It's strange hearing someone describe your body – your skin, your bones, your fear of food. She was being completely honest. I remember those mornings dabbing concealer under my eyes, praying it would make me look less haunted, less ruined.

Keith: *"After the abuse ended, I had sexual dysfunction. I had emotional dysfunction. I was a physical wreck."*

Diane: *"Maybe for the first fifteen years of our marriage, he didn't like to be touched. I still to this day, if I try to even hug him, it will last maybe half of a minute, if indeed. He is not one for physical contact. He loves, he likes sex, but he doesn't like to be touched. If we are in bed, I am never allowed to have my legs touch his. He can never allow him to feel me in bed with him after* *we make love.*

He said that when he met me, that he knew that I had a ready-made family and he was fine with that. He had no problem with that at all, and for someone who was eighteen, to take on the responsibility of two young sons, he said that he was not supposed to have children of his own, he said 'I know I'm not.' He seemed more upset at the thought of having a child than not having a child."

It was never that I didn't want Diane to touch me. I loved making love to Diane. It was that my body had long ago been wired to flinch at love. Love for me had always come with a price tag. A betrayal. A kiss and kick. Hands that said one thing and then took another. So even in safety, even in her arms, my body still recoiled. Not because it didn't want to be held, but because it couldn't understand that it was safe now. It had forgotten how to be held without a cost.

Diane had seen that I was afraid to become a biological father. I didn't know if I wasn't meant to have children, or if I just believed that I was too broken, too damaged to raise someone.

Keith: *"I just felt that I didn't physically have the stamina to bring a child into this world, let alone the fact that I really did think that it was possible that I had AIDS, and that I could pass it on to the person that I loved, and then have children come from that relationship? It was just horrifying to me. I ended up having two terrific stepchildren, that I consider to be my own, and I've helped raise them too. She did the majority of the work, but I was* *there since I was eighteen, nineteen, and I couldn't have a closer relationship with any two boys like I have with them, but still aside from that, I will never know what it is like to have my own biological child and my own biological grandchildren. I will never know what that is like, and I do now looking back, I do attribute it to that, to what I went through and what happened to me.*

I would just want them (Pecklers and Stanford) to know that while they were having vacations, and writing books, and enjoying life and having homes, that they killed me – to a certain extent when the abuse started, that it was more than just sexual abuse, that they destroyed a young boy's hope, career, affected my marriage, my family. Because of the abuse I knew that I would never have my own children, I made a conscious decision that I wouldn't have children, and that it has affected every area of my life. After the abuse ended, I thought I had AIDS for about ten years, because it was right when AIDS started in the early eighties. I was convinced that I had given it to Diane. It was just horrible. It just encompassed so many different aspects of someone's life, of a young life, that never should have been. And we are not talking like fondling or one time or ten times or even fifty times. We are talking upwards of one-hundred and fifty times. This went on for four years. It wasn't just a small period of my life; it was a huge part of my life. And I just would want them to know that for whatever reason they chose to do it, for their own gratification, that they in turn murdered somebody's soul."

A tightness formed behind my eyes while watching this part. I paused the film there. Not because I couldn't watch it, but because I needed to. I needed to sit in the silence that followed. To let those words sink in – *"they killed me to a certain extent."*

I listened to myself speak the truth, that the abuse had gone on for years, hidden behind the mask of pretending everything was fine. This was what remained. They had tried to murder my soul, but something inside of me refused to die. They stole years I'll never get back. They shattered the natural arc of a boy's life, scorched my dreams before they ever had a chance to bloom. But they didn't destroy me. I'm still here. I made it out alive and lived to tell the story.

Fr. Tom told me – on the last day I ever saw him, in his rectory bedroom at Our Lady of Perpetual Help, placing his hands on my shoulders and looking straight into my eyes.

"I'll be there to pick up the pieces of your broken dreams."

But there are no broken dreams to gather. To pick up. There are only the ones I reclaimed, the ones I still dare to create, and the ones that he and Pecklers will gather when this is all over.

They *did* kill something – my blueprint for life. They killed the natural rhythm of growing, of dreaming, of trusting, of building. They ended my education and put a stop to my fundamental development. They took a grenade, pulled the pin, and blew up my foundation. I was recreated into something fragmented and broken. They had managed to change the chemistry in my brain, but they could not kill my imagination.

I listened to myself explain that the abuse went on for years, pretending that nothing was happening. And this was what was left. They may have attempted to murder my soul, but something inside of me was stronger than that. Stronger than them. They may have stolen precious years from me, they may have disrupted the normal trajectory of a boy's life, but they did not kill me. They did not erase me.

Steve: *"If you could speak to the church leaders, what would you say?"*

Keith: *"We want to know that there is going to be real change. I'm not against the institution, I'm against the people who run the institution."*

I still have some wonderful memories of being in the church. It's not the parishioners, it's the men who are running the church. The cardinals, bishops, and priests.

Billy: *"If I had an opportunity to speak to the Archbishop, I would first hope that there would be steps in place so that this type of thing wouldn't happen again, and I'm not confident as I sit here today that that's the case. So that concerns me (sniff). And I would try to express to him how this has had such a wide-ranging impact on our family. It's not just Keith. You know, it's my mother, it's my father, it's me. It's his children. It's people in his life, his wife, other people that are close to him that don't even know about this. But you can't change the heart, compensate your heart, or your head, or give him back a life that he didn't have (emotional, voice quivering). He'll just never get that back."*

Diane: *(angry) "I would say to them, that my God wants* *their God to know that something is wrong. The Catholic Church religion – that I have known and that I have loved, was a big disappointment (emotional, heated). Because I have a faith, I have a very deep faith, I don't go to church anymore. I want to go to church (more emotional), but I don't trust the people that I see. (Diane's voice ends on a higher, quivering, vibrato, note.)*

And it's hard for me now, because I have a grandchild; and I want his spirit to be nurtured, but, I know what I don't want to happen to him, and Keith feels the same way."

Dad: *"The Catholic Religion was a disappointment to me. The way everybody treated and protected, that I found out, of all these here priests, and what they did to young kids, and yous never did a thing. Cardinal Law and the rest of them, it just tore my guts out, got me sick. I still believe in my Lord and Savior Jesus Christ (voice quivering, near tears), but I don't have too many feelings (having difficulty speaking) for…(stammering) for the church."*

And then the screen goes dark. A final stillness settles over me and Diane.

I sat motionless with my eyes staring into the black screen. There is no – *The End*. I realize that there never will be an ending to this. It felt like my life had been exorcised. We had answered all of Steve's questions. Billy with his calm attorney demeanor, Diane with her stoicism and shaken faith. Dad, with his grieving disgust at the church that he so desperately loved. Mom, trying to remember, but tired and unemotional. And me, with my hope for change, still clinging to the idea that the soul of the church might survive its shepherds. But this film wasn't for the church, it was for every family that was split open in silence. Every mother and father, who blamed themselves. Every brother, who didn't know how to help. Every spouse, who stood in the fire. And for every boy and girl – for every survivor, who still had not said a word about what had happened to them, who still believed that they were alone, who still believes the lie was their fault, or that nobody would believe them, or that healing means pretending that nothing ever happened. And maybe if there is any justice still breathing in the burning ashes of the church caused by decades of monstrous secrets, maybe it would be part of a slow change that would reach the congregations, not just the ones wearing red and gold vestments and pointy hats with streamers, but the people who show up in the pews.

    We had bared it all.

    No more secrets.

    No more shame.

Me, Mom, Dad & Billy (2005)

Chapter 30

The letter and DVD that Steve sent prompted a response sooner than we had expected. Within weeks, the sacred Society of Jesus and the Archdiocese of Newark requested a meeting. They wanted to mediate. Steve told us that we'd be entering into something called the *"Star Chamber."* I had never heard the term before. Steve explained that the original Star Chamber was an English court that met in secrecy from the 15th to the 17th centuries. Named for the gilded stars that once decorated the ceilings of its hidden room, the court's purpose was to enforce the king's will, often bypassing legal norms. It became a symbol of arbitrary power, hidden proceedings, and quiet punishments.

Our Star Chamber was in a bland office building in Hackensack, New Jersey. No gilded ceiling, no gold stars – just a dropped ceiling with fluorescent bulbs, but the secrecy remained. Steve, Diane, and I sat on one side of a long cherry finished wooden conference table, across from attorneys for the Society of Jesus, the Jesuits, and lawyers representing the Archdiocese of Newark. A retired judge presided as mediator, neutral in tone, but heavy with decades of practiced detachment.

What followed was a ninety-minute exorcism.

I had to say it all out loud again, and this time, in front of Diane.

I had never told Diane the evil, vile things that had been done to me. I had purposely kept those visuals from her. The thought of what they had done to me was enough. I had kept the letter that Steve had written to the attorneys from Diane as well. To that day, she had never heard the graphic, disturbing details. She had never asked. She already knew how broken I was.

At one point the judge asked us to step out of the chamber. Steve, Diane and I waited in a small conference room down the hall while the attorneys erupted behind closed doors. It wasn't about what had happened anymore, it was about who would pay for it. They screamed about percentages and liabilities. We were shocked that they were so completely out of control. An hour and a half later, they agreed to split it evenly. Half from the Jesuits, half from the Archdiocese. The final number was $120,000. One third went to Steve, and that left me with $85,000. I did the math. It worked out to $7.27 a day paid over 32 years of suffering.

Fr. Tom was immediately fired from his positions as manager of the Holy Sepulchre Cemetery in Totowa, New Jersey and music director for Holy Cross Parish in Wayne where he also taught children's CCD classes. When questioned by the church's attorneys, Fr. Tom said *"What's done is done. You can't change the past."* Fr. Keith Pecklers had become a prominent Jesuit scholar and the world's foremost authority on the liturgy. A professor of theology at the Pontifical

Gregorian University of Rome, he had written, contributed to or edited nine books, and was the *ABC News Correspondent for Vatican Affairs* – often commentating on the sexual abuse crisis. Pecklers remained in ministry; however, his ministry had been restricted to adults only. Unsupervised and ridiculous.

Diane and I used the money to pay off our 2003 Honda Element. We had already been making payments for five years and we were finally able to pay down some of the debt that had accumulated while I chased a life that I couldn't catch up with. I had been made aware not to expect a large settlement. But it was never about the money, it was about the truth. About the act of saying it in front of the people who had spent decades pretending it didn't happen. It was about standing up in the Star Chamber. I had been chasing stars my entire life. This was now about regaining power.

When Diane and I got back into our car to drive home, I expected silence. Instead, Diane said, "I know now. I didn't know it all before, but I know now." She took my hand, gripped it tight, and added "You're still here – that's worth more than any amount of money."

My last meeting with Steve was at his office in Margate. I had come to sign off on the settlement agreement – the final formality in a process that had opened the lid to decades of silence. Diane was by my side, as she had always been. The check was sitting there on the desk between us, but that wasn't what was on my mind. I looked at Steve and asked him gently but firmly, "Am I allowed to speak about this? What happened to me? Am I allowed to write a book or make a film?" I assured Steve that I had no idea how to do either, so it wasn't exactly imminent, but then again, I had never known how to design clothes and yet I had done that for twenty-five years. I managed to stitch together a life, a business, a name. I had learned to make something from nothing. That was the one thing that they could not take from me: my innate ability to create. I was already being prompted by the universe to create something from all of this.

Steve didn't hesitate. "We didn't sign an NDA," he said. "I never allow them in my cases. You're free to speak your truth however you choose." He paused. "You're free to do with it what you will." I nodded, absorbing it.

"I will say this," Steve continued as we made our way to the door, "there's more string on this ball."

I knew most survivors weren't ready to talk about their abuse out loud. Most carried it in their bones, in the guts, in their souls, in shadows. But that wasn't going to be my story. That was never going to be my story. I didn't walk out of Steve's office that day with just a check. I walked out with a choice. And for the first time, I knew that I would use my voice – not just for myself, but for anyone still trying to find theirs.

Six months later, I began filming my own full-length documentary, a self-shot film starring Diane and me. It was a story of survival. A horror film in many ways, but ultimately, it was a love story. *Our love story.* I already knew the title – *Of God and Gucci*. It felt right fusing the trauma I had endured at the hands of men who claimed to represent God, and the inner strength and resilience I had found through my creativity and my life in fashion. The career that I managed to build in spite of it all – through the love I had found with Diane.

My intention was simple – to share my story so that other men and women might begin to heal. To see that it was possible to not only survive, but to love and to build a beautiful life.

I set up my camcorder on a tripod and began filming our story. I would turn on the camera, run to my chair and film myself. I worked on it every day and every minute that I was not working at Neiman Marcus. I filmed Diane answering my off-camera questions. I used the original mediation video that Steve filmed of me, Diane, my parents and Billy. I edited it into sections of our voices, adding a sense of professionalism to my otherwise admittedly amateur film. The finished product, complete with narration, film clips from my fashion design career, and a soundtrack, became a fifty-eight-minute documentary. I had no idea what I was going to do with it.

And then another miracle.

I read on Facebook that a film festival was forming in Jersey City. *The Golden Door International Film Festival.* It was founded by actor Paul Sorvino's nephew. The moment I saw the post, I raced to finish my film, working late into the night, editing and trimming, so that I could enter it into the documentary category. On the very last day for submissions, Diane drove me to the address in Jersey City, and I hand delivered the DVD myself, heart pounding, hoping that I was not too late. Then came the wait. Every day I checked my email. And then finally, it happened.

Of God and Gucci had been accepted into the festival. I was stunned. Overjoyed. My self-shot film, made for $500 on a camcorder, had made it into the documentary category. The festival would unfold over three days in Journal Square and nearby venues, right at the very spot where I had first met Diane. In this lifetime anyway.

It was rare for any film at *The Golden Door International Film Festival* to get more than one screening, but *Of God and Gucci* was screened twice, each time at a different venue. That alone felt like a miracle. Word had spread. There was buzz. Something about our story was resonating. We sat in the dark, watching our lives unfold on the screen, surrounded by strangers who gasped, cried, and even laughed in the right places. And at the end of each showing, when the credits rolled, and the final frame faded out, the audience erupted into applause.

Then Diane and I stood. We stepped in front of the crowd not as actors, or filmmakers, but as survivors. The applause softened into silence as people leaned forward in their seats. We took questions. We talked about the abuse, the silence, the years of shame – and how this film, this five-hundred-dollar patchwork of courage and grit, was my act of rebellion. My way of bringing light into the darkest corners of human experience. We spoke from the heart, unscripted and unpolished. And the audiences responded with reverence and support.

And then on the second day of the festival, the

announcement came. *Of God and Gucci* had been officially nominated for Best Documentary. I couldn't believe it. I stood there, stunned, like someone had just called my name over the loudspeaker in a dream.

There was real buzz that we could win Best Documentary. People were talking. Hugging us. Asking about my next project. But for me, just to be nominated was enough. At least for the moment.

It was powerful.

It was validating.

It was prolific.

Not just for me, but for every person who had lived in silence. For every survivor who had never spoken a word. Had yet to find their voice. The nomination wasn't just an accolade. It was a flag planted in the ground. And for me, my new direction. I had told my truth. And people were listening.

I didn't win Best Documentary.

I have to admit, I was very disappointed. After all of the applause, the questions, the conversations and buzz in the lobby, I had allowed myself to believe for a moment that I could win. That maybe, *Of God and Gucci* would walk away with top honor. But instead, the award went to a documentary about bugs – beautifully shot in the filmmaker's Jersey City backyard. It was professionally done, no question, and it deserved to win. Still, I couldn't help but wonder if something else had been at play.

As I had mentioned, actor Paul Sorvino was connected with the film festival. I later learned that Mr. Sorvino was also a devout Catholic. Somewhere in my mind, I couldn't help but wonder if my film, so unflinching in its confrontation of the Church, had been too much. Too controversial. Too close to home. I'll never know. But it was hard not to wonder. And then – just as I was trying to quiet that ache of loss, came a shock.

Of God and Gucci was announced, along with another film, as Best of the Best!

I was stunned and grateful beyond words. Not only had it been nominated, but it was getting two more screenings the following month. Another chance to speak, another chance to act. I knew I had to do something more.

I had seen firsthand how the film affected people. So, I created a 5x8 postcard, and on it I printed the contact information of every state Senator in New Jersey with their emails and their office numbers. We wanted to give people something immediate, something tangible that they could hold in their hands and act on at the end of each screening. After the final frame and the credits rolled, Diane and I stood up again and spoke. We educated the audiences on why they mattered. Why stories like mine had to be told. So, we handed out the postcards and asked people to call the Senators to demand that the statute

of limitations on child sexual abuse in the State of New Jersey be changed, and to get the bill on the Assembly floor.

And then came the real impact. At each screening, men and women approached us – hesitantly at first, but then with trembling honesty, they told me things they had never said out loud. One woman in her late sixties pulled me aside, her hand shook as she spoke.

"I've never told anyone this, not even my husband of fifty years, but I was abused too. And tonight…tonight, you're the first person I've told."

Men too. Some stoic, others undone by tears they hadn't allowed themselves in decades. They looked me in the eyes. "That happened to me, too." Shame still etched into their faces, like it was tattooed there. I recognized the look. I realized then that *Of God and Gucci* was no longer just my story.

I knew that the sexual elements in the film were hard to watch. I didn't write around them. I didn't film around them either. I didn't soften them with euphemisms. Because I believe that people don't truly understand what phrases like "molestation" or "inappropriate touching" actually mean. I know I didn't. I needed them to understand – not just the act, but the aftermath. The ripple effect. What it does to a family, to a marriage, to a soul. To a boy. Left untreated, *"abuse festers"* as Steve said. It leaks out sideways into addictions, alcohol, drugs, affairs, rage. Suicide. Sometimes it turns survivors into abusers themselves. And perhaps most of all, I was guided by something that I had learned in confirmation class.

The final gift of the Holy Ghost – *Fear of the Lord*.

Not fear as in terror. Not fear of punishment. But *awe*. A deep and reverent desire not to offend the sacred. A desire to walk upright, even through fire. It's what kept me going. It's what told me that my story, no matter how hard or ugly, had to be told. Because the *truth* is Holy, and silence, in the face of suffering is its betrayal. And to be perfectly honest, I wanted Fr. Tom and Pecklers to experience this particular gift.

Chapter 31

The phone buzzed in my hand, Billy's name lighting up the screen. It was a Tuesday afternoon, and I wasn't expecting a call for him. Especially while I was now working as the designer clothes manager at Saks Fifth Avenue. I answered, bringing the phone to my ear.

"Hi Bill."

"Hey Brother. I have something important to ask you," his voice was calm but there was an urgency beneath it.

"Yeah, what's up." I asked, shifting in my chair.

"So, listen – a senator, a friend of mine, is working on the bill to change the statute of limitation for childhood sexual abuse cases in New Jersey. Right now, it's only two years from discovery which is total bullshit. They're hearing testimonies on Thursday down in Trenton. Would you be willing to testify before the Senate Judiciary Committee?"

I sat up straighter.

"This Thursday? That's the day after tomorrow." My stomach turned, tightening like a fist.

"I know it's short notice." Billy said, sensing my

hesitation. "But this is huge. Your story could really help push this legislature forward."

I swallowed. The thought of standing in front of lawmakers telling them about the darkest parts of my past turned my stomach, but if it meant real change, it was worth it.

I told Billy yes.

"Ok great, I'll call the senator now and get you on the list. I want to prep you though, so you know what to expect."

Billy explained the committee members might ask some questions afterwards, but the most important thing is telling your story and why this change is necessary. I took a deep breath. "I know exactly why it's necessary." My voice was steady even as my thoughts raced. "Too many survivors never get the chance to hold their abusers accountable. The law protects them more than it protects us."

"And you have the experience to back it up. Keith, your story is powerful. It's time for the people in charge to hear it."

I pressed my fingers against my temple, my anxious mind was already playing out every possible scenario, every question they might ask, every emotion I might feel standing before the judiciary committee. I started to tear up, standing in between two racks of Chanel, not because I was afraid to testify.

"Are you crying?" Billy asked.

"Yes. I am."

"Why? You'll do great." Billy responded.

"It's not that." I responded. "Thank you...for everything. I love you."

"I love you too. OK, let me call the senator to get you on the list. I'll call you later to walk you through."

Later that night, Billy called and began walking me through the logistics. His prep always made me feel like I was on a jury. I was already imagining it, standing before the committee, standing before the senators – using my voice to fight for those who still felt silenced. And to hold Fr. Keith Pecklers and Fr. Tom Stanford responsible. To be able to say their names out loud, in the light of day. It was time to speak, and this time the whole State of New Jersey would be listening.

Diane and I left for Trenton after our morning coffee and tea.

"I printed out three copies of your testimony," she said, glancing at the manilla envelope on my lap. "One for you, one for the clerk, and one to leave behind in case they forget your face but need to remember your words."

"Thanks. I'm sure that they must record everyone's testimony, but it's better to be over prepared. I still don't know if it's enough. It's five minutes. Five minutes to change the law."

"Yeah, five minutes and thirty-four years to find your voice." Diane said.

"I've been waiting my whole life to say out loud what Pecklers and Fr. Tom had done to me. They picked the wrong kid. I'll manage somehow to get it all in."

"Well, you'll have a microphone now. And the lawmakers will be listening."

Traffic picked up near New Brunswick and then slowed

to a crawl.

"God," I hope we get there in time." I said.

"We'll get there in time. Even if it means I have to drive on the shoulder." Diane said and then picked up speed and wove us through the traffic.

We continued in silence, allowing me to go over my speech. Diane periodically looked over at me as she drove. "I'm so proud of you. I remember when you couldn't even speak on the phone. You're not that same person anymore. You're not surviving anymore, Keith. You're leading."

I blinked fast. The road blurred. I didn't answer. I couldn't. I would start crying and there was no time for it.

We passed the *Welcome to Trenton* sign not long after. The dome of the State House glinted gold in the distance.

"Okay," Diane said, shifting gears. "Let's rewrite some history."

The State House chamber smelled of old wood and waxed floors. I checked to make sure that I was on the list. And then we waited. And waited. And waited. It was creeping up to 5 p.m., and the fluorescent lights had taken on a sickly yellow tint. I kept checking my phone, my retail shift had started at twelve and the anxious knot in my stomach twisted tighter each time I glanced at the time. I still had to prep the floor, touch the tables, fold the denim, reset the shoes and finger space Ready-To-Wear. But this – this was more important.

I had waited decades for this moment. A lifetime. The stories before mine were brutal. Shattering. One by one, survivors approached the microphone and shared their stories with the Senate Judiciary Committee – tales of betrayal, of systemic silence and cover-ups, of stolen innocence, and in one case, a mother who testified on behalf of her only son who had committed suicide at the age of forty-five because he could no longer live with the guilt, the pain, the shame. Some senators leaned forward, others had begun to drift, fatigue setting into their faces, their bodies slouched beneath the weight of hour after hour of human  agony. I saw one of them gently nodding off. And then suddenly, my name was called. The sound rang through the chamber like a bell.

    I stood up. My chair scraped against the floor as I realized that every eye had turned to me. My knees were a little shaky and I could feel the sweat beginning to form under my shirt, but I made my way up to the long table and microphone facing the senators.

    I had written my testimony in less than two days – just a day and a half to distill decades of trauma, shame, silence, survival, into five minutes of truth. But I had survived, and I knew how to effectively tell it.

    I took a deep breath.

    And then I spoke.

Man's story, revelation of six-figure settlement,

startle Senate hearing

December 12, 2010

It was another day of endless hearings in Trenton.

The Senate Judiciary Committee was taking testimony on a proposed bill that would do away with a two-year statute of limitations on lawsuits alleging child sex abuse. There were a few dozen spectators in the gallery – and one reporter.

Then a 48-year-old man leaned into a microphone. And delivered a bombshell.

"My story begins in 1976, St. Paul's Church in the Greenville section of Jersey City," said Keith Brennan.

Speaking about his experiences publicly for the first time, Brennan, of Bayonne, recalled four years of sexual abuse by church staff, starting with Keith Pecklers, the church's young musical director. Brennan said he was 14 at the time and that Pecklers was about three-and-a-half years his senior.

After about a year of the abuse by Pecklers, Brennan said, he reported it to the church deacon, Thomas Stanford, who then took over abusing Brennan, plying him with drugs and alcohol before abusing him repeatedly over the course of three years.

"Thirty-four years have gone by but I have not forgotten a single day, a single detail of my abuse," said Brennan. "While my abusers were having careers and vacations and writing books and enjoying their lives, they killed me to a certain point. They destroyed a young boy's hope, career, what could have been."

Pecklers, who became a priest, is now a prominent Jesuit scholar. A professor of liturgy at the Pontifical Gregorian University of Rome, he has written, contributed to or edited nine books, according to his Facebook page, and is a frequent commentator on Vatican affairs for American media outlets–including the sex abuse scandals.

In 2008 – after decades of suffering from depression, anxiety, panic attacks, self-mutilation, an eating disorder and the fear that his abusers may had given him AIDS – Brennan said he contacted attorney Stephen Rubino, an expert on child sexual abuse cases. Rubino forwarded Brennan's accusations to the Roman Catholic Archdiocese of Newark, along with a DVD of Brennan and his family describing how the abuse had harmed him. Within weeks, the archdiocese entered into mediation with Brennan and eventually settled for an undisclosed six-figure sum, Brennan said. He provided a partially redacted letter from his attorney outlining the distribution of the settlement amounts, dated Sept. 24, 2008, as proof.

Though Brennan testified in an open hearing Thursday, the Ledger deferred publication of his story until efforts could be made to contact people and institutions he accused in his session before the Senate committee.

Reached by phone in Italy, Pecklers would not say whether he ever had sexual contact with Brennan, but said actual abuse could not have taken place because he was not an adult at the time.

"In the 1970s, I was a student – I was a minor myself –so it would be impossible to be accused of that type of thing. I was 17 years old, so that's the end of the story," said Pecklers.

Brennan said in a later interview with the Star-Ledger that Pecklers began molesting him against his will about a month before Pecklers turned 18, and continued well past his birthday.

Jim Goodness, a spokesman for the Archdiocese of Newark, said he could not discuss anything related to litigation matters. However, he confirmed Pecklers had worked in the parish as a layman until he left to become a Jesuit priest.

Stanford, he said, had been a priest within the diocese until he left the priesthood on his own for unknown reasons in the mid-1980s.

"He asked for leave from parish work sometime around '85 or '86 and never came back," said Goodness.

Until 2008, according to the Paterson Diocese, Stanford worked as manager of the Holy Sepulchre Cemetery in Totowa and as a part-time music manager for Holy Cross Parish in Wayne.

Richard Sokerka, spokesman for the Paterson Diocese, said officials there were told two years ago by the Archdiocese of Newark that Stanford had been named in a sex abuse case. "He was immediately terminated from both positions," said Sokerka. Attempts to get comments from Stanford were unsuccessful.

The Star-Ledger located the address of Thomas Stanford in northern New Jersey. Independently, Brennan supplied a description of Stanford's car and its license plate, having written it down during an encounter two years earlier. When the Star-Ledger visited the apartment Friday and Saturday, the car was in the allotted parking spot. Occupants inside the apartment did not come to the door.

Brennan was one of several victims of childhood sexual abuse to testify at the Senate Judiciary Committee hearing Thursday in favor of a bill that would do away with the state's two-year statute of limitations on lawsuits for such sex abuse.

Currently, victims have two years from the time they realize that the abuse damaged them to file suit before the statute runs out. Brennan said he would not have had a case if he actually filed a lawsuit, but suspects the archdiocese settled the abuse through arbitration because of how well he recalled his abuse and the detailed account of it he gave.

Patrick Brannigan, executive director of the New Jersey Catholic Conference, testified against the bill, arguing that it would make institutions responsible for abuse that happened decades ago, long after critical evidence had disappeared. Proponents testified that the burden of proof remains the same no matter how old the case is, and that evidence has disappeared only makes it harder to successfully sue.

Catholic bishops have opposed similar bills in other

states, and earlier this year were instrumental in a successful effort to stop Connecticut from easing its 30-year statute of limitations.

Brennan, who left the church when he was 17, told the senators that he considers himself an "estranged Catholic." He said he spoke publicly to encourage other victims to come out.

"When you are no longer victim to the secret, you can take control of your life. If more men and women could be encouraged to come forward, healing would be contagious. This is my reason for coming forward after 34 years," he said.

I rose from my seat as the last words of my testimony echoed faintly behind me, already being replaced by the next name called, the next survivor stepping into the light. I turned and caught Diane's eyes. She was seated halfway down the row, her hands folded tight on her lap. I gave a small nod just enough for her to understand. She moved gracefully, excusing herself down the row, whispering soft apologies as she passed other survivors and their families, many of whom were wiping away tears or staring straight ahead, frozen in their own thoughts.

I grabbed Diane's hand the moment we cleared the gallery doors.

"Let's go," I said. "If we hit the turnpike fast enough, I could still make it to work by 7:00 p.m."

We were almost at the stairs when I heard a voice behind me.

"Excuse me! Excuse me – sir!"

I turned around to see a man in the navy blazer jogging toward me with a press badge flapping against his chest.

"I'm sorry to chase you down," he said, slightly breathless. "My name is Matt Friedman. I'm with the *Star*

Ledger. I just heard your testimony. Powerful stuff. Really powerful."

I was still catching my breath, still buzzing from what I had just said in that chamber.

"I'm sorry," I said, glancing at Diane, who had her hand on the stair rail, eyes scanning for her car keys. "I have to be at work."

"Can I call you tomorrow?" He asked. "I'd love to talk more. What you said today – it needs to be heard. I think it's a story that our readers need to read. I'd run it in the Sunday edition. But I need to fact-check everything. I need more details."

I hesitated. I hadn't thought that far ahead. I'd only just gotten through the moment.

"I'll talk," I said finally. "Call me tomorrow. I'll tell you everything."

He reached into his pocket and handed me his card. "I'll be in touch first thing. Thank you for your bravery today."

I nodded, my face tight, trying to keep it all together.

Diane and I bolted down the stairs and out into the late-afternoon light. By the time we reached the car, my tie was loosened, and the top button of my shirt was undone. I exhaled, deep and full, for the first time that day. I was glad it was over. Diane grabbed me by my waist and pulled me close to her.

"You did it. You really did it." We kissed and then took off.

The next day the reporter called me as promised. But that was not the end of the story. Steve was right. There *was* more string on the ball.

Nine years had passed. Nine long years of waiting, hoping, of mourning every legislative session that came and went with no vote. No change, no justice. But also, nine years of fighting, of writing, of telling my story. Unwinding the string. And then, here we were again. March 2019. At the State House. Deja Vu.

The same Senate Judiciary Committee. The same hallways with clerks. Their hushed voices and coffee breath. The same long rows of survivors clutching manila folders, trembling notes, old photographs of victims who had killed themselves, having become too tired of the fight. But this time we were grayer, angrier, clearer. Diane was seated by my side where she had been through all of it. Her presence – a constant anchor through every hearing, every interview, every silent car ride home.

When they called my name again, I didn't hesitate. I knew the walk. I knew the mic. I knew my voice. And it had grown stronger. This time I didn't just speak as a survivor. I spoke as someone who had already told them everything once before.

I leaned in.

Calm.

Controlled.

"In 2010, I sat here before you and told you the truth. I told you about the two men who had stolen my childhood.

My teenage years. My education. My relationships. My blueprint for life. I told you about the silence that nearly killed me. I told you that we needed this bill to protect the children who would come after us, and to give justice to those of us still carrying the weight of these crimes."

"And you did nothing."

A few senators bowed their heads. Some nodded. I kept going.

"We are not here today to ask you. We are here to tell you – that time's up."

My breath was steady and slow. My voice did not shake. I looked straight into their eyes.

"We urge you – pass Bill S-477. Let the healing finally begin."

And then I stepped back.

Two months later, on May 13, 2019, it happened. The bill passed. The law changed.

No longer would survivors be boxed in by an impossible timeline. No longer would the door be slammed shut before most of us were even able to open our mouths to tell someone what had happened to us. Now survivors would have seven years from discovery of the abuse, or until age fifty-five, to file civil claims. And a two-year lookback window would be opened, giving those long silenced a final chance to speak their truth.

It was done. We had done it. Not with vengeance, not with firebombs or banners. But with slow determination, testimony. Truth. And grit – with whatever tools we'd salvaged from our broken childhoods.

My tools came from my playroom. The same room I had retreated to after the abuse began. The same playroom that was my safe haven from whatever happened in *the Keeping Room*. The only place in the house where I felt I could breathe. Where I began to assemble my toolbox – with nothing but fabrics, scraps, crayons, cardboard, tape, and imagination. I created characters, imagined scenes, and wrote whole narratives that carried me far beyond the reach of what had been done to me. I didn't know it then, but I was crafting more than characters and stories. I was crafting survival. Every time I disappeared into a world of my own making, I was reclaiming something that had been stolen from me. Piece by piece. It was also in my playroom that I first discovered the magic of film. Where I'd storybook entire plots in my notebooks, then gather the neighborhood kids together and direct them in my homemade movies transforming parts of our neighborhood into a Hollywood backlot. I'd film them on my Super 8mm camera, edit the reels by hand – splicing scenes together – creating my own vision. Once my film was ready, I'd call everyone together in a basement venue, dim the lights and turn the projector on. Even back then, I had this basic instinct to create. To show.

My playroom wasn't just a sanctuary. It was a laboratory for transformation. A sacred space where I learned how to turn silence into a story, story into truth, and truth into change. And for that, I have my parents to thank. Because even if I couldn't change what had happened to me, by using my creativity, I could change what I did with it. I could reframe it. And now, decades later, those same tools I first picked up in my childhood playroom – the imagination, storytelling, a camera lens, a sketchpad, and a notebook –became instruments of justice. I brought them into courtrooms and committee chambers, fitting rooms, film sets, and even into the *Star Chamber,* turning my truth into something that could no longer be ignored. And through it all, at every moment of doubt and every triumph – was Diane – my angel, my partner, my mirror – who stood beside me not just as a witness, but as a co-creator of the life that we built together. Diane had helped me stitch the broken pieces of my soul into something bold and strong.

And together…we turned that into something that they never saw coming.

State House (May 13, 2019)

Acknowledgements

Thank you to my editor Karalynn Brancatella, whose gift for hearing my voice and strengthening it was nothing short of a miracle – arriving at exactly the moment in my life when I needed her the most.

To my parents, Bill and Colette – who gave me the space, encouragement, and freedom to believe that anything I could imagine – I could create.

To my grandparents, Nanny and Poppy, who filled my toolbox with love and lessons – from Nanny's gentle hands teaching me to sew, and Poppy, for teaching me to be rigid, and reminding me that nothing was impossible.

To my brother Bill for guiding me toward the next steps on my journey – and for proving that the love between brothers can rise to the surface and endure.

To my *fairy godwomen*, especially Madeline, Connie Anton, and "Aunt Cookie" – Agnes Dicken – for believing in me when I needed it the most.

To my faithful assistant Kelly Gowers – for your loyalty and friendship. I could not have done it without you.

To Erica Collucci and Digital Planets Media – for bringing my vision to life through design.

To Paul Rocheny, for assisting me in shaping my early cover ideas.

To my attorney, Stephen Rubino – the warrior, advocate, and steadfast voice for survivors, who carried me closer to justice and reminded me when it was over, that there was "more string on this ball."

And lastly to Diane, the angel who saved me – whose love became the light that guided our path, and who helped me weave the torn threads of my life, and the broken patterns of my past, into a masterpiece of love, healing, and strength.

About the Author

Keith Rennar Brennan is a survivor, author, artist, and advocate, whose work transforms silence into storytelling and trauma into purpose. His memoir, *Of God And Gucci,* recounts his childhood sexual abuse at the hands of Catholic clergy, his decades-long fight for justice, and the redemptive love that healed him. He also produced the award-winning documentary of the same name. Keith Rennar testified before the New Jersey Senate Judiciary Committee, helping to reform the state's statute of limitations for survivors of sexual abuse. He is currently working on a screenplay for *Of God and Gucci,* as well as a self-help book exploring how creativity can be a lifeline for trauma survivors, *Trauma to Transformation: Your Blueprint to Creative Recovery.* His work – whether on the page, the screen, or the stage – is driven by a single purpose, to break the silence and remind survivors that their stories matter. Keith Rennar resides in New Jersey with his wife Diane.

Stay Connected
Email: info@ofgodandgucci.com
Facebook: facebook.com/ofgodandgucci
Instagram: @ofgodandgucci

www.ingramcontent.com/pod-product-compliance
Lightning Source LLC
Chambersburg PA
CBHW031424160426
43195CB00010BB/606